The Cambridge Companion to Chaucer

The Cambridge Companion to Chaucer is a revised version of the first edition, which has become a classic in the field. This new volume responds to the success of the first edition and to recent debates in Chaucer studies. Important material has been updated, and new contributions have been commissioned to take into account recent trends in literary theory as well as in studies of Chaucer's works, although the structure of the book has basically remained the same. Chapters cover such topics as the social and literary scene in England in Chaucer's time, the literary inheritance traceable in his works to French and Italian sources, comedy, pathos and romance in the *Canterbury Tales*, and Chaucer's style. The volume now includes a useful chronology, and the bibliography has been entirely updated to provide an indispensable guide for today's student of Chaucer.

Piero Boitani is Professor of Comparative Literature in the Department of English at the University of Rome 'La Sapienza'. He is the author of many volumes including *The Tragic and the Sublime in Medieval Literature* (Cambridge, 1989), *The Shadow of Ulysses. Figures of a Myth* (1994) and *The Bible and its Rewritings* (1999).

Jill Mann is Notre Dame Professor of English at the University of Notre Dame and Life Fellow of Girton College, Cambridge. She has written extensively on Geoffrey Chaucer and medieval authors including Langland, Malory and the *Gawain*-poet. Her most recent book is *Feminizing Chaucer* (2002).

THE CAMBRIDGE
COMPANION TO
CHAUCER

Second edition

EDITED BY

PIERO BOITANI *and* JILL MANN

PUBLISHED BY THE PRESS SYNDICATE OF THE UNIVERSITY OF CAMBRIDGE
The Pitt Building, Trumpington Street, Cambridge, United Kingdom

CAMBRIDGE UNIVERSITY PRESS
The Edinburgh Building, Cambridge, CB2 2RU, UK
40 West 20th Street, New York, NY 10011–4211, USA
477 Williamstown Road, Port Melbourne, VIC 3207, Australia
Ruiz de Alarcón 13, 28014 Madrid, Spain
Dock House, The Waterfront, Cape Town 8001, South Africa

http://www.cambridge.org

First published 2003
Third printing 2005

Printed in the United Kingdom at the University Press, Cambridge

Typeface Sabon 10/13 pt.   *System* LaTeX 2_ε [TB]

A catalogue record for this book is available from the British Library

Library of Congress Cataloguing in Publication data
The Cambridge companion to Chaucer / edited by Piero Boitani and Jill Mann. – 2nd ed.
p.   cm. – (Cambridge companions to literature)
Rev. ed. of: The Cambridge Chaucer companion / edited by Piero Boitani and Jill Mann. 1986.
Includes bibliographical references and index.
ISBN 0 521 81556 8 – ISBN 0 521 89467 0 (pb.)
1. Chaucer, Geoffrey, d. 1400 – Criticism and interpretation.   2. Chaucer, Geoffrey,
d. 1400 – Handbooks, manuals, etc.   I. Boitani, Piero.   II. Mann, Jill.   III. Cambridge
Chaucer companion.   IV. Series
PR1924.C28 2003   821′.1 – dc21   2003051485

ISBN 0 521 81556 8 hardback
ISBN 0 521 89467 0 paperback

CONTENTS

CONTRIBUTORS

C. DAVID BENSON, University of Connecticut

JULIA BOFFEY, Queen Mary, University of London

PIERO BOITANI, University of Rome 'La Sapienza'

J. A. BURROW, formerly University of Bristol

ARDIS BUTTERFIELD, University College, London

CHRISTOPHER CANNON, University of Cambridge

CAROLYN DINSHAW, New York University

A. S. G. EDWARDS, University of Victoria

JOERG O. FICHTE, University of Tübingen

† ROBERT WORTH FRANK JR, formerly Pennsylvania State University

MARK LAMBERT, Bard College, New York

JILL MANN, University of Notre Dame

DEREK PEARSALL, Harvard University

JAMES SIMPSON, University of Cambridge

A. C. SPEARING, University of Virginia

PAUL STROHM, Columbia University

DAVID WALLACE, University of Pennsylvania

BARRY WINDEATT, University of Cambridge

PREFACE

This second edition of *The Cambridge Companion to Chaucer*, like the first one, is intended for students, teachers, and all general readers who wish to approach Chaucer's works with the help of an introduction to his texts, and to the contexts in which he composed them. Its main aim is to suggest ways of reading, furnish necessary explanations, and offer first-hand literary criticism, by means of which readers may test their own responses to one of the greatest English poets. The views offered in each essay are individual and to a large extent original ones; they are not meant to be résumés of the current state of Chaucer scholarship or criticism, although Carolyn Dinshaw's contribution explores the ways in which new critical approaches to literary texts put pressure on Chaucer's works. We feel now, as we felt at the time we produced the first edition in 1986, that the reader is best served by a clearly pursued line of argument, which may set off his or her own thinking, rather than an exhaustive survey of the field.

We have kept the basic structure of the old volume, asking contributors to rewrite or update their essays as necessary, but we have also included specially commissioned new essays in order to respond to changing currents in Chaucer criticism. About half the articles in the collection are then, here as before, focussed squarely on one or more of Chaucer's major works, identifying their themes and styles, moods and tones, in such a way as to help the reader to an appreciation of Chaucer's aims and artistry in each case. Alongside these essays are others of a more general kind – focussing on literary or historical background, on style, structure, and afterlife – which not only present the major works in ever-different lights, but also explore their links with many of the minor poems and with other medieval literature. We hope that the combination of the two types of essay will not only give a sense of a larger context for discussion of the individual works, but will also make clear that there is no 'definitive' interpretation of, say, *Troilus and Criseyde* – rather, it can be constantly re-approached via fresh lines of enquiry.

Paul Strohm's essay sketches the general scene, both social and literary, in fourteenth-century England. Ardis Butterfield and David Wallace trace the impact on Chaucer of the cultural and literary reality of France and Italy. Piero Boitani leads the reader through Chaucer's early development in the dream poems, in which books are not just the sources but the subject of his poetry. Mark Lambert discusses the densely textured narrative style of *Troilus*, while Jill Mann focusses on its philosophical themes, on the questions of chance and destiny which Chaucer encountered in Boethius. Julia Boffey and A. S. G. Edwards address the problems presented by the incomplete state of the *Legend of Good Women*, the possibility that it was a royal commission, and the uncertainties of its genre and tone. The next five essays are devoted to the *Canterbury Tales*: first, David Benson discusses the tales in relation to the pilgrimage-frame, and then the four succeeding contributions, by J. A. Burrow, Derek Pearsall, the late Robert Worth Frank Jr, and A. C. Spearing, examine selected tales grouped by mode or genre. Barry Windeatt and Christopher Cannon range widely through Chaucer's works, using comparison and contrast to engage with larger questions of structure and style. James Simpson surveys the principal English and Scots responses to Chaucer between Hoccleve and the 1542 statute permitting the reading of Chaucer's works; and Carolyn Dinshaw takes up the issues of feminist, queer, and postcolonial readings of our author.

Because this book has an introductory function, notes have been kept to a minimum, and it has not been possible to give exhaustive documentation of the history of every critical view presented or discussed. The Guide to Chaucer Studies provided by Joerg Fichte will lead the interested reader to the important works in this field whose influence has helped to shape the individual discussions in this collection, and will also clear several pathways through the dense forest of modern Chaucer criticism. The contributors to this book are the inheritors of a long and rich tradition of Chaucer scholarship, to which they feel themselves indebted. Yet in order to write freshly and freely on works which have been read and written about for six hundred years, they have inevitably had to banish from their texts and their notes many of the very works which have done most to create their own enjoyment. We hope that the final Guide to Chaucer Studies will stand as an acknowledgement of our gratitude to the labours of others. We hope also that this second edition of the *Cambridge Companion to Chaucer*, the joint effort – like the first one – of an English and Italian editor, and the product of an international team of scholars, will help to foster in new generations of readers in all countries a love of Chaucer and an interest in Chaucer studies.

PIERO BOITANI   JILL MANN
Cambridge, June 2002

NOTE ON THE TEXT

The text of Chaucer used throughout for quotation and reference is the *Riverside Chaucer*, gen. ed. L. D. Benson (Boston, 1987/Oxford, 1988). References are normally to individual works, with Book- and line-number; for the sake of concision, however, references to the *Canterbury Tales* are occasionally given by Fragment- and line-number (e.g. I, 3450 = *Miller's Tale*, 3450).

Abbreviations

BL	British Library
CFMA	Les Classiques Français du Moyen Age
EETS os, es	*Early English Text Society* original series, extra series
MED	*Middle English Dictionary*, eds. H. Kurath, S. M. Kuhn, *et al.* (Ann Arbor, Mich., 1954–)
PL	*Patrologiae cursus completus*, series latina, ed. J. P. Migne
PMLA	*Publications of the Modern Language Association of America*

CHRONOLOGY

1367	Black Prince defeats mercenary army under Bernard de Guesclin at Najera, Spain, gains throne for Pedro the Cruel (*Monk's Tale* 2375–90)
1367	Chaucer granted life annuity by Edward III
1368	Possible first visit of Chaucer of Italy
c.1369–70	*Book of the Duchess*
1371	French reclaim Gascony, Poitiers
1372–3	Chaucer visits Genoa and Florence
1374	Death of Petrarch
1374	Chaucer appointed Controller of Customs in London
1375	Death of Boccaccio
1376	Good Parliament condemns waste and profiteering by high government officials
1377	Rye and Hastings burned by French
1377	Death of Edward III; succeeded by Richard II
1377	Chaucer travels to France for negotiations toward marriage of Richard to Princess Marie of France
1378	Chaucer visits Lombardy; appoints John Gower as attorney in his absence
1378	Great Schism in Papacy; Urban VI at Rome (recognized by England); Clement VII at Avignon (recognized by France)
c.1378–80	*House of Fame* and *Anelida and Arcite*
c.1380–2	*Parliament of Fowls*
1380–6	Gower, *Vox Clamantis*
1380s	First version of Lollard Bible
1381	Peasants' Revolt (*Nun's Priest's Tale* 3394)
1382	Wycliffe's teachings condemned by Blackfriars Synod
c.1382–6	*Boece* and *Troilus and Criseyde*
1385	Death of Bernabò Visconti of Milan (*Monk's Tale* 2399–406)
c.1385–7	*Legend of Good Women*
1385–7	Thomas Usk, *Testament of Love*
1386	Chaucer a Member of Parliament for Kent
1387	Death of Philippa Chaucer
c.1387	Chaucer begins *Canterbury Tales*
1388	Chaucer's annuity transferred to John Scalby, perhaps at instigation of Merciless Parliament
1388	Merciless Parliament; Appellants gain impeachment of officials close to Richard

I

PAUL STROHM

The social and literary scene in England

Social structure

Ideas of medieval social organization have much to contribute to the study
of Chaucer. Socially and politically inflected topics are manifest within his
writings, and socially grounded issues of literary taste and reception are
thematically important as well. But, looking beyond particular matters of
content, generally held notions about the structure of society also exert a
tacit but persistent influence on the structure of his literary works.

Medieval social descriptions are very conscious of degree, and tend to
emphasize the relatively small number of people at the top of the social
hierarchy. The thirteenth-century legal commentator Bracton is representative when he divides society into those high in the ecclesiastical hierarchy
(the pope, archbishops, bishops, and lesser prelates), those high in the civil
hierarchy (emperors, kings, dukes, counts, barons, magnates, and knights),
and those remaining (a general category of 'freepersons and bondpersons'
or *liberi et villani*).[1]

Bracton's concentration on prelates and magnates is consistent with formal theory in his day, but we must remember that his category of 'freepersons
and bondpersons' comprised an overwhelming majority of the fourteenth-
century populace. After the cataclysmic Black Death of 1348–9, the population of England levelled off at about 3,500,000, where it remained for
the rest of the century and most of the next.[2] Among these persons the 150
lords and 2,000 knights and their families upon whom Bracton concentrates
would have totalled no more than 8,000–10,000, or considerably less than
one-half of one per cent of the whole.[3] He is undoubtedly correct in his half-
stated assumption that most of the remainder were agricultural workers,
with many still bound in some fashion to the land, but other groups are apparent to the modern observer. Taken together, ecclesiastical orders probably
included some 50,000 members, or just under two per cent of the whole.[4]
Esquires and other lesser gentry and their families probably comprised about

30,000–40,000 additional persons. Cities were small and city-dwellers were few by standards of today. London and nearby Westminster had a population of some 40,000, and lesser cities (which we might be more inclined to call 'towns') such as Bristol, York, Norwich, Gloucester, Leicester, and Hull had populations between 5,000 and 10,000. All told, though, we might suppose that about 100,000–125,000 additional persons were 'urban' in some sense of the word.

Latent even within Bracton's commentary is another way of viewing society which encouraged more recognition of such constituent groups. His division of society into the ecclesiastical hierarchy, the civil hierarchy, and the mass of other persons is based upon the traditional medieval view of the three estates (clerics, knights, and peasants).[5] Even when treated most hierarchically, the estates of society were also seen as interdependent, with each group contributing in its own way to the good of all. This notion of interdependence issued at times in an alternative view of society, as organic rather than hierarchical. This organic view – often conveyed through extended metaphors of the social estates as members of the body politic – permitted recognition of new classes of persons not clearly accommodated in the more traditional tripartite system. It is to be found less in formal statements than in sermons, statutes, ordinances, and a variety of other irregular and occasional documents.

A sermon delivered in the 1370s by Bishop Thomas Brinton of Rochester supplements the hierarchical view of society with a more organic view of the interdependence of its estates. We are all, he says, the mystical members of a single body, of which the head (or heads) are kings, princes, and prelates; the eyes are judges, wise men, and true counsellors; the ears are clergy; the tongue is good doctors. Then, within the midsection of the body, the right hand is composed of strenuous knights; the left hand is composed of merchants and craftsmen; and the heart is citizens and burgesses. Finally, peasants and workers are the feet which support the whole.[6] Similar views of society crop up in other occasional and relatively informal papers of the time. A Norwich gild ordinance of the 1380s, for example, takes note in its opening prayer of a ruling stratum composed of the king, dukes, earls, barons, and bachelors; a middle stratum composed of knights, squires, citizens and burgesses, and franklins; and a broader category of tillers and craftsmen.[7]

The middle groupings in Brinton's sermon and the Norwich prayer embrace persons of different social outlook. The knights – and, in the second half of the fourteenth century, the new class of esquires – enjoyed the same *gentil* status as the great aristocrats, though clearly without enjoying the benefits conferred by the hereditary titles and accompanying revenues of the latter group. Although non-*gentil*, the urban merchants (whose free status and prosperity entitled them to the titles 'citizen' or 'burgess') often enjoyed wealth considerably greater than that of most knights.[8] And even these distinctions mask variations. Many knights and esquires of the period held no land at all and had few or no military obligations, but earned their status through civil and administrative tasks which we might consider essentially 'middle class'.[9] While not *gentil*, citizens and burgesses were eligible to serve their cities and shires as 'knights' in Parliament, and some were knighted for royal or military service.[10] The ultimate standard for inclusion in these middle groupings would seem not to be rank or title, but simply civil importance and responsibility, however defined.

Chaucer's own position

Chaucer himself was a member of this middle social grouping, his place within it secured by various forms of what might be called 'civil service'. He was born in the early 1340s, in a family situation appropriate to a career of royal service.[11] His father, John Chaucer, was not only a prosperous London vintner, but had himself served Edward III in such capacities as deputy chief butler (with responsibility for certain customs collections). Chaucer's own career began in 1357 with his appointment to the household of Elizabeth, Countess of Ulster, and her husband Prince Lionel. In the service of the latter he journeyed between France and England (and was captured and ransomed during a 1359–60 military campaign in France), inaugurating a series of journeys which would take him frequently to France, twice to Italy, and elsewhere in the course of his career. Like many in his station, he married rather advantageously, to Philippa de Roet, daughter of a knight of Hainault (who had come to England in the service of the queen) and sister of Katherine Swynford (soon to be mistress and eventual third wife of John of Gaunt). In 1367, soon after his marriage, he is listed as *valettus* to King Edward III, and by 1368 he is listed among *esquiers* of the royal household. While remaining an esquire and never entering the inner circle of chamber-knights, he nevertheless continued in respected service of one sort or another until the end of his life. In 1374, he shifted from the precincts of the household to the post of controller of customs in London, assisted both by preferment from Edward III and by a timely annuity to him and to his wife from John of Gaunt. Posts and assignments continued after the accession of Richard II in 1377. The latter 1380s marked a period of comparative withdrawal from London activity, possibly tactical in nature since it roughly coincided with the years 1386–9 in which Richard II was severely challenged by an aristocratic coalition. Richard reasserted his royal prerogatives in 1389, and Chaucer soon after received his next royal appointment as clerk of the king's works. He continued in various capacities – though none of greater lustre – through the 1390s. When Henry IV supplanted Richard II in 1399, a year before Chaucer's death, he confirmed Richard's annuities and added a grant of his own.[12]

Even so spare a summary of Chaucer's civil career suggests several interesting perspectives on his life and place in society.

(1) Chaucer's position as an esquire of the royal household would have conferred *gentil* status, though he was among the more ambiguously situated members of that somewhat fluid group. Lacking the security from possession of lands and rents enjoyed by the great aristocrats and even by some of his fellow knights and esquires, Chaucer depended for his living upon his career in service. In this sense, the posts and assignments which he held in the course of what Sylvia Thrupp has called his 'versatile' career were not just an expression of his energies or his zest for politics, but were essential to his livelihood and to the maintenance of his station in life.[13]

(2) Chaucer appears to have had a representative career, both as an esquire of the king's immediate household and as a member of the royal party beyond the immediate confines of the court.[14] He would seem to have been rather good at what he did; while not lavishly rewarded, he enjoyed frequent appointments and re-appointments while weathering the extreme and sometimes dangerous factional vicissitudes of his day. His service bridged successfully the careers of three monarchs, and he managed the extremely difficult task of being on good terms both with Richard II and with John of Gaunt and the Lancastrians, even during such points of extreme tension as Richard's clash in 1386–9 with the Appellants, an aristocratic coalition headed by the Duke of Gloucester and including Gaunt's son Henry. In a period of what Thomas Usk called 'confederacie, congregacion, & couyne',[15] Chaucer was necessarily something of a factionalist, allied like Mayor Brembre of London and Chief Justice Tresilian and others with Richard's royal party. Yet – unlike such fellow partisans as Brembre, Tresilian, and Usk, who were beheaded by the Appellants in 1388 – Chaucer seems to have understood the limits of faction, and to have tempered his activity in 1386–8 and possibly in other crucial periods as well.

(3) Patronage based on his literary accomplishments seems not to have been a major factor in Chaucer's civil career. Later we will consider several literary works which may have been written in part to console, compliment, or please his superiors, but most of the facts of his civil career are comprehensible in terms of strictly non-literary talents and exertions. Chaucer's poetry fosters an impression of separation between his public and literary lives, as when the garrulous Eagle in the *House of Fame* chides him for his

habitual withdrawal from the world of affairs to that of books and private reading:

> For when thy labour doon al ys,
> And hast mad alle thy rekenynges,
> In stede of reste and newe thynges,
> Thou goost hom to thy hous anoon,
> And, also domb as any stoon,
> Thou sittest at another book
> Tyl fully daswed ys thy look . . .   (652–8)

The principal communities of readers

Solitary as Chaucer's own habits of reading and writing might have been, his poetry still shows a notable concern with issues of reception: with situations of telling and listening, of writing and reading, of audience reaction. This concern, in turn, encourages us to imagine the circumstances into which Chaucer actually launched his literary works – for whom he wrote them, and in what ways he expected them to be promulgated. Any attempt to answer these questions is, however, complicated by a number of situations peculiar to the society of Chaucer's day, including the coexistence of older 'oral' and newer 'literary' presuppositions; the relative infrequency of literacy in Chaucer's England; and, especially, the fragmentation of the literate populace into small and relatively self-contained communities of readers, based on considerations of language, geography, production and distribution of manuscripts, vocation, and social class.

The task of determining the boundaries of Chaucer's contemporary audience is complicated by the fact that the circumstances of oral narration in Chaucer's day could have permitted people to *hear* his work without having the occasion (or perhaps even the ability) to *read* it.[16] Chaucer himself seems occasionally unsure about whether he is primarily an *oral* or a *written* poet. We might loosely conceive of his earlier vision-poems as composed to be read aloud to an intimate audience and his *Canterbury Tales* as intended to reach a larger audience in manuscript form, with the mid-career *Troilus and Criseyde* as a watershed. Even so broad a formulation is, however, subject to uncertainties. Chaucer's tone of address to his audience is nowhere more intimate among his narrative poems than in *Troilus*, yet this poem concludes with an apostrophe ('Go, litel bok . . .') which certainly anticipates the circulation of his poem to an enlarged audience in manuscript form. The *Canterbury Tales* are laced with different sorts of references to hearing and reading, often within a single passage. Apologizing for his plain speech in the *Miller's Tale*, Chaucer seems to imagine his audience both as hearers and as readers of a bound manuscript:

> . . . whoso list it nat yheere,
> Turne over the leef and chese another tale.   (I, 3176–7)

We might provisionally imagine Chaucer writing for an immediate, oral audience and an ultimate audience of readers, though we must add this matter of oral/written to the list of uncertainties which urge caution upon us.

If oral rendition enlarged the possible audience of fourteenth-century works, other considerations were decidedly narrowing in their effect. The already small body of literate persons in England (probably no more than five to ten per cent of the population, even including what M. B. Parkes has called exclusively 'pragmatic' or non-literary readers[17]) was further segmented by other criteria into a number of separate 'communities of readers'. Several literary languages remained in competition throughout the second half of the fourteenth century. Though English was gradually coming to the fore, the last quarter of the century still saw Latin as the language of ecclesiastical and theological discourse, and French as the language of statecraft and civil record-keeping, as well as a literary language in some circles. Such geographically based considerations as the different dialects of English, local preference for different forms (such as alliterative as opposed to metrical verse), and physical distance were also centrifugal in their effect. Different vocational and social groupings, while anything but rigid at their outer margins, still fostered divergent tastes among such groups as the aristocracy, the gentry, and the urban middle classes. Such segmentation of the literate populace into different communities or reading publics is most dramatically illustrated by the fact that the three greatest writers of English of the later fourteenth century – Chaucer, Langland, and the *Gawain*-poet – may not have known each other's work. (Chaucer perhaps echoes the opening scene of *Sir Gawain and the Green Knight* in his *Squire's Tale*, and his Parson's dismissive allusion to poetic alliteration or 'rum, ram, ruf' may possibly embrace both writers, but neither these nor other suggestions that they knew each other's work are very persuasive.) In order better to understand how such a situation could occur, we might examine the principal literate communities of fourteenth-century England.[18]

The upper levels of the *clergy*, and especially those connected with monastic libraries and scriptoria, were naturally literate. As surviving booklists show, their continuing concern throughout the century was with theological and ecclesiastical matter written in Latin – though literature in all three languages is encountered. Some fourteenth-century manuscripts of likely ecclesiastical provenance include works in Latin, French, and Middle English, and occasionally both divine and secular works as well; London, BL, MS Harley 2253, for example, not only contains a generous selection of Middle English secular and religious lyrics, but also secular works in French and devotional works in Latin.

Members of the royal family and the fourteenth-century *aristocracy* were drawn to works in chivalry, statecraft, and occasionally theology, particularly in French. In the middle of the century, Henry, Duke of Lancaster, had written a devotional treatise entitled 'Le Livre de Seyntz Medicines'. In that work, he apologizes for the quality of his native or Anglo-Norman French, on the ground that he is more familiar with English: 'Si le franceis ne soit pas bon, jeo doie estre excusee, pur seo qu jeo suit engleis et n'ai pas moelt hauntee le franceis.'[19] In style and thrust Henry's work was somewhat of the older fashion, since the mid-century provided members of the court with ample opportunity to polish their Continental French. A series of lustrous marriages brought Continent-born and -educated wives and their trains to the royal household in the course of the century, including Isabella of France (wife of Edward II and mother of Edward III), Philippa of Hainault (wife of Edward III), and Anne of Bohemia (first wife of Richard II). Additionally, the series of conflicts between England and France known as the Hundred Years War brought the two countries into inevitable association through legations, missions, and – especially – the practice of holding prisoners for ransom (after the battle of Poitiers in 1356, King John of France and a virtual court-in-exile were resident in England throughout most of an eight-year period which lasted until his death in 1364). Extant booklists throughout this period testify to a continuing interest in French literature. At the time of her death, Isabella of France bequeathed to Edward III a number of French books, including a *Brut*, deeds of Arthur, and *Tristan and Isolde*; she owned copies of *Aimeri de Narbonne*, *Percival*, *Gawain*, and other narratives as well.[20] Although no bibliophile, Edward III seems to have had some interest in French romance; in one case the Issue Rolls of his reign specify 100 marks 'for a book of romance . . . for the King's use, which remains to the chamber of the Lord the King'.[21] Booklists of Richard II include similar romances (some possibly from his great-grandmother's bequest), and others including a 'Romance de la Rose' and a 'Romance de Perciuall & Gawyn', as well as a Bible written in French or *lingua gallica*.[22] Froissart, presenting a volume of his poems to Richard, comments that he spoke and read French very well ('moult bien parloit et lisoit le franchois'), and we have no reason to doubt his word.[23] The interest of the aristocracy was not confined to French. The Duke of Gloucester's library contained both French romances and Latin theology, and Henry IV was a reader of Latin as well.[24] Chaucer's contemporary, John

Gower, claimed some encouragement from Richard II in undertaking his English *Confessio Amantis*.[25] Yet only with evidence of Henry V's preference for literature in his native tongue does English emerge clearly as the preferred literary language of the royal and aristocratic group.[26]

The situation was different among the lower echelons of the *gentry* – especially among those knights and esquires of the royal household and/or chancery clerks and secretaries and lawyers who comprised what might be considered the 'civil service' of the day. There, an emergent public for English literary works provided a receptive milieu for Chaucer and others as well.[27] One such writer was Thomas Usk, initially a scrivener or professional scribe who became a political factionalist and convert to the royal party. In the period 1385–7, while in temporary eclipse and awaiting the royal preferment which was to be his undoing, Usk composed a political and spiritual allegory entitled *Testament of Love*, in which he explained his still unusual choice of English as a literary language:

> Trewly, the understanding of Englishmen wol not strecche to the privy termes in Frenche, what-so-ever we bosten of straunge language. Let than clerkes endyten in Latin, for they have the propertee of science, and the knowinge in that facultee; and let Frenchmen in their Frenche also endyten their queynt termes, for it is kyndely to their mouthes; and let us shewe our fantasyes in suche wordes as we lerneden of our dames tonge.[28]

Usk's probable intention in choosing English was to reach an influential audience of persons who could further his civil and factional activities. Less involved in self-promotion, but no less concerned with finding an appropriate audience for his works, was John Gower – a landed esquire with legal training, and a friend and associate of Chaucer. Gower wrote major works in French, Latin, and finally English – not, as one might suppose, from confusion, but with respect to different generic traditions and to different intended audiences. His motive in composing the *Mirour de l'Omme* in 1376–8 was comparatively devotional and private, and his linguistic choice was appropriately conservative. His *Vox Clamantis*, completed about 1385, was written in the voice of Old Testament prophecy, and the choice of Latin, which John Fisher calls 'the language of serious political discussion', suits his intended audience of influential clerics and, ultimately, the court. His *Confessio Amantis* (1385–93) addresses its message of political reconciliation to a still wider audience, and is thus written in English, 'for Engelondes sake'.[29] The deliberateness of Gower's respective choices of Latin, French, and English is underscored by the fact that, even after composing his *Confessio* in English, he returned to Latin for his *Cronica Tripertita*, with its serious political motive of Lancastrian revisionism.

The *citizens and burgesses* of London and other urban centres were (in Parkes's phrase) 'pragmatic readers' in the course of their business activities.[30] The question is, whither their interests turned when they engaged in more general reading. Throughout most of the fourteenth century, the answer seems to be that they turned toward service books and works of lay devotion in Latin. Study of the wills of London merchants and other gildsmen of the later fourteenth century shows them in possession of numerous service books (missals, breviaries, and graduals), works of pious devotion (psalters and legends of the saints), and occasional legal compilations.[31] Little wonder that, turning to English in the later fourteenth and fifteenth centuries, this audience sought devotional compendia (such as the *Prick of Conscience* – more popular than the *Canterbury Tales*, if we are to judge from over one hundred extant manuscripts), translations of Bonaventure, and mystical treatises. Segments of this audience seem, as well, to have given encouragement to Chaucer's fervent contemporary, Langland. Langland's ardently reformist poem *Piers Plowman* would seem initially to have envisioned an audience of clerics, including many in minor orders, as suggested by its theological preoccupations and its frequent interjection of scriptural and other Latin quotations. Yet its choice of Middle English embraces a larger possible audience, and most of its Latin quotations are paraphrased for that audience's benefit. The B-version of Langland's poem may even, to his possible consternation, have stimulated rebellious designs among the rebels of 1381.[32]

We must remind ourselves that boundaries between communities of readers tended to shift. While probably aimed at civil servants and literate gentry, Gower's *Confessio* was at least partially encouraged by the king; if *Piers Plowman* was first read by clerics, it was soon taken up by literate laypersons. An instance of how very far we are from establishing a 'sociology' of fourteenth-century taste is the case of the *Gawain*-poet, whose audience has been variously located with equal plausibility in baronial courts, among the country gentry, among Cheshire servants of Richard II, and in the monastic houses of the south-west Midlands.[33]

Chaucer's audience

Chaucer appears to have found his own community of readers among his fellow gentlepersons and civil servants, though several considerations argue against oversimplification. The embedded or fictionalized audiences within Chaucer's own poetry – such as his created audience of Canterbury pilgrims – are socially mixed, and at times his *gentils* and non-*gentils* engage in what appear to be socially based literary disagreements. We may assume at least a modest degree of social mixing within his actual audience, and several of his works do indeed appear to have been directed toward social superiors. The *Book of the Duchess* shows definite signs of intent to console John of Gaunt for the death of Duchess Blanche of Lancaster in 1368, both in the grieving knight's final return to a 'long castel' ['Lancaster'] (1318) and reference to the lost lady as 'White' ['Blanche'] by name (948). The narrator of this poem is himself somewhat more elevated socially than those of Chaucer's later efforts; unable to sleep, he bids a servant bring him a book (47), and riding forth to join a hunt he displays some hauteur in demanding of an attendant, 'Say, felowe, who shal hunte here?' (366). He is nevertheless deferential to the grieving knight, finding him neither curt nor formal and marvelling to find him 'so tretable . . . for al hys bale' (533–5). The relation of the narrator to the grieving knight in fact shares some characteristics of Chaucer's own probable relation to John of Gaunt: familiar in the sense that both are gentlepersons, but yet with a recognition of the rather considerable social gap between one who is simply a gentleperson and one who is at once a gentleperson and an aristocrat second in wealth and power to none in the kingdom.

Only in his short poem 'Lak of Stedfastnesse' does Chaucer appear to address Richard II directly, but Richard and Queen Anne may have been partially responsible for his ambitious but incomplete *Legend of Good Women*, with their relation to Chaucer wryly restated in his portrayal of a God and Queen of Love who set for him a trying (if not impossible) narrative task. This presumption is further fortified by the *Legend*'s points of coincidence with Gower's *Confessio Amantis* (each written in English and containing a collection of narratives of love held together by a frame which secularizes a traditional devotional form), raising the possibility that Richard and Anne were sufficiently interested in the course of English letters to give parallel charges to the two poets. If the portrayals of the God of Love and Queen Alceste are indicative, however, then certain attentions from persons in socially authoritative positions were at best to be politely endured. After all, the imperious threats of the God of Love and the inadvertent insults of Alceste ('Hym rekketh noght of what matere he take': F 365) leave Chaucer little choice but to withdraw into the defensive irony which Alfred David has seen as his characteristic strategy for dealing with socially secure members of his audience with 'limited and established literary tastes'.[34]

Chaucer's impulse to direct works beyond his immediate circle might not have been exhausted with these two efforts. Works such as his translation of Boethius and his *Tale of Melibee* may belong to the general category of 'advice to princes',[35] and the peaceable sentiments of Dame Prudence in the *Tale of Melibee* may be seen as supportive of King Richard's interest in peace with France.[36] Although we have no particular evidence that Chaucer found a bourgeois readership prior to the fifteenth century, this possibility must also be entertained. Chaucer certainly had numerous associations in the London merchant classes, such as his Port of London association with Nicholas Brembre (several times mayor, and chief among the London merchant-oligarchs) or his legal surety for John Hend (prosperous draper, eventual mayor, and also member of the royal party).[37] No documents suggest that such men were members of Chaucer's literary audience, but forums and contexts existed in which they might have been. John Gower's biographer has discussed the existence in fourteenth-century England of the French-derived merchant *Pui*, an assembly of prosperous *bourgeoisie* devoted to the cultivation of *ballades* and other *belles-lettres*.[38] Many social fraternities and gilds of the later Middle Ages provided a common meeting-place for *gentils* and merchants (for instance, the membership rolls of the Gild of St George at Norwich contain bishops and knights as well as mayors and the generality of merchants and other gildsmen and their wives).[39]

Despite such possible diversity, Chaucer's immediate circle was almost certainly composed of persons in social situations close to his own. Its members are to be sought among fellow knights and esquires of the royal household, and civil servants and lawyers of similar station in the London/Westminster area.[40] We see the outlines of such a circle in the names of those contemporaries familiarly mentioned in Chaucer's poetry: Scogan (Henry Scogan, an esquire, apparent tutor to the sons of Henry IV, and poet in his own right), Bukton (probably Peter Bukton, knight in Richard II's household and later close associate of Henry IV), Vache (Philip de la Vache, Richard's chamber-knight and eventual Knight of the Garter), Gower (lawyer, esquire, and fellow poet), and Strode (Ralph Strode, a London lawyer, who – unless we are dealing with two persons – enjoyed some standing as an Oxford philosopher-theologian earlier in his career). This circle may be filled out by our sense of other *littérateurs* in and about the court: Richard Stury (Ricardian chamber-knight and friend of the French chronicler and poet Froissart), Lewis Clifford (chamber-knight, suspected Lollard, and literary intermediary between Chaucer and the French poet Deschamps), John Clanvowe (chamber-knight, close contemporary, and author of 'The Boke of Cupid', probably the first consciously 'Chaucerian' poem in English), and more. We may also presume the presence in this circle of educated women of similar station. Philippa of Hainault (queen of Edward III) and Anne of Bohemia (queen of Richard II) and other ladies of the court were attended by *damoiselles*, and – while court records suggest they were fewer in number than household knights and esquires – a document of 1368 lists six ladies and thirteen *damoiselles* (including Philippa Chaucer) and a document of 1369 lists forty-seven ladies, *damoiselles*, and *souz-damoiselles*.[41]

Our sense of this circle is further amplified by the familiar tone in which Chaucer often addresses members of his audience – especially in his earlier poems, and most of all in certain of his verse epistles and other occasional works. One such poem is his *Envoy to Scogan*, in which a portentous opening reference to broken statutes in heaven and a consequent deluge gives way to the jesting explanation that Scogan has upset Venus with his matter-of-factness in love. As Chaucer reminds him, Scogan has in fact gone so far as to give his lady up (instead of serving patiently like the knights of literary convention), simply because she did not respond to his overtures or 'distresse':

> Hastow not seyd, in blaspheme of the goddis,
> Thurgh pride, or thrugh thy grete rekelnesse,
> Swich thing as in the lawe of love forbode is,
> That, for thy lady sawgh nat thy distresse,
> Therfore thow yave hir up at Michelmesse? (15–19)

Associating Scogan's situation with his own (both are evidently 'rounde of shap': 31), Chaucer fears that both will suffer Cupid's revenge – consisting not of Cupid's assault, but rather his decision to leave them alone:

> He wol nat with his arwes been ywroken
> On the, ne me, ne noon of oure figure;
> We shul of him have neyther hurt ne cure. (26–8)

Chaucer concludes with reflections on his poetry (he suggests that he has recently been inactive) and friendship (he asks Scogan, kneeling 'at the stremes hed' – that is, presumably, the court – to remember him, living dully downstream). Although not quite as wide-ranging, Chaucer's 'envoy' to Bukton is similarly familiar in its jocular warning of 'the sorwe and wo that is in mariage' (6). Cited as an ostensible authority on the subject of marriage is one of Chaucer's own literary creations, here as elsewhere assuming an autonomous existence outside the confines of the *Canterbury Tales*; 'The Wyf of Bathe I pray yow that ye rede / Of this matere' (29–30), Chaucer warns the prospective groom.[42]

These two poems, probable survivors of a much larger body of occasional verse now lost, confirm the existence of an 'inner circle' of Chaucer's audience which was on intimate and confidential terms both with Chaucer's store of literary devices and with Chaucer the person. Other occasional poems addressed both to men and to women – along with such moments as his address to 'every lady bright of hewe' in *Troilus* v, 1772ff – support and extend our sense of such an audience. Nimble enough to follow Chaucer's tonal shifts, acquainted enough with his verse to appreciate intertextual reference, easy enough with his company to accept and encourage jests in potentially sensitive areas – it is an audience which, in the words of Bertrand Bronson, 'must compel our admiration'.[43]

While confident in his manner of address to his immediate *hearers*, Chaucer seems less certain about the nature of his reception by those unknown persons who will be *readers* of his works in manuscript form. His ambition for such an audience has already been noted, in reference to such passages as his closing address to *Troilus* when he imagines his 'bok' entering the larger realm of 'poesye'. This imagined transition is, however, accompanied by certain anxieties, both about simple matters of transcription and also about more fundamental matters of understanding:

> . . . prey I God that non myswrite the,
> Ne the mysmetre for defaute of tonge;
> And red wherso thow be, or elles songe,
> That thow be understonde, God I biseche!   (v, 1795–8)

Nice questions of interpretation aside, Chaucer need not have worried about his embrace by an enlarged fifteenth-century readership. A progressive enlargement of his readership is suggested by the evidence of manuscript dissemination: the absence or near-absence of manuscripts from Chaucer's lifetime suggests that he prepared only a limited number of copies and used them mainly as texts for oral delivery; the first extant copies of *Troilus* and the *Canterbury Tales* are relatively fine productions, evidently intended mainly for nobility in the opening decades of the fifteenth century; by 1430–40, well before Caxton's first printed edition, the rapid proliferation of less sumptuous manuscripts in paper rather than vellum suggests that his acceptance by a truly national public was complete. All told, *Troilus* exists in sixteen fifteenth-century manuscripts; the *Tales* exist in fifty-five relatively complete manuscripts (and in Caxton's two printed editions), together with eighteen segments in miscellanies and nine more fragments. Dream visions and shorter poems circulated in numerous collections of the mid-century. Moreover, these manuscripts and fragments are distributed widely, both geographically and socially. *Troilus* exists in a vellum manuscript prepared for Henry V while he was Prince of Wales and also in paper miscellanies; the *Tales* enjoyed a fifteenth-century readership so diverse as to include a future king (Richard, Duke of Gloucester) as well as London gildsmen (as exemplified by a bequest from John Brinchele to William Holgrave, citizens and tailors of London).[44]

Chaucer as a social poet

Chaucer's poetry is complexly situated in the social context of his own time. Unlike his contemporaries Gower and Langland, he rarely if ever treats his poetry as a forum for the direct discussion of social issues of his day. The burning subject of peace with France might be addressed by Prudence's wise and pacific counsel in the *Tale of Melibee*, but only in an elliptical and proverbial way. The widespread social upheaval of 1381 known as the Peasants' Revolt – in the course of which peasants and their allies from Kent and elsewhere stormed London, burned John of Gaunt's palace, and killed Archbishop Sudbury – is a subject only for glancing and bemused comment (particularly in the *Nun's Priest's Tale*: 3394–7). Richard's near-deposition by the aristocratic Appellants and the accompanying execution of Brembre, Usk, and other of Chaucer's associates and acquaintances is mentioned not at all. As these illustrations might suggest, Chaucer is not a very topical poet. Neither, for that matter, is he a particularly historical poet, in the sense of committing himself to faithful representation of individuals or assemblies of persons or events which he might actually have seen. While his vivid portrayal of thirty-odd pilgrims has tempted scholars to propose historical identifications, the tendency of current critical theory is to see even those characterizations most apparently drawn from life as derived largely from 'estates satire' and other literary sources.[45] Yet, granting that Chaucer is neither particularly topical nor particularly historical, in certain respects he is nevertheless profoundly social.

The pilgrims gathered at the Tabard Inn seem intended to represent neither a complete census of fourteenth-century English society nor an enumeration of its most influential ranks: the great majority of the populace who worked the land is represented only by the Ploughman; entirely missing are the great aristocrats who still controlled most of England's land and wealth. Present at least by implication, however, are all three traditional estates of medieval society: the seigneurial (represented by the Knight), the spiritual (represented by the Parson), and the agricultural (represented by the Ploughman) – together with assorted other *gentils* (such as the Prioress and the Monk), and a very full review of the middle strata. While admittedly not very faithful to the numbers or proportions of fourteenth-century society, this modestly varied gathering is nevertheless presented in a way which confirms a vital premise about the relationship between social position and worldly behaviour. Jill Mann points out that the behaviour of the pilgrims on the road to Canterbury and the kinds and styles of tales they tell suggest 'a society in which work as a social experience conditions personality and the standpoint from which an individual views the world'.[46]

The pilgrimage itself is, after all, a social as well as religious event, with individuals interacting according to their social perspectives as expressed by their class (or rank) and vocation. One notices, for example, that the representatives of those traditional estates whose social responsibilities are prescribed by their place in a hierarchy mainly hold themselves aloof from the badinage of their fellow pilgrims. The Knight confines his interventions to different adjudicatory roles. The Parson chides Harry Bailly for his swearing (II, 1171) and refuses to depart from truthfulness to tell a fable (X, 31). The Ploughman does not speak. Even quasi-*gentils* like the Prioress and the Monk stand on ceremony in the end, as reflected in the Prioress's choice of a miracle for her tale and the Monk's stubborn refusal to 'pleye' (VII, 2806). In the cases of the Knight and Parson, we see evidence of the selflessness which accompanies their acceptance of the responsibilities of their social roles. Even in the case of the more self-absorbed Prioress and Monk, a certain aloof and attenuated sense of *noblesse oblige* still seems to inform their relations with their fellow pilgrims. Such restrained social conduct is at considerable variance with the bonhomie and good fellowship exhibited by their fellows. If the five gildsmen in livery are silent in the tale-telling, theirs is nevertheless the social ethic of the pilgrimage: fraternity, expressed through vital and egalitarian social interchange, is the order of the day. Certainly, quarrels based on vocational difference and other animosities constantly threaten to erupt. But the ideal of the pilgrimage is still one of amity, based on turning 'rancour and disese / T'acord' (IX, 97–8), much in the mode of those gild ordinances which seek to banish 'grucching' and 'rebellious tongues'.[47] The Merchant, in short, is not the only character attracted to 'chevyssaunce' or good deals (I, 282) – the behaviour of many of the pilgrims shows the emergence of forms of civility well suited to the advancement of transactions in an increasingly mercantile and profit-oriented society.

No less socially based are emergent issues of gender and sexual orientation; issues brought into focus by recent critical and theoretical emphases, but already evident in medieval society as well.[48] Non-normative figures like the Wife of Bath (with her commando approach to gender relations) and the Pardoner (whose unclassifiable sexuality chimes disturbingly with his religious apostasy) create their own variety of havoc on the pilgrimage, posing a challenge to the status quo.

Finally, social orientations of the pilgrims are reflected in the kinds of tales they tell.[49] The Knight, the Parson, the Prioress, and the Monk all favour traditional and edifying genres – as does their apologist, the Clerk, with his unabashed endorsement of social hierarchy. Other pilgrims more clearly identified with the middle strata of society tell tales more racy in content and more situational in ethics, culminating at one extreme in the *Shipman's Tale* with its firm satiric equation of surface civility with the furtherance of 'chaffare' and the profit-motive. To be sure, Chaucer somewhat simplified the actual state of affairs in order to suggest this socially conditioned view. While contemporary evidence *does* suggest a split in literary taste between *gentils* and others in the middle strata, that split was (as suggested earlier in this essay) probably actually grounded more on the inclination of the *gentils* toward both secular and devotional literature versus the inclination of the others toward devotional literature alone, rather than (as Chaucer seems to suggest) a clash between the *gentils'* taste for hagiographical and other elevated genres on the one hand and the taste of the non-*gentils* for fabliaux or other 'ribaudye' (VI, 324) on the other.[50] Nevertheless, Chaucer is faithful to the state of literary affairs in fourteenth-century England when he suggests that literary tastes often diverged, and that social considerations underlay the divergence.

The mingling of styles and perspectives in Chaucer's poetry has another, deeper fidelity to his social reality. The opening sections of this essay suggested that social description and social practice in Chaucer's day were moving from the static and the hierarchical to a more fluid and less hierarchical state. The penetration of new groups (such as Chaucer's own class of esquires) into the previously existing hierarchy resulted in conceptions of society as more and more internally diverse. This adjusted view in which society embraces a broadened spectrum of social groups finds a counterpart in the stylistic variety of Chaucer's own poetry – from his earlier vision poems (such as the *Parliament of Fowls*, in which the Garden of Love is divided into the regions of Venus and Nature, with each further subdivided into competing qualities and perspectives) to the *Canterbury Tales* itself (with its receptivity to a maximum variety of styles, genres, and their accompanying presuppositions). Again and again, Chaucer's poetry offers us an experience in which a hierarchy is postulated and then penetrated or otherwise qualified – as when the lower fowl of the *Parliament* interrupt the gentle pleas of the tercils with their 'kek's and 'quek's and pragmatic analysis (499) or when the drunken Miller of the *Canterbury Tales* will not abide Harry Bailly's intended order of tellers and introduces his own brand of comic 'harlotrie' (I, 3184). Chaucer's bold juxtaposition of personal and literary styles may take some liberties with the facts of personal behaviour and literary preference in his day. Even so, these stylistic juxtapositions offer an apt analogue to the complicated, varied, and dynamic social situation in which Chaucer lived and worked.[51]

NOTES

1. Bracton, *On the Laws and Customs of England*, eds. and trans. G. E. Woodbine and S. E. Thorne, vol. 2 (Cambridge, Mass., 1968), p. 31.
2. The estimates given in the pioneering study of Josiah Cox Russell, *British Medieval Population* (Albuquerque, N.Mex., 1948), are now generally regarded as too low; see, among others, John Hatcher, *Plague, Population and the English Economy, 1348–1530* (London, 1977).
3. See N. Denholm-Young, *The Country Gentry in the Fourteenth Century* (Oxford, 1969), pp. 1–40.
4. Based on Russell's analysis of the 1377 poll tax, *British Medieval Population*, pp. 133, 146.
5. The rise of the theory of the three estates between the eleventh and the thirteenth centuries in France is described by Georges Duby, *The Three Orders: Feudal Society Imagined*, trans. A. Goldhammer (Chicago/London, 1980).
6. Printed in G. R. Owst, *Literature and Pulpit in Medieval England* (Cambridge, 1933), p. 587.
7. *English Gilds*, ed. L. Toulmin Smith, EETS es 40 (London, 1870), p. 23.
8. The relative prosperity of the different estates of the realm is suggested by the different categories of the graduated poll tax of 1379; see *The Anonimalle Chronicle*, ed. V. H. Galbraith (Manchester, 1970), pp. 127–9.
9. The 1379 poll tax specifies a category of esquires who do not possess lands, rents, or chattels, but who earn their livelihood *en service* (*Anonimalle Chronicle*, p. 127).
10. M. M. Crow points out that only six of the twenty-three shire-knights in Parliament for Kent during the reign of Richard II were dubbed or formally knighted. See *Chaucer Life-Records*, eds. M. M. Crow and C. C. Olson (Oxford, 1966), p. 364.
11. Supporting evidence for this brief summary of Chaucer's career is to be found in *Life-Records*, eds. Crow and Olson.
12. Subsequent examination of the evidence suggests, however, that Henry IV's response to Chaucer's needs might not have been particularly prompt. See Sumner J. Ferris, 'The Date of Chaucer's Final Annuity and of the "Complaint to His Empty Purse"', *Modern Philology*, 65 (1967–8), 45–52.
13. Sylvia Thrupp, *The Merchant Class of Medieval London, 1300–1500* (1948; repr. Ann Arbor, Mich., 1968), p. 282. On the general matter of Chaucer's social position, see Derek Brewer, 'Class Distinctions in Chaucer', *Speculum*, 43 (1968), 290–305, at p. 304.
14. As suggested by James R. Hulbert, *Chaucer's Official Life* (1912; repr. New York, 1970).
15. In 'The Appeal . . .' in *A Book of London English, 1384–1425*, eds. R. W. Chambers and M. Daunt (Oxford, 1931), p. 29.
16. Joyce Coleman, *Public Reading and the Reading Public in Late Medieval England and France* (Cambridge, 1996).

17. M. B. Parkes, 'The Literacy of the Laity' in *The Medieval World*, eds. D. Daiches and A. Thorlby, vol. 2 (London, 1973), pp. 555–78.

18. On 'textual communities' see Brian Stock, *Listening for the Text* (Baltimore, 1990), pp. 16–29.

19. Ed. E. J. Arnould, Anglo-Norman Text Society (Oxford, 1940), p. 239.

20. Edith Rickert, 'King Richard II's Books', *The Library*, 4th ser., 13 (1933), 144–5.

21. *Issues of the Exchequer*, ed. R. Devon (London, 1837), p. 144.

22. Rickert, 'King Richard II's Books', pp. 144–5; *Issues*, ed. Devon, p. 213.

23. *Chroniques*, ed. J. B. M. C. Kervyn de Lettenhove, vol. 15 (Brussels, 1871), p. 167.

24. 'Inventory of the Goods . . . Belonging to Thomas, Duke of Gloucester', *Archaeological Journal*, 54 (1897), 275–308; William Dugdale, *Monasticon Anglicanum*, vol. 1 (London, 1846), p. 41.

25. Gower, *Complete Works*, ed. G. C. Macaulay, vol. 2 (Oxford, 1901), Prol., 48*–52*.

26. Arguments may be made for Henry V and his brothers as readers of Latin, French, and English. Indications of his preference for English include the fact that Edward, second Duke of York, translated Gaston de Foix's *Livre de Chasse* for him during 1399–1413 and that he possessed a copy of Chaucer's *Troilus* during the same period. See *The Master of the Game*, eds. W. A. and F. Baillie-Grohman (London, 1909).

27. See T. F. Tout, 'Literature and Learning in the English Civil Service in the Fourteenth Century', *Speculum*, 4 (1929), 365–89.

28. W. W. Skeat, *The Complete Works of Geoffrey Chaucer*, vol. 7 (Oxford 1897), p. 2.

29. *Complete Works*, ed. Macaulay, Prol., 24. On Gower's career and literary objectives see John H. Fisher, *John Gower: Moral Philosopher and Friend of Chaucer* (New York, 1964). The quotation is on p. 106.

30. Thrupp, *Merchant Class*, p. 161.

31. *Calendar of Wills, Court of Hustings, London*, ed. Reginald R. Sharpe (London, 1889); discussed by Thrupp, *Merchant Class*, pp. 162–3.

32. According to John Burrow, 'We must think . . . of *Piers Plowman* reaching two kinds of audience – the old audience of clerks, and the new one of prosperous, literate laymen'. See 'The Audience of Piers Plowman', *Anglia*, 75 (1957), 373–84. On Langland's Latin, see Tim Machan, 'Language Contact in *Piers Plowman*', *Speculum*, 69 (1994), 359–85. Wider dissemination of his poem is discussed by Anne Hudson, '*Piers Plowman* and the Peasants' Revolt', *Yearbook of Langland Studies*, 8 (1994), 85–106.

33. Argued, respectively, by James R. Hulbert, 'A Hypothesis concerning the Alliterative Revival', *Modern Philology*, 28 (1930–1), 405–22; Thorlac Turville-Petre, *The Alliterative Revival* (Cambridge, 1977), pp. 40–7; Michael J. Bennett, '*Sir Gawain and the Green Knight* and the Literary Achievement of the North-West Midlands', *Journal of Medieval History*, 5 (1979), 63–88; Derek Pearsall, 'The Origins of the Alliterative Revival' in *The Alliterative Tradition in the Fourteenth Century*, eds. B. S. Levy and Paul Szarmach (Kent, Ohio, 1981), pp. 1–24.

34. Alfred David, *The Strumpet Muse: Art and Morals in Chaucer's Poetry* (Bloomington, Ind., 1976), p. 122.

35. See Richard F. Green, *Poets and Princepleasers* (Toronto, 1980), p. 166.

36. Gardiner Stillwell, 'The Political Meaning of Chaucer's *Tale of Melibee*', *Speculum*, 19 (1944), 433–44.
37. *Life-Records*, eds. Crow and Olson, pp. 281–4. Additional materials on Brembre, Hend, and other mercantile associates of Chaucer are found in Ruth Bird, *The Turbulent London of Richard II* (London, n.d.).
38. Fisher, *John Gower*, pp. 78–83.
39. *English Gilds*, ed. Toulmin Smith, pp. 443–60.
40. The argument that this group provides Chaucer's principal 'point of attachment' has been made by several writers; the evidence is admirably surveyed by V. J. Scattergood, 'Literary Culture at the Court of Richard II' in *English Court Culture in the Later Middle Ages* (London, 1983), pp. 29–43. Additional information on the persons mentioned in the next paragraph is available in the *Dictionary of National Biography* and in K. B. McFarlane, *Lancastrian Kings and Lollard Knights* (Oxford, 1972).
41. *Life-Records*, eds. Crow and Olson, pp. 94–9. Less persuaded that women represented a substantial portion of Chaucer's audience is Richard F. Green, 'Women in Chaucer's Audience', *Chaucer Review*, 18 (1983), 146–54.
42. More extensive discussion of these poems, in a similar vein, is offered by R. T. Lenaghan, 'Chaucer's *Envoy to Scogan*: The Uses of Literary Conventions', *Chaucer Review*, 10 (1975–6), 46–61, and Paul Strohm, *Social Chaucer* (Cambridge, Mass., 1989), pp. 71–83.
43. Bertrand Bronson, 'Chaucer's Art in Relation to his Audience', *Five Studies in Literature*, University of California Publications in English 8 (Berkeley, Calif., 1940).
44. On manuscripts of the *Canterbury Tales*, see John M. Manly and Edith Rickert, *The Text of the Canterbury Tales*, vol. 1 (Chicago, 1940), esp. pp. 606–20. On manuscripts of *Troilus* see Robert Kilburn Root, *The Book of Troilus and Criseyde* (Princeton, N.J., 1926), pp. liii–lxi.
45. Jill Mann, *Chaucer and Medieval Estates Satire* (Cambridge, 1973), esp. pp. 1–16.
46. *Chaucer and Medieval Estates Satire*, p. 202.
47. *English Gilds*, ed. Toulmin Smith, p. 97.
48. Carolyn Dinshaw, *Chaucer's Sexual Poetics* (Madison, Wis., 1989); Elaine Tuttle Hansen, *Chaucer and the Fictions of Gender* (Berkeley, Calif., 1992); Dinshaw, *Getting Medieval* (Durham, N.C., 1999).
49. For the intriguing suggestion that Chaucer created pilgrims for his tales, rather than the other way round, see C. David Benson, *Chaucer's Drama of Style* (Chapel Hill, N.C., 1986).
50. The argument that courtly audiences enjoyed fabliaux and other narratives in everyday settings has been advanced by Per Nykrog, *Les Fabliaux: étude d'histoire littéraire et de stylistique médiévale* (Copenhagen, 1957) and has been restated in modified form by Jean Rychner, 'Les Fabliaux: genre, styles, publics' in *La Littérature narrative d'imagination* (Paris, 1961), pp. 42–52.
51. On poetic style and civic order see David Wallace, *Chaucerian Polity* (Stanford, Calif., 1997).

2

ARDIS BUTTERFIELD

Chaucer's French inheritance

It is not easy for English speakers now to believe that their language can ever have been reduced to humble stammerings by another vernacular. A complacent assumption of linguistic superiority was never felt by the English in the Middle Ages: that privilege belonged to those who wrote and spoke in Latin and French. We can come nearer to imagining this linguistic climate if we compare the relation of modern French to English and American, or of modern Swiss-German to German and French, or of Marathi to Hindi and English. All of these are subtly different situations, but in each, certain languages are perceived as dominant, and this provides a cultural model that is at once a source of aspiration and of complex feelings of insecurity. I think something like this is part of what provokes the frequent comments in Chaucer's poetry about the inadequacy of his English. Here is one example, from the *Book of the Duchess*:

> Me lakketh both Englyssh and wit
> For to undo hyt at the fulle. (898–9)[1]

Any writer indulges, from time to time, in self-deprecatory remarks about his or her skill: that Chaucer links this instinct for apology to his choice of language six times across his works is a sign that for him this is a cultural, and not merely a personal, problem.

The cultural dominance of French and its meaning for Chaucer is the topic of this essay. This is not the same as treating French writing as a 'background' for Chaucer. If, from the hindsight of history, Chaucer appears as the great father figure of English literature, from the perspective of the late fourteenth century, he appears as a rare example of otherwise small-scale English brilliance in the powerfully substantial production of medieval writings in French. For this reason, rather than look at French writing as a means of understanding Chaucer, I am going to ask what it was about French writing that was so enduring, glamorous, and foundational for Chaucer (and, by implication, his contemporaries). For Chaucer not only drew deeply from French writing, he also participated in a broad literary culture across medieval Europe that was shaped and inspired by writers in French. From a medieval point of view, Chaucer is part of the history of French culture, rather than French culture being part of the history of Chaucer.

I want to illustrate this, first of all, in two connected ways, one taking a wider political view, the other a more minutely detailed linguistic one. In broad terms, the story begins with the Norman invasion of England in the eleventh century. After 1066 England and France conducted a relationship of familiarity and aggression so closely mingled that it is often hard to tell one from the other. This is partly caused by terminology: to talk of 'England' and 'France' is to imply a sense of difference between them which only emerges later, and retrospectively. More accurately, literate cultures in England were made up of a shifting population of nobles and ecclesiastics, people who travelled widely across Europe, who used French and, if they were clerics, Latin, for the purposes of power and administration, but who also worked and lived with people from many other linguistic groupings, such as Italian, Flemish, German, Catalan, and Spanish. French itself is a term that can be misleading if it appears to apply to a single linguistic group: only in the late fourteenth and fifteenth centuries did the dialect Francien, spoken in and around Paris, become more widely dominant, and therefore synonymous with 'French'. Before that there were many kinds of 'French': Breton, Artois, Picard, and Norman, and this did not include dialect languages spoken in southern regions. The French that was used in England was also varied. Naturalized Norman French is commonly known as Anglo-Norman. This developed specific dialectal characteristics during the twelfth and thirteenth centuries; these are blurred by the mid-fourteenth century, however, since Anglo-Norman was constantly supplemented by new influxes of continental French speakers and writers. In Chaucer's London, and in court circles, the French that was used was not local but international.

The quarrelsome closeness between England and France was also a matter of kinship and possession. English kings, from Henry II on, were liege lords in France as well as England, and spent varying amounts of energy asserting their right to this title and to maintaining direct rule over Aquitaine, the large region in southwest France which was brought into English possession by Henry's marriage to Eleanor of Aquitaine in 1152. Edward II, Edward III, and Richard II all had queens from France, or neighbouring Hainault, Isabella, Philippa, and Isabella respectively. Richard II was born in Bordeaux in 1367; his father, the Black Prince, held a glittering court in Aquitaine during his extensive periods of rule in France. The issue of English rule over Aquitaine was a main source of conflict in the so-called Hundred Years War: that Richard was born there shows how interwoven his sense of identity must have been with France. Many aspects of Edwardian and Ricardian court life did not so much draw on France as were directly French: large numbers of aristocrats from France and the Low Countries lived in or in association with the royal household. This included the retinue of courtiers that Philippa, Edward III's queen, brought with her from Hainault, and the further retinues that accompanied the French royal hostages who were kept in England after the battle of Poitiers in 1356: Jean II of France (Jean le Bon) and, after the Treaty of Brétigny in 1360, his three sons, the Dukes of Berry, Burgundy, and Anjou.

One immediate impact on Chaucer of this situation was that he married one of Philippa's ladies-in-waiting, also named Philippa. With these people, and many more diplomats, ecclesiastics, soldiers, clerks, and financiers who regularly travelled on business between England and the continent, came shared social values, hard goods, and aesthetic expectations. From clothes design, cooking styles, textiles, architecture, and manuscript layout to grand tournaments and civic processions, court and city practice was characterized by an international French style. Chaucer's own domestic life, one presumes, was spent negotiating in and between English and continental French, just as it was in his diplomatic and business roles (here combined with Latin).

If this is a glimpse of the larger picture of linguistic exchange, caused by political movements of personnel across the Channel, then Richard's own use of courtly language gives us a more specific sense of the way French patterns of thinking structured English courtly life. It provides us with a way of grasping the depth of meaning in the very word *curteisye* – a key French term. Richard cultivated a more ceremonious style in court than Edward III did. Like the French kings Jean II and particularly Charles V, who insisted on a display of deferential behaviour from those who approached him, Richard demanded both increased protocol and a more elaborate form of address to himself as king. Such phrases as 'your majesty' (vostre majeste) and 'your highness' (vostre hautesse) were introduced during Richard's reign, where previously 'your rightful and gracious lord' would have sufficed. Courtiers wove these modes of address into lengthy phrases filled with flattering adjectives. 'Tresexcellent, tresredoubte et mon soverein seignur, je me recommanc a vostre haut roiale majeste' (Most excellent, most revered and my sovereign lord, I recommend myself to your high royal majesty); so begins a letter written by a bishop in 1394.[2] Such language established a subordinate role for the writer or speaker, the use of superlatives and metaphors of vertical height creating a sense of distance between subject and king.

This letter is a pure example of high courtly style. *Curteisye* is an example of French culture operating at the finest level of detail. It shows us that Chaucer's French inheritance is part of a much wider process of cultural permeation than literary influence alone. He does not merely draw from specific writers, he shares in a vocabulary that witnesses to a common history of social as well as linguistic usage.

It would be a mistake, however, to assume that to speak or write 'curteisly' in Chaucer is simply to copy the bishop's letter-writing style. There are certainly many examples where 'curteisye' finds its place alongside a whole set of related French words, 'honour', 'vertu', 'bountee', 'gentilesse', 'fraunchise', 'benyngnytee', and so on. In one case, the emperor in the Monk's tale of Nero is described as having a 'maister . . . / To teche hym letterure and curteisye' (2495–6), which illustrates how 'curteisye' is both a skill taught in royal circles and one that is associated with writing letters. Yet Chaucer also sets 'curteisye' in some wonderfully incongruous places: 'Curteys she was, discreet, and debonaire' is the phrase used to describe the hen Pertelote in the *Nun's Priest's Tale* (2871); the deceitful friar in the *Summoner's Tale* speaks 'curteisly and softe' to his host just before, 'ful curteisly', he kisses the host's wife with blatant familiarity (1771; 1802). Perhaps the most outrageous example is Alison's archly anguished request to her lover Nicholas in the *Miller's Tale*, 'Do wey youre handes, for your curteisye!' (3287). How do we reconcile all these different, often comic contexts for 'curteisye' in Chaucer's writings with the high ideal circumstances of addressing kings?

Part of the answer to this question relates to social status: the language of 'curteisye' has different functions lower down the social scale. The play of social distinctions can be carried out at all levels of society, between knights and millers, and millers and reeves, between carpenters and clerics as well as kings and bishops. With brilliant economy, Chaucer conducts an investigation into the social power of language right across his writings. My argument here is twofold: he does not lose hold of its connection with the highest forms of social behaviour, and second, his means of investigation are thoroughly French.

In the next section of this essay, after introducing the French material in general terms, I am going to focus on one of the principal gifts it offers to Chaucer and other late- and post-medieval writers, the legacy of a highly sophisticated exploration of the language of love.

It may be helpful to sketch an outline of some of the main authors and works in French medieval writing. The first authors are still the most celebrated: the troubadours. From *c.*1100–*c.*1300, they composed and performed songs, largely on the topic of love, which have resonated through nine centuries of Western imagination. Concentrated in southern France, they were followed in the thirteenth century by their northern French equivalent, the trouvères. Together, the troubadours and trouvères left nearly 5,000 songs, many with music, which, in their exquisite, allusive, and highly analytic approach to love, are the source of the language and thinking that are central to later French culture.

Alongside the trouvère songs, two main genres, romance and fabliau, dominate the thirteenth century. Let me take these in turn. French romance encompasses all the Arthurian narratives, as well as many other tales of knights, ladies, and orphaned children wandering through forests, escaping from perils, encountering magical or mysterious events, and returning finally to various forms of civilization or reconciliation. Yet by far the best-known thirteenth-century romance is rather different. The *Romance of the Rose* (*Le Roman de la Rose*) by Guillaume de Lorris and Jean de Meun is somewhat confusingly titled if we have these expectations in mind. The first surprise is that it is written in the first person, by a lover; the second that the adventure is all internal; and the third that it has two quite unequal parts, with the second (by Jean de Meun) purporting to be the same work, but emerging as a vast, ironic, coruscatingly intelligent commentary on the first.

It is hard to overemphasize the importance of this double-authored work to European medieval writing: it survives in nearly 300 manuscripts (compared to the 55 complete copies of the *Canterbury Tales*), it was translated into several European languages, and was imitated and rewritten by dozens of writers. I shall shortly describe it in more detail; here I want to emphasize its links with troubadour and trouvère lyric. For what gives it a unique quality and formal audacity is that Guillaume has turned lyric into narrative. Instead of a song with five to seven artfully constructed stanzas, articulating through the first-person voice the psychological and emotional traumas of love, Guillaume creates a 3,000-line vision, stretching and recasting the song's tight structural shape into something ostensibly linear and open-ended. It thus succeeds in being both diametrically opposite to lyric, and utterly founded on it.

Guillaume's stroke of originality was not isolated. In approximately the same decade, another *Romance of the Rose* was composed. More like a traditional adventure story, this romance acts as a double to the other *Rose*. For this *Rose*, by Jean Renart, also feeds off lyric, this time by incorporating a large number of songs within the narrative frame. Renart's decision proved to be as far-reaching as Guillaume's. Throughout the thirteenth century, romance authors continued to cast songs into narrative, and by the fourteenth century, love narrative, such as Chaucer's *Troilus and Criseyde*, looks like a cross between the two *Roses*, a narrative generated out of lyric that is also cut into by lyric. The two most significant figures in the fourteenth century are Guillaume de Machaut (1300–77) and, Chaucer's exact contemporary, Jean Froissart. Machaut, a brilliant composer of music as well as poetry, was a master of love narrative (known in French as the *dit amoureux*) and lyric, both as independent genres and in combination. For him, Froissart, and Chaucer, poetry was about exploring the limits of form, its potential as a means of articulating subtle variations in self-projection and identity. Machaut and Froissart were instrumental in establishing a newly settled set of patterned structures in lyric form, known as the *formes fixes*, or fixed forms: principally *rondeau*, *ballade*, and *virelai* (cf. *Legend of Good Women*: F 423). Froissart, unlike Machaut, abandoned poetry in middle age, and spent the remainder of his days as a writer composing prose history (the celebrated *Chroniques*).

If there is a clear line of connection between the twelfth-century troubadours, the thirteenth-century *Rose(s)*, and the fourteenth-century lyrics and *dits amoureux*, then this must be set in context against other, more satiric, didactic, and comic types of writing. Jean de Meun's elaborately lengthy extension to the *Rose* is an example of this, in its intensive use of satire and comic character portraits. He wrote his work in the 1270s; the great period of the fabliau (pl. fabliaux) dates from the middle of the century. The majority of fabliaux are associated with northern French towns, particularly with Arras, at the time an artistic centre of international repute. Hundreds survive, with plots that tend to involve low cunning, marital triangles, and obscene humour. Probably largely composed by clerics, the fabliaux are an important reminder of an anti-courtly style in French writing. The urban setting of many of the narratives complicates our reading of them: as with the large collection of stories about Renart the Fox (*Le Roman de Renart*), they show us a world in which courtliness acquires a material, mercantile edge. High ideals are shown to be compromised by worldly desires through writing that is not so much sternly moralistic as comically knowing. This kind of writing comes less to the surface in Machaut and Froissart than it does in the work of Eustache Deschamps, a slightly younger contemporary of Froissart and Chaucer, whose lyrics range through all kinds of satiric and comic material.

As well as these writers and genres, Chaucer also drew on the vast amount of didactic writing in French: sermons, saints' lives, treatises, and translations of moral philosophy, of science, medicine, and alchemy. Encyclopaedias were compiled; Latin poetry, such as Ovid's *Metamorphoses*, was both translated and supplied with extensive moral commentary.

The traditional way of relating this material back to Chaucer is through source study. We look for the texts that Chaucer appears to have worked with most closely, starting with ones that he translates or echoes verbally. In the case of French writing, Chaucer's acts of most direct translation consist in rendering Guillaume's *Roman de la Rose* into English,[3] and making frequent borrowings from Guillaume, Machaut, and Froissart in the *Book of the Duchess* and the Prologue to the *Legend of Good Women*, as well as in *Troilus and Criseyde*. His short poem *The Complaint of Venus* is translated from three *ballades* by the fourteenth-century Savoyard soldier-poet Oton de Grandson. He seems to have worked with French translations of Latin and Italian books, such as the source for his *Tale of Melibee*; French fabliaux provide analogues to the plot and structure of the Reeve's and Shipman's tales (and indeed all his fabliaux); the *Nun's Priest's Tale* is drawn from the fox fables in *Le Roman de Renart*; the Man of Law's tale of Constance is based on part of an Anglo-Norman chronicle. Correspondences of plot, structure, theme, and specific passages occur between the *Physician's Tale*, the *Wife of Bath's Prologue*, the *Merchant's Tale* and parts of Jean de Meun's *Roman de la Rose*. The looser correspondences are, naturally, numerous. As the relationship becomes more indirect, as source slips to analogue, its significance becomes harder to assess; we also have to reckon with the possibility that sources may have been lost.

As a result of this kind of investigation, it used to be widely repeated that Chaucer had an early French phase which he then outgrew in favour of Italian authors, before finally finding his own true English voice. This was matched to a simple chronology: early dream poems (French); middle dream poems and *Troilus and Criseyde* (Italian); *Canterbury Tales* (English). Yet this schema is profoundly misleading. Chaucer undoubtedly based *Troilus* heavily on Boccaccio's *Il Filostrato*, as well as Boethius's *Consolation of Philosophy*, and read far more widely than just in French throughout his writing career. But none of his specific phases of reading cancelled out earlier interests and influences. In particular, French patterns of thinking were too pervasive in European culture to be 'outgrown'. This chronology is not merely reductive about a writer's patterns of reading, it relies on crude notions of 'French', 'Italian', and 'English'. It is also dependent on a model of source study that has come to look increasingly inflexible as a means of understanding how one text interacts with another. I want to illustrate this by way of the text that has traditionally been seen as Chaucer's most visibly 'French' piece of writing, *The Book of the Duchess*.

The well-tried tactics of source criticism involve a kind of weighing exercise. Taking the source text in one hand and the 'new' text in the other, one asks how heavy is the 'new' text compared to the source? What does it retain; what does it reject? What can we deduce from the kinds of changes the author has made? All are sensible, indeed important questions, but we should also be aware that they can carry dubious assumptions. For example, the exercise can degenerate into arithmetical banality: subtract *Il Filostrato* from *Troilus* and you will end up with the 'true' Chaucer. It is difficult for most of us not to suppose that the most interesting parts of a poem are the ones without the supporting scaffolding of a source. All we have to do, it seems, to interpret Chaucer, is to measure his difference from other texts.

The *Book of the Duchess* lends itself to some of these tendencies. Nearly 1,000 lines out of 1,334 have a verbal parallel in a range of mostly French and some Latin poems. Chaucer worked principally with Guillaume de Lorris's version of *Le Roman de la Rose*, three poems by Machaut, and one by Froissart. The Machaut poems comprise *Le Jugement dou Roy de Behaingne* (*The Judgement of the King of Bohemia*), *La Fonteinne Amoureuse* (*The Fountain of Love*), and *Le Remede de Fortune* (*The Consolation of Fortune*); Froissart's is entitled *Le Paradys d'Amour* (*The Paradise of Love*). From one perspective, Chaucer's poem is a close translation of these French works. Yet a detailed study of the borrowings shows a kaleidoscopic pattern rather than blocks taken from individual passages. Ironically, therefore, the English is so intricately based on French lines that we have to stand back to gain any overall impression of the compositional process.

We discover that the apparent precision with which we can observe Chaucer handling line after line of French poetry is something of an illusion: the verbal parallel is the overt sign of a much larger, and less immediately visible, network of relationships. Chaucer's compositional choices are not being made merely in reaction to Machaut or Froissart or Guillaume de Lorris, they are choices made in parallel with them and born out of a similar cultural standpoint. An illustration of this is the description of the richly painted and glazed chamber in which the dreamer finds himself as he wakes into his dream. The windows show the story of Troy, and the walls are covered with the illuminated text of the *Roman de la Rose*. Streams of golden light pour through the windows onto his bed. In this vivid, visionary scene Chaucer presents an image of the author flooded on all sides by the colours of the *Rose* and classical myth. His access to this inspirational material is exuberantly direct and shows how he, Machaut, and Froissart are all working within larger and older cultural frameworks. It thus provides a sense of multiple histories of reading: Machaut and Froissart respond to the *Rose* just as fully as Chaucer responds to them and to the *Rose* together. Classical myth underpins all of this reading and writing. This image of an author physically surrounded by a text is a better way of grasping literary relationships than a list of parallels. As an image of immersion, it guides us towards encompassing, as well as specific, moments of cultural acquisition.

Authors are also readers; in addition, they have their own chronology of reading. And if, turning to the source of *Troilus and Criseyde*, the early fourteenth-century Italian poem *Il Filostrato* by Giovanni Boccaccio, we try to find out what Boccaccio's sources were, we discover (unsurprisingly) that several of them again coincide with Chaucer's. For example, Boccaccio, like Chaucer, read French poets avidly, alongside Boethius and Dante. Boccaccio, Machaut, and Froissart are not inert 'sources', but poets, like Chaucer, reacting dynamically to a wide range of texts.

Although finding a source or realizing that Chaucer's text is a close translation of another is an essential step towards understanding its context, we also need to consider the kinds of cultural assumption that inform source as well as text. To say that Chaucer turns away from French poetry to Italian when he composes *Troilus and Criseyde* is to forget that Boccaccio was also writing under the spell of the *Roman de la Rose*. My effort in this essay is to concentrate on the deeper rather than the more superficial elements of French influence. The specific moments of French borrowing in Chaucer may be interesting in themselves; they are also worth reading as significant traces of the larger cultural atmosphere in which Chaucer and other late-medieval writers worked.

The *Book of the Duchess* again provides a starting point, indeed, its very first word, 'I':

> I have gret wonder, be this lyght,
> How that I lyve . . .   (1–2)

As far as I am aware, this is the first narrative poem in English to start with 'I'.[4] What might be the significance of this? The first point is that it is (after all) a borrowing. The poem's opening lines are taken from *Le Paradys d'Amour* by Jean Froissart, who is himself innovating by starting a love narrative with 'je':

> Je suis de moi en grant merveille
> Comment je vifs . . .   (1–2)

In one sense this could be seen as a piece of slavish imitation by Chaucer: an English *dit amoureux* is about to begin. Yet once we probe deeper, we find that the frame of reference for the decision to start a poem in this way reaches back very far. To understand both the English and French fourteenth-century use of the first-person voice in a love poem we need to go back to the troubadours.

I remarked earlier of the troubadours that their approach to love is the foundation for later medieval notions of European courtliness. Yet the model provided by the troubadours is riven with tensions and unresolved dichotomies. The singer may start his song claiming to be in love, but may end it with flashes of misogynistic comment that question the credibility of his opening star-struck pose. Or he may complain that the season is not corresponding properly to his situation: May is supposed to be a time when lovers feel inspired and joyful but the obduracy of his lady in refusing him causes him to curse its flowers. The concept of courtly writing is itself questioned: how can the rancour caused by female inconstancy produce courtly verse? Love provokes contradiction: in uttering his love, the singer sometimes reveals that, far from being ennobled by his sentiments, he is compromised or abased by them. The poet may be exposed, often humorously, as a fraud. A fissure opens up between his identity as a poet and his identity as a lover: it turns out to be impossible for him to be both.

Troubadour song cannot be described as a vehicle for the expression of ideal love if this means claiming for it a consistent purity, refinement, and height of expression. None of the positions of high striving are left unqualified for long, and they are often shown to be susceptible to satire, contradiction, or confusion in the very next breath. One of the few exceptions to this lies in the verse form itself: in subtlety, technical difficulty, and aural craftsmanship the songs remain at a consistently superlative level. It follows that the figure of the speaker or singer is hard to characterize as a stable voice. He (sometimes she, as some songs by female troubadours – the *trobairitz* – survive) has a shifting identity, that is sometimes defined in opposition to the lady, or a patron, or the audience, or his own torn state of mind. The identity of the first-person speaker is thus always at issue; it cannot be taken for granted.

These characteristics of troubadour song are worth emphasizing to prevent the easy assumption that only in later writers, perhaps even only in Chaucer, did a genuinely ironic voice develop, one that was capable of mocking or destabilizing high seriousness. It is hard to find any rhetorical sleight, device of performance, literary self-consciousness, or instinctive ironic deflection in Chaucer that is absent from the troubadours.

In going back this far, we have met a 'background' that is far from inert or static. On the contrary, it warns us away from thinking that there is a kind of natural progression in literary history from the simple to the sophisticated. Subsequent explorations of the language of love are never merely an advance on the troubadours: they are best seen as different ways of articulating a similar sense of crux about feeling and expression. Two of the perceptions about love language voiced by troubadour poets provoke an especially vivid response in later poets. One is that writing about love is a profound analogy for the creative process *per se*; another is that just as courtesy is a way of living as well as of writing, so love poetry is a brilliant means of expressing the ironies involved in trying to live as well as write at the same time.

The *Roman de la Rose* explores both of these ways of thinking with subtlety and remarkable imaginative potency. From the first, Guillaume presents the work as a book that contains the art of Love:

Et se nule ne nus demande
comant je veil que li romanz
soit apelez que je comanz,
ce est li Romanz de la Rose,
ou l'art d'Amors est tote enclose. (34–8)

[And if any man or woman should ask what I wish this romance, which I now begin, to be called, it is the *Romance of the Rose*, in which the whole art of love is contained. (Horgan, p. 3)]

The subject of the poem is thus love, not just as an emotion or experience but as an art. For subsequent readers of the *Rose*, this was also true in reverse: the *Rose* was held up as the supreme illustration of how the subject of love is the art of writing. It takes the languages of identity and love articulated in troubadour song and exposes them to the more extended temporal and spatial scrutiny of narrative. As part of this process, Guillaume adds an infrastructure of abstractions, symbols, and personifications, set within the framework of a dream. The Lover/dreamer walks in the Garden of Delight in the blissfully sensuous season of May. He sees a wall covered in images of vices (Hate, Felony, Envy, Sadness); allowed in through the narrow gate by Oiseuse (Leisure), he meets and dances with Beauté, Largesse, Courtoisie, and many other beautiful women. He gazes into the Fountain of Narcissus: there, reflected in two crystals, he sees a rose garden and a rose. He wants to pick the rose, but is repulsed and wounded by the God of Love. Twice more he approaches, with the encouragement of Bel Acueil (Fair Welcome), Franchise (Generosity), and Pitié (Pity), but each time he is beaten off by Danger (Resistance), Honte (Shame), and others. Though he is granted a kiss with Venus's help, Jalousie then builds a castle around the Rose; locks Bel Acueil in, and keeps him under the watchful guard of an old woman (La Vieille). Guillaume's 4,000-line version of the poem ends here with the Lover left complaining his fate.

Jean de Meun now adds nearly 18,000 lines. The God of Love comes with an army to help the Lover. Male Bouche (Evil Gossip) is killed. After a long siege, Venus leads an attack right into the castle and sets the inner sanctuary on fire. The Lover manages to pluck the Rose just before waking from his dream. Jean's narrative is generated by a restlessly energetic desire to add argument, learning, philosophical discussion, satire, and comedy to Guillaume's vision. It is also a narrative designed to invent himself as a writer: paradoxically, by continuing and promoting the authorship of Guillaume's romance, Jean sought to proclaim his own authority. Once again, in an idiosyncratic style, the topic of love becomes the occasion for a poet to examine his own identity and status.

What is it about this (double) work that made it so deeply influential and attractive? Of the many factors, three stand out. First, the dazzling opening images of springtime: the birdsong, new blossom and green growth, the limpid light and warmth. None of these images is new; as I have already commented, they were a familiar set of tropes for the troubadours. Yet Guillaume gives them special radiance in his description, setting them within the transforming power of a dream-world and making them part of an emotional journey. The dream itself is a key element: it distances, yet also liberates the lover's experience. Third, Guillaume achieves an astonishingly powerful collision of the emotional and the intellectual: love is turned into something abstract but without losing its intensity. He does this partly through concentrating on certain mythic images – rose, garden, castle, fountain, and crystals. Through a combination of images of enclosure, of circles within circles, and sight, he expresses the pain and joy of deferred desire in a highly visual counterpoint to the abstract world of the intellect.

Machaut and Froissart take hold of all these aspects. Both poets develop further ways of playing with the boundaries of life and art. Thus in *La Fonteinne Amoureuse*, Machaut's poet-narrator and the lord he encounters both turn out to have the same dream. They fall asleep by the fountain; when the lord wakes up, both he and the poet see that the ring that his lady had given him in his dream is still on his finger. Machaut's last great narrative work, *Le Livre dou Voir Dit*, imitated by Froissart in his *La Prison Amoureuse*, revolves entirely around the ironies involved in living and writing. The plot is divided between two characters, Guillaume, the aged poet, and a young girl, Toute Belle, who writes to him, seeking friendship because she has fallen in love with his poetic reputation. They exchange forty-six prose letters and over sixty lyrics; the narrative couplets that describe the progress of their relationship are also gradually exchanged, so that the writing down of the love affair in due course becomes indistinguishable from the affair. Froissart takes this one stage further by dividing his narrative between the poet and a friend who is asked to comment on the poet's work. The work becomes indistinguishable from the commentary on the work.

We can see Chaucer reflecting on these perceptions concerning love poetry at many points in his writings. The start of the *Book of the Duchess* is one example. It presents a speaker who through the conversational, disjointed nature of his speech dramatically communicates his depression and evasiveness. He says he cannot feel or write; yet if we re-read the poem, we find that these opening lines are the result of his decision at the end to put his dream in writing. Like Marcabru or Girart de Borneilh, he plays a kind of trick or sleight of hand. The poet is speaking, but is claiming to be inarticulate; his identity is also obscure. Is he really the poet? Is he perhaps a lover? Or is he only the person who had the dream? Moreover, however artless these lines seem, they are taken from an extremely tightly wrought poem: Froissart wittily replays a single rhyme sound in the first six lines. Again, in classic troubadour-fashion, surface confusion is underpinned by a taut and precise verse form.

The start of the *Parliament of Fowls* plays the same trick, this time by teasing the reader with an inverted sentence structure that makes it seem as if the speaker is talking about poetry rather than love:

> The lyf so short, the craft so long to lerne,
> Th'assay so hard, so sharp the conquerynge,
> The dredful joye alwey that slit so yerne:
> Al this mene I by Love ...   (1–4)

But of course, the answer is itself teasing, since to talk of love is to talk of poetry. What we have here is a literary relationship that goes well beyond that of source or analogue. Chaucer is not borrowing a form of words so much as a cultural habit.

I want to finish by drawing attention to a correlative of this poetry of love. It is characteristic of the language of love and identity in the troubadours to use irony and hyperbole. At first sight, this may seem surprising. If we have been led to think of the Middle Ages as a period of high ideals, including the ideal of courtly love, then it may seem odd to find the early masters of vernacular love language resorting so freely to irony. And yet, as our own experience of popular culture reminds us, the commonplace expression 'I love you' has a tricky purchase on meaning. It is no guarantee of meaning, but it is not necessarily a disavowal of meaning either. Hyperbole is essential (I love you more than words can say; you are more beautiful than any woman who has ever lived), but its extravagance makes it both more likely to mean something, and less likely. In one very subtle song, Arnaut de Maruelh insists that his words of praise can mean something, because the empty boasts of other troubadours have ensured that no one will ever realize that his words are not empty. That is, the truth of his love will never be betrayed because no one will ever expect to take his words seriously.

Hyperbole and irony are strangely related in the language of love; one does not cancel the other out. It is hard to find any French love poet of the thirteenth or fourteenth century who does not take this as axiomatic. Unsurprisingly, similar assumptions are at work in Chaucer's poetry. Even moments of high seriousness, such as the ecstatic songs of love exchanged by Troilus and Criseyde in Book III, are riven with this sense of ultimate joy over-pitching into doubt.

'But natheles, myn owen lady bright,
Were it so that I wiste outrely
That I, youre humble servant and youre knyght,
Were in youre herte iset so fermely
As ye in myn – the which thyng, trewely,
Me levere were than thise worldes tweyne –
Yet sholde I bet enduren al my peyne.'

To that Criseyde answerde right anon . . .

'Ye ben so depe in-with myn herte grave,
That, though I wolde it torne out of my thought,
As wisly verray God my soule save,
To dyen in the peyne, I koude nought.
And, for the love of God that us hath wrought,
Lat in youre brayn non other fantasie
So crepe that it cause me to dye!'   (1485–92; 1499–1505)

Chaucer's ability to express the pain in such a moment, in observing experience fail to measure up to language, is matched only by his talent at showing how easily this experience can also be exquisitely comic. One thinks of John the carpenter in the *Miller's Tale*, imagining his wife drowned in the flood predicted by Nicholas:

This carpenter answerde, 'Allas, my wyf!
And shal she drenche? Allas, myn Alisoun!'
For sorwe of this he fil almoost adoun.   (3522–4)

And her reply:

But nathelees she ferde as she wolde deye,
And seyde, 'Allas! go forth thy wey anon,
Help us to scape, or we been dede echon!
I am thy trewe, verray wedded wyf;
Go, deere spouse, and help to save oure lyf.'   (3606–10)

This is irony caught up in a web of social relationships that qualifies and deepens its force. To appreciate its depth of reference we need to have some memory of the kind of language that Alisoun is faking: here, the use of death as a hyperbolic intensifier ('she ferde as she wolde deye'). What makes it poignant rather than bathetic or cynical is that her false use of hyperbole counters John's sincere attempt to live up to high courtly poses ('For sorwe of this he fil almoost adoun'). In both cases, they are missing the high note, but the result is not shallow. The closeness of the false gesture ('she ferde as she wolde deye') to the genuinely felt near-swoon ('he fil almoost adoun') plays with the fine difference between life and art in a fundamentally French manner. Chaucer is not mocking a pretension to French high style here; he is participating in a French linguistic and social perspective which was always able to handle the potentially devastating relationship between high seriousness and high language with intelligent sympathy.

I have sought to show that understanding Chaucer's French inheritance is a matter of sounding the depths as well as enjoying the brilliance of the surface allusions and echoes. This reveals how far Chaucer is always 'already' French: he cannot move on or away from these cultural habits because they are not just ingrained in his own domestic and professional circumstances, but embedded in ways of thinking and writing that extend back several hundred years. His French reading is more than a source or a phase; it is a habit of mind and of language. By allowing ourselves to see French as a natural language for Chaucer rather than an imported or alien tongue, we can better appreciate the truly international character of his English.[5]

NOTES

My thanks to Jill Mann, and also to John Mullan and Kate Mossman, colleague and student of mine respectively, for their generous and pertinent advice on the essay.

1. For other examples, see *Knight's Tale* 1459–60; *Man of Law's Tale* 778–9; *Squire's Tale* 37–41; Prologue to the *Legend of Good Women* F 66–7; *Complaint of Venus* 80.
2. John Waltham, Bishop of Salisbury. See Nigel Saul, *Richard II* (New Haven/London, 1997), pp. 340–1.
3. The Prologue to the *Legend of Good Women* describes Chaucer as having translated the *Rose* (F 329–30; G 255–6); it is uncertain whether (or how much of) the surviving Middle English translation is by Chaucer.
4. I don't include here narrative songs (one or two start with 'I'), or *The Owl and the Nightingale* (early thirteenth century) which is a debate poem built on an opening narrative song motif.
5. The following is a list of primary works referred to in this essay, and selected secondary works for further reading.

Primary:

Guillaume de Lorris and Jean de Meun, *Le Roman de la Rose*, ed. F. Lecoy, CFMA, 92, 95, 98, 3 vols. (Paris, 1965–70); trans. F. Horgan (Oxford/New York, 1994).

Guillaume de Machaut, *Guillaume de Machaut: The Fountain of Love (La Fonteinne Amoureuse) and Two Other Love Vision Poems*, ed. and trans. R. Barton Palmer (New York/London, 1993).

Le Jugement du Roy de Behaigne; and, Remede de Fortune, eds. and trans. J. I. Wimsatt and W. W. Kibler (Athens, Ga., 1988).

Le Livre dou Voir Dit (The Book of the True Poem), ed. D. Leech-Wilkinson, trans. R. Barton Palmer (New York/London, 1998).

Jean Froissart, *Le Paradis d'Amour*, ed. Peter F. Dembowski, Textes Littéraires Français, 339 (Geneva, 1986).

La Prison Amoureuse (The Prison of Love), ed. and trans. Laurence de Looze (New York, 1994).

B. A. Windeatt, trans., *Chaucer's Dream Poetry: Sources and Analogues* (Cambridge, 1982).

Samuel Rosenberg, Margaret Switten, and Gérard le Vot, *Songs of the Troubadours and Trouvères: An Anthology of Poems and Melodies with Accompanying CD* (New York/London, 1998).

Secondary:

William Calin, *The French Tradition and the Literature of Medieval England* (Toronto, 1994).

Simon Gaunt and Sarah Kay, eds. *The Troubadours: An Introduction* (Cambridge, 1999).

David F. Hult, *Self-Fulfilling Prophecies: Readership and Authority in the First Roman de la Rose* (Cambridge, 1986).

Charles Muscatine, *Chaucer and the French Tradition* (Berkeley/Los Angeles, Calif./London, 1957).

Elizabeth Salter, *English and International: Studies in the Literature, Art and Patronage of Medieval England*, eds. Derek Pearsall and Nicolette Zeeman (Cambridge, 1988).

Nigel Saul, *Richard II* (New Haven/London, 1997).

James I. Wimsatt, *Chaucer and the French Love Poets* (Chapel Hill, N.C., 1968).

Chaucer and His French Contemporaries: Natural Music in the Fourteenth Century (Toronto, 1991).

3

DAVID WALLACE

Chaucer's Italian inheritance

Viewed from continental European perspectives, Chaucer's England and its poetry appear both eccentric and retarded. Its eccentricity is geographical: from classical times onward, the British Isles had been mapped as the last stop before *ultima Thule* and the end of the world. In Boccaccio's *Decameron* II, 3, England is regarded as more exotic and fantastical than Barbary (the north African coast, just two hundred miles from Sicily): a place where a savvy young Tuscan might be seduced by an abbot (a princess in disguise), mortgage barons' castles and become Earl of Cornwall.[1] The vernaculars of these distant islands were thus seen as eccentric and of scant literary consequence: the French chronicler Froissart, who spent the years 1361–7 in England, apparently never troubled to learn English, getting by in the European *lingua franca* (French). Over two centuries earlier, Chrétien de Troyes had written the great romances foundational to the values of chivalry celebrated by Froissart in his *Chronicles*; around 1275, the *Roman de la Rose* was approaching completion. Inspired in part by Italian receptions of the *Rose*, Dante composed not only the greatest European poem of all – his *Commedia* – but also a series of works to guide its future reception and interpretation. Petrarch, while championing Latin rather than Italian, nonetheless assembled a collection of Italian lyrics – the *Canzoniere* – that English poets would not fully fathom until the early sixteenth century. Boccaccio's greatest legacy to English literature, his framed collection of tales, was also not absorbed until the sixteenth century (when it eased the path to Shakespeare). Chaucer, however, made early and precocious use of Boccaccio and was ultimately inspired to fashion a framed collection of his own.

Growing up in a mercantile family close by the Thames, Chaucer early acquired a familiarity with Italian shipmen, traders, and financiers that was put to good use in later professional life; and through his actual visits to Italy, he gained sophisticated, first-hand knowledge of the social and political settings from which the writings of Dante, Boccaccio, and Petrarch had emerged.[2] In considering the highly complex matter of 'Chaucer's Italian inheritance', however, I here concentrate on one topic of fundamental importance to Chaucer's development as a poet: namely, the very idea that poetry might be written in one's mother tongue to the highest European standards; the aspiration (even) that such a modern poet might associate with the great literary masters of antiquity. To say this is not to suggest that Chaucer ever sought to become (as his Victorian admirers suggested) the 'poet of England': for 'there is one circle of common interest,' Derek Pearsall observes, 'which Chaucer never seems desirous of moving in or even recognizing, and that is England'.[3] Chaucer's native ground, for both his poetry and his royal service, is not 'England', but rather a territory extending from the south-east quadrant of the island into continental Europe (Calais remained in English hands until 1558). As Ardis Butterfield has argued in the previous chapter, the cross-Channel cultural terrain of Chaucer's lifetime is saturated in French values. Chaucer's achievement, I shall argue, is not to declare independence as a poet of England, but rather – and here his strategy seems Joycean – to evolve a distinctively localized poetry *even as* he draws it further and deeper into crosscurrents of European cultural exchange. He was fortuitously helped here by the companionable marriage of Richard II to Anne of Bohemia, daughter of the Holy Roman Emperor, Charles (whose city and court of Prague, still visible today, hosted an internationalist culture rivalled only by that of Avignon). But Chaucer was further helped by being born at just the right time: for English, in his lifetime, was gradually superseding French as the normative language of royal, legal, and parliamentary business.[4] If there is one opportunity in the history of any language to fashion a poetic determinative of future 'makinge', it comes while that language remains sufficiently plastic and responsive to all kinds of experiment. In this regard, then, the retardedness and eccentricity of English served Chaucer well.

At this point we should note that, even as Chaucer was spinning out his European ambitions, a great phase of English poetry was actually unfolding around him: the alliterative verse of Langland, the *Gawain*-poet, and other unknowns. Langland, too, wrote versions of framed narrative (whose successive beginnings invite the closest comparison to the opening of the *Canterbury Tales*). And this, too, is a poetry of Westminster and London (rather than of baronial castles and the provinces). The relations of Chaucer to this tradition, or of this tradition's European filiations, remain remarkably uncertain. But there is one aspect of kinship between Chaucer and his alliterative peers that explains why Italian, rather than French, would prove of greater utility to his verse making. Both Chaucer and Langland fashioned a poetic line relying upon stresses either side of a medial caesura. French, a syllabic poetry, does not work like this: but Italian does. Thus it is that the entrance to Dante's hellmouth can be introduced with a half-line followed by a terrible pause ('PER ME SI VA', *Inferno* I, 3); thus too that Chaucer can imitate this line precisely ('Thorgh me men gon', *Parliament of Fowls*, 127 and 134), an effect less easily achieved by the quicker shuttling movement of French lines. Thus Chaucer's aspirations for Europeanized English verse would lead him to discover peculiar kinship and possibilities in Italian poetry not to be found in French.

But not all such experiments to fashion what Dante calls an 'illustrious vernacular' can end in success. The twentieth century, for example, saw some determined attempts to revive Scots, a literary tradition which flourished with great vigour in the later Middle Ages. Such attempts produced some brilliant early successes, such as Hugh MacDiarmid's *A Drunk Man Looks at the Thistle* (1926). But MacDiarmid, like Edwin Muir before him, was finally driven to embrace a variety of standard English by his need to explore scientific, technical, and philosophical complexities. Chaucer shared such a need: his translations of Boethius's *Consolation of Philosophy* and the *Treatise on the Astrolabe* stimulated him to incorporate philosophical and scientific terms into his own poetic writings. The limited capacities of fourteenth-century English must occasionally have driven Chaucer close to despair – especially when he came to read the pyrotechnic brilliance of Dante's *Paradiso* and realized what fourteenth-century Italian was already capable of.

Luckily for us, Chaucer did stick with English. The tradition of English metrical romances offered some sort of foundation, albeit a shaky one, for his experiments in extended narrative. Chaucer quickly recognized, however, that his first priority as an English 'makere' was to catch up with what had been learned in France. Chaucer's Englishing of distinguished French precedents began, quietly and appropriately enough, with a diligent, literal imitation of the *Roman de la Rose*.[5] But within a remarkably short space of time – and several years before reaching his thirtieth birthday – Chaucer produced a work of original genius. The *Book of the Duchess* patently aligns itself with the *dits amoureux*, a narrative tradition that was developed out of the *Roman de la Rose* by several generations of French poets and then brought to perfection by Machaut and Froissart.[6] The alignment of the *Duchess* with the *dits* is so convincing that Froissart appears to have drawn upon Chaucer's poem for one of his own efforts in this genre.[7] But even within this larger context, the originality and distinctiveness of Chaucer's dream poem is unmistakable. Chaucer's lifelong interest, for example, in communication between disparate social levels is already in evidence: the poem's centrepiece sees a narrator of middling social status and, apparently, of less than middling intelligence attempting to make sense of the metaphorical language of a Black Knight, a figure representing John of Gaunt, the most powerful lord of the realm. The poetic texture of the *Duchess* is not of uniform excellence: the workaday diction characteristic of the English romances shows through in several patches of threadbare dialogue. But the poem's structure could hardly be improved upon. The *Book of the Duchess* is an extraordinarily assured piece of writing.

Such hard-won assurance must have been devastated by Chaucer's first full encounter with the greatest poem of the age, and perhaps of any age: the *Divina Commedia* of Dante Alighieri. Chaucer may have heard something about Dante from those many Italian merchants who passed through London, or even from the French lyricists he had imitated and admired since his youth.[8] But in 1373 he was offered the chance of finding out for himself when he travelled to Florence on a trade mission.[9] The timing of this visit was extremely fortunate. Following a lifetime of energetic lobbying by Dante's most devoted disciple, Giovanni Boccaccio, the Florentine civic authorities finally decided (by a majority of 167 votes) to commemorate the great poet they had voted into exile some seventy years before. This commemoration was to take the form of a series of lectures, starting on 23 October 1373, to be delivered by Boccaccio himself at the Florentine church of Santo Stefano di Badia.[10] The public petition seeking these lectures was submitted in June 1373, just one month after Chaucer's return to England. Since these first *lecturae Dantis* were to appeal to a broad, mixed audience, it seems reasonable to suppose that they were a topic of current interest in literary, civic, and mercantile circles during Chaucer's stay in Florence. In any event, it is quite clear that Chaucer did discover Dante at some point in the 1370s, and that this discovery was to have a profound effect on his artistic future. The poem which acts out and meditates upon this discovery is, of course, the *House of Fame*.

The *House of Fame* contains less systematic imitation of French material than the *Book of the Duchess*; Dante displaces Machaut as Chaucer's guiding light. But Machaut and the French poets are never far from Chaucer's mind at any stage of his career; their influence on the *House of Fame* is still profound.[11] Chaucer sticks with the short couplets that are the English equivalent of the *Rose*'s octosyllabics, frames his narrative within the familiar French-derived dream framework, and speaks through a faintly comical narrator who, as in the *Duchess*, is led to the poem's central locale by an animal guide – in this instance by a schoolmasterly bird. But within the comfortable confines of this familiar format, Chaucer is evidently struggling with something new; something so new, in fact, that the narrator himself can barely grasp or articulate what that something might be. He tells us, repeatedly, that he is in search of 'tydynges', 'tidings', or 'news'.[12] News about what? News about love; news about fame; news about poetry. In the interests of keeping our primary focus on tracing Chaucer's evolving relations with Italian authors, we may without further discussion assume the *House of Fame* to be 'about' these newsworthy, interrelated topics of love, fame, and poetry, even though no single set of assumptions about this complex poem is ever likely to unlock its enigmas and reveal a simple, essential meaning.[13] Chaucer himself seems not to have known what this poem finally amounted to: the poem ends incomplete, and the 'man of gret auctorite' (2158) who might have answered all our questions is left without a speech.

Of these three key concepts – love, fame, and poetry – the most problematical within this English context of the 1370s is poetry. P. M. Kean has written that the main theme of the *House of Fame* is 'the relation of poetry to the traditions which form its material'.[14] The problem here is that there is no antecedent tradition of English poetry for Chaucer to relate to. No English 'makere' before Chaucer had dared to call himself a poet. Even in Italy, Petrarch, 'the lauriat poete . . . whos rethorike sweete / Enlumyned al Ytaille of poetrie' was crowned with laurel for his achievements in Latin, not in the vernacular.[15] What Chaucer first saw in Dante was the hope or dream of raising his own humble English 'makinge' to the level of poetry. Such an act might win him the fame enjoyed by the great Latin 'auctores'. Being of a modest disposition (and knowing, at this stage of his career, that he has much to be modest about), the Chaucerian dreamer ignores a request to name himself within Fame's House and denies that he has come in search of fame for himself:

> . . . 'Frend, what is thy name?
> Artow come hider to han fame?'
> 'Nay, for sothe, frend,' quod y;
> 'I cam noght hyder, graunt mercy,
> For no such cause, by my hed!
> Sufficeth me, as I were ded,
> That no wight have my name in honde.
> I wot myself best how y stonde;
> For what I drye, or what I thynke,
> I will myselven al hyt drynke,
> Certeyn, for the more part,
> As fer forth as I kan myn art.'   (1871–82)

Not surprisingly, this huffy and evasive little speech only serves to exasperate Chaucer's interlocutor. So what *are* you looking for, within a House of Fame, if not fame? The dreamer struggles to explain. He resorts to his magical word 'tydynges' as if, by repeating it in an incantatory sort of way, he might suddenly be supplied with some sort of answer:

'But what doost thou here than?' quod he.
Quod y, 'That wyl y tellen the,
The cause why y stonde here:
Somme newe tydynges for to lere,
Somme newe thinges, y not what,
Tydynges . . .'   (1883–8)

Such awkwardness and self-consciousness is not surprising in a poem which sees Chaucer trying on the poet's toga for the very first time. Dante has shown him what vernacular poetry might resemble; but Dante's Italian has forced him to realize that his own vernacular, English, is, by comparison, a blunt instrument. Chaucer, to his credit, does not shrink from such comparisons. In beginning *Paradiso*, the third and final *cantica* of his *Commedia*, Dante informs Apollo that he – Dante – upon successful completion of his poetic task, will approach Apollo's tree and crown *himself* with laurel. Chaucer, in beginning the third and final Book of his *House of Fame*, informs Apollo that he – Chaucer – upon successful completion of his poetic task, will approach Apollo's tree . . . and plant a big kiss on its trunk. This pattern of retreat into self-parody recurs throughout the *House of Fame*; Chaucer cannot yet take himself seriously as a poet. And if we juxtapose just a portion of these last two passages we can see why. Heard against the sonorous background of Dante's magisterial *terzine*, Chaucer's English couplets amount to little more than a nervous squeak:[16]

O buono Appollo, a l'ultimo lavoro
fammi del tuo valor sí fatto vaso,
come dimandi a dar l'amato alloro.
   Infino a qui l'un giogo di Parnaso
assai mi fu; ma or con amendue
m'e uopo intrar ne l'aringo rimaso.
   Entra nel petto mio . . .   (I, 13–19)

[O good Apollo, for this final labour make me such a vessel of your worthiness as you require for granting your loved laurel.

Up to this point the one peak of Parnassus has serviced me; but now both peaks are needed as I enter the arena that remains.

Enter my breast . . .]

O God of science and of lyght,
Appollo, thurgh thy grete myght,
This lytel laste bok thou gye!
Nat that I wilne, for maistrye,
Here art poetical be shewed,
But for the rym ys lyght and lewed,

> Yit make hyt sumwhat agreable,
> Though som vers fayle in a sillable . . .   (1091–8)

Chaucer makes no mention of fame here, and even the idea of 'art poetical' makes him nervous. Following a resolute start, his invocation to Apollo shrinks to an appeal for assistance in covering up the defects of a lightweight and recalcitrant medium. Chaucer clearly sees that if such a medium is to become authentically poetic – and hence capable of encompassing themes of Dantean scope and grandeur – a major overhaul is in order. Interestingly enough, Dante himself had written a treatise on how an illustrious vernacular (*vulgaris illustris*) might be forged from existing Italian dialects. This Latin treatise, entitled *De Vulgari Eloquentia*, makes diligent (but not slavish) imitation of the great Latin masters (*poetae magni*) an urgent priority for the attainment of true vernacular eloquence.[17] So it is that Dante hails Virgil as 'my master and my author' in the *Commedia*'s very first canto, confides that 'long study and great love' have compelled him 'to search your volume', and proceeds to follow in his footsteps (literally and metaphorically) through the various landscapes of Hell and of Purgatory.[18] And in the opening Book of the *House of Fame*, Chaucer too makes a valiant attempt at 'following after' Virgil:

> I wol now synge, yif I kan,
> The armes and also the man
> That first cam, thurgh his destinee,
> Fugityf of Troy contree . . .   (143–6)

This literal rendering of the *Aeneid* soon contracts to become a paraphrase (149–238), a romantic interlude (239–382), a series of exempla (388–426), and then becomes a paraphrase again (427–65) before expiring with a romancer's formula (466–7). Again, after a resolute start Chaucer's attempt at an English poetry runs rapidly downhill, offering further ironic contrasts with Dantean models and prescriptions. Another such contrast is offered in Chaucer's middle Book. In the second *cantica* of the *Commedia* Dante dreams of a golden eagle that swoops down and then carries him up into the heavens.[19] In the *House of Fame*'s second Book Chaucer dreams of a golden eagle that swoops down and then carries *him* up into the heavens. But Chaucer's Eagle, having cursed and complained about Chaucer's excessive weight (Chaucer was plump), then proceeds to bore Chaucer into glassy-eyed indifference with a tedious sightseeing commentary. So from yet another serious Dantean starting-point, Chaucer's narrative takes another turn for the comic: the would-be poet is presented as one who dangles, fat and hapless, from the claws of a big, boring bird.

But it is the very insistence and intensity of such self-parodying that most forcefully conveys Chaucer's excitement and agitation over the possibilities of the Dantean project. Within the familiar bounds of the French-derived dream poem format, Chaucer is able to measure the capabilities of his native English against the newly discovered standards of Dante's Italian. At the same time he begins exploring the complex interrelations of love, fame, and poetry. This exploration is to be carried forward into *Troilus and Criseyde*, Chaucer's heroic attempt at achieving a work of Dantean stature in English. In the *Troilus*, the interrelation of our three key concepts might be formulated as follows: love inspires poetry; poetry wins fame for both poet and lovers. At first glance, the neatness of this formulation might lead us to believe that Chaucer's artistic uncertainties evaporated the moment he abandoned the *House of Fame*. But this formulation raises some awkward questions. Why labour to win fame for one lover who fears infamy and for another who is finally as indifferent to fame as he is to everything else? Why pin your best hopes for poetic fame on a secular tale of pagan love and infidelity? Such questions are not passed over in the making of the *Troilus*, but are taken up and worried over even as the poem is taking shape. The lively but limited self-assurance of the *Duchess*, transformed into perplexed uncertainty in the *House of Fame*, was never to be fully recovered.

Chaucer recovered from the 'narrative débâcle'[20] of the *House of Fame* by emerging from the restrictive confines of short couplets to experiment with a longer line in various forms of verse; he even tried his hand, albeit briefly, at Dantean *terza rima*.[21] But it was a Boccaccian verse form that proved most helpful and instructive to Chaucer at this time: the evolution of Chaucerian rhyme royal, the seven-line verse form (rhyming ababbcc) of the *Parliament of Fowls* and the *Troilus*, owes much to a careful study of Boccaccian *ottava rima*, an eight-line stanza of hendecasyllabic (eleven-syllable) lines rhyming abababcc. Chaucer realized the narrative potential of such a stanza in reading the *Filostrato* and *Teseida*, two Boccaccian texts which he may have brought back from Florence in 1373 or acquired a few years later. Chaucer put these two texts to very different uses. The *Filostrato* must have been put aside and mulled over in private moments for many years in preparation for the long labour of the *Troilus*. The *Teseida* was drawn upon time and again as a rich repository of narrative and iconographic motifs in a whole host of works.[22] Its story-line was ultimately to provide a source for Chaucer's *Knight's Tale*. But the *Teseida* was put to work long before this in *Anelida and Arcite*, a distant forebear of the *Knight's Tale* which has the appearance of a poetic workshop in which various stanzaic, narrative, and lyric forms are put to the test.[23] The *Anelida* sees Chaucer taking his poetic role somewhat more seriously; too seriously, in fact, since the work (as Robinson so neatly puts it) is 'conspicuous among Chaucer's writings for a tendency to poetic diction'.[24] This disconcerting tendency is evident from the first in this somewhat stiff-jointed rendition of a Boccaccian invocation:[25]

> Thou ferse god of armes, Mars the rede,
> That in the frosty contre called Trace,
> Within thy grisly temple ful of drede
> Honoured art . . .   (1–4)

C. S. Lewis, in comparing Chaucer's diction with 'the plain style' of Gower, detects within such lines from the *Anelida* 'the germ of the whole central tradition of high poetical language in England'.[26] Such artificial diction, with its rows of tidy iambics pulling against a forced separation of subject from main verb, was much to the liking of Chaucer's fifteenth-century admirers: Lydgate, for one, commended 'the golde dewe dropes of speche and eloquence' that Chaucer 'made firste, to distille and rayne . . . Into our tunge'.[27] But in this, as in much else, the fifteenth-century reception of Chaucer represents a radical departure from Chaucer's own poetic agenda. The mature Chaucer strove not to gild his diction with Latinate qualities, but rather to liberate and organize those natural rhythms and energies that were peculiar to his own native tongue. The experimental *Anelida* was left incomplete, and thereafter we see Chaucer's diction becoming ever less Latinate and ever more finely attuned to the various registers and natural nuances of an English-speaking voice. The classical world of *Troilus and Criseyde*, which is underpinned by a host of Continental and Latin texts, was to offer Chaucer endless opportunities for high-flown Latinity: but to study Chaucer at work on his sources in the *Troilus* is to see him turning down such opportunities by the dozen.[28] The *Troilus* does, of course, have its grandiloquent moments. But for the most part, the poem's first-person narrator speaks in a voice which, through painstaking art, is made to seem thoroughly natural to him. This ideal of artful naturalness in poetic diction again reflects Chaucer's diligent adherence to Dantean principles. Dante acclaims Virgil as his master, author, and guide, but he never sounds like Virgil; his diction is always Italian, never Latinate. For Dante it is of fundamental importance that a poet should labour to perfect his own voice; he should not seek to borrow a voice from books or from strangers. Love of your homeland and of the language you grew up with is, after all, the most natural thing in the world. So it is that Dante's Purgatory, the most authentic homeland of poetic struggle and of artistic endeavour, is thickly peopled with poets from all over Continental Europe. At the very entrance of the Ante-Purgatory, Dante, Virgil and their companions are held spellbound by one Casella, singing one of Dante's own songs (II, 112–17). One Bolognese poet, on being acclaimed by Dante as a supreme exponent of vernacular poetry ('l'uso moderno'), points to one of his poet companions as the 'miglior fabbro del parlar materno' (XXVI, 117). And this 'better craftsman of the mother tongue' is accorded the honour of speaking in his native Provençal (which Dante has troubled to learn) even within Dante's Italian masterpiece. Arnaut's greeting of Dante, his fellow poet, is respectful, friendly, and fraternal:

> *Tan m'abellis vostre cortes deman . . .*   (XXVI, 140)
>
> [Your courteous question pleases me so much . . .]

Chaucer must have hungered for such intelligent appreciation of his own poetic enterprise; he might also have thought that there was nobody alive in England capable of offering it to him. He continued, nonetheless, to struggle towards a Dantean standard of artful naturalness in vernacular diction; and in the *Parliament of Fowls* he finally achieved it:

> The lyf so short, the craft so long to lerne,
> Th'assay so hard, so sharp the conquerynge,
> The dredful joye, alwey that slit so yerne:
> Al this mene I by Love . . .   (1–4)

This voice, so perfectly expressive of a mind that wanders distractedly beneath the burden of a weighty, all-consuming subject, sounds quite unlike the voice which made such a stilted start to the *Anelida*. This speaker seems more vulnerable and hence more human, and less concerned with striking poetical postures. He seems, at first, to be unaware of any audience, only pulling himself together in the fourth line to tell us what his main subject is to be. From his opening lines we might have guessed his subject to be art itself: but it is love, a subject which is always intimately bound up with art in medieval writing. And although these opening lines seem so artlessly natural (even in talking around or about the subject of art), they are actually highly crafted: the opening line translates the Latin maxim *ars longa, vita brevis*; the next two lines continue the rhetorical themes of *contentio* (contrast) and *circumlocutio*; and taken together, all three lines add up to an example of *interpretatio*, saying the same thing in different ways.[29]

The opening sentences of medieval poems (and this includes the *Troilus* and the *Canterbury Tales*) are often exceptionally complex and highly wrought: it is as if the poet needs to convince us of his credentials before we commit ourselves to following his text. This holds true for the *Parliament*, too. But the *Parliament*'s opening lines, which speak with an apparently spontaneous and lifelike voice that conceals painstaking elaboration of a foreign source and quiet mastery of rhetorical techniques, are also suggestively emblematic of the poem as a whole. Like the *House of Fame*, the *Parliament* offers three differing views of its declared subject, love: the first from a distant, cosmic perspective; the second from within a house of art; and the third from within a more freewheeling, densely peopled (or birded) milieu. Each of these three major narrative segments builds upon a major Latin or Continental, ancient or modern, source.[30] As Piero Boitani indicates in the following essay, the first utilizes the fifth-century Latin of Macrobius (the 'auctour' who supplies the dream lore with which the *Roman de la Rose* opens); the second the fourteenth-century Italian of Boccaccio's *Teseida*; and the third the twelfth-century Latin of the Frenchman Alan of Lille. To complicate matters further, the transition between the second and third domains here seems to owe something to another Boccaccian text, a dream vision in *terza rima* called the *Amorosa Visione*.[31] Such a weight of source material might seem oppressive; and within the hothouse atmosphere of the temple of Venus, Chaucer himself becomes somewhat disgruntled and disaffected by the sheer weight of past writing on love. Towards the end of his temple tour he does little more than name names:

> Semyramis, Candace, and Hercules,
> Biblis, Dido, Thisbe, and Piramus,
> Tristram, Isaude, Paris, and Achilles,
> Eleyne, Cleopatre, and Troylus . . .   (288–91)

Chaucer wanders out of this art gallery in search of 'solace' (297); and Nature rescues him. He discovers a parliament of fowls, a gathering of birds representing every class and subclass of contemporary London society. This parliament, loosely governed by Nature herself, is initially monopolized by aristocratic voices. Such high-born birds, operating within the framework of an idealized world, would naturally sympathize with the likes of Helen of Troy, Cleopatra, and Troilus. But this idealizing conception of love is soon exposed to some pungent criticisms by birds of lower degree. Duck logic may not be pleasant – it is the logic of Pandarus once Criseyde has flown – but it does ask some awkward questions about the wisdom of fidelity in a case of unrequited love:

> 'Wel bourded,' quod the doke, 'by myn hat!
> That men shulde loven alwey causeles!
> Who can a resoun fynde or wit in that?
> Daunseth he murye that is myrtheles?
> Who shulde recche of that is recheles?'
> 'Ye queke,' seyde the goos, 'ful wel and fayre!
> There been mo sterres, God wot, than a payre!'   (589–95)

This movement from art-monument to a contest of impetuous, disparate voices retraces the movement from Fame's hall, where the poets stand on their metal pillars in silent rows, to the noisy, disorderly house of Rumour, a place which

> Was ful of shipmen and pilgrimes,
> With scrippes bret-ful of lesinges,
> Entremedled with tydynges,
> And eek allone be hemselve.
> O, many a thousand tymes twelve
> Saugh I eke of these pardoners . . .   (2122–7)

And such a movement seems prophetic of its author's entire career, as Chaucer himself was to move from the classical, noble, and delimited realm of the *Troilus* to the more open territory of the *Canterbury Tales*, with its shipmen, pilgrims, and pardoners. But it would be foolish to equate this with a movement from art to life, or from imitative art to art from life, or even from a derivative Englishness to a declaration of English independence. Chaucer himself warns us against forming such an equation in the latter part of his *Parliament*. Nature may look and sound like an Englishwoman but she is, Chaucer insists, of Franco-Latin origin, born out of Alan of Lille's Latin text (316–18). These English birds may sound spontaneous and unrestrained, but they still manage to keep within the bounds of a seven-line stanza rhyming ababbcc. And in concluding their parliament, these boisterous birds select a choir from within their own number, change their rhyme scheme, and forget their differences in singing a roundel. Such a musical resolution to the vehement conflicts of a London parliament is, of course, a fantasy of art, not a record of life. This art is not as natural as birdsong; it is a patiently negotiated marriage between English voices and Continental forms. These birds sing in English to a tune that is borrowed not from nature but from Machaut or Deschamps:

> The note, I trowe, imaked was in Fraunce,
> The wordes were swiche as ye may heer fynde . . .   (677–8)

Once the *Parliament*'s roundel ends the dream dissolves and Chaucer wakes up. Offering no comment whatsoever on his dream, he returns at once to the studious pursuit of reading. These long years of study were to bear fruit in *Troilus and Criseyde*, Chaucer's magnificent attempt at achieving an English classic of extended narrative that might survive comparison with serious works of any age or language, ancient or modern. In the *House of Fame*, struggling with a vernacular which is far from illustrious, Chaucer can only eye the great 'auctores' in passing as they look down on him from their pedestals (1419–1512). Not until he has worked his way to the end of *Troilus and Criseyde* does Chaucer dare to post a claim to stand in their company. This claim, made with characteristic modesty, invites us – for the very first time – to consider the English art of an English writer as poetry, 'poesye':

> Go, litel bok, go, litel myn tragedye,
> Ther God thi makere yet, er that he dye,
> So sende myght to make in som comedye!
> But litel book, no makyng thow n'envie,
> But subgit be to alle poesye;
> And kis the steppes where as thow seest pace
> Virgile, Ovide, Omer, Lucan, and Stace.   (V, 1786–92)

Chaucer clearly wishes us to relate his *Troilus* to those famous texts of antiquity which share his serious concern with the great themes of warfare, love, and moral virtue.[32] But, at the same time, he also wishes us to associate his poem with the major texts of those medieval poets he most admired and made most use of: Boccaccio, Dante, and the poets of the *Rose*. For in placing himself sixth in a poetic confraternity of six, a grouping which extends from the pagan past to the Christian present, Chaucer is deliberately upholding a precedent established by Jean de Meun and then adopted within Dante's *Commedia* and Boccaccio's *Filocolo*. Jean represents himself as following after Tibullus, Gallus, Catullus, Ovid, and Guillaume de Lorris; similarly, Dante joins the company of Homer, Horace, Ovid, Lucan, and Virgil as 'sixth among such intellects' ('sesto tra cotanto senno'); and Boccaccio describes himself as following in the wake of Virgil, Lucan, Statius, Ovid, and Dante.[33] The 'sixth of six' topos that is pinned to the end of Chaucer's poem functions, then, both as a badge of independent merit and as a sign that points us towards a greater, Continental context for *Troilus and Criseyde*.

This wider European context within which the *Troilus* situates itself is unified by the fundamental and pervasive influence of one key text: the *Roman de la Rose*. Chaucer remained a diligent student of the *Rose* through-out his life; Deschamps chose his words advisedly in addressing Chaucer as the 'great translator' who had 'planted the *Rose* tree' in England.[34] And Chaucer's movements between the poetic territories of Italy and France were eased by the formative and long-lasting influence exerted by the *Rose* in both countries.[35] The Italianization of the *Rose* had got under way by 1266, several years before Jean de Meun set to work on extending the text that Guillaume de Lorris had left incomplete some forty years before. The year 1266 saw Brunetto Latini, Dante's celebrated teacher, returning to Florence after six years of political exile in France. During this period of forced idle-ness Brunetto had composed a poem in seven-syllable couplets known as the *Tesoretto*, which takes its inspiration from the *Rose*. This first effort at learning from the French poem was taken up by a second generation of Italian poets in a number of transitional works. One of these, the *Intelligenza*, paved the way for the Boccaccian *Amorosa Visione* and, ultimately, for the Petrarchan *Trionfi*. Another, the *Fiore* (a sequence of sonnets by a certain 'ser Durante' which imitates both parts of the *Rose*), helps clear the way for Dante's *Commedia*. It is possible that Durante and Dante are one: so Chaucer and Dante might actually have begun their poetic careers in parallel, as translators of the *Rose*. In any event, Chaucer (who had brought his own vernacular tradition through so many evolutionary stages in such a short space of time) was uniquely qualified to perceive the presence of the *Rose* within Italian texts, including Dante's *Commedia*.[36]

Chaucer thus experienced little difficulty in detecting the presence of both the *Commedia* and the *Rose* within Boccaccio's *Filocolo*, a monumentally lengthy, Italian prose version of the French romance of *Floire et Blancheflor*. It was the *Filocolo*'s fourth Book that Chaucer made most use of.[37] *Filocolo* IV appropriates landscapes from the *Commedia* and the *Rose* to explore the problematic status of a young pagan hero struggling to consummate his love-affair and, at the same time, to understand that greater love which orders and governs the universe. The central Book of the *Troilus*, in taking up this exploration of the uncharted territory between pagan consummation and Christian revelation, borrows from and alludes to all three of these texts in ways that criticism has barely begun to understand.[38] Although such borrowing and allusion is at its most intense in Book III, it continues throughout the *Troilus*. Allegorical personifications from the *Rose*, such as 'Kynde', 'Daunger', and 'Feere', war within the minds of Chaucer's lovers; the conflicting views of love which separate the idealist Troilus from the pragmatist Pandarus recall the differing attitudes which separate the two authors of the *Rose*. Certain Dantean figures, often of classical origins, inspire the most complex and suggestive allusions; certain Dantean moments such as *Inferno* V (Paolo and Francesca) or *Inferno* XXX (the juxtaposition of Troy and Thebes) cast long shadows over the entire poem. Troilus's praise of 'Benigne Love' at the height of the consummation scene (III, 1261–7) is inspired by St Bernard's prayer to the Virgin in *Paradiso* XXXIII (14–15), and the beautiful image of Criseyde's eyes as a vision of Paradise (V, 817) reminds us of Beatrice's admonition to Dante in *Paradiso* XVIII (21). Even the poem's final stanza begins with a studied imitation of lines from the *Paradiso*.[39] And the poem's tragic conclusion seems the more poignant when viewed within this Continental context, since all of its companion texts are comedies, pilgrimages to truth or love that reach their religious or erotic terminus, their designated shrine. The *Troilus* goes against the European grain: perhaps this helps to account for the narrator's acute discomfiture during the last two Books.

Within his *Filocolo*, Boccaccio purports to be following the 'true testimony' of an ancient author, one 'Ilario' (v, 97, 10). Chaucer, similarly, insists that he is bound to follow the ancient, Latin text of 'Lollius'. Both Ilario and Lollius are, of course, pious fictions, cultural ciphers expressive of a common commitment to revivifying an ancient past. They disguise the fact that both Boccaccio and Chaucer are actually reworking more modern, vernacular texts which they choose not to name. The actual source of Chaucer's *Troilus* is, of course, another Boccaccian text, the *Filostrato*. At first glance, the *Filostrato* seems a curious choice as the source of Chaucer's most serious and sustained effort at mature 'poesye'. Boccaccio was barely twenty when he wrote it; his text bears obvious signs of immaturity. Boccaccio entertains himself by striking authorish postures within the *Filostrato*; he particularly enjoys advising his youthful peers, once his love story is spent, to put a brake on their eager steps towards sexual gratification.[40] His text makes little effort to homogenize its diverse literary sources: phrases picked up, magpie-like, from writers such as Cino da Pistoia, Andreas Capellanus, and Dante (especially Dante) are stuck on to the narrative surface with great complacency and little concern for context. According to its prose preface, Boccaccio's poem discovered its originary impulse within an assembly of courtly young lovers, the kind of assembly (real or imagined) that Chaucer was obviously at home with. But the basic narrative technique of Boccaccio's poem is actually developed out of the *cantare*, a tradition of popular narrative in *ottava rima* which has much in common with the English tradition of tail-rhyme romance.[41] The *Filostrato* did not suit Chaucer as a poetic exemplar: the English poet turns repeatedly to Dante, Machaut, and the *Rose* poets when seeking more suitable models of lyric prosody or more authentic accounts of courtly sensibility.[42] But the *Filostrato* did suit Chaucer admirably as a poetic source. The *Commedia* and the *Rose*, after all, can hardly be improved upon as poetic sources. They are completed, universal texts; after hell, purgatory, and heaven there is nowhere much to go. The youthful *Filostrato*, on the other hand, allowed generous room for improvement.

In choosing the *Filostrato*, Chaucer was making a deliberate, far-reaching decision about the kind of poet he wished to be and, consequently, about the kind of audience he expected to reach. He did not wish to be the kind of poet who makes things difficult for his readers and ends up by reaching only a favoured few. Petrarch anticipates that very few men will find their way into his Academy; and women are not invited. Dante is more generous: everyone is welcome at his banquet, his *Convivio*.[43] But not everyone will make it to the end of his *Commedia*; those who grow faint-hearted on entering the *Paradiso* are actively encouraged to give up reading (II, 1–9). *Troilus and Criseyde*, by contrast, is a generous, inclusive, reader-friendly text that could (and did) find a home almost anywhere: at court, at the quayside, or even in the convent. It is a text which finds room for cheerful bedside banter as well as for anguished philosophical reflections. Its narrator remains on easy, familiar terms with his readership; his evolving relationship with his readers forms part of the poem's subject. These readers or listeners may, then as now, thoroughly enjoy Chaucer's poem whilst remaining blissfully ignorant of its larger cultural context and voluntarily indifferent to its learned allusions. Unlike Petrarch or Dante, Chaucer does not strive for perpetual, ingenious variety in his rhyming. He achieves moments of high drama, demanding close concentration from his readers, but he also budgets for moments when our concentration may slacken. To this end he borrows numerous tags, epithets, oaths, asseverations, and other such resources from popular narrative tradition; the reader or listener may nod for a line or two. The *Troilus* employs variations of the romancer's simile 'stille as any ston' on five occasions and rhymes on 'ston' six times. Chaucer rhymes on 'two' on over twenty occasions; these include the romance tags 'eyen two' (III, 1352; IV, 750) and 'armes two' (IV, 911). And he takes full advantage of having a heroine whose name rhymes with 'seyde'.

Chaucer seems, then, to assume a double identity within *Troilus and Criseyde*. He wishes to align himself with the greatest European poets, ancient and modern. Yet he also wishes, when it suits him, to speak like an English romancer. Perhaps this is why he chooses to represent himself within the *Canterbury Tales* first as the teller of an English stanzaic romance and secondly as the translator (who avoids a Latin source when he can find a French one) of a 'moral tale vertuous' (VII, 940) from ancient times. Taken together, the tail-rhyme of *Sir Thopas* and the learned, pedagogical prose of the *Tale of Melibee* do amount to a recognizable caricature of their author: Chaucer as a dog who knows two tricks, romancing and translating. Perhaps we should respect Chaucer's defence of *Sir Thopas* as 'the beste rym I kan' as a candid half-truth. *Troilus and Criseyde* is, after all, Chaucer's 'beste rym'.

It is of course in the *The Canterbury Tales* that Chaucer most boldly mixes and juxtaposes differing social voices and genres within a single poetic structure. Such promiscuous ambition, we have noted, is already scented among 'shipmen and pilgrimes' at the end of the *House of Fame* (2122) and more substantially explored in the *Parliament of Fowls*. But it is Boccaccio's example, it would seem, that finally encourages Chaucer to organize a travelling company of tellers under a single narrative structure; fully one-quarter of Chaucer's tales find analogues in the *Decameron*.[44] Boccaccio certainly takes on a remarkable range of literary genres, beginning with a scurrilous saint's life (I, I), working through tales of Mediterranean voyaging (compare his Gostanza in V,3 to Chaucer's Custance, *Man of Law's Tale*) and urban trickery (Day Six) to end with patient Griselde (X, 10). But although there is considerable variety of social content, there is also homogenization of literary form: whereas Chaucer lets his tales establish multiple worlds of generic expectation, in different forms of verse and prose, Boccaccio produces one hundred *novelle*. And whereas Chaucer, the royal servant, imagines taletellers from a remarkable range of professions, Boccaccio (lifelong servant of the Florentine Republic) gives us a rotating monarchy governed by young aristocrats. There is one moment of rebellion in the *Decameron*, however: a furious noise ('romore') erupts from the kitchen, and Licisca – who may be a slave – is dragged before the Queen (Sixth Day, 'Introduction'). Although Licisca's torrent of lascivious talk is considered amusing (supplying material for later tale-telling), she is threatened with whipping and sent back to her pots. The equivalent moment of rebellion in Chaucer, of course, has quite different results: the Miller gets to speak and the *Tales* changes course for good. Critics habitually label Chaucer as a social conservative, but by European standards the Miller's successful rebellion is a pretty bold move. Bolder still is Chaucer's final deployment of the European 'sixth of six' topos: for in the *General Prologue*, he puts himself sixth in a company of six 'miscellaneous predators', namely the Reeve, Miller, Summoner, Pardoner, Manciple, 'and myself – ther were namo' (I, 544).[45] At once self-deprecating, socially precarious, and endlessly ambitious as an English author, Chaucer here seems suddenly a lot like Langland.

It is not difficult to see why Chaucer made more use of Boccaccio than of any other writer. Boccaccio shares Chaucer's ambition of establishing himself as a poet of European stature who, in company with a few Continental contemporaries, joins hands across the centuries with the great authors of antiquity. This ambition was first fired by a diligent reading of Dante. But Boccaccio also shares Chaucer's willingness to draw narrative inspiration from more popular quarters, fashioning complex texts which appeal to a broad range of readers. This willingness on Boccaccio's part was somewhat short-lived, however. Gradually succumbing to the influence of Petrarch and the early humanists, Boccaccio channelled most of his mature energies into Latin encyclopedism. But although he gave up vernacular verse in mid-career, Boccaccio retained a deep personal devotion to Dante. And in 1373 he was finally offered the opportunity of conducting a public celebration of Dante's great poem. But this opportunity caught Boccaccio in an awkward dilemma. He wished to honour Dante as the great poet of the Florentine vernacular. But by 1373 excessive enthusiasm for the vernacular had become unfashionable in Florence. Boccaccio struggles with this dilemma throughout the *accessus* (or introduction) to his Dante lectures. Finally he proposes that Dante actually began his *Commedia* in Latin but then switched to Italian, an inferior medium, because few noble and educated men could or would read Latin. So Latin could not make him famous; and a Latin *Commedia* 'might fall into the hands of plebeians and men of low degree'.[46] These fantastic propositions, a comprehensive betrayal of Dante's most deeply held artistic principles, mark Boccaccio's final capitulation to the cultural pressures exerted by Petrarch and the Latin humanists.

Perhaps the very fact that Florence was finally able to rehabilitate Dante in 1373 suggests that by that time Dante's text had lost something of its revolutionary resonance. Its politics were outdated; its leading figures were long since dead, if not entirely forgotten. Its theology was outmoded; its zealous championing of vernacular poetry had passed out of fashion. And the Florentine vernacular had settled down. It had become more polished and accomplished, but could hold fewer surprises.[47] Present utterance was already conditioned and restricted by the weight of past history. English, by contrast, had little to weigh itself down with in 1373. English poetry was scarcely aware of its own existence before Chaucer's discovery of Dante. The first effects of this discovery, acted out in the *House of Fame*, were to reduce Chaucer to a state of comically ambivalent, self-conscious agitation. But, as we have seen, Chaucer's self-assurance quietly grows in the course of writing the *Anelida* and the *Parliament*; and in *Troilus and Criseyde* he finally draws English into the mainstream of European poetry.

Chaucer is Dante's truest fourteenth-century continuator because it is in Chaucer's hands that Dante's text rediscovers its revolutionary potential. Chaucer came across the *Commedia* at precisely the right moment: that moment near the beginnings of a vernacular tradition when a language, although inchoate and unstable, seems (in the hands of a genius) to be marvellously malleable, infinitely adaptive, capable of almost anything. Chaucer learned many things from Dante but the most important was, quite simply, to keep faith with his own language: a vernacular must be revolutionized from within, not patched and amended from without. The cultural prestige of French need not and (despite Petrarch's best efforts) could not be disputed: French precedents were fundamental to European literary culture. And no vernacular could hope to match the authority of Latin: for unlike Latin, no vernacular could shield itself from the effects of passing time. But it is this very inability to resist or be indifferent to changes over time that guarantees the vernacular's peculiar glory: for human experience is, after all, an experience of continual change, of growth, decay, and renewal. The vernacular, not Latin, provides the most accurate mirror of the human condition.

Languages change, Chaucer reminds us, 'withinne a thousand yeer';[48] and this is natural and appropriate, Dante's Adam argues, since

> ... l'uso d'i mortali è come fronda
> in ramo, che sen va e altra vene.[49]   (*Paradiso* XXVI, 137–8)

> [... the usage of mortals is like a leaf
> on a branch, which goes away and another comes.]

NOTES

1. See *The Decameron*, trans. G. H. McWilliam, 2nd edn (Harmondsworth, 1995), II, 3; David Wallace, *Giovanni Boccaccio: Decameron* (Cambridge, 1991), pp. 34–5.
2. See Robin Kirkpatrick, *English and Italian Literature from Chaucer to Shakespeare* (London, 1995); David Wallace, *Chaucerian Polity* (Stanford, Calif., 1997); Wallace, 'Italy' in *A Companion to Chaucer*, ed. Peter Brown (Oxford, 2000), pp. 218–34.
3. 'Chaucer and Englishness', *Proceedings of the British Academy*, 101 (1998), 77–99, at p. 86. On Victorian and post-Victorian Chaucers, see Steve Ellis, *Chaucer at Large. The Poet in the Modern Imagination* (Minneapolis, 2000).
4. See Alfred Thomas, *Anne's Bohemia. Czech Literature and Society, 1100–1420* (Minneapolis, 1998); Wallace, *Chaucerian Polity*, pp. 357–64; Susan Crane, 'Anglo-Norman Cultures in England, 1066–1460' in *The Cambridge History of Medieval English Literature*, ed. David Wallace (Cambridge, 1999), pp. 52–8; Derek Pearsall, *Old English and Middle English Poetry* (London, 1977), pp. 189–91. Crane, like most other experts, considers it 'likely that Geoffrey Chaucer began writing in French' (p. 55).
5. Chaucer refers to his translation of the *Rose* in the *Legend of Good Women*, F 327–31, G 253–7. See Ronald Sutherland, *'The Romaunt of the Rose' and 'Le Roman de la Rose'. A Parallel Text Edition* (Oxford, 1967). Sutherland affirms that there is 'no reason to doubt that Fragment A of the *Romaunt*, save for a few revisions, is Chaucer's genuine work' (p. xxxiv).
6. James I. Wimsatt, *Chaucer and His French Contemporaries* (Toronto, 1991); and see ch. 2 above.
7. See James I. Wimsatt, *Chaucer and the French Love Poets: The Literary Background of the Book of the Duchess* (Chapel Hill, 1968), pp. 129–33.
8. See James I. Wimsatt, *Chaucer and the Poems of 'Ch'* (Cambridge, 1982), pp. 51–60, 66–8.
9. For details of Chaucer's 1373 visit to Genoa and Florence, see *Chaucer Life-Records*, eds. M. M. Crow and C. C. Olson (Oxford, 1966), pp. 32–40; D. S. Brewer, *Chaucer and His World* (London, 1978), pp. 119–31.
10. See *Esposizioni sopra la Commedia di Dante*, ed. G. Padoan, in *Tutte le opere di Giovanni Boccaccio*, ed. Vittore Branca, 12 vols. (Milan, 1964–98), vol. 6; G. Padoan, 'Boccaccio, Giovanni' in *Enciclopedia Dantesca*, ed. Umberto Bosco, 6 vols. (Rome, 1970–8), vol. 1, pp. 645–50; A. Vallone, 'Lectura Dantis', *Enciclopedia Dantesca*, vol. 3, pp. 606–9; *Medieval Literary Theory and*

Criticism, c.1100–c.1375. The Commentary Tradition, eds. A. J. Minnis and A. B. Scott, with the assistance of David Wallace (Oxford, 1988), pp. 453–8.

11. See W. O. Sypherd, *Studies in Chaucer's Hous of Fame* (London, 1907), p. 13.
12. The word *tydynges* appears some twenty-two times in the *House of Fame*.
13. For summaries of recent views, see *Riverside Chaucer*, ed. Benson, pp. 977–8. See also Piero Boitani, *Chaucer and the Imaginary World of Fame* (Cambridge, 1984).
14. *Chaucer and the Making of English Poetry*, 2 vols. (London, 1972), vol. 1, p. 111.
15. See *Clerk's Prologue*, 31–3. Petrarch was crowned with the laurels of a Latin poet at Rome in 1341.
16. I follow the text of the *Commedia* established by Giorgio Petrocchi (Turin, 1975): my translation. One of the two peaks of Parnassus that Dante speaks of here was regarded as sacred to Apollo, the other to the Muses.

    For a detailed consideration of Chaucer's indebtedness to specific Dantean contexts and phrasings, see Howard H. Schless, *Chaucer and Dante: A Reevaluation* (Norman, Okla., 1984). See further *The Cambridge Companion to Dante*, ed. Rachel Jacoff (Cambridge, 1993); Richard Neuse, *Chaucer's Dante* (Berkeley, 1991).
17. See the edition (with facing Italian translation) by A. Marigo, 3rd edn, updated by P. G. Ricci (Florence, 1957), esp. II, iv, 1–3. For a convenient translation see *Literary Criticism of Dante Alighieri*, ed. and trans. Robert S. Haller (Lincoln, Nebr., 1973), pp. 3–60; see further *Medieval Literary Theory*, eds. Minnis and Scott, pp. 376–7, 381–2.
18. See *Inferno* I, 83–5. This passage is deliberately recalled by Christine de Pizan in her *Livre du Chemin de Long Estude* (1402–3), a dream vision in which Christine 'explicitly conceives her literary career as a learned continuation of the poetic achievement of Virgil', Christine de Pizan, *The Book of the City of Ladies*, trans. E. J. Richards (New York, 1982), pp. xliii–xliv. See further *The Selected Writings of Christine de Pizan*, eds. and trans. Renate Blumenfeld-Kosinski and Kevin Brownlee (New York, 1997).
19. See *Purgatorio* IX, 13–42.
20. Derek Brewer, *Towards a Chaucerian Poetic*, British Academy, 1974 (London, 1974), p. 8.
21. See *A Complaint to His Lady*, lines 15–22; and see *Riverside Chaucer*, p. 1078.
22. See Piero Boitani, 'Style, Iconography and Narrative: The Lesson of the *Teseida*' in *Chaucer and the Italian Trecento*, ed. Piero Boitani (Cambridge, 1983), pp. 185–99.
23. For a differing view of this poem, see John Norton-Smith, 'Chaucer's *Anelida and Arcite*' in *Medieval Studies for J. A. W. Bennett*, ed. P. L. Heyworth (Oxford, 1981), pp. 81–99.
24. See *The Works of Geoffrey Chaucer*, ed. F. N. Robinson, 2nd edn (London, 1957), p. 304.
25. See *Teseida delle Nozze d'Emilia*, ed. A. Limentani, in *Opere di Boccaccio*, ed. Branca, vol. 2 (Book I, stanza 3).
26. The *Allegory of Love* (Oxford, 1936), p. 201.
27. From *The Life of Our Lady*, c.1410, Book II, lines 1632–4 (Derek Brewer, ed., *Chaucer: The Critical Heritage*, 2 vols. (London, 1978), vol. 1, p. 46).

28. See David Wallace, *Chaucer and the Early Writings of Boccaccio* (Cambridge, 1985), pp. 94–140. And see *Troilus and Criseyde: A New Edition of 'The Book of Troilus*, ed. B. A. Windeatt (London/New York, 1984), which juxtaposes texts of the *Filostrato* and the *Troilus*; *Chaucer's Boccaccio: Sources of Troilus and the Knight's and Franklin's Tales*, ed. and trans. N. R. Havely (Cambridge, 1980), which provides the most recent and reliable translation of the *Filostrato*. See further Thomas C. Stillinger, *The Song of Troilus: Lyric Authority in the Medieval Book* (Philadelphia, 1992).

29. See *The Parlement of Foulys*, ed. D. S. Brewer (London, 1960), pp. 48–9.

30. See B. A. Windeatt, *Chaucer's Dream Poetry: Sources and Analogues* (Cambridge, 1982).

31. See Wallace, *Early Writings*, pp. 143–6. The *Visione*, which attempts to accommodate the influence of Dante within the French-derived framework of a dream vision, has much in common with the *House of Fame*: see Wallace, *Early Writings*, pp. 5–22.

32. On this division of subject materials, see *De Vulgari Eloquentia* II, ii, 6–10 (Haller, *Literary Criticism*, pp. 34–6).

33. See *Le Roman de la Rose*, ed. F. Lecoy, 3 vols. (Paris, 1975–9), lines 10477–644; *Inferno* IV, 80–102 (102); *Filocolo*, ed. A. E. Quaglio, in *Opere di Boccaccio*, ed. Branca, vol. I, V, 97, 4–6: and see Wallace, *Early Writings*, pp. 46–53.

34. See Brewer, *Heritage*, vol. I, pp. 40–1 (Brewer's translation).

35. See David Wallace, 'Chaucer and the European *Rose*' in *Studies in the Age of Chaucer. Proceedings, No. 1. 1984: Reconstructing Chaucer*, eds. Paul Strohm and Thomas J. Heffernan (Knoxville, Tenn., 1985), pp. 61–7.

36. Both Laurent de Premierfait (who translated Boccaccio's *Decameron* into French) and Christine de Pizan (who was born in Venice and worked in various parts of France) explicitly compare the *Commedia* and the *Rose* in the early years of the fifteenth century: see John V. Fleming, *The 'Roman de la Rose'. A Study in Allegory and Iconography* (Princeton, N.J., 1969), p. 18; Maxwell Luria, *A Reader's Guide to the 'Roman de la Rose'* (Hamden, Conn., 1982), p. 201. See further *The Fiore in Context: Dante, France, Tuscany*, eds. Zygmunt G. Barański and Patrick Boyde (Notre Dame, Indiana, 1996).

37. *Filocolo* IV, 31 provides a source for Chaucer's *Franklin's Tale*: see *Sources and Analogues of the Canterbury Tales*, eds. Robert M. Correale and Mary Hamel, vol. I (Cambridge, 2002), pp. 220–39 (with translation). The parliament of courtiers in which this source story appears is immediately preceded by a dream vision assembly of some thirty birds: the same female figure (in different symbolic disguises) governs both gatherings (IV, 12–72). The latter part of *Filocolo* IV, featuring the long-delayed consummation of a pagan love affair, influences *Troilus* III, 442–1309, that part of Chaucer's poem in which the *Filostrato* exerts virtually no influence: see Karl Young, *The Origin and Development of the Story of Troilus and Criseyde* (Chaucer Society, 1908; repr. New York, 1968), pp. 139–81.

38. See Winthrop Wetherbee, *Chaucer and the Poets: An Essay on Troilus and Criseyde* (Ithaca, N.Y., 1984). See also Young, *Development*, pp. 139–51; Wallace, *Early Writings*, pp. 133–40.

39. See Wetherbee, '*Troilus and Criseyde*', pp. 37–43, 95–6, 111–78; Wallace, *Early Writings*, pp. 133–40.

40. See *Filostrato*, ed. Branca, in *Opere di Boccaccio*, ed. Branca, vol. 2, esp. VIII, 29: 'O giovinetti . . .'.

41. See Wallace, *Early Writings*, pp. 73–93, 146–50. For a different view, which aligns the *Troilus* with the illustrious tradition of French romance, see Barbara Nolan, *Chaucer and the Tradition of the 'Roman Antique'* (Cambridge, 1992).

42. See James I. Wimsatt, 'Guillaume de Machaut and Chaucer's *Troilus and Criseyde*', *Medium Aevum*, 45 (1976), 277–93.

43. The courses of Dante's *Convivio* ('banquet') are commentaries upon his own *canzoni* served to those who, through familial or civic commitments, or through being far from a university or scholarly company, have found little time or opportunity for 'speculazione': see *Il Convivio*, ed. Maria Simonelli (Bologna, 1966), I, i, 2–4. For an excellent translation (which does, however, predate more reliable editions of the Dantean text) see *Dante's Convivio*, trans. W. W. Jackson (Oxford, 1924).

44. See now *The Decameron and the Canterbury Tales. New Essays on an Old Question*, eds. Leonard Michael Koff and Brenda Deen Schildgen (London, 2000).

45. See Wallace, *Chaucerian Polity*, pp. 80–2, 100; Wallace, 'Humanism, Slavery, and the Republic of Letters' in *The Public Intellectual*, ed. Helen Small (Oxford, 2002), pp. 62–8. On the 'rogue's gallery of miscellaneous predators, associated only in the skill with which they batten upon the society that has just been described', see Derek Pearsall, *The Canterbury Tales* (London, 1985), p. 80.

46. See *Esposizioni, accessus*, 74–6.

47. See Erich Auerbach, *Literary Language and Its Public in Late Latin Antiquity and in the Middle Ages*, trans. Ralph Manheim (London, 1965), p. 318.

48. *Troilus and Criseyde* II, 23. Compare *Convivio* I, v, 9, where Dante claims that 'were those who departed this life a thousand years ago to return to their native cities, they would believe them occupied by a foreign people, so different would be the language from their own' (Haller's translation, pp. 62–3). As is pointed out by Robinson in *Works of Chaucer*, p. 818 and Windeatt in *Troilus*, p. 153, the ultimate source of *Troilus* II, 22–5 is Horace, *Ars Poetica* 69–72. The phrasing of the *Convivio* passage is, however, closer to *Troilus* II, 22–3 than any other source; and it is obviously vastly more suggestive.

49. For a helpful guide to Dante's evolving views on the relationship of Latin to the vernacular, see J. Cremona, 'Dante's Views on Language' in *The Mind of Dante*, ed. U. Limentani (Cambridge, 1965), pp. 138–62. And for an illuminating comparison of the views of Dante and Petrarch on this relationship, see Kenelm Foster, *Petrarch. Poet and Humanist* (Edinburgh, 1984), pp. 23–48.

4

PIERO BOITANI

Old books brought to life in dreams: the *Book of the Duchess*, the *House of Fame,* the *Parliament of Fowls*

When, in a May dream, the mighty God of Love appears to the poetic persona of Geoffrey Chaucer in the Prologue to the *Legend of Good Women,* he angrily reproaches the writer for having translated the *Roman de la Rose* ('an heresye ageyns [Love's] lawe') and composed the 'bok' of Troilus and Criseyde, which shows 'how that wemen han don mis' (G 256, 266). In the tirade that follows, Love asks the poet whether, among all the books he owns, he could not have found 'som story of wemen that were goode and trewe' to serve as a literary model (G 271–2). The God is quite specific in his description of these books:

> Yis, God wot, sixty bokes olde and newe
> Hast thow thyself, alle ful of storyes grete,
> That bothe Romayns and ek Grekes trete
> Of sundry wemen, which lyf that they ladde,
> And evere an hundred goode ageyn oon badde.[1]   (G 273–7)

He cites 'Valerius', Livy, Claudian, St Jerome, Ovid, Vincent of Beauvais – indeed 'al the world of autours' both Christian and pagan could confirm to the poet that women can be true and good.

In his typically light, half-jocose, but erudite manner (he will soon mention and borrow from Dante, too), Chaucer seems to be telling us that he owns sixty books. We cannot be sure that the figure corresponds to reality – it is too round a number, and the context is not completely clear: are the sixty books exclusively 'Roman' and 'Greek', and do they deal only with 'sundry wemen'? And what does 'olde and newe' mean? Chaucer's personal library can be expanded almost *ad infinitum* by people who take every literary al-lusion in his works to imply knowledge of a 'book', and reduced to far less than sixty volumes by those who consider the way in which many works of literature or philosophy circulated throughout the Middle Ages as fragments in anthologies and miscellanies. A more historical approach to these prob-lems is outlined in Paul Strohm's essay above. What interests me here is the image of himself and his library that Chaucer seems keen on presenting to his readers in this passage, the very fact that he makes Love talk to us about his books.

The God's words are extremely appropriate to the present circumstances and to this particular dreamer. For, at the very beginning of his poem (and this time in both versions), Chaucer had launched into a long hymn in praise of books and prefaced his dream of the God of Love with the portrait of himself as a fanatic bibliophile, who puts down his volume only when the overwhelming power of spring prompts him to choose the meadow and its flowers instead:

> And as for me, though that I konne but lyte,
> On bokes for to rede I me delyte,
> And to hem yive I feyth and ful credence,
> And in myn herte have hem in reverence
> So hertely, that ther is game noon
> That fro my bokes maketh me to goon . . .   (F 29–34)

Books are for him a delight, a faith, a passion full of reverence. The Eagle who carried him to the House of Fame had reproached Geoffrey for exactly the same reason. In his view, the poet lives a hermit's life, he ignores the real world around him and indeed his very neighbours:

> For when thy labour doon al ys,
> And hast mad alle thy rekenynges,
> In stede of reste and newe thynges
> Thou goost hom to thy hous anoon,
> And, also domb as any stoon,
> Thou sittest at another book
> Tyl fully daswed ys thy look . . .   (*House of Fame*, 652–8)

Neither Richard De Bury, who wrote a *Philobiblon* to celebrate the might of books and the love we should have for them, nor his friend Petrarch, the greatest non-religious collector of books in fourteenth-century Europe, ever wrote anything like this. The comic overtone of this picture, the fact that the bibliophile is characterized as a bookworm, should not prevent us from seeing the deep seriousness which is hidden behind it and which is confirmed by the self-awareness implicit in the image. What Chaucer has the Eagle tease him for is the very source of his inspiration – not the 'tydynges of Loves folk' nor the reality of either 'fer contree' or his 'verray neyg*hebores*', but books. The very journey to the House of Fame, begun in a temple that contains an 'Aeneid' and the purpose of which, the Eagle says, is to show the poet 'wonder thynges' and tidings of Love's folk (674–5), will become a visit to the world of books, writers, and Muses, before turning into an exploration of tidings as such.

Literature is Chaucer's inspiration. A book is at the beginning and end of each of his poems until he starts composing the *Canterbury Tales. Troilus* is born out of a book, Boccaccio's *Filostrato,* and ends with a reference to the 'litel bok', *Troilus and Criseyde* itself. What takes place in the *Troilus* is but an expansion and a change into a direct source–product relationship of a phenomenon which governs Chaucer's dream poems in a more indirect fashion. After his 'labour', Geoffrey goes back home and sits at another book. In the *Book of the Duchess,* he suffers from insomnia, asks for a book to 'drive the night away' as reading is 'better play' than 'ches or tables' (49–51). He reads his book, falls asleep, dreams, wakes up with his book beside him, and decides to write a book. In the *House of Fame,* he dreams a book as a pictorial experience (the 'Aeneid' on the walls of the temple of Venus), flies, thinking of books, through the air, and encounters in the Palace of Fame the writers of books themselves. In the *Parliament of Fowls,* he reads a book, falls asleep, dreams, in his dream is promised 'mater of to wryte' (168), visits a garden and a temple of Venus, witnesses a parliament of birds, wakes up, and resorts to other books. In the Prologue to the *Legend of Good Women* he celebrates books, falls asleep, dreams about the God of Love and Alceste, wakes up, takes his books (in the F version), and starts composing his 'Legende'.[2]

The repetition of this pattern is as significant as the variations Chaucer plays on it, and constitutes a phenomenon of great cultural relevance. For Chaucer, the book (literature) both causes the dream and exists within it. He is the first European writer to use this formula, which was to become a distinctive feature, if not a topos, of Western culture. At the beginning of the fourteenth century Dante, in the episode of Paolo and Francesca, had consecrated the book as an occasion for love, sin, murder, and eternal damnation; now, in the second half of the century, Chaucer consecrates it as the key and integrating element of the dream experience – one of the fundamental activities of the human psyche – and of the creative process itself. Thus, independently of Petrarch's humanism, literature becomes one of the driving forces of European civilization. And Chaucer does indeed seem to catch and to announce, though without ostentation and as if unconsciously, the essence of all humanisms when, in the Prologue to the *Legend,* he proclaims that 'if that *olde* bokes weren aweye, / Yloren were of remembrance the keye' (G 25–6), and when, in the *Parliament,* he explains that 'out of *olde* bokes' comes the '*newe* science' (24–5).

It is to the mechanisms, the meaning, and the implications of Chaucer's dream-books and book-dreams that the following pages are devoted. And we begin with an obvious consideration. Books can be used as sources, as pure references, or as a mixture of the two.[3] As two essays in this volume show, Chaucer uses French and Italian authors as sources of several passages in his dream poems. However, he never explicitly acknowledges his verbal indebtedness to, say, Machaut, Froissart, or Boccaccio. He begins the *Book of the Duchess* with the quotation and summary of the episode of Ceyx and Alcyone from Ovid's *Metamorphoses,* but calls this a romance. He quotes the opening lines of Virgil's *Aeneid* when, at the beginning of his dream, he enters the temple of Venus in the *House of Fame.* Again, he does not acknowledge his source, but later, when he describes Dido's complaint in his summary of the *Aeneid* in Book I, tells his readers that if they want to know more they should resort to 'Virgile in Eneydos' and to the 'Epistle of Ovyde' – that is, the *Heroides* (378–9). Later in the *House of Fame* he does not point out that the description of Fame is indebted to Virgil and that of the House of Rumour to Ovid. In the *Parliament,* instead, he mentions 'Tullyus of the Drem of Scipioun' just before giving us a summary of it (31), but carefully keeps silent on the fact that the description of the temple of Venus is translated straight out of Boccaccio's *Teseida.*

What emerges from all this is a fairly clear strategy of hide and seek. People who read or listened to Chaucer's dream poems were invited to find out where the stuff came from and were or were not, depending on the author's judgement of what was appropriate to his text and possible to his audience, given, in an exciting literary game, a clue. Would not John of Gaunt, the Black Knight who in the *Book of the Duchess* quotes 'al the remedyes of Ovyde' (568), be able to guess that the dreamer's romance is in fact an episode of the *Metamorphoses*? Readers of the *House of Fame* who were told to look up the 'Eneydos' would undoubtedly suspect that the 'table of bras' contains a translation of the most famous lines of Virgil's poem, *arma virumque cano* (142–4). They would be sent off on research of their own when they heard the poet say that he saw Homer, Statius, Virgil, Ovid, Claudian, and others stand on the pillars of the hall of Fame. On the other hand, no one probably could imagine that an as yet unknown vernacular author like Boccaccio was behind the *Parliament*'s temple of Venus.

From the beginning, then, Chaucer plays with his audience a game of intertextuality, raising expectations, stimulating cultural awareness, puzzling and overwhelming his readers with displays of erudition and at the same time relieving them with clues and a light tone. He 'translates' and popularizes, incarnating that tendency which has been seen as the culmination of the encounter between the chivalric culture of the courts and the clerical culture of the schools in fourteenth-century Europe.[4] But he often does more than that – he drops hints or explicitly refers to books which are not, strictly speaking, his sources. For instance, in the *Book of the Duchess* he says that in his dream he found himself in a chamber whose windows were 'yglased' with the story of Troy and whose walls were frescoed with 'al the Romaunce of the Rose' (321–34). In the *House of Fame* he tells his readers that if they want to know more about hell, they should turn to Virgil, Claudian, and Dante (447–50). In the *Parliament* he declares that Nature appeared to him exactly as 'Aleyn, in the Pleynt of Kynde' (Alan of Lille, in the *De Planctu Naturae*) describes her (316–18). It might be interesting to glance at a complete list of these implicit (but easily recognizable) and explicit references in the four dream poems:

> *Book of the Duchess:* Ovid, *Metamorphoses* (Ceyx and Alcyone, 62ff); Bible, Genesis (Joseph's dream, 280–2); Macrobius, *Commentarii in Somnium Scipionis* (284–6); story of Troy (Benoit's *Roman de Troie?*, 326–31); *Roman de la Rose* (334); 'remedyes of Ovyde' *(Remedia Amoris?*, 568); Bible, Esther (987); Dares Phrygius (1070); Livy (1084); Peter Riga's *Aurora (Biblia Versificata*, 1169); Ovid, *Metamorphoses* (1326–7).

> *House of Fame:* Virgil, *Aeneid* (378); Ovid, *Heroides* (379); Virgil, Claudian, Dante (449–50); *Somnium Scipionis* (916–18); Boethius, *De Consolatione Philosophiae* (972–8); St Paul, 2 Corinthians (980–2); Martianus Capella, *De Nuptiis Mercurii et Philologiae* (985); Alan of Lille, *Anticlaudianus* (986); Virgil (1244); St John, Apocalypse (1385); Josephus Flavius (1433); Statius, *Thebaid* and *Achilleid* (1460–3); Homer, Dares Phrygius, Dictys Cretensis, Lollius (Boccaccio?), Guido delle Colonne, Geoffrey of Monmouth (1466–70); Virgil, *Aeneid* (1483); Ovid (1487); Lucan, *Pharsalia* (1499); Claudian, *De Raptu Proserpinae* (1509).

> *Parliament of Fowls:* Cicero, *Somnium Scipionis* (*De Re Publica* VI) (29); Macrobius, *Commentarii in Somnium Scipionis* (111); Dante, *Inferno* III (the gate, 127 and 134?); Alan of Lille, *De Planctu Naturae* (316).

> *Legend of Good Women*, Prologue G: Chaucer, *Romance of the Rose* (255); Chaucer, *Troilus* (264–5); 'Valerius', Livy, Claudian, St Jerome (280–1); Ovid, *Heroides* (305); Vincent of Beauvais, *Speculum Historiale* (307); Dante (336); Chaucer, *House of Fame, Book of the Duchess, Parliament of Fowls*, 'Palamon and Arcite', *Boece*, Innocent III's *De Contemptu Mundi* (translation), 'Lyf of Seynt Cecile', 'Orygenes upon the Maudeleyne' (405–18); Agathon (514).

This list must be read carefully: it is fairly obvious, for instance, that Chaucer did not have a first-hand knowledge of Livy,[5] that the reference to Macrobius in the *Book of the Duchess* is probably indebted to the *Roman de la Rose* as is that to the *Somnium* in the *House of Fame*,[6] and that the mention of Agathon, the Athenian tragic poet of the Prologue to the *Legend*, is almost pure name-dropping. It is also clear that the list itself can (and will in the following pages) be supplemented by numerous references which, taken in their context, reveal knowledge of other 'books'. When the Black Knight of the *Book of the Duchess* mentions 'Genelloun', 'Rowland', and 'Olyver', he takes for granted that his interlocutor and his audience know some form of the *Chanson de Roland* or at least of the Charlemagne romances. On the other hand, the quotation from the opening lines of *Inferno* III (the threefold repetition of *per me si va* – 'through me one goes') for the *Parliament*'s gate poses a problem. If we think that Chaucer expected his audience to recognize it even if he did not give the author's name, we must also assume knowledge of the *Commedia* to have extended beyond the circle of his acquaintances. Or was Chaucer playing a 'private' game with his intellectual friends (like Gower, who mentions Dante in the *Confessio*), whom he himself might have introduced to the great Italian poem?

Whatever we are inclined to believe on this and other issues, the list gives a fairly clear overall view of the direction towards which, within a persistently Ovidian and 'classical' horizon, Chaucer's culture moves in his dream poems. In the phase that goes from the *Book of the Duchess* to the *Parliament of Fowls* there are two general shifts – one from a culture basically founded on Ovid and the romances to an enormous widening of the *literary* spectrum in the *House of Fame* (which includes Ovid, but also relies heavily on Virgil, consecrates a number of Latin classics and medieval authors, and explicitly refers to Dante); and another from an essentially literary culture to a more philosophically inclined one, which emerges clearly in the second Book of the *House of Fame* with the mention of Boethius, Martianus Capella, and Alan (and *en passant* Aristotle and Plato, 759), and predominates in the *Parliament*, where Cicero's and Macrobius's *Somnium*, and Alan's *De Planctu Naturae* are the only two explicit references.[7] It goes without saying that Chaucer's perusal of some Old and New Testament texts is constant. In the *Legend*, Virgil, Ovid, and Dante take over again, but the most interesting feature here is that Chaucer's own previous works are discussed in a context dominated by a meditation on the value of books 'old' and 'new'. Chaucer's dream poems begin with a book and end with a book, generally his own. His dreaming begins with Ovid's *Metamorphoses* and ends with Chaucer's own books. In this double pattern there is an extraordinary circularity and an equally staggering direct pointedness: when Chaucer dreams, a book inevitably produces another book. The 'old' book becomes 'new'. Ovid becomes Chaucer.[8]

It is the functions of this transformation that we must now explore. In the *Book of the Duchess*, Chaucer is supposed to offer to John of Gaunt a 'consolation' for the death of his wife Blanche of Lancaster, and there are indeed several details, including the name of the Black Knight's Lady, White, to confirm this eminently 'private' occasion.⁹ Yet if one reads the actual poem Chaucer has written, one hardly notices this, but rather has the impression that the images and the narrative sequence of the book raise far wider, 'public' issues such as those of love, fortune, and death. The transformation of private occasion into public concern is effected by Chaucer through a series of operations basically centred on the fictionalization of certain motifs. The fundamental 'private' nucleus – the relationship between Gaunt and Blanche and her death – becomes the second, and longest, section of the dream, in which the protagonist meets a knight in black mourning his loss and complaining against Fortune, and forces him to tell the story of his love for White and finally reveal her death. But this nucleus, to which we shall soon return, is preceded by an introduction that makes the fiction much more complex. At the beginning, the poetic 'I' tells us that he suffers from insomnia, the reason of which he does not know unless it be a 'sicknesse' he has suffered for the last eight years. Apparently, this is love. At this point, the poetic persona relates that he asked for a book, 'a romaunce', to 'drive the night away':

> And in this bok were written fables
> That clerkes had in olde tyme,
> And other poets, put in rime
> To rede and for to be in minde,
> While men loved the lawe of kinde.
> This bok ne spak but of such thinges,
> Of quenes lives, and of kinges,
> And many other thinges smale. (52–9)

'Amonge al this' he finds a 'tale' which is the Ovidian story of Ceyx and Alcyone. In this story Ceyx loses his life at sea and his wife, Alcyone, asks Juno to put her to sleep and to show her husband's fate to her in a dream. Morpheus, summoned by Juno's messenger, takes the mortal form of Ceyx and appears to Alcyone, who dies within three days. The sleepless reader, amazed and rather sceptical, decides to offer a feather-bed to Morpheus and Juno if they will put him to sleep. Hardly has he formulated his vow when he falls asleep over his book and begins to dream.

The function of the Ovidian tale is, structurally, to connect the themes of sleep and insomnia (the protagonist's problem) with the story of Gaunt and Blanche fictionalized in the second part of the poem. For in the episode from the *Metamorphoses* we have a kind of mirror-version of the Black Knight–White sequence – the story of a deep love between wife and husband, one of whom (in this case the latter) dies – and also a tale in which sleep and dreams occupy a central position. Like Alcyone, the poem's protagonist will sleep and dream, and his dream will in some way be the projection of his book and of the Gaunt–Blanche story.

The two fictionalized nuclei of the poem, preceded by the introduction, are thus thematically linked at a deep level. On the surface, they are joined to each other by an intermezzo where the logic of dreams reigns supreme. Here, as soon as he falls asleep, the dreamer finds himself, on a May morning, lying in bed naked, with birds singing all around him, in a room whose walls are covered with frescoes depicting the *Roman de la Rose* and whose windows are storiated with scenes from Trojan history and its heroes. The sun is shining and the air is 'blew, bryght, clere'. Suddenly he hears a horn, shouts, dogs, and horses. The protagonist mounts a horse, rushes out, and hears that the emperor Octavian is going on a hunt. He follows the company and ends up near a tree with a small dog. Trying to catch the animal, he goes down a 'floury grene wente', a grassy path in the full bloom of spring. At its end, leaning against a great oak, stands a man dressed in black, a knight, reciting a 'compleynte' for his dead lady.

Apparently, this intermezzo has nothing to do with the first and third parts of the poem (the story of Ceyx and Alcyone and that of the Knight and his lady). In fact, it picks up at least two themes common to both. One is that of literature, represented in the first part by the romance itself, the book full of 'fables' which the protagonist reads, and in the second by the allusion to the *Roman* and the story of Troy. In the third part, this will be taken up by both Knight and dreamer. The latter invokes Socrates (717) and mentions the 'fables' of Jason and Medea, Phyllis and Demophon, Aeneas and Dido, Narcissus and Echo, Samson and Delilah (726–38). The former, in five formidable *tours de force* which establish both a common cultural ground with, and his superiority to, the protagonist (both would have been pleasing to John of Gaunt), manages to evoke the 'remedyes of Ovyde', Orpheus, Daedalus, Hippocrates, and Galen (568–72), Alcibiades, Hercules, Alexander, the great cities of the ancient world, Trojan heroes and heroines, Dares, Penelope, Lucretia, and Livy (1057–84), Achitofel, Antenor, Ganelon, Roland and Oliver (1118–23), Lamech, Pythagoras, and Peter Riga's *Aurora* (1162–9), culminating in a display of geographical-imaginary erudition which is really a jibe at the conventions of romance. Here, the Knight makes clear that Blanche was never the type of lady who sent her faithful cavaliers off to the ends of the earth, as happens in the romances (1020–33). Literature, sensibly put in its place in this passage, ties up the three parts of the poem.

The second theme common to them is that of nature. When, in the introduction, the protagonist describes his insomnia, he makes clear that this 'sickness' goes against nature:

> And wel ye woot, agaynes kynde
> Hyt were to lyven in thys wyse,
> For nature wolde nat suffyse
> To noon erthly creature
> Nat longe tyme to endure
> Withoute slep and be in sorwe. (16–21)

Opposed to this is the book our sleepless reader picks up at night, which was written to be read and remembered 'while men loved the lawe of kinde' (56). The book, the *Metamorphoses*, sets the reader on the path of natural law, that sleep which has been denied him by his illness; in the same way this very book, with the dream of Alcyone it contains, also provides the Knight indirectly with an example of how to recover that harmony with nature which he has lost through his lady's death (466–9 and 511–13): because death is, precisely, the 'lawe of kinde', as the story of Ceyx and Alcyone demonstrates. Nature reigns supreme in the intermezzo, in the *locus amoenus*, the 'floury grene wente' that displays its vegetable and animal plenitude, where the 'povertee' and the 'sorwes' of winter are forgotten in the quasi-celestial triumph of spring on earth:

> For hit was, on to beholde,
> As thogh the erthe envye wolde
> To be gayer than the heven,
> To have moo floures, swiche seven,
> As in the welken sterres bee. (405–9)

Likewise, Nature later dominates the ideal portrait of the lady, a 'chef patron of beaute' according to the best poetic and social models, and 'chef ensample' of Nature's work (869–73, 908–12, 1194–8). Little wonder, then, that the story of the Knight's love for Blanche, recounted in typically courtly terms (the 'worship and the servise' the man pays to the woman), ends in union, supreme 'natural' bliss (1289–97). Once more, the 'private' (John of Gaunt's marriage with Blanche of Lancaster) takes on a general, 'public' significance: *amour courtois* culminates in the happy union of man and woman, who share joy and sorrow until death parts them.

Against Nature and Love fight the forces of grief, Fortune, and death. In the splendid meadow where the 'sorrow' of winter is forgotten, the dreamer suddenly hears a complaint where sorrow and death dominate (475–86), and comments, with a phrase that reminds us of one used earlier for his insomnia (18–21):

> Hit was gret wonder that Nature
> Myght suffre any creature
> To have such sorwe and be not ded. (467–9)

The story of the Knight's love for Blanche is prefaced by his long complaint against Fortune, who played a chess game with him and who is accused of being the epitome of deception and false appearances (598–709) – Chaucer's first utterance on the theme of destiny, examined by Jill Mann later in this volume. And Blanche's beauty and the perfect union of love is destroyed by death, the 'natural law' which had killed Ceyx, and at the announcement of which the dream abruptly and realistically ends. When, at the end of the series of questions and answers that characterizes their exchange, the Knight cries to the dreamer, 'She ys ded!', the hunt is suddenly 'doon' (1309–12). The Knight walks off homewards to 'a long castel with walles white' (1318). The bell strikes twelve, and the protagonist wakes up in his bed, with the book of Alcyone and Ceyx in his hand, ready to put his 'queynt sweven' into rhyme, to turn the book into *his* Book – the *Book of the Duchess*.

The themes of love and nature, at the centre of the three-part-plus-introduction structure of the *Book of the Duchess,* are even more overtly prominent in the three-part-plus-introduction structure of the *Parliament of Fowls.* Here, however, there seems to be no 'private' occasion behind the poem,[10] and the level of discussion is much less concrete than in the *Book of the Duchess.* We have no Knight and no lady with a story of love and death, but, instead, a dreamer-reader led by the protagonist of his dream-book, Scipio Africanus, to a garden-park of nature and love, to a temple of Venus, and to the hill where personified Nature herself presides over a parliament of birds. The central problems of the poem are examined in three successive abstract stages – the summary of a book, Cicero's *Somnium Scipionis*; the iconography of garden and temple; the animal parable of the parliament.

Throughout these phases the poet's focus is on the theme of love announced in the first two stanzas as a polyvalent and comprehensive dimension. Love is 'dredful joye alwey that slit so yerne', 'assay . . . hard' and 'sharp . . . conquerynge'; its 'werkynge' is 'wonderful'; its phenomena are 'myrakles' and 'crewel yre'. It is an ambiguous world, in which one lives in perpetual uncertainty (6–7) and in absolute impotence ('I can na moore', 14). But Love is also a power that dominates everything: even one who, like the narrator, does not know love 'in dede', can get from books an idea of how 'he wol be lord and syre' (8, 12). Love is really human life – all of it, albeit short; it is an art – the *ars amandi* – that is long and difficult to learn. And finally, as is implied by the reference to *ars longa, vita brevis*, love is the art of poetry itself, and often the object of literature:

> Yit happeth me ful ofte *in bokes reede*
> Of his myrakles and his crewel yre. (10–11)

In other words, love is not only a feeling, but also a real culture, with its conventions and its laws.

When the narrator of the *Parliament*, who is – 'what for lust and what for lore' (15) – an inveterate reader, picks up his book of the day, the *Somnium Scipionis*, the problem of love acquires a metatemporal and cosmic dimension.[11] We are now brought, through Scipio's dream, to the galaxy whence one can contemplate 'the lytel erthe that here is' and where the music of the spheres is heard (56–63). And we are told of life after death, of heaven, of a 'blysful place' 'there as joye is that last withouten ende' (48–9). The love that is rewarded here is love for the 'commune profyt' (46–9 and 73–7), a love which must be exercised on earth but must be detached from worldly pleasure (64–6). Clearly, this is not sensual love – it is, rather, love directed towards the *bonum commune*, love that goes beyond the individual, whose object is society and the state. The latter should be understood in the Roman sense, to which the *Somnium* obviously refers, and which was partly incorporated into the language of the English Parliament. Love is the salvation and aggrandisement of the *res publica* – or, in a wider sense, of the whole of mankind.

One understands why the narrator, deprived of his book by the falling of night, and 'fulfyld of thought and busy hevynesse' as he starts getting ready for bed, declares that he has something he did not want and does not have what he wanted (89–91). It is not exactly this kind of love that he was looking for. Nor will he be any luckier in the dream which promptly begins as soon as he falls asleep after perusing his 'olde bok totorn' (110), the *Somnium*. For here Africanus, the very protagonist of Cicero's and Macrobius's book, appears and leads him, through a Dantean gate, into a park where love reigns in a very particular fashion. As the double inscription over the gate announces, and as the visit confirms, the dreamer enters a garden which is at once a happy and a deadly place, an Eden of eternal, flourishing life and a world of total sterility; it is both a source of grace, the way to a happy end (127–33), and a 'sorweful were' where the fish die in aridity (134–40). The 'blysful place' of the *Somnium*, ultramundane and heavenly, becomes a 'blysful place' (127) in an earthly paradise, where love for the 'commune profyt' is replaced by the love with which the birds 'besyede hem here bryddes forth to brynge' (192), that is, by procreation, and where the harmony of the spheres becomes 'ravyshyng swetnesse' of 'instruments of strenges in acord' and angelic voices of singing birds (59–63, 190–1, 197–203). Here is the eternal joy the reader found in the vision of the *Somnium* (49 and 208), here is immortality (50–6 and 207), perennial day, constant spring, the plenitude and variety of the vegetable and animal kingdoms (172–5 and 206). Here, finally, is harmony between the world of nature and that of man, indicated subtly by the function each tree has in human life and activity – the oak to build with, the fir to sail on, the 'olyve of pes' and the 'asp for shaftes pleyne', the 'cipresse, deth to pleyne' (176–82).

Yet, as the dreamer's view penetrates deeper into the garden, this Edenic universe changes. We enter the human cosmos, an artificial world where myth and courtesy – civilization as distinct from nature – are in full bloom. Here, we find Cupid and the personifications and incarnations of Eros – Beauty and Pleasure, Courtesy and Gentilesse, and many others – from the *Roman de la Rose* and Boccaccio's *Teseida*. We visit the temple of Venus, where angelic harmony is replaced by a 'swogh' of sighs hot as fire (246–7). Priapus stands 'in sovereyn place', all naked and 'with hys sceptre in honde' (253–6). The phallic image provides a prelude to the inner recesses of the temple, where the darkness thickens. There Venus, wrapped in a golden aura, with her hair unbound, her body half-covered by a film of transparent lace, reclines on her couch 'til that the hote sonne gan to weste' (265–73). Planet and goddess, courtly and sensual, Venus also represents tragic love. All around her lie the broken bows of the virgins of Diana who have sacrificed their chastity in her service, and the walls of the temple are frescoed with the stories of love and death consecrated by literature and mythology – Semiramis, Dido, Cleopatra, Helen, Tristan and Isolde, Troilus himself. Love, which is part of life – desire, which is necessary to nature – is also the negation of life, the reversal of nature. The gold that surrounds Venus is far from the flowers of white, blue, yellow, and red, far from the red fins and silvery scales of the fish in the garden.

So far, love has appeared as service of the *bonum commune*, Edenic plenitude, supreme moment of sensual infatuation. It has been described by means of a book, a vision, a series of images. Now, the poet introduces a lively debate between birds, an animal parable. But the implications of this are as vast as those of the preceding sections. The specific case – that of the eagle loved by three birds at once – is a courtly contest *par excellence*, but it is broadened by the introduction of Nature and the extension of the discussion to all the birds, including the less noble ones. The occasion, the annual mating of the birds on St Valentine's day, already places the *demande d'amour* within the context of natural order in general, and the problem of love itself in a perspective that is more properly philosophical. The eagle's courtly love becomes but one aspect of the general economy of nature – mating, procreation, and the perpetuation of the species. The presence of both 'lower classes' and 'nobility' (here represented by the different ranks and 'degrees' of birds) brings the problem into the sphere of the social order.

By opening the debate to the representatives of the lower classes, who have not all absorbed the courtly experience, Nature makes the *demande d'amour* apparently unsolvable. For some of the lower birds suggest solutions that contrast with the code (thus the goose maintains that the rejected suitor should choose another mate; the cuckoo recommends that all three should remain celibate; the duck scornfully rejects the whole code, 589–95), but all of them indicate, first by their noisy impatience (491–7) and then by flying away satisfied, the basic irrelevance for them of the problem itself and the socio-cultural convention it represents.

On the other hand, Nature, the 'vicaire of the almyghty Lord' (379), follows her own logic in favouring the choice of the royal eagle, whom she herself has fashioned to her full satisfaction (636) and who is 'the gentilleste and most worthi' (635). The Nature of Alan's *De Planctu Naturae* (and of Boethius's *Consolatio*) 'keeps all things in balance and accord and . . . embodies their moral-natural norm'[12] – a feature that Chaucer's goddess faithfully incarnates (379–81). For her, the social order, and hence the courtly culture which it includes as an aspect of the ideal of the upper classes, is but a part of the natural order. The perfection of the universe requires plenitude and plurality – the increase and multiplication of living beings proclaimed by Genesis – as well as 'inequality'. 'It concerns the perfection of the universe', says Thomas Aquinas,[13] 'that there be not only many individuals, but that there be also different species of things, and consequently different degrees in things.' Chaucer's parliament of birds incarnates these ideas:

> For this was on Seynt Valentynes day,
> Whan every foul cometh there to chese his make,
> Of every kynde that men thynke may,   [plurality]

> And that so huge a noyse gan they make
> That erthe, and eyr, and tre, and every lake
> So ful was that unethe was there space
> For me to stonde, so ful was al the place.   [plenitude]

> . . .

> That is to seyn, the foules of ravyne
> Weere hyest set, and thanne the foules smale . . .   [inequality]
>   (309–24)

In assembling before Nature to choose a mate, the birds fulfil the supreme law of the universe, that of 'generation', which is the one 'natural act' to be pre-eminently directed to the common good. Hence, what we witness in the third section of the *Parliament* is the preparation for something that already took place in the second (the birds' procreation, 192), a direct consequence of the 'desire' pictured in the temple of Venus, and an interestingly wider version of the 'commune profyt' propounded in the first. Love is now complete.

Nature's problem, however, is still unresolved, for if reason and natural (including social) law suggest that the eagle choose the 'royal tercel', Nature herself 'prike[s] with plesaunce' all three of the lovers, so none of them can claim a greater natural right than the others. The solution might look simple to us, but is at once novel, realistic, and sensible in a fourteenth-century context:

> . . . she
> Shal han right hym on whom hire herte is set,
> And he hire that his herte hath on hire knet.   (626–8)

But the lady is not ready for this, yet, and asks for a year in which to make up her mind (647–9). Delay is a characteristic of all parliaments that cannot decide. And the birds, singing a roundel in honour of Nature, fly away. Their shouting awakes the dreamer, who immediately picks up other books in the hope of some day reading something 'that [he] shal mete som thyng for to fare / The bet' (698–9). Reading a book can be unsatisfactory. Indeed, before falling asleep the protagonist of the *Parliament* had revealed that the *Somnium Scipionis*, which he had taken out 'a certeyn thing to lerne', was not exactly what he wanted (20, 90–1). The reading of the *Somnium* produced the dream, the first part of which mirrors, with the presence of Africanus, the book itself (106–8). Soon, however, this is forgotten, and the dream develops as a visit to the park of love and the temple of Venus. At this point, the reader's memory of another book, Alan's *De Planctu Naturae*, seems to start off the second section of the dream. This, too, is somehow unsatisfactory, in that it offers only a partial solution to the problem it poses. Hence, more reading is required. We have here two interrelated fundamental mechanisms. One is that of the endless quest, the search for an ever-receding object that the reading of books implies. The other is the transformation of 'olde bokes' into 'newe science' – the way in which the poet, both satisfied and dissatisfied with what he has read, produces his own book by connecting his texts, relating them to each other, integrating them with his own images and ideas, by finding in them 'mater of to wryte' and supplementing it with his own 'connyng for t'endite' (167–8). For the first time in European literature, a poet lays bare before our very eyes the intellectual, cultural, and creative processes by which 'tradition' is transformed by 'individual talent'.[14]

The 'newe science' consciously propounded by the discussion of Love and Nature in the three-part-plus-introduction structure of the *Parliament of Fowls* had already been at the centre of the incomplete three-part-plus-introduction structure of the *House of Fame,* where the themes of love and nature also occupy an important place. In fact, Chaucer's three early dream poems all share a series of important images. For instance, we realize that the theme of 'generation' which dominates the second and third sections of the *Parliament* is also present in the *House of Fame,* where, during the flight with the Eagle, Geoffrey beholds the 'ayerissh bestes', clouds, mists, storms, snows, and 'th'engendrynge in hir kyndes' (965–8). Like the Scipio of the *Parliament* and of the *Somnium* (explicitly recalled in *House of Fame,* 916–18), Geoffrey also sees the galaxy, and the earth reduced to no more 'than a prikke' (907). The 'halles' and 'boures' of Nature in the *Parliament* are made of 'braunches'; the House of Rumour in *Fame* is made of multicoloured twigs. Yet the former are 'iwrought after [the] cast and [the] mesure' of Nature herself (305), whereas the latter are the product of a labyrinthine imagination. The cave of sleep described in the *Metamorphoses* story of the *Book of the Duchess* is the first image we encounter in the *House of Fame* (66–76). The garden-park is present in both *Book of the Duchess* and *Parliament of Fowls.* A temple of Venus appears in both *Parliament* and *Fame.* The *Book of the Duchess* ends with the view of a castle, the castle of Fame dominates the first part of the third book of the *House of Fame.* Frescoes on the walls feature in all three poems. We are obviously in the presence of an imagination constantly at work on the same images. Poring over his books, Chaucer is fascinated and intrigued by the 'archetypal loci' of the Western mind they present.[15]

The exploration of these in the *House of Fame* is one of the most interesting poetic enterprises of fourteenth-century Europe – a journey through tradition, myth, literature, thought, language, and poetry. The self-consciousness with which Chaucer embarks on this adventure is witnessed by at least four highly significant features of his poem. First comes the discussion of the nature and causes of dreams in the long Proem to Book 1. Here, in an apparently light manner, the author examines the very medium of his poetry – the dream as mode of apprehension of reality and as type of discourse, the world removed from everyday concerns yet somehow representing their sublimated or distorted projection. Then the invocations prefaced to each book attract our attention, both as conscious manifestations of a desire to enter the mainstream of 'high' tradition and as indications of a thematic programme:

the God of Sleep and the Christian God introduce the entire poem; Venus, the Muses, and Thought the second book; Apollo, 'god of science and of lyght', the last. Third is the fact that the protagonist is called by his real name, 'Geoffrey'. And, finally, this very poet takes here full responsibility for his sufferings, thoughts, and 'art':

> For what I drye, or what I thynke,
> I wil myselven al hyt drynke,
> Certeyn, for the more part,
> As fer forth as I kan myn art.   (1879–82)

If one adds to this the fact that Geoffrey compares his vision and flight in Book II with those of Isaiah, Scipio, Nebuchadnezzar, Pharaoh, Enoch, Elijah, Romulus, Ganymede, Alexander, and Daedalus, and evokes for his situation the names of Plato, Boethius, St Paul, Martianus Capella, and Alan of Lille, one has a full idea of how serious, in his slightly ridiculous pedantry and bookish exaggeration, Chaucer really is.

With a stroke of genius, Chaucer chooses as his central theme that of Fame, a concept which Western tradition develops throughout antiquity and the Middle Ages as omnicomprehensive. A goddess from the time of Hesiod's *Works and Days,* Fame embraces the spheres of nature, death, heroism, love, chivalry, wisdom, conscience, virtue, fortune, myth, language, and poetry – the very themes Chaucer explores in his book.

A series of triads, following the tripartite structure of the *House of Fame,* will illustrate the development of these themes in the poem. The clearest sequence connects Love, Nature, and Fame.[16] The temple of Venus and the story of Dido and Aeneas in Book I are Love's domain, but, together with its pictorial and iconographic triumph, Love celebrates here its defeat. Aeneas, followed by Dido's complaint and cursed for his inconstancy, love of fame, 'delyt', and 'synguler profit' (and one thinks, by contrast, of the 'commune profyt' of the *Parliament*) leaves the queen, who kills herself. And the dreamer, going out of the temple, finds himself not in a garden, but in another *locus classicus* of the imagination – a waste land, a sterile desert where Nature is totally absent (489–90). When the golden Eagle lifts the dreamer up into the air, the flight they begin is precisely one through the world of Nature, where 'every kyndely thyng that is / Hath a kyndely stede' (730–1), where 'th'engendrynge in hir kyndes' can be contemplated, and where the 'fetheres of Philosophye' are almost on the point of overwhelming the poet with thoughts of Boethius, St Paul, Martianus Capella, and Alan's *Anticlaudianus.* The travellers, however, do not reach the heaven of the *Somnium* nor the earthly paradise of the *Parliament,* but the House of Fame, where the goddess of renown celebrates her triumph in wealth and splendour with the Muses, the poets, and the heroes and heroines of myth. But Fame, too, is not totally positive. In her judgement of nine companies of people, she denies, grants, and changes fame in a completely erratic, fickle, and unjust manner. The dreamer passes from her castle to the House of Rumour, an enormous rotating cage where crowds of anonymous, 'common' people gather to communicate and distort their news and stories to each other, and where tidings become an inextricable mixture of true and false, fly away and reach back to Fame, who gives them 'name' and 'duracioun'.

A principle of de-composition and re-composition seems to work throughout the *House of Fame*. Fame is glory, ill-repute, and rumour. Another triad to appear in the poem is that governed by Fortune, closely associated with Fame, and indeed called her 'sister' in Book III (1547), and who figures as 'destinee' in the story of Aeneas and as Chance in the House of Rumour. The truth of love is polluted by deception, lack of truth (330–1), 'apparence . . . fals in existence' (265–6). The truth, the philosophical and scientific reality of Book II, does not withstand the action of fame, which magnifies everything (1290–2). The precise laws of nature which rule the propagation of sound are completely upset by the castle, whose foundations rest on ice. Fame herself is a mutable monster, infinitely small and infinitely great, and her Triumph is contradicted by her Judgement. In the world of Rumour, finally, 'fals' and 'soth' are 'compouned' (2108–9).

A similar process dominates in the oneiric sphere which characterizes Chaucer's journey to Fame. After discussing the nature and causes of dreams, the *House of Fame* passes through several phases that seem to find, and immediately to abandon, a correspondence with traditional types of dreams: *somnium coeleste* or *visio* as a whole, it seems to be a love-dream in Book I and to turn, at the end of the Book, into a *phantasma* ('fantome', 493). Book II, with its quotation of Scipio and Alexander, is more clearly a *visio*, but, with its reminiscences of Dante and St Paul, comes close to a beatific vision. In Book III, elements of the apocalyptic vision (1383–5) merge with those of the Triumph. Finally, with the apparition of the man of great authority, the poem breaks off with what may be seen as the overture to an *oraculum*.

On one more level – that of poetry and literature – an oscillating and circular movement is a fundamental feature of the *House of Fame*. This poem begins with a poem, the 'Aeneid' painted on the walls of the temple of Venus. In Book II the Eagle gives Geoffrey an explanation of the physical nature of language – sound – and of the ambiguity that distinguishes meaning, that is, the relationship between a word and what it signifies and between a word and the speaker (765–81, 1066–82). 'Fama', say medieval etymologies, 'a fando, i.e., a loquendo' – the word 'fame' comes from *fari*, to speak. The poets and their cycles – 'Jewerye', Troy, Aeneas, Love, Rome, Hell – figure in Book III. Finally, the tidings which the protagonist was promised by the Eagle appear in the House of Rumour as the oral molecules of narrative, covering the whole universe of nature and human activities (1960–76) already contained by the 'book', the 'Aeneid' of Book I.[17]

From the cave of sleep of the Proem to the cave of Aeolus in Book III (1583–7), the House of Fame is, moreover, an encyclopedia of myths both ancient and medieval and an exploration of various literary genres. Aeneas's behaviour towards Dido is but the most illustrious example of that 'untrouthe' in love which recurs in endless stories of myth, from that of Demophon and Phyllis to that of Theseus and Ariadne (388–426). Daedalus, Morpheus, and Aeolus dominate the imaginary world of Chaucer's poem. The entire 'chevalrie' of Africa, Europe, and Asia (1338–40) exhibits its 'armes' in Fame's hall. But myth is literature. When Chaucer recounts the 'Aeneid', he is obviously thinking of a great narrative poem such as those which, in the disguise of poetic cycles, are 'borne up' by the poets on their shoulders in Book III. But he also mentions 'olde gestes' (1515) and the popular literature of 'mynstralles' and 'gestiours', Orpheus the Ur-poet together with 'Bret Glascurion' (1197–1208). The scientific culture shown off by the Eagle agrees with the philosophical and didactic poetry of Boethius, Martianus, and Alan. When Geoffrey undergoes the mystical temptation during which, like St Paul, he knows no more whether he is there, up in the sky, 'in body or in gost' (979–82), it is hard not to remember that fourteenth-century England is full of mystical treatises. When the Eagle tells him about the 'poetrie' in which 'goddes gonne stellifye / Bridd, fissh, best, or him or here', and mentions the Raven, the Bear, Castor, Pollux, and Atalanta (1000–8), we must imagine that a courtly and cultured audience such as that for which Chaucer wrote the *Book of the Duchess* would catch the allusion to Ovid's *Metamorphoses*.

In this context, it might seem paradoxical that myth and poetry disappear in the House of Rumour, which is explicitly compared to one of the mythological, archetypal buildings *par excellence*, the 'Laboryntus', 'Domus Dedaly' (1920–1), where tidings represent the oral roots of literature. But the labyrinth is for Ovid and Virgil the place where signs are lost, unrecognizable, false like Chaucer's tidings, and the all-encompassing traditional image of life, art, the world.[18]

What Dante saw in the essence of God was, 'legato con amore in un volume, ciò che per l'universo si squaderna' (bound by love in one single volume, that which is dispersed in leaves throughout the universe).[19] Chaucer's journey to the House of Fame is a secular and partly ironical version of this vision – a movement from the Book at the beginning (the 'Aeneid') to the oral fragments of it at the end. These in turn go back to Fame to be ordered by her and find themselves inserted in the great cycles of poetry. Soon the shipmen, pilgrims, pardoners, and messengers who crowd the House of Rumour with their 'tydynges' will begin another journey during which they will tell each other tales to be collected in a book – the *Canterbury Tales*. Meanwhile, through the cave, temple, desert, flight in space, castle and labyrinth of the *House of Fame*, the world has become a book.[20]

NOTES

1. The whole passage, G 267–312, is absent in the F redaction of the Prologue, supposedly written earlier than G.
2. The structure of the dream poems thus appears as a vertiginous 'mise en abyme': see S. d'Agata d'Ottavi, *Il sogno e il libro. La myse en abyme nei poemi onirici di Chaucer* (Rome, 1992). At the same time, the 'books' constructed by Chaucer's early poems remain 'open': see R. P. McGerr, *Chaucer's Open Books. Resistance to Closure in Medieval Discourse* (Gainesville, Fla., 1998).
3. When considered together, these operations outline what would be called an 'intertext'. The best analysis of this in Chaucer's dream narrative is the volume of the Oxford Guides to Chaucer by A. J. Minnis, *The Shorter Poems* (Oxford, 1995).
4. G. Duby, *The Age of the Cathedrals*, trans. E. Levieux and B. Thompson (London, 1981), ch. 8.
5. Unless the mention of Livy here and elsewhere in Chaucer's works indicates that he shares the general European, and particularly Anglo-Italian, passion for this author, who was being 'rediscovered' in the fourteenth century. See G. Billanovich, *La tradizione del testo di Livio e le origini dell'Umanesimo* (Padua, 1981).
6. Chaucer says that 'Macrobeus' 'wrot al th'avysyoun / That he mette, *kyng* Scipioun' (*Book of the Duchess*, 284–6; and see *House of Fame* 916–18). The *Roman de la Rose* (ed. F. Lecoy (Paris, 1968) lines 7–10) says that 'Macrobes' 'ançoit escrit l'avision qui avint au *roi* Scipion'.
7. Chaucer's philosophical concerns and learning in the dream poems are rightly emphasized by K. L. Lynch, *Chaucer's Philosophical Visions* (Cambridge, 2000).
8. This double pattern is mirrored in what R. R. Edwards terms 'representation' and 'reflection': see his *The Dream of Chaucer. Representation and Reflection in the Early Narratives* (Durham/London, 1989). Two very different approaches to the dream poems are to be found in L. J. Kiser, *Truth and Textuality in Chaucer's Poetry* (Hanover/London, 1991), and J. Chance, *The Mythographic Chaucer. The Fabulation of Sexual Politics* (Minneapolis/London, 1995).
9. For various correspondences, see Paul Strohm's essay, pp. 1–19 above.
10. For speculations on this point, see L. D. Benson, 'The Occasion of *The Parliament of Fowls*' in *The Wisdom of Poetry*, eds. L. D. Benson and S. Wenzel (Kalamazoo, Mich., 1982), pp. 123–44; and H. A. Kelly, *Chaucer and the Cult of Saint Valentine* (Leiden, 1986).

11. See J. A. W. Bennett, *The Parlement of Foules: An Interpretation* (Oxford, 1957), pp. 25–61, and E. S. Kooper, *Love, Marriage and Salvation in Chaucer's Book of the Duchess and Parliament of Foules* (Utrecht, 1985).

12. P. Dronke, 'Chaucer and the Medieval Latin Poets', part A, in *Writers and Their Background: Geoffrey Chaucer*, ed. Derek Brewer (London, 1974), p. 165.

13. *Summa contra Gentiles* II, xlv, 6.

14. 'Tradition and the Individual Talent' is the title of a famous essay by T. S. Eliot published in *The Sacred Wood* (1920 and 1928).

15. For this and several other aspects of the *House of Fame* discussed in the following paragraphs, see P. Boitani, *Chaucer and the Imaginary World of Fame* (Cambridge, 1984), pp. 180–216; and Chaucer, *The House of Fame*, ed. N. R. Havely (Durham, 1994).

16. See J. A. W. Bennett, *Chaucer's Book of Fame* (Oxford, 1968), chs. 1–3. A different approach can be found in S. Delany, *Chaucer's House of Fame and the Poetics of Skeptical Fideism* (Chicago, 1972).

17. This 'Aeneid' has a plot organization which resembles that of the *Roman d'Eneas*: see Minnis, *The Shorter Poems*, pp. 188–9.

18. See P. R. Doob, *The Idea of the Labyrinth from Classical Antiquity through the Middle Ages* (Ithaca, N.Y., 1990), pp. 307–39.

19. *Paradiso* XXXIII, 86–7.

20. See G. Josipovici, *The World and the Book*, 2nd edn (London, 1979), chs. 2–3.

5

MARK LAMBERT

Telling the story in *Troilus and Criseyde*

Especially in its first three books, *Troilus and Criseyde* is a wonderfully textured poem: places, talk, people, are rendered with a mastery of nuance, a love of the suggestive detail, unexampled in earlier English literature. Nor is the art of the *Troilus* only an art of detail, of charming cornices and misericord carvings: *Troilus and Criseyde* has a large, clear architectural plan; it is a structure of emphatic bilateral symmetry. It is also a work which knows, and makes sure the reader knows, that it has important thematic concerns: fortune and the good things of this world; human love; fidelity. The *Troilus*, in short, has the elements of a well-made work of serious literature. But perhaps the most subtle of the things which make it not merely a worthy but a truly great poem, a poem both exhilarating and disturbing, is the way these elements are combined with and related to one another. Texture does not merely echo, enhance, unproblematically enrich the meaning suggested by thematic statements and by structure. Almost the reverse proves to be the case; particularly as we read the second half of Chaucer's poem, our response to texture interferes with our 'proper' response to bilateral symmetry and to theme – particularly the theme of fidelity. As we move toward the conclusion of the work, *trouthe* has become both truly admirable – almost what Arveragus calls it in the *Franklin's Tale*, 'the hyeste thyng that man may kepe' (1479) – and also something we covertly dislike and are ashamed of ourselves for disliking. In the present essay I shall be discussing some of the salient features of narrative technique in the *Troilus* and also trying to show some of the ways in which texture, theme, and structure are related. I shall also want to speak of the place of the poet-narrator – who, like the reader, will have trouble responding properly to the story – in the *Troilus*. Here my special concern will be the interworkings of the poet's commitment to his task and the commitment of the poem's hero and heroine to one another – their fidelity, their *trouthe*.

I begin with the poem's remarkably efficient, tightly focussed opening stanza, in which the narrator makes an implicit commitment both of and to considerable elegance:

> The double sorwe of Troilus to tellen,
> That was the kyng Priamus sone of Troye,
> In lovynge, how his aventures fellen
> Fro wo to wele, and after out of joie,
> My purpos is, er that I parte fro ye.
> Thesiphone, thow help me for t'endite
> Thise woful vers, that wepen as I write.   (I, 1–7)

'That wepen as I write': the audience prepares itself for a poem with a strongly dominant (for all one can yet tell, perhaps an unvaried) mood. But even earlier in the stanza there is a statement about the overarching shape of experience: 'double sorwe . . . Fro wo to wele, and after out of joie'. The poem which follows, one is perhaps gratified but certainly not surprised to discover, will indeed be symmetrical in structure, with various features of the rising (in medieval terms, 'comic') action of the first half recalled by features of the falling ('tragic') action of the second half.[1] One notices also, perhaps, what is *not* in this stanza: no superlatives, no suggestion of any extraordinary qualities in Troilus, Priam, or Troy, to distract us from the dominant mood and that idea of double sorrow. There is also, of course, no Chaucerian indirection: no frame of dreaming or reading or setting out on a pilgrimage to suggest that an attentive reader may choose to align in a number of different ways the various things the poet is telling him or her. No, as the old lady says in *David Copperfield*, let us have no meandering: Chaucer's initial emphases are upon the mood of the story, the shape of the story, and – thanks to the artful syntax which emphasizes 'my purpos' (the grammatical subject of the main clause of the first sentence) by holding it back for four lines – upon the poet's own commitment to something, his willing and implicitly promising the poem to follow. And this implicit promise is made, like all serious promises, to particular people for a particular time: 'er that I parte fro ye'.

The opening stanza, then, draws our attention both to the bilateral symmetry of Troilus's experience in love, and to the poet's commitment to the telling of Troilus's story. It should be noted that the two things are related: that is, self-commitment which proves successful, the kept promise, is itself a thing of bilateral symmetry: even-song and morning-song accord; what I said I would do, I have done. And like the symmetry of 'fro wo to wele, and after out of joie', the symmetry of a successful human promise is likely to entail a second half which is more difficult, oppressive than the first: it is generally easier to give our word than to keep it.

The reader who is on some level aware of these harmonics of the opening will be particularly alert to the lines which end the introduction to Book I and subtly align the heroine's fidelity with the narrator's commitment, story content with story-telling:

> For now wil I gon streght to my matere,
> In which ye may the double sorwes here
> Of Troilus in lovynge of Criseyde,
> And how that she forsook hym er she deyde. (53–6)

The phrase 'double sorwes' brings us back to the initial stanza, and the association is made a bit stronger by the use of 'tag-ending' *ere*-clauses in the two sentences: 'er that I parte fro ye'; 'er she deyde'. The storyteller's foreseen good parting from his audience, painful task faithfully completed, is put into some kind of relationship with a bad, faith-breaking parting of hero and heroine. (We should notice Chaucer's selection of 'forsook', a word which suggests betrayal as movement away.)

Thinking further about the relationship of telling the story and the material of the story, love which goes bad, or is not strong enough, we find a special poignancy in something Chaucer reveals shortly after his first stanza has displayed its elegance. We are made to realize that the narrator has undertaken this difficult literary task out of a generous impulse; the poem is to be a gift of love, an act of charity:

> . . . if this may don gladnesse
> Unto any lovere, and his cause availle,
> Have he my thonk, and myn be this travaille! (19–21)

Moreover, the poem will come into being, or the poet wishes it to come into being, not through the efforts of purposeful writer and helpful fury alone; *Troilus and Criseyde* should emerge from a context of common and loving human effort. The writer will try to 'don gladnesse' to lovers, but his chosen audience should themselves contribute to the work by praying; praying both for other lovers and for the poet himself (22–46). As, in the early books of *Troilus and Criseyde*, the reader savours the busyness of Pandarus and, more generally, the atmosphere of Chaucer's Troy, the atmosphere in which the love of hero and heroine is fostered and consummated, it will be good to remember that the poem itself was to grow out of charity and a like generosity of feeling. We should also recall this general goodness of heart when, late in our reading of *Troilus*, we are disturbed to find that our responses to the story have ceased to be entirely generous.

I want now to look at the characteristics of Chaucerian Troy, that city in which the love of Troilus and Criseyde grows. It is in the presentation of this city that Chaucer shows his astonishing mastery of atmosphere and texture. This poet's Troy is the city of kindness and friendship, of an unheroic and, because not free of foibles, unintimidating loving-kindness. Minor characters are important here. Hector helps Criseyde in a socially difficult situation: he is 'pitous of nature' (I, 113), but Criseyde's beauty also has its influence upon him (115); Deiphebus loves his brother Troilus and is not only eager to help Criseyde out of a difficulty, but indignant when Pandarus speaks of her, this friend of his, as though she were a stranger (II, 1422–4); later on in the poem, when bad news comes, Trojan ladies – like all ladies, given to visiting with friends – gather at Criseyde's house to offer the solace of unexceptionable sentiments (IV, 680–730); Helen of Troy, in an astonishing transformation, becomes the very nicest lady in an affluent suburb; Troilus is the beneficiary of the human habit – still with us, the reader is glad to learn – of responding to someone's praise of a given person with still higher praise (II, 1582–9). Physically, this Chaucerian Troy is of course walled, enclosed; it is under siege, but the state of siege serves to heighten by contrast the life of peace within (cf. I, 148–50). The fighting itself is essentially off-stage, summarized rather than narrated. This city is peculiarly one of commodious, welcoming, well and discreetly staffed households: we have scenes set in the homes of Troilus, Criseyde, Pandarus, Deiphebus, and, later, Sarpedon. It is a city where a kneeling hero will have a friend ready and solicitous enough to fetch him a cushion and that cushion which Pandarus brings for Troilus (III, 960–6), almost as touching as it is absurd, might be the very emblem, as Pandarus is the most extraordinary representative, of Trojanness.

This Troy is a city – or this *Troilus* is a poem – where characters, especially the hero, retreat to bed remarkably often; bed as a place of Eros is, in the *Troilus*, ambiguously related to bed as the place of infantile refuge. More generally, heroic love, the grand passion *Troilus and Criseyde* would seem to be about, is made to appear at once quite different from warm-hearted decency, and something which grows from and is nurtured by such instinctive benevolence.[2]

We are charmed, but also a bit disconcerted; which is to say we are being educated. When we began this narrative of double sorrow and weeping verses, we expected to hear about the intensity of love, and of course we do hear about it. Still, this story is not quite what we had anticipated: we have had to learn to experience intense love within the peculiar setting of the first books, heroic love in the context of niceness. Texture as rich as the texture of the *Troilus* does not simply enhance our response to theme and structure: it inevitably changes that response.

One feature of Chaucer's technique which deserves special attention both for its contribution to our sense of texture in the poem and for its intrinsic interest is his mastery of dialogue. In *Troilus and Criseyde*, talk is vitality. The association is strongly, delightfully made in the first half of the work, and variously played upon in the second half. Pandarus, the Trojan *genius loci*, is the famed and very effective speaker; when, towards the end of the poem, we learn 'a word ne kowde he seye' (v, 1729), we know that there is no hope left. The love-fostering scene at Deiphebus's house (II, 1555ff) presents diverse folk speaking diversely; in the 'falling-action' scene which is balanced against this one, the visit to Sarpedon (v, 435ff), all characters except Pandarus and Troilus are left unquoted, and thus, in contrast to the minor characters of the earlier gathering, are rather pallid, more data than persons. And there are still subtler (though, in view of the place in this work of the code of lover's secrecy, not necessarily more important) things to notice about Chaucer's dialogue than the basic speech–silence contrast. Tempo and speech-size are worked with adroitly. A sunny, comic scene may make much use of rapidly exchanged short speeches, while a sombre interview is built primarily of large blocks of speech. (Compare the Pandarus–Criseyde delivery-of-letter section at II, 1093ff, with the Pandarus–Troilus duologue at IV, 372ff.) In Chaucer's greatest presentation of talk, the first interview of Pandarus and Criseyde (II, 78ff), there is a Shavian mastery of scene rhythm, a splendid utilization of both quick interchange and long declamation.

But fully to appreciate the expressive movement of talk in *Troilus and Criseyde* (and, indeed, fully to appreciate the expressive rhythm of narration in *Troilus and Criseyde*) means to consider the particular form in which Chaucer cast his narrative: the *Troilus* is a story in verse and, more particularly, a story in stanzaic verse. The basic point is this. When an author elects to tell a tale in seven-line stanzas, one expects life in that tale (including speech) to be articulated as series of seven-line and multiple-of-seven-line units; in other words, the maker of stanzaic narrative is more conspicuously committed than is the couplet-writer (or, of course, the prose writer) to finding a certain shape in experience again and again. This is not to say that 'shape' will be a special thematic concern of any rhyme-royal narrative; but there is something right in the fact that *Troilus and Criseyde* is both stanzaic and also opens by drawing our attention to a large pattern which it is going to trace. Now *Troilus and Criseyde*, wonderfully clear in its first few lines about what it is going to do, is also the poem notorious for the trouble it finally has in coming to a stop; and whatever we make of its peculiar last pages, we will not think them quite unprepared for if we attend carefully to the way we as readers (or far better, imagined auditors) experience the longer speeches of the poem. In those longer speeches, Chaucer is having a good deal of what is in two senses liminal fun with stanza boundaries. Again and again we will have thought a given seventh line concluded a speech, only to discover a couple of seconds later that it was merely a section of that speech which so ringingly terminated. (In its technical aspects, the longwindedness of Pandarus is more amusing than the longwindedness of the Wife of Bath.) To put this another way: the opening of *Troilus and Criseyde* draws partic-ular attention to the story's shape and anticipates the end of the matter, the parting of narrator and audience; but metrically, *Troilus* is a poem that keeps us saying to ourselves, 'ah no; there is more'. The articulation of stanzas pro-vides, throughout the poem, reminders of the tension between the 'first-half' values of surprising abundance and the 'second-half' values of shape-holding and promise-keeping.

Now the 'more' of the *Troilus* stanza is not a matter of quantity alone. Chaucer, in moving from speech by one character to speech by another, to narration, and perhaps back to speech again – sometimes all within seven lines – gives us effects one would have thought outside the range of stanzaic verse. Thus, the opening of that first Pandarus–Criseyde interview:

> Quod Pandarus, 'Madame, God yow see,
> With youre book and all the compaignie!'
> 'Ey, uncle myn, welcome iwys,' quod she;
> And up she roos, and by the hond in hye
> She took hym faste, and seyde, 'This night thrie,
> To goode mot it turne, of yow I mette.'
> And with that word she doun on bench hym sette.
>
> 'Ye, nece, yee shal faren wel the bet,
> If God wol, al this yeer,' quod Pandarus;
> 'But I am sory that I have yow let
> To herken of youre book ye preysen thus.
> For Goddes love, what seith it? telle it us!
> Is it of love? O, som good ye me leere!'
> 'Uncle,' quod she, 'youre maistresse is nat here.'   (II, 85–98)

This would be nice enough in prose, and perhaps charming in couplets; in stanzas, it is truly exhilarating, metrical dexterity almost become a moral good. The listener receives not something in place of what was expected, but something beyond what was expected. The rhymes of easy speech do not distort the structural logic of the rhyme scheme, but unconstrainedly emerge in the stanzaic form; talk can be both talk and well-shaped rhyme royal. Thus, Chaucer's dialogues are something which equivalent exchanges in novels (which have no responsibility, no implicit contract, to be well shaped as anything but imitations of human talk) simply cannot be: they are radically 'something more', the metrical representation of a promise being exceeded.

The first Pandarus–Criseyde interview is, I have said, Chaucer's greatest conversation scene. But this scene's mastery of stanzaic and larger rhythms is in various ways in the service of things less technical, and I do want to look here at one of those things: this is the scene where Chaucer really presents Criseyde, or presents what we might call the *other* Criseyde. Up to this time, that is, Criseyde has seemed pretty much what the original 'purpos' and indicated design required: a superlatively beautiful lady. Here one discovers that there is more to her than necessary conditions for double sorrow, more to her indeed, than her lover or anyone else in the poem can quite appreciate. She is wonderfully shrewd, agile-witted; and though we know from the beginning the one salient moral fact of her story, that she will forsake Troilus, we are endlessly interested in the nuances of her character. And we should notice also that in this interview scene and after it, our pleasure as audience involves a sort of conflict of interests, not just a combination of interests. Here Pandarus, after all, is acting to advance our hero's fortunes, and we should (unless we are trying to keep to a *very* high moral road in our reading of the poem) be on the hero's side. But we do find ourselves, for all the good we wish Troilus, taking pleasure in the fact that Criseyde is not all that easy for her uncle to manipulate, is a worthy, resourceful adversary in these verbal skirmishes. We want the scene to be a well-played match even more than we want it to be an advancing of the hero's cause. (As a good first-half scene, it will, of course, manage to be both.)

In these last pages I have been chiefly stressing the various ways in which the first half of *Troilus and Criseyde* gives its audience more than could have been expected from a poem which began by being markedly explicit about its particular concerns and insistent about its lachrymose mood: the concerns have turned out to be broader than we thought they would be, and the weeping verses proved to be not steadily weeping verses. Now a work of art is always teaching us things about ourselves while revealing things about itself, and this is certainly true of our poem: we find how easy and pleasant it is to contemplate all these unexpected, unheroic things; how responsive we are to the texture of narrative. But one might say that it is Criseyde – and, again, the Criseyde of the first interview scene – who teaches us the most flattering lesson about ourselves: if she is clever, so are we; we are clever enough to *discover* her cleverness – and thus more clever than the hero, or even her uncle, who, well into the scene, is strangely patronizing about Criseyde's intelligence (II, 267–73). We can feel more perceptive than the poet-narrator also. Chaucer is quite willing to explain, and, for comic effects, sometimes overexplain, why something is happening and what we ought to think about it. But he also knows when to leave things unexplained – sometimes because ambiguity is desirable, at other times (and this is what particularly concerns us) so that the audience may feel it understands more than the narrator, or at least does not need comments from the narrator. Exemplary in this respect is the stanza beginning at II, 141: the stanza in which Criseyde's adroitness is first discovered. Pandarus, in the part of the scene which precedes this stanza, has been arousing his niece's interest in that secret of his – Troilus's love for her – and feigning reluctance to tell the secret. There has been, thus far, no great reason to think Criseyde will be more difficult for Pandarus to manipulate than Troilus himself had been in the complementary extracting-of-the-secret scene. The first four lines of the stanza in question are, then, quite unsurprising, mere confirmation of Pandarus's ability to achieve the effects he wants:

> Tho gan she wondren moore than biforn
> A thousand fold, and down hire eyghen caste;
> For nevere, sith the tyme that she was born,
> To knowe thynge desired she so faste . . .   (141–4)

And then, in the next three lines, Criseyde comes out into the light. Rather than plead to know the secret, she becomes shrewdly acquiescent:

> And with a syk she seyde hym atte laste,
> 'Now, uncle myn, I nyl yow nought displese,
> Nor axen more that may do yow disese.'   (145–7)

The great line here is the one Chaucer abstained from writing: the one that would have explained why, feeling *that*, Criseyde came to say *this*: there is more pleasure for the audience in being left alone with the juxtaposition.

It is exhilarating to discover that we do not need more explanation; and it is altogether typical of Chaucer that he leaves us here feeling not that a clever author is flattering the intelligence of a fit audience, but that the writer somehow failed to notice that anything just here in his story required explanation: we are made to believe, as I have said, that only we are capable of fully appreciating Criseyde, of relishing her cleverness in falling back, playing the good, dutiful niece, in order to gain her end. And one should go on to stress that our discovery of this Criseyde, our clever, resourceful Criseyde, is really the type of our discovery of all the richness of texture in the poem, and particularly in the first half of the poem: we feel that there is more in the work than we could have expected to find, and also more in ourselves; that our experience keeps broadening and growing richer. And this surely is something Chaucer would have wanted the reader of any spacious narrative to feel.

The first part of the *Troilus* might be thought of as the poetry of grace: it delights by giving the reader more than was promised, more than was, perhaps, even nameable, at the poem's opening. The final part of the *Troilus* – and especially Book V – is the poetry of contract: it is itself the completing of the work explicitly described and implicitly promised by the poem's opening, and has as its subject-matter fidelity, the keeping of an agreement. The great question now is whether even-song and morning-song accord: match and symmetry are here the signs of moral health; surprises, the source of delight in the first part of the poem, are now inherently suspect or culpable. The shift here is of course in the underlying patterns of tale-telling and response rather than on the surface of the story, but it is nonetheless a very difficult shift to make, and our difficulty in making it (indeed our inability to make it completely) is part of what *Troilus* means. In his self-effacing way, Geoffrey Chaucer does have the daring of a great poet. To enrich our understanding of his matter, he will take chances, will have us feel dissatisfied: the poetry of contract is also the poetry of contraction. One may say that if the first half of *Troilus and Criseyde* is remarkable for the mastery, the ease of its narrative technique, the second half is remarkable for the riskiness, the strange moral courage of its narration. Chaucer does of course feel and want his readers to feel that, on the simplest human level, what Troilus did was right and what Criseyde did was wrong. But he also wants us to feel that on that simplest human level (that is, without any consideration of larger philosophical questions) there would be something deeply impoverished in a response that was limited to this judgement and a feeling of pity for Troilus. Human experience should be richer, human response more complex, than such a judgement allows. One feels Chaucer's unease, his artistic and moral claustrophobia, given comic expression in the narrator's celebrated statement that he would excuse Criseyde if he could (V, 1097–9). That unease becomes a thing of splendour in the final leap to a Christian vision – which of course means a contract-cancelling vision. But we find that Chaucerian unease at its most disturbing in some aspects of the tale-telling.

The reader, in the first half of the poem, develops a richly specific liking for Criseyde which, being based largely on characteristics of the heroine not pertinent to the original rise-and-fall design of the work, is one of the 'extra' things of the *Troilus*. In a sort of complement to this structurally and morally excessive liking for the heroine, the reader of the second half of the poem will come to feel, and, being a good person, try to censor, repress, deny, a sense of exasperation with the decent, suffering hero of Chaucer's narrative. We do genuinely pity Troilus (if we did not, our own exasperation would not disconcert us) but we have a nagging sense of the accuracy of his self-description in Book IV: 'I, combre-world, that may of nothyng serve, / But evere dye and nevere fulli sterve' (279–80; cf. also 517–18). For 'cumber-world' (apparently a Chaucerian coinage) one should perhaps substitute 'cumber-poem' – an aesthetic encumbrance, a drag on the narrative. Chaucer's hero is faithful (always the same) but he is also, as Chaucer sees he ought to be, more than a little boring (always the same) as one follows him through two long books of despair, of hopes the reader knows to be false, of waiting for death and wishing for death. Troilus is not given, as was his model, the hero of Boccaccio's *Filostrato*, a spectacular faint on hearing the decision to exchange Criseyde for Antenor (IV, 18–20), or a serious suicide attempt when he comes to suspect that his lady has been unfaithful (VII, 33); on the other hand, Chaucer adds a long philosophical meditation by the hero, the import of which is that there is not much Troilus can do about things: 'For al that comth, comth by necessitee: / Thus to ben lorn, it is my destinee' (IV, 958–9). At this point Pandarus is given the comic character's privilege of voicing the audience's censored exasperation (1086ff). Another Chaucerian addition to the poem is Diomede's first, wickedly brilliant courting speech (V, 106–75). The reader of that speech is disturbed to realize that s/he, like Criseyde, finds Diomede's speed and efficiency less appalling than s/he ought. If we examine our reactions closely, we see that the smile of Cassandra and the laughter of Pandarus when they recognize the dismalness of the hero's position (V, 1457; 1172) are disquieting not for what is disclosed about Troilus's sister and friend, but for what is suggested about the reader, who feels something of the same amusement – the amusement, really, of Fortune herself (IV, 6–7) at two removes. Chaucer's hero is being a true lover, faithfully going down as Fortune turns her wheel; but the reader – and indeed the narrator – are coming to feel confined and, in their exasperation, momentarily tough-minded almost to the point of feeling cruel amusement, even while they are predominantly compassionate.[3]

There is something salutary in the mere acknowledgement that one's reactions to the final, drawn-out sufferings of Troilus are decidedly mixed reactions; early in the poem we make pleasant discoveries about ourselves, and later on, some disconcerting ones. Chaucer has the great poet's ability to disturb. Our awareness of how Chaucer disturbs the reader, complicates our responses, is enhanced by a consideration of Book IV of the *Troilus* as a structural unit, a block in the composition. This penultimate book presents what may be called a ghost ending, an 'alternative', bittersweet conclusion to the story which one feels might have been the true one, but simply is rejected by an arbitrary god or fortune or author. The arbitrariness with which the

Book IV conclusion is avoided – things do not happen that way just here because things do not happen that way just here – works to lessen the authenticity, the felt inevitability, of the actual, Book V conclusion. A hint of what Chaucer is up to here comes in the lines which end the 'Prohemium' to Book IV. The author calls on Mars and the Furies for assistance:

> This ilke ferthe book me helpeth fyne,
> So that the losse of lyf and love yfeere
> Of Troilus be fully shewed heere. (26–8)

This rather suggests that the *Troilus* is to be a four-book poem, the conclusion of which we are now reaching. But what does happen in 'this ilke ferthe book'? Let me summarize in a way that will bring certain patterns out clearly. After the decision to exchange Criseyde for Antenor is made, Chaucer presents scenes with the two grieving but, in these early episodes of Book IV, separated lovers. Each of the two wishes for and is associated with death (cf. 250–2; 499ff; 816–19; 862–3). Then comes the climax of Book IV: hero and heroine are brought together, and their individual death-wishes, death-associations, combine into a structurally and archetypically important near-death, or pseudo-death, or symbolic death. Criseyde cries, 'O Jove, I deye, and mercy I beseche! / Help, Troilus!' (1149–50) and swoons; this tragic swoon of the heroine will recall the comic swoon of the hero in the earlier consummation scene (III, 1092): there the height of the lovers' bliss was fast approaching; here, one might guess, their final woe is approaching as fast. Troilus believes Criseyde is dead and lays out her body 'As men don hem that shal ben layd on beere' (1183); he is making a fine taking-leave-of-life speech (1191–1210) and is about to kill himself when Criseyde sighs and calls out his name (1213). Realizing what has happened, she says – not, perhaps, quite realistically (cf. IV, 771–2) – that if she had found Troilus dead, she would have used his sword to end her own life. This, then, is the averted ending to the story: a Romeo and Juliet, Pyramus and Thisbe ending. And this averted ending does make the real one look somewhat arbitrary, at least where the hero is concerned: he, at least, could have died in bittersweet sorrow rather than an entirely bitter sorrow. His sufferings from this point on will seem on one level the result of what might be called *deus ex machina* continuation: if Criseyde's faint had only lasted some seconds longer . . .[4]

The pseudo-death, then, makes Troilus's later sufferings appear gratuitous: sufferings to be gone through not just because one cannot keep the good of this world, but because Troilus is going to lose those goods (or his one great good) in an especially painful way. This, however, does not seem to suggest much about why we should become covertly displeased with Troilus himself – though it may suggest a good deal about why we and the narrator grow impatient with the latter part of the story. To understand our exasperation with the hero himself a little better, we must look at this pseudo-death scene in a somewhat different way. Here I would invoke the axiom that in narrative a near-death usually is a ritual death, a moment of major transition. (One might think of Dante in this connection, but it is just as useful to recall *Great Expectations* or *Our Mutual Friend*: the question is one of archetypal narrative patterns, not particular influences.) Now if we do feel that this climactic incident of Book IV of *Troilus* is a ritual death, we will also feel that, in a kind of countercurrent to what is happening on the surface, Criseyde is afterwards moving back to life again.[5] We have this movement toward life in the creaturely good sense of what she says after declaring that she would have killed herself if she had found Troilus dead ('But hoo, for we han right ynough of this, / And lat us rise, and streght to bedde go, / And there lat us speken of oure wo': 1242–4) and in the larger progress of the scene, which is from pseudo-death to Criseyde's presentation of plans to live, and to live by going from the known good place, Troy, to the frightening other place, and then returning. Her plan is, it might be said, to be not a romance heroine, but a romance hero, a Gawain or a Lancelot, undertaking a classic out-and-back adventure. (Her plans, of course, are not very good, but soundness is not the only issue here.) We should also notice that, as she begins to explain her plans, Criseyde is given one of those speeches which express the reader's censored exasperation with Troilus:

> 'Lo, herte myn, wel woot ye this,' quod she,
> 'That if a wight alwey his wo compleyne
> And seketh nought how holpen for to be,
> It nys but folie and encrees of peyne;
> And syn that here assembled be we tweyne
> To fynde boote of wo that we ben inne,
> It were al tyme soone to bygynne.'   (1254–60)

Briefly, then, one may say that Chaucer has arranged his narrative so that the reader will on one level, the surface, always know that Criseyde forsakes the faithful Troilus, and that this is a bad thing. But on another level one senses that these two characters, Troilus and Criseyde, respond to a crisis by wishing for death, then undergo (in what is, structurally, *the* death scene of Chaucer's long, weeping love-poem) a symbolic or near-death from which one, Criseyde, emerges predominantly ready to live again and encounter new experiences, while the other seems comparatively timorous (*his* plan is for an unheroic 'stealing away') and chiefly ready to continue waiting for death even after he has, symbolically, had that death: 'But evere dye and nevere fulli sterve'. It is worth noticing also that in the early part of Book IV Chaucer even makes Criseyde seem morally superior to Troilus: she is notably more concerned with the pain he must be feeling than he is with the pain she must feel. It is especially striking that Criseyde's sympathy here transmutes the elegant double sorrow formulation of the poem's opening into something emotionally generous: 'Kan he for me so pitously compleyne? / Iwis, his sorwe doubleth al my peyne' (902–3).

The latter part of *Troilus and Criseyde* is about fidelity, but it focusses the issue of Criseyde's faithfulness in a particular way: the question of whether Criseyde will be true to Troilus, the real question, becomes for a good part of the narrative the more contractual question of whether or not Criseyde will return from the Greek camp *within ten days*. It is worth noticing that that figure of ten days starts out in what is clearly a conversational, approximating way: Criseyde says first, 'withinne a wowke or two / I shal ben here' (IV, 1278–9) and then, 'By God, lo, right anon, / Er dayes ten' (IV, 1319–20) (Boccaccio's heroine is from the beginning more precise: cf. *Filostrato* IV, 154). Thus in the *Troilus*, a lover's wish to be reassuring produces a legalistic condition which both represents and also displaces the true issue of love. There is one interesting moment, in fact, where Criseyde seems pushed toward despair not by her inability to remain faithful to Troilus, but by her difficulty in keeping to the ten-day agreement, and her certainty that Troilus will interpret the small failure as the great infidelity:

> And if so be that I my terme pace,
> My Troilus shal in his herte deme
> That I am fals, and so it may wel seme:
> Thus shal ich have unthonk on every side –
> That I was born, so weilaway the tide! (V, 696–700)

That part of the ten-days stipulation which is the contractualization rather than the representation of love is indirectly commented upon in Book V by the dispute Troilus and Pandarus have about the need to stay the 'contracted-for' full week amid the delights of Sarpedon's house even when it is clear that the visit is doing nothing to make Troilus feel better (V, 475–97). Pandarus prevails; Troilus is, as one would have expected him to be, a man of his word, and stays the full week. It is not clear here (as it was in Boccaccio) that the host indeed would have been offended by his guests' early departure; it is not clear in Chaucer's version that this keeping to an agreed time accomplishes anything at all.

During his visit to Sarpedon, Troilus begins to impose another kind of shape on his misery: he ritualizes his grief by returning to the things associated with his time of joy. Thus he rereads the letters Criseyde sent to him in better days 'an hondred sithe atwixen noon and prime' (V, 472); he will revisit the places associated with earlier experiences (519ff; 562ff). Having doubled, symmetrized the happy part of his love, Troilus goes on to his more recent, unhappy experiences, and moves physically to the city gates. One remembers the pathos of Troilus on the walls, but there is also something morbid here, the movements (not suggested in *Filostrato*) of a caged animal: 'And up and down ther made he many a wente' (605); 'And up and down, by west and ek by este, / Upon the walles made he many a wente' (1193–4). In this ritualizing, this doubling of his experience, Troilus is doing something distinctly like what the poet Chaucer does when he traces on-the-way-up, on-the-way-down symmetries in Troilus's adventures in love; and the suspicion that the art of telling nicely shaped stories and the art of intensifying one's misery are closely related is made a bit stronger when one notices that it is after he has ritualized and symmetrized his experiences that Troilus realizes his life has the stuff of a narrative in it:

> . . . 'O blisful lord Cupide,
> Whan I the proces have in my memorie
> How thow me hast wereyed on every syde,
> Men myght a book make of it, lik a storie.'   (582–5)

In the meantime, the narrator, who has in fact undertaken to make such a book, suffers his own, smaller miseries: how painful it is for this story-teller to go through with it, to trace the pattern he proposed to trace! In the opening stanzas of Book IV, his heart bleeds and his pen quakes because of what he must now write (12–13); but perhaps, somehow, Criseyde did not quite forsake Troilus, but was only unkind – perhaps no more than that 'moot hennesforth ben matere of [his] book' (15–17); perhaps the authorities on whom this author relies have slandered the heroine (19–21). In the final book of *Troilus and Criseyde*, the narrator will move with painful, source-citing slowness through the stanzas in which he must tell of Criseyde's favours to Diomede (1030–50). These celebrated attempts to mitigate or evade the heroine's guilt are charming and humane, doing credit to the narrator's heart if not to his head. More disturbing and meaningful are the moments when he attempts to get through his self-imposed, charity-imposed obligation to deal with this final misery by emotionally disengaging himself; disengaging himself by recalling that he does, after all, know what is going to happen (e.g., v, 27–8; 766–70) or by facile moralizing (1432–5; 1748–50). Too much compassion leads to protective self-anaesthetizing: leads to it in the narrator and, even more disturbingly, leads to it in ourselves, creates that undercurrent of impatience in our reaction to the hero's world-encumbering misery. It is also this sense of a nemesis of the emotions – a lack of feeling, and unresponsiveness to love, that counterbalances long fidelity and excessive feeling – which makes the late stanza on the now world-unencumbered Troilus feel terribly right; whatever we think about the particular philosophical position taken, intuitively, we know this is, indeed, the very thing that happens:

> And in hymself he lough right at the wo
> Of hem that wepten for his deth so faste,
> And dampned al oure werk that foloweth so
> The blynde lust, the which that may nat laste,
> And sholden al oure herte on heven caste. (1821–5)

Brilliantly, our censored exasperation with and hostility toward the hero seem transformed into his hostility toward us.

With Troilus's terrible laughter we have a sort of emotional nemesis at work. With Chaucer's audacious sequence of lurching, sputtering 'concluding' stanzas (1765ff) we discover an artistic nemesis: the poem that begins by being too sure of what it is going to be ends rather unsure of what it has, after all, been – or, more precisely, unsure of how to return from this story to the real world. Love and art require fidelity; but also room to grow and change. As a love story, *Troilus and Criseyde* overtly celebrates – and exemplifies – fidelity; covertly, it makes us feel something of the claustrophobia which comes with fidelity rigidified, gone wrong.

NOTES

1. On this symmetrical structure, see Barry Windeatt, *Oxford Guides to Chaucer: Troilus and Criseyde* (Oxford, 1995), pp. 189–191, and Ian Bishop's *Troilus and Criseyde: A Critical Study* (Bristol, 1981), pp. 43–4 and ff.
2. I have dealt at greater length with Chaucer's Troy and Trojans in 'Troilus, Books I–III: A Criseydan Reading' in *Essays on Troilus and Criseyde*, ed. Mary Salu (Cambridge, 1979), pp. 105–25. See also C. David Benson's *Chaucer's Troilus and Criseyde* (London, 1990).
3. With the present discussion of Troilus in Books IV and V, compare Winthrop Wetherbee's *Chaucer and the Poets: An Essay on Troilus and Criseyde* (Ithaca, N.Y./London, 1984), pp. 205–23.
4. Compare the discussion of this 'Pyramus and Thisbe' scene, 'in a way . . . the climax of the poem', in E. Talbot Donaldson's *The Swan at the Well: Shakespeare Reading Chaucer* (New Haven, Conn./London, 1985), pp. 22–6.
5. See in connection with this movement back to life the provocative treatment of the poem's hero, heroine, and author in Alfred David's *The Strumpet Muse: Art and Morals in Chaucer's Poetry* (Bloomington, Ind./London 1976), pp. 27–36.

6

JILL MANN

Chance and destiny in *Troilus and Criseyde* and the *Knight's Tale*[1]

At a crucial moment in Book II of *Troilus and Criseyde*, Criseyde is left alone
to reflect on Pandarus's astonishing revelation that Troilus is dying with love
for her. And as chance would have it, at this very moment Troilus rides past
her window.

> But as she sat allone and thoughte thus,
> Ascry aros at scarmuch al withoute,
> And men criden in the strete, 'Se, Troilus
> Hath right now put to flighte the Grekes route!'
> With that gan al hire meyne for to shoute,
> 'A, go we se! Cast up the yates wyde!
> For thorwgh this strete he moot to paleys ride;
>
> For other wey is fro the yate noon
> Of Dardanus, there opyn is the cheyne.'
> With that com he and al his folk anoon
> An esy pas rydyng, in routes tweyne,
> Right as his happy day was, sooth to seyne,
> For which, men seyn, may nought destourbed be
> That shal bityden of necessitee.   (610–23)

The vision that passes before Criseyde's eyes is a powerfully attractive one: a
handsome warrior, young and strong, whose battered armour and wounded
horse bear witness to his daring and bravery, and whose blushing response
to the people's cheers bears witness to his humility. As she watches, Criseyde
finds her emotions instinctively aroused by the sight.

> Criseÿda gan al his chere aspien,
> And leet it so softe in hire herte synke,
> That to hireself she seyde, 'Who yaf me drynke?'
>
> For of hire owen thought she wex al reed,
> Remembrying hire right thus, 'Lo, this is he

> Which that myn uncle swerith he moot be deed,
> But I on hym have mercy and pitee.'   (649–55)

There is no such window-scene at the corresponding point in Chaucer's narrative source, Boccaccio's *Filostrato*.[2] There, Pandaro's departure is immediately followed by a description of Criseida's solitary reflections, in which the handsome exterior of Troiolo exercises its due influence, but which are not interrupted by his actual appearance. Only after this do we hear how Pandaro goes to Troiolo to tell him that the wooing of Criseida has been begun, and Troiolo, full of gratitude and hope, allows Pandaro to lead him to Criseida's window, where he receives a favourable glance from his lady. His gentle and amiable looks remove her remaining fears, and henceforth she fixes all her desires on this new love (*Filostrato* II, 82–3).

On first comparing Chaucer's version with Boccaccio's, we might simply assume that Chaucer's change is made with an eye to dramatic immediacy. Instead of the imagined appearance of Troilus, Chaucer introduces the hero himself, and he places the window-scene before rather than after Criseyde's internal deliberations so as to increase its influence on her thoughts. But Chaucer does not merely move the position of the window-scene; he also doubles it. On returning to Troilus, Pandarus advises him to write Criseyde a letter, declaring his love; he suggests that Troilus should ride past Criseyde's window *as if* accidentally, while he is delivering the letter to his niece, so that he can draw her into the window to impress her with the sight of her admirer (II, 1009–22). This plan is duly executed (II, 1247–74), and Troilus's reward is an outward blush and inward admiration from Criseyde. This second window-scene is clearly, like the first, born of the single window-scene in Boccaccio, which indeed it resembles even more closely in being a calculated move on Pandarus's part, designed to establish contact and some kind of tacit understanding between the two young people.

Why did Chaucer go to such trouble to expand and duplicate the single brief window-scene (described in only two stanzas) in Boccaccio? Why did he fashion his narrative in such a way that the interview carefully arranged by Pandarus is preceded by an earlier encounter, dictated by nothing more than chance? The first answer, I believe, is that he wanted the comparison of the two scenes to reveal human efforts as negligible when weighed against the role of chance. The second window-scene confirms and strengthens Criseyde's attraction to Troilus (1271–4), but it is the first window-scene that has created this attraction ('Who yaf me drynke?'), and it is of key significance in the process because of its crucial positioning, occurring as it does at the moment when Criseyde is momentarily thrown off balance by the novelty of the situation, and thus most vulnerable to impressions one way or the other. Having initiated Criseyde's internal deliberations by one chance occurrence, Chaucer follows them with two more, neither of which has any precedent in Boccaccio's narrative. Fluctuating between fear and desire, Criseyde goes to walk in her garden, and hears her niece Antigone sing a song, written by 'the goodlieste mayde / Of gret estat in al the town of Troye' (880–1), which praises love in terms that answer all Criseyde's doubts and fears (899–903).[3] She then goes to bed, with the nightingale singing beneath her window, and dreams that a white eagle tears her heart from her body, without causing her any pain, and leaves his own in its place. These experiences too have a contributory role in the 'proces' (678) by which Criseyde turns to love. We shall better understand the reasons for their introduction if we return to the initial account of Troilus riding past the window and scrutinize it more closely.

I have said that this first encounter is dictated by nothing more than chance; Chaucer makes this clear by using the adjective 'happy' ('his happy day': 621), whose root is the noun 'hap', meaning 'chance'. As Chaucer presents it, Troilus's riding past the window at that particular moment is nothing more than 'a piece of good luck'. In doubling the window-scenes, Chaucer is emphasizing chance as the crucially important determinant in the course of the love-affair. The scope of human agency is correspondingly restricted; Pandarus, fondly imagining himself the omniscient and omnipresent director of the drama, is in fact merely a contributor to, not the controller of, the dynamics of the narrative. The chance which he carefully simulates in the second window-scene has already been independently at work, making his own efforts superfluous. His skilful manipulations begin to look less like vital contributions, and more like baroque flourishes on an independently worked design.[4] Looking back to the beginning of the story, we realize that chance appropriately guides the love-affair, since it was chance that initiated it; it is 'upon cas' (I, 271) that Troilus's gaze falls on Criseyde in the temple, with such dramatic effects. Troilus himself thinks of his love as an 'aventure' (another Middle English word for chance; see I, 368), and it is consistently referred to as such by Pandarus (II, 224, 288) and also Criseyde (II, 742). Indeed, Pandarus's own intervention in the affair is dictated by the 'cas' or 'aventure' that causes him to break in on Troilus's solitary languishing (I, 568).[5]

But no sooner has Chaucer established Troilus's ride-past as due to chance, than he goes on to refer this chance to an underlying 'necessitee'.

> Right as his happy day was, sooth to seyne,
> For which, men seyn, may nought destourbed be
> Thal shal bityden of necessitee. (II, 621–3)

And it is of 'necessitee' that Troilus complains at the other end of the narrative, in his much-discussed soliloquy on free will in Book IV. Here the sense of casualness associated with 'luck' or 'chance' has entirely disappeared; the relentless rhyming of 'necessitee' and 'destinee' that ushers in Troilus's lament (958–9) expresses his sense of being imprisoned in a tyrannical world of fate which leaves no room for the exercise of the human will or the realization of human desires. What then is the nature of the 'necessitee' that underlies the episode in Book II, and the 'necessitee' confronting Troilus in Book IV? What is the nature of the connection between this destinal 'necessitee' and chance? And what room is left for the exercise of free will in the face of these powerful forces?

Troilus and Criseyde itself testifies to the fact that Chaucer's thinking on these questions was stimulated and directed by his reading of Boethius's *Consolation of Philosophy*, which he himself translated.[6] Boethius, confronting disgrace, imprisonment, and possible death, is brought, like Troilus, to raise questions of cosmic order – 'questiouns of the symplicite of the purveaunce of God, and of the ordre of destyne, and of sodeyn hap, and of the knowynge and predestinacioun devyne, and of the liberte of fre wil' (*Boece* IV pr. 6). As he ponders the arbitrary injustice manifested in his own loss of good fortune, he observes that such injustices would better sort with a theory that the world was governed by blind chance ('fortunows hap') than with a belief in the ordering control of divine providence (IV pr. 5). Philosophy's answer to these doubts addresses itself first to the questions of providence and destiny (IV pr. 6), and then to the question of chance (V pr. 1-m. 1); finally she reaffirms the freedom of the human will (V pr. 2-pr. 6).

Crucial to Philosophy's explanation of providence and destiny is the role of time. Providence, the 'pure clennesse of the devyne intelligence', is outside of time – a separation expressed in the image of the tower, from the height of which the divine intelligence surveys all together the events which are for us arranged in temporal succession. This atemporal providence disposes all things in an order; destiny is the manifestation of that order in time – it is a 'temporel ordenaunce'. To express this idea, Philosophy uses the analogy of a craftsman who first conceives the object he is to make, and then produces it according to his design; his conception of the object as a whole 'governs' its final form, but exists separately from its execution at all stages of the process. Using a different analogy, we could say that the relation between providence and destiny is something like the relation between a bus timetable and the actual running of the buses. The analogy is not perfect in either instance, because it is difficult to rid ourselves of the notion that the workman's design, and the bus timetable, *precede* the temporal realization that they govern – in other words, that they too belong to a temporal process. The point at which the analogies hold good is the perception that the conception and its execution exist on different planes, and that the conception embraces as a whole and immediately what can only be executed as a reality gradually and over time.

The difference between providence and destiny can thus be expressed as a difference of *perspective* – as is suggested in the text by the image of the tower, and Philosophy's repeated use of the word 'lokynge' for the divine thought (IV pr. 6). Although Philosophy talks of destiny as 'subgit' to providence, it is misleading to think of them only as two separate links in a chain of command. On the contrary, destiny and providence are merely two different names given to the same thing, which is called providence when considered as a unity out of time, and destiny when it is manifested in the linear succession of events in time. It is precisely this difference of perspective that gives rise to human doubts about providence. Bound to a temporal existence, human beings are denied a vision of the unity in which the order of providence is visible; they can glimpse only a part of the whole pattern, which inevitably appears to them as fragmentary and confused. Philosophy speaks of 'destinal ordenaunce' as 'ywoven and acomplissid' (IV pr. 6), and the image of weaving is a helpful one. In the weaving of tapestry, the design of the whole will be perceptible only when the weaving is completed; while it is in progress, the shifts in shape and colour may well seem random and confusing.

This conception of destiny helps solve the problem of necessity inasmuch as destiny is no longer perceived as the direct imposition of a divine will (whether the divinity be pagan or Christian) on helpless humanity. On Philosophy's definition, the free exercise of the human will is *part of* destiny; it is simply one of the 'moevable thinges' (IV pr. 6) whose constant interplay makes up the temporal unfolding of destiny. For us the term 'destiny' implies a predetermining of the future, outside the human will, whereas for Boethius, events take their place in the 'destinal cheyne' (V pr. 2) as a result of their own natural developments. The existence or non-existence of 'necessitee' is a matter of perspective; it exists only when the destinal chain is seen as a whole from the perspective of providence, since that which God sees must necessarily exist to be seen. As Philosophy puts it a little later (V pr. 6): 'thilke thing that is futur, whan it is referred to the devyne knowynge, than is it necessarie; but certis whan it is undirstonden in his owene kynde, men seen it outrely fre and absolut fro alle necessitee'. It may help us to understand this differentiation between the freedom of events within the temporal process, and their necessity within the atemporal sphere of the divine intelligence, if we consider for a moment the status of the past, rather than the future, in relation to divine knowledge. Human beings are quite happy to think of the past as fixed and determined, merely by virtue of the fact that it has happened; it is only the future that they feel must be undetermined – that is, open to the influence of their own will. Now since divine providence 'enbraceth alle thinges to-hepe' (IV pr. 6), it makes no distinction between past, present, and future. If then it is to consider the future as undetermined, the past must be considered undetermined also; conversely, the future must be perceived as determined in exactly the same way as the past is. The future is 'necessary' only in the sense that it exists (not pre-exists) in the atemporal vision of divine providence, which beholds past, present, and future in the timelessness of the eternal moment. 'Thilke God seeth in o strok of thought alle thinges that ben, or weren, or schollen comen' (V m. 2). From the human point of view, we could express the upshot of this argument by the paradoxical proposition that things are destined only when they have happened. ('The thingis thanne . . . that, whan men doon hem, ne han no necessite that men doon hem, eek tho same thingis, first *or thei ben don*, thei ben to comen without necessite': V pr. 4, my italics.) Only after they have happened are portions of the destinal pattern realized in time and made perceptible to human observers. 'Necessite', then, does not represent the intrusion of divine control into human affairs; it is the pattern achieved by the totality of temporal units, working according to their own causes and effects.

The role of chance in this scheme of things is easily explained. Like destiny and providence, chance is a matter of perspective. 'Hap', explains Philosophy, is a name that men give to occurrences not embraced by their own intentions in initiating actions (V pr. 1). If a man ploughs a field and discovers a buried cache of gold, the discovery was intended neither by himself nor by the burier of the treasure; we therefore call it chance. Yet the event is not without causes – in this case, the hiding of the treasure and the ploughing of the field, both of which play an instrumental role. It is simply that the result of these two actions was not envisaged by either of their human performers. 'Hap' arises, therefore, from 'causes encontrynge and flowynge togidere to hemself, and nat by the entencioun of the doere' (V pr. 1). In the following metre, Philosophy illustrates this idea with the image of the two mighty rivers, Tigris and Euphrates, in whose waters a multitude of floating objects are swept together or pushed apart, as the whole mass rushes onward to the sea; in the same way, the shifts of Fortune are made one with the inexorable course of 'destinal ordinaunce'.

Turning back to our starting-point, we can see how brilliantly Chaucer has fashioned the scene in which Troilus passes Criseyde's window so that it embodies Boethius's notion of 'causes encontrynge and flowynge togidere to hemself', independent of human intention. The impression that Troilus makes on Criseyde is not only unintended by him, he is not even conscious of it; nor was it envisaged by Criseyde as she went into her closet for private thought. Even less was it foreseen or intended by Pandarus, despite his confidence that the whole world will proceed to execute his 'purpos'. Yet Pandarus is *one* cause within the larger confluence; it is his introduction of the idea of Troilus's love into Criseyde's mind that has created in her a susceptibility to a sight that would at other times have evoked no more than polite admiration. The 'flowynge togidere' of causes is thus rightly called chance ('his happy day'), since it lies outside what was envisaged by the human actors. But it can also be accurately called 'destiny', since the confluence of causes realizes a pattern. All the other occasions on which Troilus rode up this very street are not important; this one assumes significance because it connects with another contingent circumstance – Criseyde's first response to Pandarus's revelation – and thus forms part of the pattern that we are to call Troilus's destiny. The 'opyn cheyne' of the gate of Dardanus is a surrogate for the chain of destiny; open as Troilus embarks on his ride home, it closes as his passing links with Criseyde's watching. Thus the term 'necessite' can be justified by reference of the event to its presence in the destinal pattern, out of time, in the divine thought.

The readers of Chaucer's poem are in a privileged position, since they can perceive this destinal necessity in a manner analogous to, if not identical with, that of the divine intelligence. For the pattern of destiny is, in literary terms, the pattern of the story. We feel it therefore as 'inevitable' that Pandarus's revelation should be followed by Troilus's impressive appearance, and that this in turn should be followed by Antigone's song, the nightingale, and Criseyde's dream, all insensibly steering her towards love. But we feel it as inevitable only because we know already that this is a love story, and because we are observing these individual occurrences with their known end in mind; it is because the story has, in a sense, already happened for us – we see it in 'o strok of thought' – that we can perceive its course as inevitable. The occurrences recounted are not necessary in themselves; Troilus could have ridden up some other street or returned an hour earlier; Antigone could have chosen to sing a melancholy song in which a lady lamented the loss of her lover or the torments of jealousy; it could have been a rainy night on which the nightingale uttered not a note and Criseyde fell into a dreamless sleep – the result of all this being that she woke next morning in a mood of bracing common sense determined to hear no more romantic tales. These are not undisciplined speculations; they are justifiable precisely because this is a narrative in whose dynamics chance plays a crucial role. In order to register with full appreciation the brilliance of Chaucer's depiction of 'causes encontrynge and flowynge togidere to hemself', we must be alive to the possibility that the confluence of chance events could at every point have taken on a different form. The 'openness' of the story, our present sensation of suspense as we live through each event as it happens,[7] gives us a sense of its fluidity, its vulnerability to chance, even as our knowledge of its eventual end gives us a sense of inevitability, of its final shape as destiny. Through narrative suspense, Chaucer makes us alert to the possibility of a different story – that is, a different destiny. For *this* destiny is realized only through the confluence of contingent events; it is not fixed in advance, but in retrospect, when the pattern of 'temporel ordenaunce' (*Boece* IV pr. 6) has been worked out.[8]

Love is an area of human experience in which the retrospective nature of the realization of destiny is particularly easy to grasp, precisely because it is an experience about which it is next to impossible to use the future tense. The future-tense formulation 'I will/am about to fall in love with you' is patently absurd, while the present 'I am in love with you' implies not so much the consciousness of a present happening as of a past event – 'I have fallen in love with you' – which is achieving belated recognition. That is why Criseyde's expression of surrender to Troilus in the consummation scene of Book III – 'Ne hadde I er now, my swete herte deere, / Ben yolde, ywis, I were now nought heere!' (1210–11) – is not, as some critics have held, a coy revelation that her mind had been consciously made up at some earlier date; it is rather a realization that her present situation and feelings imply – and therefore reveal – an earlier unconscious surrender, now to be made explicit.[9] Thus it is, also, that after the consummation the lovers – like all lovers – rehearse the events that have led up to this climactic end:

> Thise ilke two of whom that I yow seye,
> Whan that hire hertes wel assured were,
> Tho gonne they to speken and to pleye,
> And ek rehercen how, and whan, and where
> Thei knewe hem first, and every wo and feere
> That passed was; but al swich hevynesse –
> I thank it God – was torned to gladnesse. (1394–1400)

They reinterpret previous events as part of the pattern of destiny, their significance – the direction in which they were tending – now being established by the end that has been reached.[10]

The lovers have here no complaints of a destiny being forced on them; when Troilus (echoing the lover's perennial cry, 'we were meant for each other') tells Criseyde that 'God hath wrought me for I shall yow serve' (III, 1290), he is not expressing a consciousness of tyrannical control, but rather a sense of having discovered his true nature and function in life for the first time, of finding what it is that most fully expresses and engages his individual being. Their free assent, that is, is not only part of the 'confluence of causes', it is also accorded to the confluence as a whole. Free will and destiny are thus inextricably united; destiny, as I said earlier, works through the will in the subtle coalescence of outward event and inward desire.

This subtle coalescence is portrayed with extreme delicacy by Chaucer in Book II, as he traces Criseyde's response to Troilus's love. So far I have concentrated on the external occurrences – Pandarus's revelation, Troilus's riding past, Antigone's song, the dream. But equally important in the confluence of causes are the inner workings of Criseyde's mind and emotions, which are as it were the eyes into which the hooks of external incident can fall. Between Troilus's riding past and Antigone's song, Chaucer places his long account of Criseyde's deliberations (703–812). The details of what she thinks are less important than the fact that her mind appears as a seething mass of different possibilities, jostling and giving way to each other with the spontaneous movement of her emotions.[11] Within these possibilities, we can perceive the instincts towards love – and specifically, towards an ennobling love – which find an echo and a confirmation in Antigone's song. But we can also see the instincts *against* love – the fears of jealousy, emotional torment, and betrayal – which could equally have found a chance echo and confirmation in the outside world; the different nature of the coalescence would have given a different turn to the story. The chances and changes that Boethius contemplates in the *Consolation* are chances and changes in the external world – loss of riches, family, or friends. Chaucer adds to his representation of these instances of 'moevable destinee' the *inner* mutations which are ceaselessly at work in every human being. It is on these inner mutations that the external occurrences work; it is from the coalescence of the two that the shape of the action is born. A spherical object placed at the top of a slope will roll to the bottom because of its own sphericity as well as because of the declivity; its own nature is 'expressed' in the rolling just as much as the nature of the surrounding circumstances.[12] So Criseyde is 'expressed' in her motions towards love, even though external circumstances are needed to bring her potentialities into being.

In describing this process, I am not merely saying that Criseyde chooses to fall in love, exercising her free will in a matter presented to her for decision. This description fits Boccaccio's Criseida fairly accurately, but not Chaucer's Criseyde. For Chaucer's brilliance lies precisely in the way he makes us alive to the *in*voluntary elements involved in the exercise of the will. Criseyde certainly imagines that Pandarus has presented her with a case in which she is free to choose one way or the other – she comforts herself, when he has left her, that she need not fear because

> . . . man may love, of possibilite,
> A womman so, his herte may tobreste,
> And she naught love ayein, but if hire leste.   (II, 607–9)

But it is at this very point that Troilus rides past, and Criseyde finds herself unable to view the sight with the detachment she has just described; she is inevitably affected by the new knowledge she possesses.

> For of hire owen thought she wex al reed,
> Remembrying hire right thus, 'Lo, this is he
> Which that myn uncle swerith he moot be deed,
> But I on hym have mercy and pitee.'   (II, 652–5)

Tolstoy's brother Nicholas used to tell him that his wishes would come true if he first fulfilled certain conditions; the first of these conditions was to stand in a corner and *not* think of a white bear. Tolstoy commented: 'I remember how I used to get into a corner and try (but could not possibly manage) not to think of a white bear.' Criseyde's case as she thinks about *not* falling in love with Troilus seems to me of the same sort; the more she considers not doing so, the larger the position occupied in her mind by the possibility. The revelation of Troilus's love inevitably creates a new entity in her mind, a new set of emotions, of circumstances ready to form a nexus with external incidents and thus to take on the configurations of destiny.

The long and patient observation of this process in Books II and III teaches us to understand how it can be repeated, with contradictory results, in the movement towards betrayal in Book V. The changed external circumstances again exert their own pressure on Criseyde's mind, linking with her fears and her sense of emotional desolation to bring different possibilities to the fore. Again, there is no decision; the moment of betrayal is diffused through a long-drawn-out process that renders it invisible. The gloomy stanza describing the internal state of mind which is to coalesce with Diomede's external pressure in the shape of betrayal –

> Retornying in hire soule ay up and down
> The wordes of this sodeyn Diomede,
> His grete estat, and perel of the town,
> And that she was allone and hadde nede
> Of frendes help; . . .

– does not conclude 'and thus she decided to stay'. Rather, it emphasizes that this is the beginning of a process whose conclusion is dispersed through a series of minute readjustments:

> . . . and thus *bygan to brede*
> *The cause whi*, the sothe for to telle,
> That she took fully *purpos for to dwelle.* (v, 1023–9)

We are now in the position to appreciate, not only Chaucer's debt to Boethius, but also his most original development of Boethian ideas. Boethius, as I have already suggested, sees Fortune as largely external; Chaucer on the other hand sees the processes of mutability as permeating the inner life of humankind to the very depths of being. The adjective 'slydynge', which Boethius applies to Fortune (1 m. 5), Chaucer applies to Criseyde's mind, telling us that she was 'slydynge of corage' (v, 825). Fortune, for Chaucer, is not merely apparent in the larger, more readily observable mutations in worldly affairs, it is a name we can also apply to the moment-by-moment mutations in Criseyde's mind, observable in her long soliloquy in Book 11, to the opalescent shifts as one impulse or another spontaneously emerges. It is from these minute and ceaseless fluctuations that the larger movements of change are formed. In addressing Fortune with a capital F, human beings deceive themselves into thinking that Fortune is an independent entity, existing apart from themselves and from other agencies, whereas Fortune is simply the name for (what is to them) the random, the unplanned, the unforeseen, for mutability in all its manifestations, which include not only the accidents of the external world, but also the momentary oscillations within their own minds.

There is, however, a moment in *Troilus and Criseyde* where Fortune is associated with an external agency which apparently overrides human will – and that is the influence of the planets. At the moment when Criseyde is about to leave Pandarus's supper-party, Chaucer suddenly breaks the cheerful mood with two stanzas of gloomy foreboding.

> And after soper gonnen they to rise,
> At ese wel, with herte fresshe and glade;
> And wel was hym that koude best devyse
> To liken hire, or that hire laughen made:
> He song; she pleyde; he tolde tale of Wade.
> But at the laste, as every thyng hath ende,
> She took hire leve, and nedes wolde wende.
>
> But O Fortune, executrice of wierdes,
> O influences of thise hevenes hye!

Soth is, that under God ye ben oure hierdes,
Though to us bestes ben the causez wrie.
This mene I now: for she gan homward hye,
But execut was al bisyde hire leve
The goddes wil, for which she moste bleve.

The bente moone with hire hornes pale,
Saturne, and Jove, in Cancro joyned were,
That swych a reyn from heven gan avale
That every maner womman that was there
Hadde of that smoky reyn a verray feere;
At which Pandare tho lough, and seyde thenne,
'Now were it tyme a lady to gon henne!'   (III, 610–30)

How does this view of planetary influence sort with the views on chance and destiny that I have already outlined? And does it contradict or undermine the supposition that human will is an element in the 'causes flowynge togidere to hemself', in its assertion that 'the goddes wil' is executed regardless of Criseyde's 'leve'?

The first step in answering these questions is to identify the nature of the planetary conjunction described. Critics have, astonishingly, spent more time in trying to use this passage as a means of dating the composition of *Troilus and Criseyde* (by relating it to the real occurrence of such a conjunction) than in attempting to analyse its poetic function.[13] Poetically, the most important feature of the conjunction is that it is a malevolent one. The benevolent influence of Jupiter is outweighed by the malign effects of Saturn (described at length by the planet himself in the *Knight's Tale*), in combination with the Moon, in the unpropitious house of Cancer.[14] The conjunction therefore bodes eventual ill for the love-affair that is consummated under its auspices. But the description of the conjunction tells us more than this – it also tells us what it is that will bring about this ill. Saturn was traditionally interpreted in medieval mythic allegoresis as Time, since his Greek name, Cronos, was identified with the Greek word *chronos*.[15] The Moon is a traditional symbol of change, because of her constant waxing and waning.[16] Time and change hang threateningly over the love-affair which is shortly to be consummated; time and change bring it into being, time and change will destroy it. When understood, the planets appear not as agents of an independently exercised 'goddes wil', but as emblems (as well as representatives) of the natural forces through which the 'goddes wil' – the pattern of destiny – realizes itself. As in the Boethian scheme of things, destiny is executed by Fortune ('executrice of wierdes'), by the individual chances that weave together the 'temporel ordenaunce' of destiny.

If this passage represents the planets as dominating human will, it is in order to show that the destinal ordinance that is being woven is one that *goes beyond* the wishes and predictions of the human contributors to it. Troilus and Criseyde are shortly to commit themselves to a consummated love as to their (beneficent) destiny, as we have seen; they assume that the pattern is now completed, it has achieved its final shape at that point. This passage reminds us that the destinal process will continue, and that the 'cas or aventure' (IV, 388) of Criseyde's exchange for Antenor will be the first in a different confluence of causes which will seal the final destiny of Troilus. The planetary conjunction images to perfection this 'double destiny'; its immediate effect is to bring the rain, cause of Criseyde's decision to stay the night, and thus eventually, of the blissful consummation, while its ultimate effect is to subject the love-affair to the forces of time and change by which it is destroyed. Pandarus sees only the immediate effect; he rejoices in the rain that enables the execution of his will. Forgetful of the astrological calculations which he had taken care to complete before making his first approach to Criseyde (II, 74–5), he sees only that portion of the cosmological whole which is useful to his immediate purposes. The description of Pandarus's preparations for the supper-party shows his powers of control at their apparent zenith; directing Troilus, coaxing Criseyde, picking a moonless night when rain is threatening, so that the cosmos itself seems merely a tool of his grand design. The words used of him at this point represent him as a kind of mini-providence; his planning is referred to as 'purveiaunce', and it is 'Forncast and put in execucioun' just as divine providence is executed by destiny (III, 533, 521). The stanzas on the planetary conjunction reveal that this appearance of all-embracing control is a pathetic sham. The solemn apostrophe of Fortune introduces not only a note of foreboding but also a sobering shift in perspective, as our vision widens with dramatic speed from the cosy domestic interior of the dinner-party to the dizzying heights of the cosmos, whence we glimpse humans crawling like 'bestes' on the surface below. This dramatic effect makes clear with unforgettable impact the limitations of human control. Pandarus's grand design is merely a feeble fragment of a far vaster pattern, woven by mightier forces than he.

Chaucer's attempt to render the operations of chance and destiny in human affairs was not confined to *Troilus and Criseyde*. They assume importance in several of the *Canterbury Tales* – notably the *Man of Law's Tale*, the *Wife of Bath's Tale*, the *Franklin's Tale*, and the *Nun's Priest's Tale*, but most of all in the *Knight's Tale*, to which I shall devote the brief remaining space of this essay.

As in *Troilus*, Chaucer takes pains in the *Knight's Tale* to alter his Boccaccian source in order to emphasize the role of chance in the events of the
narrative.[17] The most striking example can be found in his altered account
of Palamon's escape from prison. In the *Teseida*, Palemone is driven to make
the attempt by discovering that Arcita has returned to Teseo's court in disguise and is serving Emilia as her page (v, 1–8). The mechanics of the escape
are carefully and plausibly recounted, and once he is free, Palemone goes
straight to the grove outside Athens because he knows that it is a favourite
haunt of Arcita (v, 22, 33). Chaucer patiently unravels this logically knit
narrative sequence, in order to produce a narrative dominated by chance.
Knowing nothing of Arcite's presence in Athens, Palamon simply happens
(after seven years!) to escape:

> Were it by aventure or destynee –
> As, whan a thyng is shapen, it shal be . . .   (1465–6)

The occurrence is, like Troilus's riding past the window, referred equally to
chance and destiny. Chaucer's apparent casualness in proposing the two as
alternatives is a mere narrative disguise, for here as in *Troilus* we shall see
that the one is a component of the other. Palamon goes to the grove to hide
himself, and 'by aventure' (1506) Arcite makes for the same place. Not only
that, but 'by aventure' (1516) he wanders into the very path by whose side
Palamon lies hidden, and then reveals his true identity in soliloquy. Chaucer's
motive in creating this inherently improbable narrative can only have been
to illustrate 'causes flowynge togidere to hemself' and creating destiny out of
'fortuit hap'. The final chance necessary to complete the pattern – in that it
turns the knights' private squabble over Emily into a public contest capable
of practical resolution – is the arrival of Theseus, which is duly heralded by
an emphasis on destiny.

> The destinee, ministre general,
> That executeth in the world over al
> The purveiaunce that God hath seyn biforn,
> So strong it is that, though the world had sworn
> The contrarie of a thyng by ye or nay,
> Yet somtyme it shal fallen on a day
> That falleth nat eft withinne a thousand yeer.   (1663–9)

The thousand-to-one chance fixes the shape of the destinal pattern for good
or ill.

The rest of the narrative is equally full of chance events, most often signalled as such by the use of the key-words 'aventure', 'cas', or 'hap'. It is 'by
aventure or cas' (1074) that Palamon first sees and falls in love with Emily,

his fate, like that of Troilus, being sealed by chance – and Chaucer here alters the *Teseida*, in which the first glimpse belongs to Arcita (III, 11–12), as if to stress that it *is* simply the chance of being first-comer that will often determine a man's success in love. It is chance ('It happed', 1189; cf. 'aventure' at 1235) that brings Perotheus to Athens and thus effects Arcite's release. We are made conscious also of the alternative stories that chance could dictate, as Palamon and Arcite each speculate on various ways in which Fortune might produce events to favour the other's suit (1240–3, 1285–90). Finally, the tournament which Theseus decrees shall determine who is to marry Emily is a vast amphitheatre for chance ('fallyng nys nat but an aventure', 2722). Acknowledging, with true wisdom, the limitations of human control, Theseus eschews making the choice himself; not denying or combating the role of chance, he merely provides a civilized context within which it can operate. The final chance of Arcite's death after victory is thus a blow, but not a crushing one, since Theseus's role throughout the narrative constitutes an acknowledgement of the powers of chance and an illustration of readiness to adapt to it.

However, in the *Knight's Tale* as in *Troilus*, at an important moment in the poem we might be tempted to think that the course of events is *not* dictated merely by chance, but by the will of higher powers. For the *Knight's Tale*, like *Troilus*, represents human affairs as subject to planetary influence.[18] Just before the tournament, Palamon and Arcite pray to Venus and Mars respectively to grant their wishes, and Chaucer temporarily abandons the human plane of his narrative to show us the heated debate that then breaks out between the conflicting celestial powers. For Palamon and Arcite, Venus, Mars, Saturn, and the rest are 'gods'; when we look closer, however, we can see that it is not as deities but as planets that they exert power. Saturn's speech makes this plain:

> 'My cours, that hath so wyde for to turne,
> Hath moore power than woot any man.
> . . .
> I do vengeance and pleyn correccioun,
> Whil I dwelle in the signe of the leoun.'   (2454–5, 2461–2)

It is because Saturn's sphere is the outermost in the planetary order (his course thus being widest of all) that his influence dominates the planets beneath him.[19] His overruling influence means that the lesser influences exerted by Mars and Venus will resolve themselves into a malevolent pattern; his sending of a 'furie infernal' to startle Arcite's horse is an anthropomorphic representation of a cosmological phenomenon. It is *because* Mars and Venus are planets, and not independent pagan deities, that Palamon and Arcite win their favour; both knights take care to make their pleas at the astrologically correct hour, when the planet's power is at its height,[20] and response to human prayers follows according to a quasi-physical law of cause and effect. The importance of this is that we perceive that the planets act according to their nature, not according to their whims. Their representation in human shape means we can 'read' their behaviour in two ways – first, as the result of their own independent wishes, and second, as the result of inevitable natural processes. As we shift between these two views – from free agents to naturally impelled forces – we are instructed in the illusions of control; we see that the apparently independent movers are themselves moved by other powers.

The shift from the human to the cosmological plane has a similarly instructive effect. Like the dramatic widening of vision in the passage concerning the planets in Book III of *Troilus*, it expands way beyond the possible reach of any sort of human control the kinds of causes that we conceive as flowing together to make up the pattern of human destiny. We are allowed, by poetic licence as it were, a fleeting glimpse of the hidden causes behind what appears to the human onlookers as the chance ('aventure', 2703) of Arcite's fall (as if, in Boethius's example, we were privileged to see the man burying the gold and thus to know the 'cause' of its being found). But in being vouchsafed this glimpse, we are being shown only one more cause, not the final cause that lies behind all of them. We have a shift in perspective, not the complete vision which belongs only to providence, seeing 'alle thinges to-hepe'. We have left the human plane; we have not left the cosmos, or the realm of time. It is in Theseus's final speech that we perceive this most fully. His opening reference to the 'Firste Moevere' reminds us that there is a power beyond the planets, by which they are moved. They do not operate of their own volition; their power is only a secondary one. *A fortiori*, the same holds good for human beings. Only from the perspective of the First Mover, which is forever inaccessible to mortals, could the final causes of events be understood, and the shape which would give them final meaning be perceived. Theseus emphasizes our perception of 'temporel ordenaunce' as a series of individual destinies, whose end is determined by the natural processes of change and decay – the tree falls, the river runs dry, man dies. The larger shape, the whole of which these individual experiences are part, remains hidden; human beings can perceive only what Boethius calls the 'entrechaungeable mutacioun' (IV pr. 6) by which the processes of decay and renewal work themselves out. The planets too are part of this 'entrechaungeable mutacioun'; they are not the agents by which it is set in motion.

Since human beings are bound to time and change, they must embrace these conditions of their existence, for good or ill. But time and change do not always bring disaster. Theseus's humble acknowledgement of the inevitability of change and death concludes with an attempt to realize the beneficent possibilities created by the shifting kaleidoscope of chance. Arcite's death is irreversible, but it provides the chance to create a new configuration with the marriage of Palamon and Emily. Whereas at the end of *Troilus* chance works to close off possibilities, here there survives the opportunity, gladly perceived and realized by Theseus, to move forwards, to allow the process of mutability to carry one on to happiness. Caught in the realization of his tragic destiny, Troilus perceives 'necessitee' as a cruel trap; in the more optimistic configurations of the *Knight's Tale*, we can see that it is possible to 'maken vertu of necessitee' (3042) – not merely to 'grin and bear it', but to transform necessity *into* 'vertu', to respond to the pattern as it forms with a recognition of its passing chances for good, as well as the faith that its final shape will be revealed as concordant with the 'cheyne of love'.

Chaucer's thinking on the question of whether the world is governed by 'fortunows hap' or by a benign ordering power, is fundamental to his most serious poetry. In reading that poetry, we must in consequence give due attention to his presentation of *event*, rather than focussing on the 'characters' of Criseyde and Troilus, or Palamon and Arcite, as sole determinants of the narrative development. We must be alive to his use of words like 'cas', 'aventure', or 'destinee' (and to others, such as 'entencioun', 'purveiaunce', 'ordinaunce', 'governaunce', which also belong to his exploration of Boethian problems)[21] as signalling his reflections on the nature of the forces which work on human beings, and the extent of their own possibilities for action. Chaucer is outdone by none in his ability to reproduce the idiosyncratic details of human speech and action, but his deepest interest in investigating human psychology is to uncover the subtlest manifestations of time and change at work in human emotions, shaping the course of human lives.

NOTES

1. The issues dealt with in this essay have been discussed by numerous other writers, and it is not possible to indicate in detail points where my own treatment corresponds to or diverges from theirs. The reader is referred to some particularly important contributions: Howard R. Patch, 'Troilus on Determinism', *Speculum*, 6 (1931), 225–43; Morton W. Bloomfield, 'Distance and Predestination in *Troilus and Criseyde*', PMLA, 72 (1957), 14–26; Walter Clyde Curry, 'Destiny in *Troilus and Criseyde*' in *Chaucer and the Mediaeval Sciences*, rev. edn (New York, 1960), pp. 241–98. All three articles are reprinted in *Chaucer Criticism*, eds. Richard J. Schoeck and Jerome Taylor, 2 vols. (Notre Dame, Ind., 1961), vol. 2; Bloomfield's article is also reprinted in *Chaucer's Troilus: Essays in Criticism*, ed. Stephen A. Barney (London, 1980). For a study of Chaucer's translation of

Boethius in relation to the medieval afterlife of the *Consolatio*, see A. J. Minnis, ed., *Chaucer's Boece and the Medieval Tradition of Boethius* (Cambridge, 1993).

2. Comparison of the two texts is easiest in the edition of *Troilus and Criseyde* by B. A. Windeatt (London/New York, 1984), which places the Italian text alongside corresponding passages in Chaucer; here no parallel is given, but the source of the scene in *Filostrato* II, 82 is noted.

3. For a more detailed demonstration of this, see Jill Mann, 'Troilus' Swoon', *Chaucer Review*, 14 (1980), 319–35, at pp. 320–1 (repr. in *Critical Essays on Chaucer's 'Troilus and Criseyde' and His Major Early Poems*, ed. C. David Benson (Milton Keynes, 1991), pp. 149–63.

4. This is even more true of his efforts in the bedroom scene of Book III; see Mann, 'Troilus' Swoon', pp. 325–6.

5. The role played by these and connected words in the development of this theme in *Troilus* may be traced in *A Concordance to the Complete Works of Geoffrey Chaucer*, eds. John S. P. Tatlock and Arthur G. Kennedy (Gloucester, Mass., 1963), or Larry D. Benson, *A Glossarial Concordance to the Riverside Chaucer* (New York/London, 1993).

6. The most comprehensive study of Chaucer's debt to Boethius is Bernard L. Jefferson, *Chaucer and the Consolation of Philosophy of Boethius* (Princeton, N.J., 1917).

7. The most obvious example of suspense is the ending of Book II ('O myghty God, what shal he seye?': 1757), but the whole Horaste story, for example, increases narrative tension and our sense of precariousness up to the consummation scene.

8. In the preceding essay, Mark Lambert shows how Chaucer deliberately fashioned the parting scene in Book IV as an 'alternative ending' to the story; had Criseyde not revived from her swoon in the nick of time, we should have had a Romeo-and-Juliet-type ending, which would have made this a story of fidelity unto death, rather than a story of classic betrayal.

9. See further Mann, 'Troilus' Swoon', p. 330.

10. I owe this point to Dr Philip Davis of the University of Liverpool.

11. For a subtle, sensitive and full analysis of Criseyde's internal monologue and its relations to the surrounding narrative, which coincides very closely with the next section of my discussion, see Donald R. Howard, 'Experience, Language and Consciousness: "Troilus and Criseyde", II, 596–931' in *Medieval Literature and Folklore Studies: Essays in Honor of Francis Lee Utley*, eds. Jerome Mandel and Bruce A. Rosenberg (New Brunswick, 1970), pp. 173–92; repr. in *Chaucer's Troilus*, ed. Barney.

12. This analogy is based on those devised by the Stoics to express their theory of necessity and free will (see A. A. Long, *Problems in Stoicism* (London, 1971), p. 180); there is of course no question of Chaucer having direct knowledge of these theories, but he seems independently to have arrived at similar ideas.

13. See the articles listed in the note to *Troilus* III, 624–6, in the *Riverside Chaucer*. John J. O'Connor ('The Astronomical Dating of Chaucer's *Troilus*', *Journal of English and Germanic Philology*, 55 (1956), 556–62) insists on the storial significance of the conjunction, but relates it to the fall of Troy and the heavy rain, rather than to the ultimate outcome of the love-affair. Chauncey Wood (*Chaucer and the Country of the Stars* (Princeton, N.J., 1970), pp. 47–8) also emphasizes

the rain, which he sees as a bathetically deflatory result of so awe-inspiring a conjunction.

14. Cancer was the mansion of the Moon (J. D. North, 'Kalenderes Enlumyned Ben They: Some Astronomical Themes in Chaucer', *Review of English Studies*, ns 20 (1969), 129–54, 257–83, 418–44, at p. 136), and would thus strengthen her influence. Jupiter at first seems the 'odd man out' in this predominantly malevolent grouping. I suggest that here, as in the *Knight's Tale*, he has a double role: first, as one of the seven planets (in which role he brings the short-term happiness experienced by the lovers), and second, as a mythic representative of the power of the Christian God, the providence which lies behind the whole conjunction and subjects it to its own ultimate plan.

15. Isidore of Seville, *Etymologiae*, VIII, xi, 31: *Vnde et eum Graeci Cronos nomen habere dicunt, id est tempus, quod filios suos fertur devorasse, hoc est annos, quo tempus produxerit, in se revolvit . . .*

16. See *Romaunt of the Rose*, 5331–50; *House of Fame*, 2114–16; *Complaint of Mars* 235, for the moon as an image of change.

17. Excerpts from Boccaccio's *Teseida*, including those which form a source for the *Knight's Tale*, are to be found in *Chaucer's Boccaccio: Sources of Troilus and the Knight's and Franklin's Tales*, ed. and trans. N. R. Havely (Cambridge, 1980).

18. For an astrologically based interpretation of the whole poem, see Douglas Brooks and Alastair Fowler, 'The Meaning of Chaucer's *Knight's Tale*', *Medium Aevum*, 39 (1970), 123–46.

19. In the medieval cosmological scheme, the planets were thought to move in concentric spheres, arranged in the order: Moon, Mercury, Venus, Sun, Mars, Jupiter, Saturn. Then came the sphere of the fixed stars, and finally the Primum Mobile or First Moving Sphere, which moves all those beneath it. God is the First Mover of the whole cosmos. For a brief account, see Edward Grant, *Physical Science in the Middle Ages* (Cambridge, 1971), ch. 5, 'Earth, Heavens and Beyond'.

20. See John Livingston Lowes, *Geoffrey Chaucer* (London, 1934), pp. 10–13.

21. For a discussion of Chaucer's use of the last three words to develop Boethian themes, see Jill Mann, 'Parents and Children in the "Canterbury Tales"' in *Literature in Fourteenth-Century England*, eds. Piero Boitani and Anna Torti (Tübingen/Cambridge, 1983), pp. 165–83.

7

JULIA BOFFEY AND A. S. G. EDWARDS

The *Legend of Good Women*

Like much of Chaucer's *œuvre*, Chaucer's *Legend of Good Women* cannot be certainly dated and survives only in an incomplete form. Both factors bear on the larger issues of the poem's interpretation.

Certain references in the text provide evidence for the date of the poem's composition. The chief of these is in the F version of the Prologue to the *Legend*, where the narrator/poet is directed by the God of Love: 'whan this book ys maad, yive it the quene, / On my byhalf, at Eltham or at Sheene' (F 496–7). Since Eltham and Sheen were actual royal palaces, the 'quene' can only be Anne of Bohemia, wife of Richard II. Anne died in 1394 and the palace at Sheen was then destroyed. In the unique G version of the Prologue, these lines are omitted. The general scholarly assumption has been that G is the later of the two versions, and postdates Anne's death. The most obvious alternative to explain the omission of any mention of Anne in the G version is to assume it predates Richard's marriage to her in 1382. This is not impossible, but since the work involves an experiment with a related series of short narratives, it is tempting to suppose it is close in chronological sequence to the *Canterbury Tales*, which seems largely to date from the second half of the 1380s. The question, like so much else in Chaucerian chronology, remains unresolvable in any final way.

Although the allusion to the queen indicates that the F Prologue must have been completed some time before Anne's death, a more precise dating is difficult. We know from the list of Chaucer's writings in the Prologue that *Troilus* was completed before the *Legend* was composed (see F 332–5, 441, 469, etc.). And it is generally accepted that *Troilus* was written in the period 1380–5 (it was certainly completed before 1388). Near the end of the poem, the narrator announces 'gladlier I wol write, yif yow leste, / Penelopeës trouthe and good Alceste' (v, 1777–8). Some scholars have seen this passage in *Troilus* as an adumbration of the idea of the *Legend*. 'Alceste' is the name of the God of Love's consort in the Prologue to the *Legend* (F 518). And while there is no narrative of Penelope in the *Legend* as it survives, she is invoked in the 'Balade' in the Prologue (F 249–69), which has often been seen as an outline of the contents of the projected legends. Whether or not Chaucer had already conceived the idea of writing the histories of good women while finishing *Troilus*, the close sequence of the two poems seems highly probable. The question of the dating of the unique G Prologue is a separate issue and is discussed below.

In its fullest form, the *Legend of Good Women* comprises the Prologue and the nine legends (in order) of Cleopatra, Thisbe, Dido, Hypsipyle and Medea, Lucretia, Ariadne, Philomela, Phyllis, and Hypermnestra (the last incomplete). All but two of these (Medea and Philomela) are invoked in the Ballade in the Prologue (F 249–69), which mentions another eleven virtuous women: Esther, Penelope, 'Marcia Catoun' (252), Isolde, Helen of Troy, Lavinia, Polyxena, Hero, Laodamia, Canace, and Ariadne. This gives a total of twenty or twenty-one legends (depending on how one counts Hypsipyle and Medea who appear as a single legend). Even if we assume that the 'Ballade' is a valid guide to the work's design there is a large gap between what survives of the *Legend* and the apparent design that informed it.

The extent of this gap is confirmed by the manuscripts of the Retraction to the *Canterbury Tales*, which usually refer to the *Legend* as 'the book of the xxv. Ladies' (X, 1086–7) – although some manuscripts give the number of legends as either fifteen or nineteen. The latter number may have been influenced by the Prologue to the *Legend*, which depicts the God of Love as accompanied by 'ladyes nyntene' (F 283). The former may reflect the description of the 'Seintes Legende of Cupide', mentioned among Chaucer's works in the Prologue to the *Man of Law's Tale*, which lists fifteen, including some who appear in surviving parts of the *Legend*: Lucretia, Thisbe, Dido, Phyllis, Medea, and Hypermnestra (II, 60–75). Only two manuscripts of the *Legend* itself correctly record the surviving number of legends in describing it as 'the boke of the .ix. goode women'; the rest do not specify a number. In addition, there is a very early reference to the work, by Edward, duke of York, in the Prologue to his translation of Gaston de Foix's hunting treatise, *The Master of Game*, made in the first decade of the fifteenth century, where he speaks of Chaucer's 'prologe of the xxv good wymmen' and confirms his direct acquaintance with the work by quoting a version of a line from the Prologue ('for writynge is þe keye of alle good remembraunce'; cf. F 26).

These various claims for the scope of the work cannot be reconciled with the surviving manuscript evidence. Some of the manuscripts suggest that the poem may have existed, or, at least, was once believed by Chaucer's near contemporaries to have existed, in a much fuller form at an early point in its textual history. If so, we can only speculate about what was lost. What can be said is that the assertion of some critics that the surviving work is somehow 'incomplete but finished'[1] does not gain much support from manuscript evidence. A number of manuscripts of the work do have concluding rubrics, which, unsurprisingly, do not draw attention to the work's incomplete state; they take the form either of a simple 'Explicit' ('here ends') as in Cambridge, Trinity College, R. 3. 19, or 'here endyth the legend of ladyes' in British Library, Add. 12524 and Bodleian Library, Arch. Selden. B. 24. But other manuscripts offer no indication of formal closure, and some even leave space after the end of the surviving text, possibly because they had some hope of more of it turning up.

The surviving manuscripts also point to the quite wide-ranging appeal of the *Legend of Good Women*, as well as to its appearance in a variety of forms and contexts. Twelve manuscripts survive. Two of these (Bodleian Library, Rawlinson C. 86 and Cambridge, University Library, Ff. 1. 6), contain only single legends, of Dido and Thisbe respectively. The earliest of the manuscripts that contain the full range of surviving legends is Cambridge, University Library, Gg. 4. 27, which is the earliest attempt at a 'collected' Chaucer (it contains the *Canterbury Tales*, *Troilus and Criseyde*, the *Parliament of Fowls*, and other short works, in addition to the *Legend*), and was probably copied at some point in the first quarter of the fifteenth century. What is generally regarded as the best text is that preserved in Bodleian Library, Fairfax 16 (probably written in the 1440s), which contains all of Chaucer's dream visions and a number of his lyrics, together with poems by other fourteenth- and fifteenth-century English poets.

Some of the later copies are of interest for what they reveal about the reception of the *Legend*. For example, in Cambridge, Trinity College, R. 3. 19 it occurs with a number of poems to do with women, such as *The Assembly of Ladies* and *La Belle Dame sans Merci*, as well as a verse translation, by Gilbert Bannister, of the *Tale of Guiscard and Sigismonda*, which derives ultimately from Boccaccio's *Decameron*. Interestingly, another version of this last appears in two other manuscripts containing parts of the *Legend*, Bodleian Library, Rawlinson C. 86 and British Library, Add. 12524. Such collocations provide some indication of the way in which the *Legend* became linked in manuscript form with other related poems to do with wronged women.

Something of the same tendency can be found in Bodleian Library, Arch. Selden. B. 24, which is another large, late collection of Chaucer's works and other materials. This manuscript was copied in Scotland in the late fifteenth or early sixteenth century and combines the *Legend* with Chaucer's *Troilus and Criseyde*, *Parliament of Fowls*, and various of his shorter poems, and with a number of Scottish love poems, some of which seem to reflect a careful reading of Chaucer's *Legend*. In this manuscript Chaucer's poems have all been 'translated' into Scots. The manuscript provides testimony to the steadily widening appeal of Chaucer's works at the end of the Middle Ages and confirms that the *Legend* formed part of the appeal.

The manuscripts show, however, that this appeal was rarely of a kind that singled out the work itself but rather saw it in relation to other works of Chaucer or to poems related in subject-matter. This remained the case with the advent of print. Unlike many of Chaucer's works, the *Legend* never achieved any separate identity in printed form. It was not printed at all until 1532, in the first compendious collected edition of Chaucer's writings by William Thynne. (In contrast, the *Canterbury Tales* was among the earliest books printed in England, *c.*1476.) But henceforward the *Legend* was included in all such editions.[2] It may be that its evident incompleteness militated against separate publication, although Thynne and later sixteenth-century editors give the reader no indication of its state. In Thynne's edition, for example, there is an (ungrammatical) full stop after the final word 'conclusyon' and a rubric 'Thus endeth the legends of good women'. It is largely modern editions of the poem that think it necessary to specify, as the standard Riverside edition does, that it is '[Unfinished.]'.

One other aspect of the manuscript history of the *Legend* requires mention. As we have already observed, there are two versions of the Prologue: the F version survives in the majority of the manuscripts, while the G version survives only in Cambridge, University Library, Gg. 4. 27. The G Prologue is unique in Chaucer's *œuvre*: it is the only clear evidence we have of revision by Chaucer of any of his longer works. What is also clear is that revision was limited to the Prologue; it did not extend to any of the separate legends. What is less clear is the effect of these revisions.[3] Certainly G is shorter, 545 as opposed to 579 lines, and there are a number of transpositions, as well as deletions of passages in F. Quite a lot is added that insists on women's suffering and other writings about this suffering in 'storyes grete, / That bothe Romayns and ek Grekes trete' (G 274–5). The factors that may have led Chaucer to undertake such revision are unrecoverable, like much else to do with the poem's historical circumstances. Perhaps he hoped to receive the support of a different patron from the one for whom the work may originally have been commissioned.[4]

The question of a possible patron for the *Legend* is obviously linked to the question of the poem's occasion. The most recurrent indications of its occasional significance are provided by a cluster of the narrator's allusions. Early in his Prologue he requests the support of 'Ye lovers . . . / Whethir ye ben with the leef or with the flour' (F 69, 72) and defines himself as 'in service of the flour' (F 82). Later, he qualifies this:

> But natheles, ne wene nat that I make
> In preysing of the flour agayn the leef,
> No more than of the corn agayn the sheef;
> For, as to me, nys lever noon ne lother.   (F 188–91)

The casual allusiveness of such references to the flower and the leaf (see also line 2613), suggests that they would have been readily intelligible to Chaucer's audience. It is possible for a modern audience only partly to recover their force. They can be most profitably glossed in relation to other literary works of the late fourteenth or fifteenth century which contain similar allusions. These have been conveniently assembled[5] and only their implications need concern us. They seem to imply the existence of some sort of courtly 'game' in which courtiers offered service to contending amorous factions represented by the flower and the leaf. Such games may have been linked to May Day celebrations of the kind mentioned in the Prologue (F 36, 45, 108, 176), which were a recurrent aspect of courtly activity during the fifteenth and sixteenth centuries, and again often the subject of literary allusion.[6] They remind us that court life was a form of shared intimacy, one in which poet and audience coexisted in a proximity that can infuse courtly works with a tone that is at the same time palpable yet historically unrecoverable in its precise implications.[7]

The idea of a courtly game offers a context that seems to accord with the tone of playfulness that forms an insistent aspect of the Prologue. The narrator's devotion to the daisy is presented in terms of such hyperbolic intensity as to prevent it being taken seriously, especially if we consider it as reflecting the activities of some courtly environment (F 40–211). The emphasis on the controlling roles of figures of paramount authority, and the clear links between these figures and those of a real world ('yive it the quene, / . . . at Eltham or at Sheene'), and between the narrator and an actual contemporary poet, a bibliography of whose works is rehearsed for us, suggests a close relationship between 'play' and actuality.

In such an environment it seems proper to assume a crucial element of game in which the poet-narrator becomes a comic figure through his relationship to those figures of power, and to assume that this relationship is, in some way, a reflection of that within the real world. The question of power is indeed given some prominence in the Prologue. There is a long disquisition on the authority of the king, which foregrounds the question (F 369–402), and the Prologue's action turns on the resolution of the offence against love of which Chaucer stands accused by the king, an offence mitigated by the queen's intervention. This offence creates the momentum for the larger strategy of the game: to validate Chaucer's poetic credentials and to establish the subsequent structure of his poem. One of the most remarkable aspects of the Prologue is its inclusion of an enumeration of Chaucer's works (F 414–30), a listing that has no precedent in English and few parallels elsewhere in medieval European culture.[8] This enumeration foregrounds the poet as a bibliographical entity just as the larger action of the Prologue foregrounds him as a comically muted voice, one to be argued over by those with 'real' (the word means 'royal' in Middle English) power, and denied sustained direct speech until his final praise of Alceste (F 517–34). His silencing as a character in the Prologue is one aspect of its playfulness; it objectifies him but in so doing makes him and his creative anxieties the central subjects of his own dream experience.

This sense of a direct relationship between poet and audience is sustained only intermittently beyond the Prologue. At one point the narrator does seem conscious of a connection between his narrative and an immediate, physical environment when he considers the possibility 'in this hous if any fals lovere be' (1554). And there are passages of *occupatio* that draw attention to the presence of the narrator (e.g., 616–23, 953–7, 2257–8, 2454–8, 2513–15).[9] But inconsistency of tone throughout the narratives seems to be one of the *Legend*'s larger critical problems, and is one to which we will return.

If the occasion of the poem seems linked to forms of courtly activity that can be, at best, imperfectly recovered, what of the larger narrative dimensions of the *Legend*? The narrator is charged by Alceste to undertake as a 'penance' (F 479, 491, 495) the composition of a specified form of narrative:

> Thow shalt, while that thou lyvest, yer by yere,
> The moste partye of thy tyme spende
> In makynge of a glorious legende
> Of goode wymmen, maydenes and wyves,
> That weren trewe in lovyng al hire lyves;
> And telle of false men that hem bytraien,
> That al hir lyf ne don nat but assayen
> How many women they may doon a shame;
> For in youre world that is now holde a game.
> And thogh the lyke nat a lovere bee,
> Speke wel of love . . .
>
> (F 481–91)

The idea of a collection of narratives organized around principles related to gender has few precedents in medieval literature. The most obvious is Giovanni Boccaccio's *De Claris Mulieribus*, a collection of Latin prose lives of famous women, completed in 1361. This is a work that Chaucer clearly knew by the time he came to write his *Monk's Tale*, when he drew on it for his account of Zenobia (VII, 2247–374). But its possible function as a model for Chaucer's *Legend* cannot be certainly established since there are no evident traces of its influence in this work.

More relevant may be the *Confessio Amantis*, the long collection of narratives by Chaucer's contemporary, John Gower. The Man of Law speaks in the Prologue to his tale of Chaucer's 'Seintes Legende of Cupide' (II, 61), mentioning, as we have said, a number of figures in the surviving part of the *Legend*, and contrasts these with tales of incest represented by Canace and Apollonius of Tyre, both of whom figure in the *Confessio*. The tone of this Prologue is not easy to assess, but it does seem to refer to Gower and to reflect some element of comparison between two different treatments of the same kind of narrative subject, the representation of women.

There are few other English collections of female lives that offer parallels of any relevance. Those that occur have to do with saints' lives.[10] The separate lives in the *Legend* are often characterized in manuscript rubrics or running titles as lives of martyrs (*martyris*), a circumstance that suggests that at least Chaucer's copyists wanted to stress hagiographical parallels with the lives he narrates. But the stories in Chaucer's collection are, of course, stories of classical women and the 'religious' frame of reference is that of the secular religion of love, with Cupid as its God. It is quite likely that Chaucer adapted a number of the distinctive qualities of the genre of the medieval saint's life for his work, as has been sometimes argued.[11] One of the most significant differences seems to be that his 'good women' have an afterlife only insofar as the form of their stories evokes a distant pagan suffering intelligible in terms of the polarities of gender: good women and bad men. Such narratives lack the overarching Christian intelligibility of saints' lives, like Chaucer's own *Second Nun's Tale*, where past female suffering has a doctrinal significance for a contemporary audience.

Hence the general effect of his pagan legends tends toward pathos rather than piety, reminding the reader of male cruelty rather than making the suffering of such injustice intelligible or memorable in any exemplary way. Men are 'false loveres' (1236, 1368, 1385, 2180, 2226, 2565), whose treachery is typified in the account of Jason:

> For as a *traytour* he is from hire go,
> And with hire lafte his yonge children two,
> And falsly hath *betraysed* hir, allas,
> As evere in love a chef *traytour* he was. (1656–9)

The focus is not altogether coherent in the sequence of stories. The location of these stories in 'olde bokes' raises the question of Chaucer's sources for the *Legend* and the extent to which they are of relevance to his treatment of individual 'martyrs'. He names a few works in particular legends. The most recurrent is Ovid, whose *Heroides* are cited in several legends: at the end of Dido (1367), in Hypsipyle and Medea (1465, 1678), and in Ariadne ('hire Epistel', 2220); in addition, he is cited again in Dido in conjunction with Virgil ('Eneyde and Naso', 928), and with Livy in Lucretia ('Ovyde and Titus Lyvius', 1683), this last probably referring to Ovid's *Fasti*. The only explicit mention of a medieval author is 'Guido' in Hypsipyle and Medea (1396, 1464), Guido delle Colonne (d. 1287), author of a Latin prose *Historia Destructionis Troiae*.

Although such citations broadly reflect Chaucer's indebtedness, they do not give a full reflection of his use of various works of Ovid. The *Heroides* provide material as well for the legends of Phyllis and Hypermnestra, the *Fasti* for Lucretia, the *Metamorphoses* for Thisbe and Philomela, and both the *Metamorphoses* and the *Heroides* for Hypsipyle and Medea. In other respects the narrator's citations of his sources are not wholly reliable. Although Livy is cited he does not seem to have been used. For some legends, those of Ariadne and Cleopatra, there is no certain source, although the former may draw on the medieval commentary on Ovid, the *Ovide Moralisé*. Cleopatra is the only legend not to draw on any classical material; once again, there is no certain source.

To this degree, at least, the legends reflect not just the injunction to the narrator to tell stories of virtuous, wronged women, but also his own initial ruminations on the crucial necessity of 'olde bokes' (F 25) or 'olde appreved stories' (F 21).[12] But in larger terms the separate narratives seem to afford a much larger destabilization of narrative expectations in relation to their ostensible purposes.

We see this in its most extreme form at the end of the penultimate legend, of Phyllis, where the narrator follows her long letter of complaint against Demophon's cruelty (2496–554) with this conclusion:

> And whan this letter was forth sent anon,
> And knew how brotel and how fals he was,
> She for dispeyr fordide hyreself, allas.
> Swych sorwe hath she, for she besette hire so.
> Be war, ye wemen, of youre subtyl fo,
> Syn yit this day men may ensaumple se;
> And trusteth, as in love, no man but me. (2555–61)

The tonal shifts here seem bewilderingly abrupt, from the sustained indignation of Phyllis's letter, presented in direct speech, to the narrator's perfunctory recounting of her suicide and his final apostrophe to 'ye wemen' in which he presents himself as the only model of male fidelity. The overall effect seems so egregiously discordant with the preceding narrative as to signal an apparent lack of tonal sense that lays Chaucer open to a charge of narrative ineptitude.

Destabilizing moments such as this must in part relate to the double imperative with which the narrator is faced: on the one hand to tell stories that fit a common template, and on the other to supply sufficient variety to keep the attention of a reading (even perhaps of a listening) audience. Similar double imperatives are posed in both the *Monk's Tale* and the *Canterbury Tales* as a whole, and it would be possible to argue that Chaucer found some positive creative challenge in the issues of narrative construction that they raise. Certainly the legends (whose order remains consistent in all the 'complete' manuscript copies) attempt different sorts of variation as they progress. At a most obvious level this has to do with the extent to which separate legends change their focus from individuals to pairs of people: from Cleopatra to both Pyramus and Thisbe, to Dido, to Hypsipyle and Medea, to Lucretia, then Ariadne, then to both Philomela and Procne, Phyllis, and finally to Hypermnestra. Such a pattern of narrative variety seems to gesture towards the possible variations in not just the form, but also the number of love's martyrs – even to the extent of including among them a man in Pyramus, who dies for his love of Thisbe, a circumstance which requires some finessing by the narrator: 'Of trewe men I fynde but fewe mo / In alle my bokes, save this Piramus, / And therefore have I spoken of hym thus' (917–19).

As they succeed each other, the separate narratives also contrive to create a network of relationships of different kinds. Some of these depend on shared sources, with the effect, for example, that the writing women of the *Heroides* (Dido, Medea, Ariadne, Hypermnestra, Phyllis) unite in a sorority across the separate legends to offer a common model of female complaint. While this model remains fairly consistent, though, the succession of legends contrives steadily to intensify the blackening of men and to draw them together more deliberately into an indivisible body of wrongdoers. If Antony's abandonment of Cleopatra, like Pyramus's of Thisbe, might be viewed as accidental, and even Aeneas's departure from Dido might be explicable to readers of Virgil as the promptings of a divinely ordained destiny, Jason's perfidy is made to seem greedily boundless – 'There othere falsen oon, thow falsest two' (1377) – and Tarquin's rape of Lucretia incontestably 'a vileyns dede' (1824). Theseus and Demophon, linking as father and son the separate legends of Ariadne and Phyllis, illustrate a congenital male propensity for falseness which is confirmed by Hypermnestra's experience at the hands of a family network in which both father and cousin/husband turn out to be 'crewel' and 'unkynde' (2715–16). Even Mynos, not strictly a betrayer of Ariadne, is implicated in Theseus's perfidy (1886–90).

Whatever dreary sameness comes to characterize male behaviour in the legends, variety is retained in the ways in which women confront it, and in the voicing of their responses. Cleopatra and Thisbe actively choose their deaths, and meet them with asseverations of steadfastness (695–8, 910–11); Lucretia, similarly determined, takes the knife with a terse rejection of any gesture of forgiveness (1852–5). The deaths of Dido, Ariadne, and Phyllis follow on the completion of Ovidian letters, and in the stories of Hypsipyle and Medea letters are briefly summarized, although in these legends (perhaps strategically, given the difficulties of turning Medea's story into one of martyrdom) Chaucer omits any details of the women's deaths. 'The wo, the compleynt and the mone' (2378) takes in the legend of Philomela a poignantly non-verbal shape, with the sisters locked in embrace after the mute Philomela's story has come to light in its woven form, and Hypermnestra, as her legend breaks off, remains forever 'fetered in prysoun' (2722), denied death or truth to her own womanly nature.

Variation of this kind may be useful in the context of the larger narrative structure, and it clearly opens a range of possibilities in the *Legend* both for the ventriloquizing of women's voices and for their suppression. Thisbe, for example, who does not speak on her own at all through the course of her story, finds a voice only when Pyramus's apparent death persuades her to take her own life (until this point all we hear is that she speaks in unison with Pyramus at 756–66, and thinks to herself at 855–61); Lucretia's words are limited to her worries over her husband (1724–31), her sleepy questioning and then imploring of Tarquin (1788, 1804), and the resolute statement with which she dies (1852–3). But the range of women's utterance elsewhere in the narratives is comparatively wide: women speak freely to their sisters (Dido and Anna, 1170–85, 1343–5; Ariadne and Phaedra, 1978–2024, 2126–35) or their fathers (Hypermnestra, 2650–2; Philomela 2329), and both speak and write, quite extensively, to their lovers. These are not – unless for special effect – silent martyrs for love's cause, and their legends offer varied examples of women's modes of discourse, just as they do of women's stratagems, women's actions.[13] They offer, too, an accommodating sense of women's understanding of their own natures, in such a way that Thisbe's capacity to take her life ('My woful hand . . . / Is strong ynogh in swich a werk to me', 890–1) can sit alongside Hypermnestra's determination to spare that of her husband:

'Allas! and shal myne hondes blody be?
I am a mayde, and, as by my nature,
And bi my semblaunt and by my vesture,
Myne handes ben nat shapen for a knyf,
As for to reve no man fro his lyf.'   (2689–93)[14]

The sameness that a number of critics have claimed to detect in the succession of individual legends does not seem wholly easy to credit, at least in relation to the construction of individual women within them.[15] Furthermore, although all the stories conform to a certain essential pattern and are all set in the pagan past, the variety in their sources, and hence in the location and nature of their actions, permits changes of focus and tone from legend to legend. There are notable differences, for example, between the sparely constructed legends of Cleopatra and Thisbe and the much more elaborate account of Dido's history, which begins with an invocation of Virgil, compresses large swathes of the *Aeneid*, and yet still has space for rich descriptions of the attractions of Troy (1098–1125) and of the preparations for the hunting expedition (1188–1217). Similarly, there are obvious contrasts in both technique and tone between the silences in Lucretia's story and the prominence and amount of direct speech which follows in the legend of Ariadne.

At one level, nonetheless, reiteration is a quite deliberate aspect of the *Legend*'s shaping. It is entirely appropriate to Alceste's instructions that the narrator should endlessly repeat patterns in which 'goode wymmen . . . / That weren trewe in lovyng al hire lyves' should be forever betrayed by 'false men . . . / That al hir lyf ne don nat but assayen / How many women they may doon a shame' (F 484–8, G 474–8). The awkwardly admirable behaviour of Pyramus, very early in the sequence, occasions some embarrassed backtracking on the narrator's part (917–23), while the obvious manipulation of source material observable in the account of Medea, where any reference to the infanticide which was a central part of her story has been omitted, serves as a still more stark demonstration of the demands of the template according to which the legends have been shaped. Many of the legends include some form of explicit invitation to dwell on the weakness or vileness of men, whether in the form of generalized command or statement: 'loke ye which tirannye / They doon alday' (1883–4); 'Ful lytel while shal ye trewe hym have' (2391), or of the singling out of particular instances or exemplars of perfidy: 'Now herkneth how he [Aeneas] shal his lady serve!' (1276); 'Thow rote of false lovers, Duc Jasoun!' (1368). The recurrent exclamatory mode signals a narrative apportioning of gender sympathy which sets implied female virtue against male vice.

The cumulative effect of these passages is an important feature of the *Legend*'s construction, since in sequence they contribute to what may seem the narrator's growing impatience through the course of the work. Even as early as the legend of Dido, he asks whether the weight of evidence is not already sufficient to deter women from amorous involvement:

> O sely wemen, ful of innocence,
> Ful of pite, of trouthe and conscience,
> What maketh yow to men to truste so?
> Have ye swych routhe upon hyre feyned wo,
> And han swich olde ensaumples yow beforn?   (1254–8)

The increasing tone of frustration which is detectable as the work progresses seems a response to the ingrained, even innate characteristics of male and female behaviour which render possible the proliferation of stories about unhappy love. If men behave like this, what are women to do? And if women exist how can men not be men (as the legend of Lucretia seems powerfully to suggest)?

Such impatience is intensified and complicated by another aspect of the *Legend*'s construction: the requirement that, in order to allow space for the citing of as many examples as possible, each legend should be pared down to its essence, often at the cost of large-scale abbreviation of the source material. The rhetorical ploys by which this abbreviation is effected sometimes sound excessively casual, at times almost as if the narrator is grateful to be able to omit certain details: 'forthy to th'effect thanne wol I skyppe, / And al the remenaunt, I wol lete it slippe' (622–3); 'What shulde I more telle hire compleynyng? / It is so long, it were an hevy thyng' (2218–19).[16] And in combination with the expressions of frustration and impatience, they occasionally contrive to make the narrator sound weary of his material – irritated by the inevitable sameness of its patterns, grateful when the opportunity arises to compress information or to omit it altogether. The contrast between this use of *occupatio* and the notable achievement of contriving a series of miniature 'grete effectes' in narrative across a wide historical sweep seems one of the more significant tonal contradictions inherent in the *Legend*'s processes.

Of a piece with such contradiction is the instability of tone which pervades much of the narrator's discourse, especially those parts which take the form of direct address to his audience. This sometimes results from asides which work against the direction established in a particular story, as, for example, Thisbe's credulity in agreeing to an assignation with Pyramus is questioned ('allas, and that is routhe / That evere woman wolde ben so trewe / To truste man, but she the bet hym knewe', 799–801), or the speed of Dido's attraction to Aeneas is remarked ('To som folk ofte newe thyng is sote',

1077). Especially ambiguous in their tone are the passages of direct address positioned at the end of individual legends, which contrive a series of slippery variations on the theme of men's untrustworthiness. Some of these seem straightforward enough, like the sombre warning which concludes the legend of Lucretia: 'And as of men, loke ye which tirannye / They doon alday; assay hem whoso lyste, / The trewest ys ful brotel for to triste' (1883–5). Others, though, complicate their advice by drawing attention to the narrator's own gender bias:

> For it is deynte to us men to fynde
> A man that can in love been trewe and kynde.
> Here may ye se, what lovere so he be,
> A woman dar and can as wel as he. (920–3)

> Ye may be war of men, if that yow liste.
> For al be it that he wol nat, for shame,
> Don as Tereus . . .
> Ful lytel while shal ye trewe hym have –
> That wol I seyn, al were he now my brother –
> But it so be that he may have non other. (2387–93)

These questions of response and tone take us back to problems of the work as a whole.

'And yf that olde bokes were aweye, / Yloren were of remembraunce the keye' (25–6) the narrator insists near the beginning of the poem. 'Olde' is an important term in the Prologue: 'olde thinges' (F 18), 'these olde wyse' (F 19), 'these olde approved stories' (F 21), 'olde stories' (F 98), 'olde clerkes' (F 370), 'olde auctours' (F 575), as are books (F 17, 28, 30, 34, 39, 496, 510, 556, 578). Tradition and antiquity are linked to the act of creating a new book that is described in the narrative of the Prologue. We are reminded of the relationship between old and new books, between the materials Chaucer is going to be drawing on to create his 'new' book, as well as those he has himself already written. It is this attempt to create 'new' from 'old' that may lie at the heart of our difficulties as modern readers of the *Legend*. What its narratives expose are the often irresolvable situations thrown up by the disjunction between the classical worlds of these stories and the Christian world of Chaucer's audience.[17] The intermittent, but often striking lack of tonal coherence in the work stems from a lack of ethical congruence between the arbitrary sufferings of virtuous pagan women and the capacity of Chaucer's audience to remind themselves of the difference between such suffering and that in their own Christian world, as celebrated by Chaucer in his life of another female martyr, Saint Cecilia. The nature of her martyrdom and its implications reflect the ethical and historical distance that separates her world from the pagan one in terms of its moral intelligibility: in a Christian world it is possible to understand both why she is suffering and the benefits that she and those who read of her fate can gain from such suffering. The sufferings of Chaucer's good women afford no such solace; they are love's martyrs, not God's.[18]

NOTES

1. See Rosemarie P. McGerr, *Chaucer's Open Books: Resistance to Closure in Medieval Discourse* (Gainesville, Fla., 1998).
2. See Constance Wright, 'The Printed Editions of Chaucer's *Legend of Good Women*: 1552–1889', *Chaucer Review*, 24 (1990), 312–19.
3. The differences are discussed by Michael St John, *Chaucer's Dream Visions: Courtliness and Individual Identity* (Aldershot, 2000), ch. 4: 'The alterations in G have the effect of making the narrator seem . . . a little more distanced from the conventions of courtly love poetry' (p. 177).
4. It may be worth noting here that the unique G version of the Prologue formally distinguishes the narratives themselves from the dream of the Prologue in its concluding lines: 'And with that word, of slep I gan awake, / And ryght thus on my Legende gan I make' (G 544–5), something not done in the F version.
5. See the introduction to Derek Pearsall's edition of *The Flower and the Leaf and the Assembly of Ladies* (Edinburgh, 1960), pp. 22–9.
6. See John Stevens, *Music and Poetry in the Early Tudor Court* (London, 1961), pp. 184–8.
7. The playfulness of the *Legend* is stressed in the reading offered by A. J. Minnis, *Oxford Guides to Chaucer: The Shorter Poems* (Oxford, 1995), pp. 322–454, and developed in William A. Quinn, *Chaucer's 'Rehersynges': The Performability of 'The Legend of Good Women'* (Washington, D.C., 1994).
8. For other fourteenth-century examples, see Florence Percival, *Chaucer's Legend of Good Women* (Cambridge, 1998), p. 143.
9. See the discussion in Robert Worth Frank, Jr, *Chaucer and 'The Legend of Good Women'* (Cambridge, Mass., 1972), pp. 198–208.
10. See A. S. G. Edwards, 'Fifteenth-Century English Collections of Female Saints' Lives', *Yearbook of English Studies*, 33 (2002), 131–41.
11. Janet Cowen, 'Chaucer's *Legend of Good Women*: Structure and Tone', *Studies in Philology*, 82 (1985), 416–36.
12. See the extensive consideration of this aspect of the work in Lisa J. Kiser, *Telling Classical Tales: Chaucer and the Legend of Good Women* (Ithaca, N.Y., 1983).
13. With consequences that have persuaded some critics of the 'feminization' of the *Legend*'s men; see Elaine Tuttle Hansen, 'Irony and the Antifeminist Narrator in Chaucer's *Legend of Good Women*', *Journal of English and Germanic Philology*, 82 (1983), 11–31, and the later reflections in *Chaucer and the Fictions of Gender* (Berkeley/Los Angeles, Calif., 1992).
14. The *Legend*'s exploration of womanly characteristics, especially 'pitee', is discussed by Jill Mann, *Feminizing Chaucer* (Cambridge, 2002), pp. 26–38.

15. See, for example, Carolyn Dinshaw, *Chaucer's Sexual Poetics* (Madison, Wisc., 1989), p. 72: 'He edits his pagan tales . . . to conform to a single, closed, secure, and comforting narrative model.'
16. For a full list of these passages see Frank, *Chaucer and 'The Legend'*, p. 23.
17. See V. A. Kolve, 'From Cleopatra to Alceste: An Iconographic Study of *The Legend of Good Women*' in John P. Hermann and John P. Burke, eds., *Signs and Symbols in Chaucer's Poetry* (University of Alabama, 1981), pp. 130–78.
18. On the various possible implications of 'faith' for the *Legend*, see James Simpson, 'Ethics and Interpretation: Reading Wills in Chaucer's *Legend of Good Women*', *Studies in the Age of Chaucer*, 20 (1998), 73–100.

8

C. DAVID BENSON

The *Canterbury Tales*: personal drama or experiments in poetic variety?

Readers sometimes neglect what is most extraordinary about the *Canterbury Tales*: its dazzling variety of stories and styles. Although story collections were a recognized literary form long before Chaucer (and were especially popular in the late Middle Ages, as shown by Boccaccio's *Decameron* and the *Confessio Amantis* of Chaucer's contemporary John Gower), no other example of the genre contains the radical literary individuality of the *Canterbury Tales* nor creates such complex relationships among its different parts. Chaucer himself had earlier used the form in the unfinished *Legend of Good Women*, but the *Legend* is a disappointment to some Chaucerians, largely because its stories of suffering women are so alike in approach and content. Uniformity also mars for many modern readers a story-collection within the *Canterbury Tales*: the several tragedies of the Monk are finally halted by the Knight because he says they are too pessimistic, though, as the Host suggests, their real fault may be their sleep-inducing monotony. But monotony is the last word one would use to describe the *Canterbury Tales* as a whole. The work is energized by unexpected juxtapositions of styles and subject-matter, so that, for example, a long romance of ancient heroism comes before a short, witty tale of local lust and an account of alchemical swindlers follows a story about ancient martyrdom.

For many, the clearest signals of the variety of the *Canterbury Tales* are the sharply distinct tellers and their intricate relationships before, after, and sometimes during the tales. No other medieval story-collection has a frame that is so lively and dynamic. In contrast to the uniformly aristocratic company of the *Decameron* or the two speakers in Gower's *Confessio* (the Lover and Genius), Chaucer's pilgrim-tellers come from a wide range of clerical and lay estates: an exquisite squire rides next to scurrilous churls and a worldly businessman next to a poor but saintly parson. Like the rural retreat from the Florentine plague that occasions the *Decameron*, the Canterbury pilgrimage is presented as a real event, but unlike the Italian work, whose careful symmetry demands that each of the ten characters tell a tale on an assigned topic on each of ten days, the English narrative permits violent interruptions and unexpected changes in direction.

The plan of tale-telling in order of social rank that is apparently intended by the Host is quickly subverted beyond repair when the drunken Miller insists that he, and not the Monk, will tell the second Canterbury tale and 'quite' the Knight's noble sentiments (I, 3120–7). But before the Miller can begin, the Reeve angrily speaks out, vowing to answer in kind the slanders he anticipates. As the journey proceeds, more surprises occur: two tales are abruptly cut off, while two others remain incomplete, perhaps deliberately so. A dispute breaks out between the Friar and Summoner during the Wife of Bath's performance (which also contains an interruption by the Pardoner), a quarrel they continue before and within their own tales. Later, two strangers ride up to join the company, and, soon after, the Cook is called upon for a story (even though an incomplete tale had already been assigned him in the first fragment), but he falls drunkenly from his horse before he can utter a word. Chaucer puts himself among this boisterous company and attempts two tales, yet the part he plays is that of benign incompetence familiar from his earlier works and he insists that he is only a reporter with no power over the words and actions of others (I, 725–38). As a result of such narratorial diffidence, the *Canterbury Tales* contains no logical order of events or explicit hierarchy of values, but all remains in flux and on the road.

The originality of Chaucer's frame narrative has encouraged many to see the relationship between the pilgrims and their tales as the central achievement of the *Canterbury Tales*. Although such an approach had been developing for over two hundred years, the most influential modern exponent of the so-called 'dramatic theory' was undoubtedly George Lyman Kittredge. In *Chaucer and His Poetry*, Kittredge argued that the individual tales are not told in Chaucer's own voice, but that each is a dramatic expression of the personality of its particular teller: 'the Pilgrims do not exist for the sake of the story, but *vice versa*. Structurally regarded, the stories are merely long speeches expressing, directly or indirectly, the characters of the several persons. They are more or less comparable, in this regard, to the soliloquies of Hamlet or Iago or Macbeth.'[1] Kittredge's view has been adapted and developed by later dramatic critics, but his central assumption – that the Canterbury pilgrims have complex, believable personalities that intimately inform their individual tales – is still widely accepted today, with few feeling the need to justify its validity.[2] The dramatic interpretation has surely contributed much to our understanding of the *Canterbury Tales*, especially by calling attention to its diversity, but the crippling limitation of the approach is that it can lead readers to concentrate on what is less interesting and less knowable in the work: the characters of the tellers instead of the poetry itself. The special genius of the *Canterbury Tales* is not so much its frame narrative, fascinating as that may be, as it is the radical poetic experiments of the individual tales.

Those who see the *Canterbury Tales* as a drama of personality naturally make much of the magnificent descriptions of the pilgrims in the *General Prologue*; indeed, many readers in past centuries seem to have read no farther. Yet Chaucer's opening portraits are most extraordinary not because they give a full and realistic picture of late medieval English life (though they have much to tell us), still less because they contain psychologically believable individuals, but because of their literary skill and wit. The usual medieval character portrait is static and distant, as Chaucer himself demonstrates when he suddenly, and surely ironically, mimics it briefly to describe Criseyde, Troilus, and Diomede in Book v of *Troilus and Criseyde* (799–840). At its most elaborate, medieval characterization is often nothing more than an interminable list of the subject's physical parts, as in the following very brief excerpt from Paris's first sight of Helen, taken from the standard medieval history of Troy and itself adapted as a model of portraiture in an influential medieval rhetorical manual:

He also admired how her even shoulder-blades, by a gentle descent to her flat back, with a depression between them, joined each side gracefully and pleasantly. He admired her arms, which were of proper length to induce the sweetest embraces, while her hands were plump and a little rounded, and the slender tips of her fingers, which were proportionally long, revealed ivory nails.[3]

In contrast to such methodical inventories, the portraits in the *General Prologue*, while equally detailed, are dynamic and vivid. The variety that marks the *Canterbury Tales* as a whole is fully present from the very beginning. Chaucer's pilgrims are arranged in no clear order or hierarchy, as his disingenuous apology ('My wit is short, ye may wel understonde': I, 746) makes clear, and their descriptions vary in length, point of view, and tone. The longest (the Friar's) is sixty-one lines, the shortest (the Cook's) only nine; some emphasize what the pilgrim wears, some what he does, some what he thinks. Although the Knight is described quite formally from the outside, we go inside the mind of the Monk to share his private, rebellious thoughts. Chaucer does not restrict himself to a single consistent narrative voice in the *General Prologue*, as is sometimes claimed, but is variously naive and shrewd, devout and worldly – bluffly endorsing the murderous Shipman one moment, while slyly questioning the Physician's religious faith and business practices the next. The standards of judgement continually shift: the pretensions of the Merchant or the Man of Law produce social satire, while the

Pardoner is condemned and the Parson praised in strictly Christian terms. The portraits are built on memorable details and telling insights, such as the Prioress's careful table manners and unsophisticated French or the simple pleasures of municipal office enjoyed by the wives of the Guildsmen. Few readers can forget the Cook's 'mormal', the Miller's wart, and the Franklin's hospitality ('It snewed in his hous of mete and drynke': I, 345), or the terrifying countenance of the Summoner and the odd appearance of the Pardoner.

Given such diverse and energetic portraits, it is all too easy to imagine the Canterbury pilgrims as fully developed and psychologically complex characters, like those we know from the realistic novel or film. Scholars have argued that Chaucer must have had real-life models and even suggested specific names, but the best studies confirm what some earlier readers understood – the *General Prologue* describes types rather than specific individuals. In the eighteenth century, Dryden and Blake argued that the Canterbury pilgrims illustrate universal categories of human nature, and in her *Chaucer and Medieval Estates Satire*, Jill Mann has shown that the portraits are largely based on material from the traditional descriptions of different occupational 'estates'.[4] As the labels Knight, Miller, Prioress, and even Wife suggest, the *General Prologue* describes professions rather than believable personalities, and many of its pilgrims are composite portraits of an estate. No single warrior could have fought all the battles attributed to the Knight, just as the Monk and Friar exemplify the full range (and not just some) of the vices associated with their respective callings.

Even when the *General Prologue* far transcends standard medieval portraiture and seems most complex, the result is not the rounded, believable characters required for dramatic interpretations so much as intriguing, incomplete puzzles. Chaucer often creates the illusion of life-like individuality through brief insinuations, as in the famous couplet about the Man of Law ('Nowher so bisy a man as he ther nas, / And yet he semed bisier than he was': 321–2) or the observation that 'ther wiste no wight' that the Merchant 'was in dette' (280). But such lines suggest more than they actually state. They are so framed that the reader may guess, but cannot certainly know, how busy the Lawyer actually is, or whether no one recognizes the Merchant to be in debt because he is not or because he has hidden it so well. Chaucer's most subtle portraits stubbornly avoid final judgement and thus allow a range of interpretation. The courteous and 'pitous' Prioress, for instance, has been seen as everything from a corrupter of holy office to an attractive, if sentimental, woman of style. Such diversity of opinion is a tribute to Chaucer's skill, but the reader who chooses any single view, and interprets the tale in its light, runs the risk of serious distortion because of a subjective reaction to a brief and deliberately ambiguous portrait. The *General Prologue* rarely provides characterization that is specific or clear enough for the reader to have any confidence that it will be more than generally useful in understanding the tale that follows.

Chaucer's pilgrims are not developed much further in their later appearances on the road to Canterbury. When he so desires, the poet can create characters as complex and convincing as any in medieval literature, as we see most memorably in *Troilus and Criseyde*, but the frame of the *Canterbury Tales* suggests that he was not primarily concerned with the psychological depth or consistency of his pilgrim-narrators. Many of the pilgrims – such as the Squire, Physician, Second Nun, and Shipman – make only the briefest appearance, or none, outside the *General Prologue*. More revealing are the frequent inconsistencies between what we are told about a pilgrim in his or her portrait and what we discover later. Consider the contrast between the stiff, secretive Merchant in his portrait and the voluble husband who recklessly exposes his marital failure in the prologue to his tale. The pleasure-loving Monk of the *General Prologue* also seems to have little in common with the cleric of the same name who ignores the Host's suggestive repartee in order to tell his solemn tragedies; likewise, the old age of the Reeve, which is so important in the prologue to his tale, goes unmentioned in his portrait in the *General Prologue*. Of course, clever readers will be able to construct a consistent character out of even the most random and contradictory materials, but in so doing they must supplement what the poet has written with their own inventions, and thus they rarely agree with one another.

If most of the Canterbury pilgrims are relatively undeveloped and appear only briefly after the *General Prologue*, there are some striking exceptions. Three pilgrims especially, who are often at the centre of dramatic interpretations of the *Canterbury Tales* – the Canon's Yeoman, the Wife of Bath, and the Pardoner – come forward in the body of the work to give detailed accounts of their lives. Yet even though all three possess extraordinary narrative energy, and contribute much to the total effect of the *Canterbury Tales*, each is more a dramatic voice than a believable personality. We see a public performance rather than a psychological study. Like Chaucer's other pilgrims, the Canon's Yeoman, Wife of Bath, and Pardoner are essentially occupational types not individual subjects, and what they tell us about themselves has only a general relationship to their stories.

The *Canon's Yeoman's Tale* shows the flexibility of the Canterbury frame and its potential for narrative surprise. The pilgrims are travelling through 'Boghtoun under Blee' when they are suddenly overtaken by a hard-riding canon and his yeoman to whom the narrator responds strongly (for example, 'it was joye for to seen hym swete!': VIII, 579). The Host's initial questioning of the Yeoman results in extravagant praise of the Canon and his achievements, including the claim that he can pave the road 'al of silver and of gold' (VIII, 626). When Harry wonders why such a distinguished man is dressed in filthy rags, the Yeoman laments that his master will never prosper, and then begins to admit the failures that alchemy has brought. The Canon attempts to stop these revelations, but when he fails he flees the company 'for verray sorwe and shame' (702), leaving the Yeoman to tell all: 'Syn that my lord is goon, I wol nat spare; / Swich thyng as that I knowe, I wol declare' (718–19).

This scene is one of the most exciting moments in the frame narrative, and perhaps shows Chaucer extending the possibilities of the format at a late stage in the composition of the *Canterbury Tales*. But we should not confuse this with psychological realism. Why does the Yeoman change so quickly from excessive praise of his master to bitter condemnation? Why does he decide now, within minutes of joining the pilgrims, to confess everything to Harry Bailly? One could imagine circumstances and motives that would make such behaviour plausible – and many dramatic critics have – but Chaucer does not even bother to try. He is more interested in the result of the Yeoman's decision to confess than in establishing the inner motives that brought it about. As often, the primary purpose of this prologue is to introduce the subsequent tale.

The *Canon's Yeoman's Tale* itself has interested dramatic critics because its first half, which is less a story than a hodgepodge of alchemical lore, is said to be drawn from the teller's own experiences. Critics sometimes read Chaucer's tales as though they were as personally revealing as Browning's dramatic monologues, but, in fact, the *prima pars* of the *Canon's Yeoman's Tale* is the only explicitly autobiographical episode not in a prologue in the entire *Canterbury Tales*:

> With this Chanoun I dwelt have seven yeer,
> And of his science am I never the neer.
> Al that I hadde I have lost therby,
> And, God woot, so hath many mo than I.   (720–3)

As the last line of the quotation suggests, however, the *Canon's Yeoman's Tale*, though autobiographical, is only superficially personal. The Yeoman and his experiences are offered as a demonstration of the errors of many; he is not an individual but an exemplum: 'Lat every man be war by me for evere!' (737).

The first half of the tale is less about the Canon's Yeoman than about his profession. It tells us almost nothing special about the teller because its subject from first to last is the 'cursed craft' (830) and 'elvysshe nyce loore'

(842) of alchemy. Indeed, the word 'craft' occurs more often here than in any other tale. Thus dramatic narration need not mean genuine personal disclosure: as early as the *House of Fame*, Chaucer understood how effectively a vivacious speaking voice could present technical information, especially scientific lore. Although the Eagle who lectures 'Geffrey' so authoritatively on the way to the House of Fame makes the journey delightful for the reader, he is little more than a cartoon figure. Similarly, the colloquial, breathless, occasionally confused voice in the *Canon's Yeoman's Tale* defines no individual (the Yeoman has been judged at various times both stupid and shrewd), but instead illustrates the mixture of chaos and enthusiasm among all alchemists. The most memorable detail we learn about the Canon's Yeoman is purely external and generic (his leaden complexion from too much blowing on the fire). The voice performs its functions – it is flexible, aware of the audience, and lively. It has kept us interested while demonstrating the delusions of alchemy, but we have learned nothing idiosyncratic or personal about the Yeoman. The dramatic voice is nothing more, and nothing less, than a brilliant narrative device.

The second part of the *Canon's Yeoman's Tale*, about another canon who tricks a greedy priest into believing he knows how to turn base metal into silver, is told in the same animated voice, with even more moral outrage: 'This false chanoun – the foule feend hym fecche!' (1159). Despite the teller's explicit denial, dramatic critics often assume that the Yeoman is actually speaking about his master; but the narrative logic is surely wrong (why would the confessing Yeoman suddenly turn coy?), and there is no reason to believe that the Canon and his Yeoman are crooks – everything we are told suggests they are victims of sincere belief in the science. The delight some readers find in developing such faint personal hints merely distorts the purpose of the work. The *Canon's Yeoman's Tale* reveals the folly of alchemy, not the folly of one or two individual pilgrims. It is an extended occupational portrait. The first part of the tale demonstrates one of the vices of alchemy (deluding oneself), while the second part demonstrates another (deluding others); the connection between the two is thematic rather than personal. Any sense of dramatic consistency of the tale is further undermined by its conclusion, in which a more learned and thoughtful voice than we have heard before assesses the pros and cons of alchemy before advising that men should wait for God to reveal its secrets (1388–1481). The different tone will bother only those who imagine that the tale has been told throughout by a complex and believable personality. In fact, the most interesting relationships are literary rather than dramatic; not between the Canon's Yeoman and his tale, but, for instance, between the sterile work and hellish fire of the *Canon's Yeoman's Tale* and the fruitful work and divine fire of the preceding *Second Nun's Tale*.

The Wife of Bath is undoubtedly the most fully and consistently developed of the Canterbury pilgrims. Her prologue is the longest in the *Tales* and offers a clever defence of marriage as well as detailed and roughly chronological accounts of her five husbands. In addition to being of special interest to modern feminist critics, Alison was apparently a great favourite from the start. Chaucer himself cites her twice, in his *Envoy to Bukton* and within the *Merchant's Tale*, and it has been persuasively argued that her role grew over the years, perhaps in response to public demand.[5] If so, the Wife's evolution is something like that of Shakespeare's Falstaff, whom she resembles in so many other ways. Like him, she has an allegorical model, possesses great verbal powers, and represents an exaggeration of one aspect of human nature more than a convincing human being. Like Falstaff also, the Wife has moments of real pathos – the regret for her lost youth or her troubles with her fifth husband, Jankyn, for instance – but the reader never knows quite how to take these scenes because everything important we think we know about her comes from her own mouth.

Like the Canon's Yeoman, the Wife of Bath has a distinct speaking voice, though it is heard only in her prologue. In the first part, before the interruption of the Pardoner, the Wife produces a travesty of traditional Christian teachings about marriage with her brilliant spoof of medieval logic and biblical quotation. Question: Should one marry more than once? Answer: Christ's views on this are difficult to understand, but certainly God's 'gentil text' bidding us to 'wexe and multiplye' is clear enough – and look at all Solomon's wives (III, 9–44). Question: Is virginity commanded? Answer: If so, where would new virgins come from? And does not a household need wooden vessels as well as gold? And why then were humans given 'membres of generacion' (62–134)? The Wife's eclectic arguments never seriously engage orthodox belief, but their cleverness is thoroughly entertaining. Later, we see more evidence of her terrifying fluency when she repeats a speech used to overwhelm her old husbands that masterfully blends false reasoning ('And sith a man is moore resonable / Than womman is, ye moste been suffrable'), stunning vulgarity ('Is it for ye wolde have my queynte allone'?), and magnanimous generosity ('Wy, taak it al! Lo, have it every deel!': 441–5). Despite her initial claim to follow 'experience' rather than 'auctoritee', the Wife of Bath is an intellectual *manqué*, a would-be clerk, who, like Falstaff, is fully powerful only in discourse.

The other long autobiographical prologue in the *Canterbury Tales* is that of the equally verbal Pardoner. When he interrupts the Wife, the Pardoner calls her a 'noble prechour' (III, 165), a subject on which he is an expert. Now in his own prologue, he explains his use of the pulpit to impress the 'lewed peple' (VI, 437) and make them give him money. Like the expert huckster he is, the Pardoner knows all the tricks of the trade. He puts on a multimedia show that includes papal bulls and fake relics, but his most effective skill is his use of words. His verbal devices include 'olde stories' (436), 'false japes' (394), and indirect attacks on his enemies (412–22); his showy Latin quotations (344–6) are balanced by a sniggering reference to a wife sleeping with two or three priests (369–71). The Pardoner is justly proud of his command of language. With his 'hauteyn speche' he makes his words ring out 'as round as gooth a belle' (330–1), and the effect is spectacular: 'Myne handes and my tonge goon so yerne / That it is joye to se my bisynesse' (398–9).[6]

Like the Canon's Yeoman, the Wife of Bath and the Pardoner are primarily dramatic voices. Their prologues contain magnificent performances, but they do not reveal individual personality. Instead of believable human beings, the Pardoner and the Wife are verbal artists, skilled users of words. However much the reader enjoys their linguistic virtuosity, nothing that either says can be trusted. Most of what we know about them is what they themselves choose to tell us in their prologues, and a persistent theme of both is their ability to manipulate others with false speech. Because we have no way of verifying the truth of what either says, the reader who desires to define the 'real' Pardoner or Wife behind the performances can do so only subjectively. We may suspect that the Wife's final relationship with Jankyn was not as harmonious as she asserts, or wonder about the jolly wenches the Pardoner boasts of having in every town, but we can be no more certain about these claims than about anything else either says. As a result, critics can find justification for arguing that the Pardoner is everything from a damned soul to Christ-like, and that the Wife of Bath is either a lusty lover of life or a pitiful example of the wages of sin.

The mistake is to imagine that Chaucer has given a full and consistent human personality to either. Despite the many lines devoted to them, both the Pardoner and the Wife, like the other Canterbury pilgrims, are essentially occupational types. Although the Wife's *Prologue* may seem intimate because it concerns domestic life, all that she ever talks about is her profession – marriage. We hear nothing about weaving (her first vocation) and no details of the extramarital sexual encounters she hints at; other parts of her life, like her gossips or pilgrimages, are mentioned only when directly relevant to her husbands. The Pardoner is equally professional. For all his seeming revelations, his skill in the pulpit is really all that we know about him and the only subject of his apparently personal prologue. Although Chaucer has developed them far beyond their original models in the *Roman de la Rose*, the Wife and Pardoner retain an allegorical core: she is the standard nightmare of medieval antifeminism and he the corrupt preacher he boasts himself to be. This is not to say that either is dull or simple. As allegorical figures such as Gluttony or Lady Meed in Langland's *Piers Plowman* demonstrate, literary dynamism is not the same as in-depth psychological realism. In fiction, as Dickens knew, it is often the fundamental purity of a characterization that makes it memorable.

Although the Pardoner and Wife of Bath are highly developed in their prologues, the relations between these pilgrims and their tales are not especially revealing. The *Wife of Bath's Tale* is much shorter than the preceding *Prologue*. The story of the old hag who wins back both youth and a vigorous husband can be read as the Wife's wish-fulfilment, if one so desires, but the voice of the teller has changed completely. The style of the tale is more reserved and objective than that of the prologue (only an early dig at friars reminds us of the earlier tone), and the idealistic speeches in the tale on gentility, poverty, and age sound nothing like the Wife's aggressive materialism and impudent self-assertion. The *Pardoner's Tale* is more closely connected to its teller (it purports to be his standard homily), but for all its use of preaching techniques, its resemblance to an actual sermon is only general. Moreover, while the melodramatic denunciation of the three tavern sins is clearly appropriate to a corrupt preacher, the profundity and quiet austerity of the exemplum of the 'riotoures' seem far beyond his understanding. There is no reason to believe that either part reveals anything about the Pardoner as a man. As with the Canon's Yeoman, the most fruitful relationships are literary rather than personal. Rather than pursuing the elusive psyches of even these highly developed pilgrims, the reader would do better to look closely at how the *Wife of Bath's Tale* differs from experiments with romance narrative elsewhere in the *Canterbury Tales*. Similarly, one might compare the *Pardoner's Tale* with Chaucer's other forms of Christian instruction in the collection or even explore its internal juxtaposition of two very different kinds of religious poetry – the flamboyant denunciation in contrast to the haunting exemplum. We know very little that is certain about the personal lives of the Wife and the Pardoner, but the poetry of their tales is fully available for literary analysis and comparison.

Although few, if any, of the tales reveal the psychology of their pilgrim speakers in any significant way, Chaucer has so designed the *Canterbury Tales* that there is usually some kind of correspondence between teller and tale. The poet himself calls attention to this in a warning to fastidious readers before the *Miller's Tale*:

> The Millere is a cherl; ye knowe wel this.
> So was the Reve eek and othere mo,
> And harlotrie they tolden bothe two. (I, 3182–4)

Note, however, that the relationship Chaucer claims here is extremely broad and the general result of class rather than individual personality – a low-born pilgrim will naturally tell a low story.

The natural appropriateness of tale to teller is clearly demonstrated in the first fragment of the *Canterbury Tales*, the most finished part of the work and the best indication of what the whole would have been like had Chaucer lived to complete it. After the *General Prologue*, the noble Knight's philosophical story of chivalry, love, and 'gentilesse' is followed, as Chaucer warns, by three ribald fabliaux told by churls. Elsewhere in the *Canterbury Tales*, a similar congruity between estate and kind of story is common. The two nuns tell religious tales, the Squire and Franklin tell romances, and the Pardoner and Parson explore the effects of sin. Sometimes the relationship may be even more specific. The voice of the pompous Man of Law has been detected in his highly rhetorical tale of the trials of Custance and that of the plain, clever Clerk in his story of Griselda.

But despite such general agreement, the intense, personal association between teller and tale automatically assumed by the dramatic theory is rare in the *Canterbury Tales*. The classical learning of the *Knight's Tale*, the polished art of the *Miller's Tale*, the moral delicacy of the *Friar's Tale*, the subtle cleverness of the *Summoner's Tale*, and the dogged didacticism of the *Monk's Tale* – none of these qualities, but rather their reverse, is suggested by what we know of the pilgrims outside the tales. Perhaps the most extreme disjunction of teller and tale is the contrast between the rough, murderous Shipman of the *General Prologue* and the cool, sophisticated art of the *Shipman's Tale*.

Given such loose connections between teller and tale, dramatic readings of the *Canterbury Tales* are frequently either banal (the *Knight's Tale* fits the Knight because it is about chivalry) or highly imaginative (the *Prioress's Tale* has been said to reveal its teller as a frustrated mother). Even worse, the approach sometimes leads critics to assume that the supposed limitations of a pilgrim mean that the tale assigned to him or her must be severely flawed or even deliberately bad. Tales so regarded are often moral or religious works, such as the tale of *Melibee* or the Prioress's, Second Nun's, Man of Law's, Physician's, and Clerk's tales, but others, including the *Squire's Tale* and *Franklin's Tale*, have been similarly dismissed. It is possible that Chaucer wanted some of these tales to be read ironically, but it is more probable that the dramatic approach is being used to support modern assumptions about what makes a good story.

Dramatic interpretations sometimes manage to trivialize Chaucer's greatest achievements by associating them too closely with their assigned tellers. A flagrant example is the attempt to read the Merchant into the extraordinary tale of the marriage of old January to 'fresshe' May. Neither the secretive

Merchant of the *General Prologue* nor the recklessly confessional husband of the *Merchant's Prologue* has much in common with the protagonist of the *Merchant's Tale*, despite the circular reasoning by which dramatic critics derive the biography of the Merchant almost entirely from the story of January, after which teller and tale are, not unsurprisingly, found to be in remarkable agreement. The relationship between the *Merchant's Prologue*, in which the Merchant briefly and bitterly condemns his wife of two months, and the tale that follows is introductory rather than psychological. The Merchant's complaints are a conventional piece of medieval antifeminism, not a significant revelation of individual personality. They serve to prepare the reader for a tale about married woe, but they do not begin to define the specific shape of that tale – the Merchant's problems with his wife are different from and more familiar than January's. It is reductive in the extreme to derive the complexity and dark brilliance of the *Merchant's Tale* from the simple disappointments of a new husband. January is one of Chaucer's greatest achievements in moral characterization, but the pilgrim Merchant is little more than a stock figure. The *Merchant's Tale* warns us to trust the tale and not the teller.

I am not, of course, arguing that the dramatic frame has no purpose in the *Canterbury Tales*, only that it, along with the portraits in the *General Prologue*, has been given too much of the wrong kind of attention by some readers. Chaucer often uses a pilgrim's voice to make complex information more lively, as we have seen with the antifeminism of the *Wife of Bath's Prologue* or the alchemical lore of the *Canon's Yeoman's Tale*. The frame narrative offers the reader a more ordinary, frequently comic world that is something of a relief between the powerful fictions of the tales themselves. If Chaucer's prologues prepare us only generally for what is to come, the dramatic episodes between pilgrims that conclude some tales are rarely their thematic or artistic culmination, though they are commonly so regarded. The coarse foolery at the end of the *Pardoner's Tale*, for example, during which the Host angrily insults the Pardoner, has often dominated critical discussions at the expense of the infinitely greater narrative of the three revellers. Like the Host himself, who is so active in these episodes, the frame often provides indirect and deliberately misleading comment on the tales, something like the grotesques in the margins of medieval manuscripts. For all its value and originality, the pilgrimage story should not become more important than the tales it encloses.

Perhaps the greatest contribution of the frame is that its personal conflicts point to the more important literary conflicts of the tales themselves. When the drunken Miller interrupts to 'quite' the *Knight's Tale*, the human drama is only a brief and general moment of class antagonism (the two pilgrims never actually address one another), but the resulting juxtaposition of their two different tales initiates the extraordinary artistic variety of the *Canterbury Tales*. Imagine how different the *Tales* would be if, as originally planned, the long and philosophical *Knight's Tale* were then followed by the interminable tragedies of the Monk. How many would want to read further? Instead, Chaucer uses the Miller's rudeness to establish the principle of literary diversity that enlivens and distinguishes the entire collection.

As I have suggested throughout this essay, the Canterbury tales are a series of literary experiments rather than a drama of personalities. The undeniable variety of the collection comes from the conflicting artistries of the tales themselves. Stylistically, not one of Chaucer's tales is much like any other. Each is a unique work with its own distinct poetic, a poetic that ranges from large literary elements, such as narrator and dialogue, down to the specifics of imagery, allusion, and vocabulary. Even more remarkable, the special artistry of an individual tale remains consistent throughout, almost as if Chaucer had created an individual poetic for each. I know of no other literary work so constructed, for the various tales are not parodies or only generally different; instead, each is a fully worked-out expression of a special kind of poetry. This radical stylistic variety, and not the relations between tale and teller, is the central achievement of the *Canterbury Tales*.

The *General Prologue* first prepares us for the coming drama of style with its many different kinds of pilgrim portraits, and Chaucer further shows us how to read the *Canterbury Tales* in the two works he assigns to himself – the clever parody *Sir Thopas* and the dull if worthy *Melibee*. Although much critical ingenuity has been spent trying to define the vague and contradictory figure of 'Chaucer the Pilgrim', the significant drama in this episode is the literary opposition of the two tales themselves. *Thopas* and *Melibee* reveal no clear pilgrim personality, but they do suggest the outer boundaries of Christian literature. Though a delightful exercise in aesthetic burlesque, *Thopas* is so self-indulgent and insubstantial, so empty of theme and *sentence*, that it risks confirming the worst fears of medieval moralists about the frivolity and falsity of poetry. In contrast, the admirable but plodding *Melibee* threatens to undermine its didactic mission by putting its audience to sleep. In the sharp artistic opposition of his own two tales, Chaucer both announces the dialectic of styles in the *Canterbury Tales* and suggests that the most effective poetry combines the moral meaning of *Melibee* with the literary skill of *Sir Thopas* – 'sentence' and 'solaas' (I, 798).

Chaucer's art of literary contrast and experiment is found throughout the *Canterbury Tales*. It begins with the juxtaposition of the Knight's and Miller's tales, whose differences go far beyond the change from romance to fabliau, and near the end we find an equally complex relationship between the paired tales of the Second Nun and the Canon's Yeoman, which are opposite in form and theme, but share similar kinds of imagery. Chaucer even creates poetic variety within a single tale. The first part of the *Pardoner's Tale* (the sermon on the tavern sins) is as corrupt as it is skilful – a dazzling, manipulative, and superficial harangue designed to sell pardons, but one that offers no real understanding of sin or help against it. Yet the second part of the tale (the exemplum of the three rioters searching for Death) is completely different in tone and effect: the melodramatic rhetoric of the sermon instantly gives way at line 661 to a powerfully understated and symbolically charged narrative that succeeds as both an exciting story and a vehicle for serious Christian instruction. The two different kinds of artistry in the *Pardoner's Tale* suggest both the dangers and the opportunities of moral fiction.

The literary variety of the *Canterbury Tales* occurs even among tales that ought to be most alike. Although rarely discussed directly by critics, and then only generally, the radical stylistic differences among stories of the same genre are the clearest proof of the unique poetic sensibilities created for each of the Canterbury tales. The several romances in the collection, for example, are significantly different from one another. A similar literary variety occurs in the religious tales. The *Prioress's Tale* and the *Second Nun's Tale* both tell of an innocent martyr whose death is a triumph of Christian faith, yet the first is a lyrical exercise in affective piety, while the second is an austere and intellectual work that makes complex use of dialogue and imagery.

Perhaps the most surprising example of literary experimentation within a single genre occurs in the fabliaux. The *Miller's Tale, Reeve's Tale, Shipman's Tale,* and *Merchant's Tale* all contain the same basic situation (a husband is cuckolded by a younger man whom he himself has introduced into the household), yet no two share anything like the same artistry; rather each contains its own unique poetic voice, only a little of which can be attributed to the different tellers. The stylistic individuality of Chaucer's fabliaux is found in everything from their different narrators and wooing scenes to their special use of imagery and vocabulary. For instance, each of the fabliaux has its characteristic kind of speech: quick and witty exchanges in the *Miller's Tale,* flat and frequently inarticulate expression in the *Reeve's Tale,* sophisticated, manipulative dialogue in the *Shipman's Tale,* and long, often interior monologues of great psychological and moral depth in the *Merchant's Tale.* Or consider a more specific example: literary and learned allusions are virtually non-existent in the Reeve's and Shipman's tales, but extremely important, though completely different, in the Miller's and Merchant's tales. The allusions in the *Miller's Tale* are drawn largely from popular sources like contemporary songs or mystery plays, while those in the *Merchant's Tale* are more various and more learned (including its frequent use of biblical and classic stories), introducing new standards of judgement, and perhaps also hope, to the sordid fabliau world of January and May.

The *Reeve's Tale* has sometimes been slighted by critics in favour of the more flamboyant *Miller's Tale*. But when the two are read together and compared as experiments in the possibilities of a genre, the special virtues of the *Reeve's Tale* become apparent, such as its glorious glossary and profound understanding of the physical and social constraints of ordinary life. Perhaps the clearest proof of the unique and accomplished artistry of the *Reeve's Tale* is the northern dialect spoken by the two Cambridge students. For this one tale and its particular poet, Chaucer creates an unprecedented and sophisticated literary device he never uses again. Some critics have also dismissed the *Shipman's Tale*, mistaking its individual, understated artistry for inferiority. The work lacks some of the famous literary elements of Chaucer's other fabliaux because its special accomplishments lie elsewhere, especially in the long dialogue of seduction between wife and monk whose cool calculation is unmatched elsewhere in the *Canterbury Tales*.

Because it privileges relationships sanctioned by the frame narrative, the dramatic approach has hindered the detailed and wide-ranging literary comparisons between particular tales and among groups of tales sketched above. Such comparisons are essential to understanding the accomplishment of the *Canterbury Tales*, allowing us to recognize Chaucer's intricate drama of style. The *Canterbury Tales* is a collection of radically different kinds of poetry; each contributes a unique artistic vision, and thus a special view of the world. Even Chaucer's comic tales contain a challenging literary and thematic individuality. Too often the dramatic theory has concealed or trivialized the depth and the poetic range of the collection by asking us to dwell on the lesser thing (the pilgrims) rather than the greater (the tales themselves). Although the *Canterbury Tales* has been enjoyed for over six hundred years, the full achievement of Chaucer's experiments in poetic variety remains to be explored.

NOTES

1. George Lyman Kittredge, *Chaucer and His Poetry* (Cambridge, Mass., 1915), p. 155.
2. Influential recent studies of the *Canterbury Tales*, for all their theoretical sophistication, often accept many of the assumptions of Kittredge's dramatic approach: see, for example, H. Marshall Leicester, Jr's postmodern *The Disenchanted Self: Representing the Subject in the Canterbury Tales* (Berkeley, 1990), and Lee Patterson's historicist *Chaucer and the Subject of History* (Madison, 1991). Whatever its limitations, the dramatic theory will persist in the teaching of Chaucer, if for no other reason than that it is so convenient for presenting the *Canterbury Tales* to students. For a recent survey of the distorting effects of the

dramatic theory on interpretations of the *Man of Law's Tale*, and an attempt to show what is to be gained by abandoning it, see A. C. Spearing, 'Narrative Voice: The Case of Chaucer's *Man of Law's Tale*', *New Literary History*, 32 (2001), 715–46.

3. Guido delle Colonne, *Historia Destructionis Troiae*, trans. Mary E. Meek (Bloomington, Ind., 1974), p. 71.

4. Jill Mann, *Chaucer and Medieval Estates Satire* (Cambridge, 1973). The comments of Dryden and Blake are most conveniently found in *Geoffrey Chaucer: The Critical Heritage*, ed. D. S. Brewer, vol. 2 (London, 1978), pp. 66–7 and pp. 249–60.

5. R. A. Pratt, 'The Development of the Wife of Bath' in *Studies in Medieval Literature in Honor of Professor Albert Croll Baugh*, ed. MacEdward Leach (Philadelphia, 1961), pp. 45–79.

6. There is a strong modern tradition of understanding the Pardoner not only textually but also sexually (assuming him to be, in some sense, a eunuch or a homosexual), an assumption that has only been intensified by queer theory. For arguments that question this approach, however, see my 'Chaucer's Pardoner: His Sexuality and Modern Critics' and Richard Firth Green's 'The Sexual Normality of Chaucer's Pardoner', *Mediaevalia*, 8 (1985), 337–49 and 351–8.

9

J. A. BURROW

The *Canterbury Tales* I: romance

The term 'romance' is not an exact one. Applied to medieval writings it denotes a large area whose outer limits are by no means easy to define. Yet most readers of English literature have some notion of what a typical romance is like, a notion derived mainly from the tales of Arthur and the Round Table. The hero of such a romance will be a knight who engages in perilous adventures, riding out and frequently fighting, sometimes to win or defend a lady, sometimes to defeat enemies of the realm, and sometimes for no evident reason at all. It should be said straightaway that the reader who turns to Chaucer's great story-collection in search of such a typical romance will be disappointed; for the five Canterbury 'romances' to be discussed in this chapter are all, in one way or another, divergent from that stereotype. It is as if Chaucer, who seems so much at home in the fabliau, the miracle of the Virgin, and the saint's life, felt less easy with the very genre which we regard as most characteristic of his period, the knightly romance.[1]

The only poem of Chaucer's which has an Arthurian setting – indeed, the only poem in which he so much as mentions Arthur, apart from a passing reference derived from Guillaume de Lorris in the first fragment of the *Romaunt of the Rose* – is the *Wife of Bath's Tale*. The opening line of this tale, 'In th'olde dayes of the Kyng Arthour', holds out the promise that here for once Chaucer is going to try his hand at the most traditional kind of knightly romance. Yet by the end of the poem's first paragraph this expectation is already shaken:

> In th'olde dayes of the Kyng Arthour,
> Of which that Britons speken greet honour,
> Al was this land fulfild of fayerye.
> The elf-queene, with hir joly compaignye,
> Daunced ful ofte in many a grene mede.
> This was the olde opinion, as I rede;

> I speke of manye hundred yeres ago.
> But now kan no man se none elves mo,
> For now the grete charitee and prayeres
> Of lymytours and othere hooly freres,
> That serchen every lond and every streem,
> As thikke as motes in the sonne-beem,
> Blessynge halles, chambres, kichenes, boures,
> Citees, burghes, castels, hye toures,
> Thropes, bernes, shipnes, dayeryes –
> This maketh that ther ben no fayeryes.
> For ther as wont to walken was an elf
> Ther walketh now the lymytour hymself
> In undermeles and in morwenynges,
> And seyth his matyns and his hooly thynges
> As he gooth in his lymytacioun.
> Wommen may go saufly up and doun.
> In every bussh or under every tree
> Ther is noon oother incubus but he,
> And he ne wol doon hem but dishonour. (857–81)

The ostensible purpose of these scintillating lines is the same as that of the opening of *Sir Gawain and the Green Knight*: to set the ensuing story in Britain's great age of wonders, the reign of King Arthur. Yet, whereas the *Gawain*-poet's introduction is serious and single-minded, Chaucer's is comic and distracted. It may appear that the Wife of Bath (for the voice is distinctly hers) here turns a traditional comparison upside-down. Arthurian romancers commonly compare modern times unfavourably with the grand old days of Arthur; but the Wife at first speaks as if, for women at least, things are better nowadays. In Arthurian times women lived in continual fear of being raped by the 'elves' or fairy creatures with which the land was then filled; but now these incubi have been driven out by the pious activity of the friars: 'Wommen may go saufly up and doun'. This flattery of friars may remind us that the Wife of Bath belongs to that class of 'worthy wommen of the toun' with whom the Friar on the pilgrimage was especially 'wel biloved and famulier', according to the *General Prologue* (215–17). Such women were, in fact, notorious for their susceptibility to sweet-talking friars. Yet the Wife is a tough character, who can look after herself. Perhaps the Friar's laughing compliment at the end of her prologue irritated her ('This is a long preamble of a tale!' 83). At any rate, one may detect a note of sarcasm in her response to the Host's call for a tale:

> 'Al redy, sire,' quod she, 'right as yow lest,
> If I have licence of this worthy Frere.' (III, 854–5)

The mock submissiveness of these words prepares the way for the deceptive sweetness of the tale's opening. For the Wife does not in reality treat modern friars as an improvement on their elvish predecessors. Her description of friars blessing everything in sight 'as thikke as motes in the sonne-beem' is not merely ridiculous; it also has something of that horror of the swarm so vividly evoked later by the Summoner's dreadful account of thousands of friars swarming out of the devil's arse like bees from a hive (III, 1692–6). Nor are women, she suggests, actually safe with friars from sexual attack. Their only comfort is that the friar has not inherited the elf's power of infallibly causing conception: 'he ne wol doon hem but dishonour'. Nothing but dishonour! By comparison, the olden days of King Arthur emerge as something like a golden age for women. We may notice, looking back, that the Wife first describes Arthurian fairies, not as lustful male incubi, but as a happy band of dancing ladies:

> The elf-queene, with hir joly compaignye,
> Daunced ful ofte in many a grene mede. (860–1)

This brief but memorable glimpse of the queen of the fairies and her company of ladies does much to establish the character of the Arthurian world as the Wife is to portray it in her tale. It is essentially a feminine world, dominated by women both human and fairy. The fairy element is not obvious, for the old hag who turns into the beautiful young wife is never explained as an elf-woman. But neither does she turn out to be, as in the three other surviving English versions of the story, a human girl bewitched by a wicked stepmother.[2] Indeed, she is not explained at all. Yet the circumstances in which the knight first encounters her clearly associate her with the 'joly compaignye' of the queen of the fairies. Under the forest eaves he comes upon a company of four and twenty ladies dancing; and it is after they have mysteriously vanished that he first sees the old hag sitting on the green. This is enough, in a land 'fulfild of fayerye', to establish her true identity.

The dominance of women in the fairy world evoked by the Wife of Bath is striking. The hero of the tale is a man, a 'lusty bachelor' of Arthur's court; but he is not named, like Florent in Gower's version of the story or Sir Gawain in the other two versions. Nor is he, like Gower's Florent, a 'knyght aventurous'. The masculine activities of adventure and feats of arms play no part in his story. Riding back from a day's hawking he commits, it is true, the ultimate act of male domination, when he rapes a passing girl; but, unlike an incubus or a friar, he does not go unpunished. His act of 'oppressioun' delivers him, in fact, into the hands of the women – Arthur's queen and her ladies, and also the elf-woman. His life is made to depend on his ability to determine what women most desire; and the answer to that question, when he discovers it, proves to affirm their claim to supremacy:

> 'Wommen desiren to have sovereynetee
> As wel over hir housbond as hir love,
> And for to been in maistrie hym above.' (1038–40)

Chaucer's only 'Arthurian romance', then, turns out to be a fairy-tale, told by a woman and dominated by women. Perhaps this is how Chaucer thought of Arthurian stories – strange as that may seem to a reader of Malory. In his tale the Squire speaks of 'Fairye' as the country out of which Gawain might come again (96); and the Nun's Priest skittishly associates an Arthurian book with women readers:

> This storie is also trewe, I undertake,
> As is the book of Launcelot de Lake,
> That wommen holde in ful greet reverence. (VII, 3211–13)

Chaucer probably had in mind here the French *Lancelot*, which formed part of the great thirteenth-century Vulgate Cycle of Arthurian stories. This is the very book which, in a memorable episode in Dante's *Inferno*, the two young lovers Paolo and Francesca were reading together when they first kissed. Dante himself had certainly read the *Lancelot*, for he recalls a tiny episode from the book, to brilliant effect, in the *Paradiso* (XVI, 14–15); but it may be surmised that he, like Chaucer, regarded knightly romance as a form of agreeable light reading to which no serious fourteenth-century poet should devote more than passing attention.

If this was indeed Chaucer's attitude, it may seem strange that he should have assigned to himself, of all the Canterbury pilgrims, the tale which comes closer than any other of his works to being a story of knightly adventure; but his *Tale of Sir Thopas*, as nearly all readers have noticed, is an outright burlesque. Adventure, as it figured so largely in the romance of chivalry, seems never to have attracted Chaucer's interest. His account of how Jason and Hercules 'soughten the aventures of Colcos' occurs in a context that directs attention not to male heroism but to female suffering (as part of the legend of Hypsipyle and Medea in the *Legend of Good Women*): and the only other Chaucerian hero who sets off in search of adventure is Sir Thopas himself. Having fallen in love with an 'elf-queene' (790), Thopas rides out into the 'contree of Fairye' (802). There he encounters her monstrous guardian, a three-headed giant called Sir Olifaunt ('Elephant'), whereupon he hurries home again to fetch his armour. There follows an elaborately circumstantial arming scene, very much in the romance manner, after which the knight sets out again to meet the giant. Chaucer is careful to explain that Thopas conducts himself on this second sortie exactly as a 'knyght auntrous' or adventurous knight should – sleeping in the open with his helm as a pillow, and drinking nothing but spring water:

> Hymself drank water of the well,
> As dide the knyght sire Percyvell
> So worly under wede,
> Til on a day –   (915–18)

At this point, however, the Host can stand no more, and he tells Chaucer to stop: 'Thou doost noght elles but despendest tyme' (931). Perhaps Harry Bailly here voices his creator's thought about those shapeless and interminable adventures which occupy so many medieval romances. Yet it may be noticed that even in this ridiculous context, just as in the *Wife of Bath's Tale*, the thought of the elf-queen inspires Chaucer (himself described as 'elvyssh' in the *Prologue to Sir Thopas*) to an imaginative response:

> 'Heere is the queene of Fayerye,
> With harpe and pipe and symphonye,
> Dwellynge in this place.'   (814–16)

The strange potency of Chaucer's fairy queen, with her entourage of instrumental music and dancing ladies, impressed her on the mind of the next great English poet; for Spenser's Faerie Queene is her descendant. The episode where Spenser's Arthur falls in love with the 'elf-queene' seen in a vision as he sleeps in a forest glade (*Faerie Queene* I, ix, 8–15) is directly modelled upon the episode in *Sir Thopas* where the hero falls in love in just the same fashion.

> 'Me dremed al this nyght, pardee,
> An elf-queene shal my lemman be
> And slepe under my goore.'   (787–9)

Spenser, the devoted subject of Queen Elizabeth I, evidently found much that was congenial in the fairylands of the *Wife of Bath's Tale* and *Sir Thopas*, where knights and even three-headed giants submit themselves to mysterious female powers.

Yet Chaucer's *Sir Thopas*, whether or not Spenser realized the fact, is first and foremost a literary *jeu d'esprit* – a pointed burlesque, not of romance in general, but of the English romances of his day. Modern readers acquainted only with *Sir Gawain and the Green Knight* will miss the immediate point of the joke, for Chaucer's target was a quite different kind of fourteenth-century poem, not much read today but popular in its time: older rhymes such as the romances of Bevis of Hampton and Guy of Warwick (both mentioned in *Sir Thopas*, 899), and newer works such as the two Arthurian pieces composed by Chaucer's contemporary Thomas Chester, *Lybeaus Desconus* and *Sir Launfal*.³ Chaucer signals his intention plainly enough in the first stanza:

> Listeth, lordes, in good entent,
> And I wol telle verrayment
>   Of myrthe and of solas,
> Al of a knyght was fair and gent
> In bataille and in tourneyment;
>   His name was sire Thopas.   (712–17)

No contemporary reader, and few modern ones, could mistake this for Chaucer's own poetic voice. He nowhere else uses the tail-rhyme stanza which was such a favourite with hack poets of his day: there was evidently something ludicrous, to his more fastidious ear, in the effect of the two short 'tail' lines linked by a thumping rhyme. The appeal for attention to a listening audience, vulgarly addressed as 'lordes', strikes a popular note; and the epithets 'fair and gent' seem to owe their connection with battle and tournament helplessly to the exigences of rhyme. There are also other wrong notes in the stanza more difficult for a modern ear to detect. 'Entent', here coupled with the rhyme-tag 'verrayment' (which Chaucer does not use elsewhere), always has a final *-e* in Chaucer's serious writings: 'entente'. 'Thopas' is obviously a ridiculously fanciful name for the tale's Flemish hero; but it can also be shown, more surprisingly, that to preface a knight's name with the title 'Sir' was regarded by Chaucer, as by his French contemporaries, as a vulgarism. He employs the form only in *Sir Thopas*, where it is scattered so promiscuously that even a giant can be dubbed 'Sir Olifaunt'.⁴

The next two romances to be considered, those of the Squire and the Franklin, were intended by Chaucer to stand side by side in the completed Canterbury collection. Taken together they may be distinguished from the *Wife of Bath's Tale* and *Sir Thopas* in their treatment of that essential ingredient in romance, the marvellous. Arthurian Britain, according to the Wife of Bath, is a land full of fairy, and the Flanders of Sir Thopas, though comically mundane in itself, abuts upon the 'contree of Fairye'. Both tales accept the fairy as a potent source of marvels which require no further investigation or excuse. Things are different in the Tartary of the *Squire's Tale* and the Brittany of the *Franklin's Tale*. Here wonders have, or may have, natural causes. In the *Squire's Tale* an emissary from the King of Araby and Ind brings four gifts to the Tartar king Cambyuskan and his daughter Canacee, each possessing marvellous powers: a brass horse, an unsheathed sword, a mirror, and a ring. The people of Tartary, so far from accepting these wonders as the commonplaces of romance, look for explanations and precedents. The long passage describing their various speculations (189–262) shows Chaucer at his best. How can a brass horse fly? Some think it may be 'of Fairye'; others recall the flying horse Pegasus and the wooden horse of Troy; and one sceptic suggests that it may be nothing but 'an apparence ymaad by som magyk, / As jogelours pleyen at thise feestes grete' (218–19):

> Of sondry doutes thus they jangle and trete,
> As lewed peple demeth comunly
> Of thynges that been maad moore subtilly
> Than they kan in hir lewednesse comprehende;
> They demen gladly to the badder ende. (220–4)

Since the *Squire's Tale* is unfinished, the truth of the matter is never revealed; but we may notice that the most sceptical of the explanations canvassed by the Tartars serves in the *Franklin's Tale* to account for the great marvel of the disappearing rocks. Set the task of removing all the rocks from the coast of Brittany – apparently an 'inpossible', as he complains (1009) – the lovesick squire Aurelius first prays to Apollo for a miracle, but without result; and it is only when he consults a scholar of Orleans who has learned from his books of natural magic the science of producing 'apparences' that Aurelius is able to produce the desired effect: 'It semed that alle the rokkes were aweye.' But only 'semed'. In this tale the marvellous is an illusion, like the tricks played by conjurors at feasts (1139–51).

Although the tales of the Squire and the Franklin are coupled together and share a playful interest in the rationalization of marvels, they are otherwise very different. The *Squire's Tale* presents problems because it is unfinished. It has been suggested that the 'wordes of the Frankeleyn to the Squier', which follow the fragmentary tale in the manuscripts, are to be read as an interruption of the Squire's performance, similar to, though much more polite than, the Host's interruption of *Sir Thopas*. Certainly it is not easy to imagine how the elaborate plot projected by the Squire in lines 661–9 could have been contained within the Canterbury framework, for the story was to follow the branching adventures of Cambyuskan himself and each of his three children. Of these, we have only the beginnings of a story about Canacee and the lovesick falconess, and the promise 'of aventures and of batailles' remains tantalizingly unfulfilled, as in *Sir Thopas*. Yet the Franklin's flattering comments do not sound like an interruption ('In feith, Squier, thow hast thee wel yquit': 673), and it may be questioned whether Chaucer could have trusted either his readers or the scribes who copied the *Tales* to understand them as such. His two undoubted interruptions, when Harry Bailly stops Chaucer and when the Knight stops the Monk, are both clearly signalled by the phrase 'Namoore of this!' (VII, 919, 2767). It seems preferable, all things considered, to suppose either, with Edmund Spenser, that the rest of the *Squire's Tale* has been lost (*Faerie Queene* IV, ii, 33), or else, with John Milton, that the tale was simply 'left half-told' (*Il Penseroso*, 109). In any case, the admiration expressed by both Spenser and Milton for this 'work of noblest wit' makes one hesitate to accept the opinion of some modern critics that the *Squire's Tale*, like *Sir Thopas*, is unworthy of its author.[5]

The tale contains, in fact, some of the richest passages of poetic narrative to be found in Chaucer. The description of the arrival of the Arabian emissary at the Tartar feast is as vivid as the *Gawain*-poet's description of the Green Knight's arrival at Camelot, with which it is often compared. Even better is the account of how the great feast ends in the small hours, not long before daybreak:

> The norice of digestioun, the sleep,
> Gan on hem wynke and bad hem taken keep
> That muchel drynke and labour wolde han reste;
> And with a galpying mouth hem alle he keste,
> And seyde that it was tyme to lye adoun,
> For blood was in his domynacioun.
> 'Cherisseth blood, natures freend,' quod he.
> They thanken hym galpynge, by two, by thre,
> And every wight gan drawe hym to his reste,
> As sleep hem bad; they tooke it for the beste.   (347–56)

Later poets' personifications of Sleep use language more poetical ('O soft embalmer of the still midnight'), but none is more powerful than this. The goodnight kiss so strangely bestowed with a yawning mouth by Sleep is received by the revellers with an answering yawn. The repetition of 'galpyng', supported by the haunting repetition of 'blood' in the intervening lines, creates a powerful narcotic effect, anticipating the more famous infectious yawn which brings Pope's *Dunciad* to an end. Equally vivid is the ensuing account of how young Canacee (who has prudently gone to bed early) gets up at dawn the next day to walk in the park. It is just after six in the morning,

> And in a trench forth in the park gooth she.
> The vapour which that fro the erthe glood
> Made the sonne to seme rody and brood;
> But nathelees it was so fair a sighte
> That it made alle hire hertes for to lighte.   (392–6)

The sun, discoloured and magnified by low-lying morning mists, casts a peculiar light over the ensuing scene, in which Canacee encounters the grieving falcon, perched in a tree 'for drye as whit as chalk' (409).

It seems that the *Squire's Tale* was planned as one of those complex, multi-track stories which inspired Dante (again no doubt recalling the French *Lancelot*) to speak of the 'exquisite intricacies of Arthur' – but with oriental rather than Arthurian materials. Yet the fragmentary condition of the poem leaves its precise character in doubt. The Franklin, by contrast, clearly announces his tale as belonging to that species of romance known as the Breton lay:

> Thise olde gentil Britouns in hir dayes
> Of diverse aventures maden layes,
> Rymeyed in hir firste Briton tonge,
> Whiche layes with hir instrumentz they songe
> Or elles redden hem for hir plesaunce;
> And oon of hem have I in remembraunce,
> Which I shal seyn with good wyl as I kan. (709–15)

The Breton lay had its origin in the twelfth century, when minstrels from Brittany performed their 'lays' or songs in the households of France and England. Their lays were essentially musical performances, sung to the harp in the Celtic 'Briton tonge'; but since the emotions they expressed were commonly attributed to characters in stories (Tristan's Lament, as it might be), the performers made a point of explaining the narrative context of their songs in French. It was from these accompanying narratives that the French poetess, Marie de France, claimed to derive the matter for her collection of twelve romantic verse-narratives, written in England in the time of Henry II (1154–89). The 'diverse aventures' rhymed by Marie and her imitators are conveniently characterized in the English Breton lay *Sir Orfeo*,[6] which Chaucer probably knew:

> Sum bethe of wer and sum of wo,
> And sum of joie and mirthe also,
> And sum of trecherie and of gile,
> Of old aventours that fel while,
> And sum of bourdes and ribaudy,
> And mani ther beth of fairy;
> Of al thinges that men seth
> Mest o love forsothe thay beth. (5–12)

Among these varied subjects the English poet here gives pride of place to the fairy and especially to love – the two themes which together may be taken to characterize the Breton lay tradition which Marie established. In her poems, as in such English lays as *Sir Orfeo* and *Sir Launfal*, it is not adventure or feats of arms that interest the poet, but the world of fairy and the joys and sorrows of love.

Chaucer may not have read Marie de France;[7] but it seems that the feminine type of romance which she played a part in establishing appealed to Chaucer more than the tales of derring-do which so delighted Sir Thomas Malory. In the *Franklin's Tale*, Arveragus is presented as an adventurous knight who wins Dorigen by 'many a labour, many a greet emprise' (732); but these exploits are no more than mentioned, and when after a year of marriage Arveragus sets off, as knights were supposed to do, to escape from uxorious idleness and keep honour bright by the exercise of arms, the narrative does not follow him. We are merely told that he

> Shoop hym to goon and dwelle a yeer or tweyne
> In Engelond, that cleped was eek Briteyne,
> To seke in armes worshipe and honour –
> For al his lust he sette in swich labour. (809–12)

It is startling to hear the chief business of so many romances – seeking honour in arms – thus dismissed in a single couplet. 'Swich labour'! The heart of the *Franklin's Tale* lies elsewhere. Although the Franklin does not share with the Wife and Marie their interest in the fairy, in his tale as in theirs woman plays the dominant role. The chief concern of the tale is with Dorigen and her feelings, and its most characteristic moments are when she piteously laments her absent husband (852–94) and her present dilemma (1352–1458). In these passages especially the poem comes very close to being another Legend of Good Women. Not for nothing did the Scots poet Gavin Douglas say of his master Chaucer that 'he was evir, God wait, all womanis frend'.

Like the Breton lays described in *Sir Orfeo*, the *Franklin's Tale* deals above all with love: the married love between Dorigen and Arveragus, and the passion of Aurelius for Dorigen. In one of Marie de France's poems a lady expresses the opinion that no gentleman would seek to win love by virtue of his lordly power ('par seignurie') because love can be worthy and honourable only between equals: 'Amur n'est pruz se n'est egals' (*Equitan*, 137). The same essentially courtly thought is expressed by the Franklin:

> Love wol nat been constreyned by maistrye.
> Whan maistrie comth, the God of Love anon
> Beteth his wynges, and farewel, he is gon!
> Love is a thyng as any spirit free. (764–7)

Already in the twelfth century writers saw that this doctrine created difficulties, on the one hand because the courtly lover was supposed to be his mistress's servant, and on the other because the husband was supposed to be his wife's master. Chrétien de Troyes solved this problem by affirming that, in an ideal romantic marriage, the man is at one and the same time

superior (lord), equal (friend), and inferior (servant); and it is this mysterious paradox that the Franklin invokes in his account of the relationship
between Dorigen and Arveragus (791–8). Dorigen is at once lady (superior),
wife (inferior), and love (equal) to Averagus.[8] Such is the Franklin's solution
to the problem of sovereignty in marriage. But his tale is not, as discussions of the so-called Marriage Group (the tales of the Wife of Bath, Clerk,
Merchant, and Franklin) suggest, concerned solely with love in marriage.
The same noble principle, that 'love wol nat been constreyned by maistrye',
triumphs also in the case of the squire Aurelius. By engineering the disap-
pearance of the rocks and holding Dorigen to her rash promise, Aurelius
does indeed attempt to 'constrain' her love; but in the event he cannot bring
himself to 'doon so heigh a cherlyssh wrecchednesse / Agayns franchise and
alle gentillesse' (1523–4) as to force her against her will. He releases her from
her promise.

The behaviour of Aurelius places the refusal of mastery in love in its relation to more general doctrines of 'gentillesse'. Commonly in medieval romance one character finds himself or herself subjected to the will of another
by virtue of a vow or promise, and stands to suffer in consequence. Since
nobility of soul obliges any romance hero to keep his pledged word, the
story will seem all set for a painful conclusion; but this is averted by an
answering nobility in the adversary, who waives his rights and releases the
hero from his obligations. This pattern of reciprocal nobility or 'gentillesse' –
submission on the one hand, release on the other – can be traced in the happy
endings of many romances, most obviously in the scene at the Green Chapel
in *Sir Gawain and the Green Knight*. In the *Wife of Bath's Tale*, the old hag's
attempt to 'constrain love by mastery' seems to be leading to an unhappy
conclusion when she demands, not only that the young knight should honour
his promise to marry her, as he is prepared to do, but also that he should accept her as his love: '"My love?" quod he, "nay, my dampnacioun!"' (1067).
The impasse is comically prolonged by the hag's ensuing lecture on 'gentillesse' and the virtues of poverty and old age, as if the happy ending were
to depend on the knight's readiness to abandon his prejudices against ugly
old working-class women. And so, up to a point, it does; for in response
the chastened hero goes so far as to employ a triple form of address which
implies exactly the romantic married relationship described by the Franklin:

> 'My lady and my love, and wyf so deere,
> I put me in youre wise governance.'   (1230–1)

This improved act of submission finally triggers the moment of release. Not
only does the old hag turn into a beautiful woman, but she also appears to
have waived her claim to one-sided 'maistrye':

A thousand tyme a-rewe he gan hire kisse,
And she obeyed hym in every thyng
That myghte doon hym plesance or likyng. (1254–6)

In the case of the *Franklin's Tale*, the happy ending depends upon two such moments of 'release' (the word is used at lines 1533 and 1613), both of which manifest 'franchise and gentillesse' in the characters involved. Impressed by the resolve of both Dorigen and her husband that she should honour her promise, and moved to pity by the woman's distress, Aurelius releases her from her obligation; and he himself is released from his debt to the scholar of Orleans by a further act of 'gentillesse' on the part of his creditor:

'But God forbede, for his blisful myght,
But if a clerk koude doon a gentil dede
As wel as any of yow, it is no drede!
Sire, I releesse thee thy thousand pound.' (1610–13)

Thus the tale can end, like its closest analogue in Boccaccio's *Filocolo*, with a question: 'Which was the mooste fre, as thynketh yow?' (1622). It has been suggested that the Franklin's insistence on the fact that generosity of spirit can manifest itself in clerks and squires as well as in knights betrays some uneasiness about his own claim to be accepted as a gentleman; but this is borne out neither by the historical evidence about franklins nor by the character of the tale itself. Franklins had every justification for regarding themselves as gentlemen, albeit of the country sort; and this franklin's tale, so far from appearing the work of a social climber, may claim to express more fully than any other Middle English poem that generous and humane spirit which marks the best medieval courtly writing, from the time of Marie de France and Chrétien de Troyes onwards.

Of all the tales under discussion here the *Knight's Tale* least resembles other medieval romances, French or English. Its source is an Italian poem, the *Teseida* of Giovanni Boccaccio; and the *Teseida* claims to be not a romance but an epic. It is indeed one of the first attempts in a European vernacular to match the twelve-book epics of antiquity. Its title declares this ambition: 'Teseida' from 'Teseo' (Theseus), like 'Aeneid' from 'Aeneas'. In reality, Boccaccio's poem is something of a hybrid, for the story of the two young Thebans Palemone and Arcita and their rivalry for the hand of the beautiful Emilia might well have figured, stripped of its neo-classical trappings, in one of the popular Italian romances of the time; but the poem's epic form marks it out as an altogether more ambitious, not to say pretentious, literary production. Chaucer, of course, could not incorporate a twelve-book epic in his Canterbury anthology; yet even his version, much abbreviated and with most of the epic machinery removed, is itself a complex and many-sided work, which cannot without discomfort be described simply as a romance.[9]

Literary historians sometimes associate the rise of romance in the twelfth century with the increased interest manifested at that time in individual experience. Certainly the heroes and heroines of Marie and Chrétien are activated chiefly by personal considerations, especially the desire for honour and for happiness in love. In this respect, Palamon and Arcite may be accounted typical romance heroes. Although the *Knight's Tale* is not, like so many of Chaucer's works, dominated by a female character, it is the two young knights' love for Emily which exclusively preoccupies their minds, once they have glimpsed her from their prison window. From that moment on, they are lovers and nothing else, in the best romantic tradition. Their love turns them instantly from sworn brothers into sworn rivals; and it is for love that they fight each other, first in the grove and then at the great tournament. Some readers have seen differences in character between them, but it is doubtful whether Chaucer intended any. The prison scene in which Arcite argues that, although Palamon in fact saw Emily first, he himself was the first to love her 'paramour' since Palamon mistook her for a goddess, does not prove Arcite to be a less romantic type than his companion. The argument is obviously a desperate sophistry. Arcite loves Emily quite as much as Palamon does, and in exactly the same fashion. When he later prays to Mars for victory in the tournament, he has Emily just as steadily in mind as does Palamon when he prays for Emily herself to Venus. The only significance of Arcite's choice is that it lays him open, most unhappily, to the equivocating judgement of the planet-god Saturn, who neatly resolves the problem at his expense by granting him what he asked for, not what he wanted.

If there were no more to the *Knight's Tale* than this, it might rank as a piece of sentimental courtly casuistry, to set beside the episode in the *Parliament of Fowls* where three eagles each swear undying devotion to the same female bird – the problem in both cases being to decide how such a situation can be resolved, given that 'gentils' cannot be expected to seek consolation elsewhere when disappointed in love. But the young people in the *Knight's Tale* do not pursue their private ends in isolation: they belong to a larger world with other concerns, best represented by Theseus, Duke of Athens. The full title of Boccaccio's poem was *Teseida delle Nozze d'Emilia*, or 'The Theseid, Concerning the Nuptials of Emily'. Whilst indicating the poem's romantic subject, this title gives pride of place to Duke Theseus, whose campaigns against Amazons and Thebans occupy the first two of Boccaccio's twelve books. Boccaccio's ambition to be the first Italian poet to sing of feats of arms in a manner worthy to be compared with that of Virgil or Statius

(*Teseida* XII, 84) evidently failed to inspire a similar ambition in Chaucer, who shows his customary impatience with such subjects by cutting most of the fighting out. Yet Theseus remains a dominating figure in the English poem. The Knight begins his tale with Theseus, introducing him as 'lord and governour' of Athens and conqueror of many nations. It is in these capacities that he exerts his influence over the lives of Palamon and Arcite. First, after his conquest of Thebes, he imprisons the two young Theban princes for ever and without hope of ransom – evidently treating them as war criminals along with their dead leader, Creon, who had put himself beyond the pale of humanity by refusing burial to the bodies of the dead. Later, when he comes upon the two young men fighting in the grove, it is Theseus who decrees and organizes the tournament which is to settle their fate. And finally it is Theseus who, after Arcite's death, proposes the marriage between Palamon and Emily, so securing a bond between Athens and Thebes. By these and other actions, Theseus manifests his concern for matters of foreign relations and public order which have no place in romances such as the *Wife of Bath's Tale*. Unlike Alice's Arthurian Britain, the Knight's ancient Greece has a political dimension. Its great ceremonial occasions – the tournament, the obsequies of Arcite, the parliament at which Theseus proposes the marriage – are not mere scenes in a romantic pageant. They represent man's attempts to accommodate and civilize the anarchic and inescapable facts of aggression, death, and love, as social life requires.

The attitude of Theseus to Palamon and Arcite changes in the course of the story; they are first enemies beyond the pale, then threats to public order at home, and at last friends. Insofar as they are romantic lovers, his attitude to them is best represented in the speech which he makes when he comes upon them fighting in the grove. This oration, beginning 'The god of love, a benedicite!' (1785), opens in a spirit of outright mockery. The Duke remarks pithily on the folly of lovers who can so put their lives at risk for the sake of a woman who does not even know that they love her:

> 'She woot namoore of al this hoote fare,
> By God, than woot a cokkow or an hare!'   (1809–10)

But the speech then modulates into a tone of sympathy and forgiveness, as Theseus recalls that he himself, though now a sober married man, has in his time been made a fool of by the overpowering force of love:

> 'But all moot ben assayed, hoot and coold;
> A man moot ben a fool, or yong or oold –
> I woot it by myself ful yore agon,
> For in my tyme a servant was I oon.'   (1811–14)

Theseus speaks here as a mature man who has passed through and beyond the stage of life represented by Palamon and Arcite. Like Shakespeare's *A Midsummer Night's Dream*, which owes much to Chaucer's poem, the *Knight's Tale* displays the preoccupations of young love in a large human context, exhibiting both their utter naturalness and also their funny side. As Shakespeare's Theseus observes:

> Lovers and madmen have such seething brains,
> Such shaping fantasies, that apprehend
> More than cool reason ever comprehends.   (v, i, 4–6)

There is also a still larger context within which Chaucer sets his romantic adventure – no less than the universe itself, represented in the *Knight's Tale* by the classical gods. In the pre-Christian Brittany of the *Franklin's Tale* Apollo can evidently do nothing for his votary, but in pagan Athens the gods wield real power.[10] It is only when the issue between Palamon and Arcite is taken up by Venus and Mars that it achieves a kind of solution. Yet that solution, engineered by 'the pale Saturnus the colde', raises profound questions about the order of things – questions similar to those raised by Dorigen in her complaint to God about the black rocks which, she says, 'semen rather a foul confusion / Of werk than any fair creacion' (869–70). These two poems have a philosophical dimension lacking in the other Canterbury romances. What chiefly interests Chaucer, however, is not so much the philosophical ideas themselves as the way human beings select and adopt them according to mood or occasion. If Dorigen is prompted by the Breton rocks to reflect on problems of evil and pain in the universe (865–93), it is perhaps only because they threaten her beloved husband. Once he is safely home, one hears no more of that particular difficulty, just as in the third book of *Troilus and Criseyde* Criseyde stops thinking about 'fals felicitee' (III, 814) once she discovers that Troilus is not in fact, as Pandarus has maintained, angry with her. Similarly in the *Knight's Tale*, imprisonment prompts Palamon and Arcite to some deep Boethian reflections on the vanity of human wishes (1251–67) and the miseries of life (1303–27); but once the young men regain their freedom, such considerations are soon forgotten. Some readers have found in the more settled pessimism of Theseus's father Egeus the true voice of the tale: 'This world nys but a thurghfare ful of wo' (2847). But one might equally well see that speech as a typical old man's utterance, or as a customary half-consolatory response to the fact of death. It is rather Theseus who, from his commanding position as a mature man and a 'governour', makes the most impressive philosophical utterance in the poem, when he addresses the Athenian parliament: 'The Firste Moevere of the cause above . . .' (2987). This oration (the opening of which Chaucer derived not from Boccaccio but from Boethius) expounds a universal order in which partial and transitory things have their origin in a first cause which is itself eternal and unchanging. Since death is inevitable in the sublunary world, Theseus argues, it would be folly for Palamon and Emily to go on grieving for Arcite – especially since the circumstances of his death were so honourable:

> 'Why grucchen we, why have we hevynesse,
> That goode Arcite, of chivalrie flour,
> Departed is with duetee and honour
> Out of this foule prisoun of this lyf?' (3058–61)

Yet even these grand truths are being used – and in this case for a very practical purpose – to introduce the proposal that the Theban prince should marry Emily. Theseus speaks not as a philosopher but as a governor, whose business it is to make the best of an awkward human situation, and who is also (we may infer from lines 2973–4) interested in linking the royal houses of Athens and Thebes by marriage. He is so little a philosopher that, in flat contradiction of his earlier argument, he can go on to offer Emily and Palamon the prospect of 'o parfit joye, lastynge everemo' (3072) in their marriage.

The *Knight's Tale* does indeed end in the 'parfit joye' of mutual love in marriage:

> For now is Palamon in alle wele,
> Lyvynge in blisse, in richesse, and in heele,
> And Emelye hym loveth so tendrely,
> And he hire serveth so gentilly,
> That nevere was ther no word hem bitwene
> Of jalousie or any oother teene.
> Thus endeth Palamon and Emelye;
> And God save al this faire compaignye! (3101–8)

This is the customary happy ending of romance. Each of the two other Canterbury romances completed by Chaucer leaves its hero and heroine united in the same fairy-tale felicity: 'parfit joye' in the *Wife of Bath's Tale* (1258), 'sovereyn blisse' in the *Franklin's Tale* (1552). Yet it is a measure of the greater seriousness of the *Knight's Tale* that the happy ending here seems a fragile and questionable thing, shadowed by thoughts of suffering and death and especially by the memory of Arcite's dying words (2777–9):

> 'What is this world? What asketh men to have?
> Now with his love, now in his colde grave
> Allone, withouten any compaignye.'

NOTES

1. For fuller discussion of four of the five romances considered here, see ch. 4, 'Romances', in Derek Pearsall, *The Canterbury Tales* (London, 1985); and for the *Wife of Bath's Tale*, see pp. 86–91 there.
2. The three English analogues are printed in *Sources and Analogues of Chaucer's Canterbury Tales*, eds. W. F. Bryan and G. Dempster (Chicago, 1941). See John Gower's tale of Florent, *Confessio Amantis*, I, 1841–6; *The Marriage of Sir Gawaine*, part 2, stanzas 16–17; *The Weddynge of Sir Gawen and Dame Ragnell*, 691–3.
3. Chester was possibly an acquaintance. A Thomas de Chestre appears together with Galfridus Chaucer among those ransomed in 1360. Both men had been captured by the French. See *Chaucer Life-Records*, eds. M. M. Crow and C. C. Olson (Oxford, 1966), pp. 23–4. For all his lack of interest as a poet in fighting, Chaucer was not without military experience.
4. For details of these and other wrong notes in *Thopas*, see the annotations in the *Riverside Chaucer*. Further discussion in Helen Cooper, *The Canterbury Tales*, Oxford Guides to Chaucer (Oxford, 1989), pp. 299–309.
5. For a survey of critical responses to the tale, including those 'ironic' readings which see it as designed to expose weaknesses either in the romance genre or in the young Squire himself, see *The Squire's Tale*, ed. D. C. Baker, *Variorum Edition of the Works of Geoffrey Chaucer*, vol. 2 (Norman, Okla., 1990), pp. 59–74. David Lawton gives a strong non-ironic account in ch. 5 of his *Chaucer's Narrators* (Cambridge, 1985). On the tale as a fragment, see J. Burrow, 'Poems without Endings', *Studies in the Age of Chaucer*, 13 (1991), 17–37.
6. *Sir Orfeo*, ed. A. J. Bliss, 2nd edn (Oxford, 1966).
7. See, however, Jill Mann, 'Chaucerian Themes and Style in the *Franklin's Tale*' in *The New Pelican Guide to English Literature*, ed. Boris Ford, vol. 1, Part 1 (Harmondsworth, 1982), pp. 133–53.
8. So, at the end of *Cligès*, the romance by Chrétien de Troyes, the heroine Fénice marries the hero but is said to continue to be his *amie* and his *dame* as well as his *fame* (lines 6629–38). These terms correspond to the Franklin's 'love', 'lady', and 'wife' (lines 796–7). What Chaucer calls the 'law of love' is the same in both texts.
9. On the *Knight's Tale* in relation to the *Teseida* and to the Latin epic tradition, see David Anderson, *Before the Knight's Tale* (Philadelphia, Pa., 1988).
10. Chaucer understands the gods as representing, in modern reality, the planets which bear their names. On astrology in the *Knight's Tale*, see Jill Mann in this volume (pp. 107–8), and Cooper, *The Canterbury Tales*, pp. 77–84.

10

DEREK PEARSALL

The *Canterbury Tales* II: comedy

Comedy of one kind or another is present in a large number of the *Canterbury Tales*, and pervasive in the links between tales, but we are concerned here with those tales where the narrative structure and expectations are those of comedy as a specific genre. There are six such tales, those of the Miller, Reeve, Shipman, Merchant, Friar, and Summoner, and a seventh, that of the Cook, which is left unfinished but which was certainly going to belong to the genre. The fact that we know this, from only fifty-eight lines, is an indication of the general firmness of the initial structure of expectation of Chaucerian comedy, the codifiability of the preliminary ground-rules, whatever strain or defiance those rules may be subjected to in Chaucer's subsequent development of the story. Anticipatory indications of the nature of a particular tale are often given by what we know or suspect of the character of the pilgrim who tells it, and the comic or satirically abusive prologues to five of these tales are important in creating expectation; but even without such clues we should know, from elements built into the narrative structure, the rules of the narrative game we were being invited to play.

The time is the present, and the story is introduced as an up-to-date report on a contemporary 'slice-of-life'. There is nothing of what 'olde stories tellen us' (*Knight's Tale*, 859). The place is the homely known world of town or village, usually in England. The Miller's and Reeve's tales are slily set in or near the two university towns of Oxford and Cambridge (Trumpington is 'nat fer fro Cantebrigge': I, 3921), as if to give a broad and impartial view of the principal preoccupations and activities of university students, and the *Cook's Tale* is set in London, 'oure citee' (4365). The *Friar's Tale* speaks of 'my contree' (1301), again communicating that sense of the known and familiar, while the *Summoner's Tale* is set in Holderness, in Yorkshire. The French setting of the *Shipman's Tale* in 'Seint-Denys', with Paris and Bruges figuring in the action, would have seemed homely enough, and quite different from another French setting, that of the *Franklin's Tale*, near Penmarch, in Brittany, with all its romantic associations. The *Merchant's Tale* is set in

Pavia, in Lombardy, which may have had a reputation in English eyes as a 'city of sin': whatever the connotations, in this as in other respects the *Merchant's Tale* proclaims itself 'different'. Apart from these matters of setting, in time and place, there is also a distinctive tone about Chaucer's comic tales which helps to mark them off as a genre, a reductive tone, resembling a clinical analysis of the inhabitants of a zoo. Only in this type of tale would we be told of a merchant 'That riche was, for which men helde hym wys' (*Shipman's Tale*, 2) or of the desire of an old man for a wife, 'Were it for hoolynesse or for dotage' (*Merchant's Tale*, 1253) or be given an unoutraged description of a wife 'that heeld for contenance / A shoppe, and swyved for hir sustenance' (*Cook's Tale*, 4421–2).

More important than any of these features, however, in contributing to the distinctiveness of the sense of genre in Chaucer's comic tales are the assumptions we are asked to share in reading them. In romance, to take a contrasting type of tale, we are asked to accept for the purposes of the story that there are noble ideals of behaviour, fidelity to which is the means through which human existence is validated, through which life is shown to be meaningful. So Arveragus speaks of 'trouthe' (*Franklin's Tale*, 1479), and Arcite, in dying, of 'trouthe, honour, knyghthede' and the other values he admires (*Knight's Tale*, 2789). In religious tales and saints' legends, an equally self-transcending system of values operates, in this case proving the significance of life through the demonstration of its ultimate insignificance in relation to life eternal. Comedy sets all this aside, and asserts that there are no values, secular or religious, more important than survival and the satisfaction of appetite. Characters who may be temporarily under the illusion that things are otherwise, such as Absolon or January, are given short shrift. The injunction is not 'be noble', or 'be good', but 'be smart'. Our extreme satisfaction in seeing Nicholas, in the *Miller's Tale*, receive his comeuppance is not based on a perception of moral justice being done – the idea that he is 'scalded in the towte' (3853) because he has committed adultery is too trite for words – but on the comic justice of 'the biter bit'. Nicholas makes himself vulnerable because he ceases to be smart, and tries to play the same trick on Absolon that Alison has already played: this is not the behaviour of a cunning animal, which is what the comic hero is expected to be.

It will be seen that Chaucerian comedy, on this definition of it, differs markedly from comedy as classically defined, that is, as a socially normative literary form, working to correct our behaviour through making us laugh at the ridiculousness of vice and folly. This is the comedy of dramatists like Jonson or Molière, or of theorists like Bergson or Meredith.[1] In Chaucer, though, the social norms are not clearly displayed and moral norms are often openly subverted, as when the narrator of the *Miller's Tale*, after licking his lips over the description of Alison, comments in conclusion:

> She was a prymerole, a piggesnye,
> For any lord to leggen in his bedde,
> Or yet for any good yeman to wedde. (3268–70)

For the reader to reassert the moral norm by attributing the neglect or sub-version of moral value to the narrator's inadequacy is a trick that has often been tried, but mostly by people who think laughter unimportant or who have misunderstood the rules of this particular game. This is not to say, of course, that satire, done from well-established normative positions, is not present in these comic tales: the complacency and gullibility of John the carpenter, the ludicrous philandering of Absolon, are classics of satirical comedy. But the tales as a whole are not satirical comedies: one would have to ask, satirical of *what*? and Chaucer will not return any simple answer, or any complicated one for that matter. The case may seem different with the Friar's and Summoner's tales, but even there the satire is made part of a mutual exchange of abuse and thereby pushed away from any authoritative moral centre. The wickedness of summoners and friars remains the theme of the two tales, respectively, but not their *point*.

At the same time that one rejects moralistic interpretations of Chaucerian comedy, one should not allow one's enthusiasm for immorality to go so far as to encourage an alternative kind of assertiveness – that the comic tales are a 'celebration of life', a universal subversion of established values, a kick up the behind for all orthodoxies. The popularization of the views of Bakhtin in the West has led to a good deal of insistence on the presence of this kind of 'festive comedy' in Chaucer, as in Shakespeare.[2] In a certain basic way, of course, laughter always offers a kind of psychic release which is assertive of life, especially when we laugh at the blaspheming of what is revered, the breaking of taboos, the open practice of verbal obscenity, the explicit depiction of excretory and sexual functions. There is also release of another kind in the denouements of these comic tales, where in every case the climax, after much build-up of tension and expectation, involves the final acting-out of some trick, accompanied by delightful surprise and reversal. The moments when we realize that Nicholas's call for water – '"Help! Water! Water! Help, for Goddes herte!"' (3815) – is going to be construed by the carpenter in his tub as the announcement of the predicted deluge, or that Aleyn, thinking he has got into bed with his fellow student, has snuggled up to the miller, are moments of almost cathartic physical release. Laughter here is a renewal of vitality: it does not, however, mean anything beyond itself, in relation to life (as distinct from art), or constitute a 'celebration of life', that is, of life in its physical functions (as if those functions were more 'real' than intellectual, emotional, or spiritual functions). Chaucer's comic tales exist no more to celebrate life than to criticize immorality: 'realism' is not in question, and the narrative assumptions we are asked to make are no more realistic than those we are asked to make in romance.

It is important at this stage to introduce a distinction between the Friar's and Summoner's tales and the other four (or four-and-a-bit) tales, and to appropriate the technical term fabliau to apply to the latter group. The term is often used broadly for all comic tales of low life involving trickery, but there is much advantage in restricting it, in discussing Chaucer, to the tales involving marriage and sex, and setting aside the Friar's and Summoner's tales for later discussion. The four tales remaining are capable of quite strict definition as fabliaux, as tales, that is, in which a bourgeois husband is duped or tricked into conniving at the free award of his wife's sexual favours to a clever young man. Such tales are widespread in European tradition, and well known from being included in such numbers in Boccaccio's *Decameron* or in French collections such as the *Cent Nouvelles Nouvelles* ('A Hundred New Stories'). There are very few examples in English: indeed, Chaucer's are almost the only examples of the genre as more strictly defined. It was long believed, because of a convenient assumption about social class and social morality, that the fabliaux could only have been enjoyed by the lower classes, or the bourgeoisie at best, but this belief has been shown to be unfounded,[3] and indeed it seems on the face of it unlikely, given that the pillars of petit-bourgeois society are constantly the objects of ridicule, and that the humour of the stories often relies on quite a subtle understanding of the courtly behaviour that is travestied.

In practice, Chaucer blurs this distinctive sense of audience, this sense of a sophisticated courtly group laughing at the animal antics of their inferiors, perhaps because his idea of his potential audience in the *Canterbury Tales* is much more generous and comprehensive. He allocates the telling of the tales, by a shrewd dramatic stroke, to the kind of people that they are about, suggesting half-playfully a kind of merging of pilgrimage-reality and tale-reality (the appearance in the *Miller's Tale* of a servant who, like the Miller himself (3129), is called Robyn and has a special way with doors (3466; cf. *General Prologue* 550) is the most whimsically audacious example of this), and subsuming the real audience (us) in the fictional one (the pilgrims). He also apologizes in advance, in the *General Prologue*, for telling such coarse tales, explaining that, as an honest reporter, he must report exactly what was said, however 'rudeliche and large' (734) he has to speak, and he returns to these tongue-in-cheek excuses in introducing the *Miller's Tale*. It is hard to believe that Chaucer was genuinely embarrassed by what he was doing: it is all part of the fun, and all part of the system of dramatic subterfuges that Chaucer has worked out in the *Canterbury Tales* to give himself the freedom he needs to do what he wants to do as a writer. The freedom, however won, was worth winning, for the four fabliaux are, without exception, amongst the supreme achievements of his artistry.

The association of fabliau with romance needs a word more said about it, since the two literary forms seem to exist in a complementary relationship. Romance asserts the possibility that men may behave in a noble and self-transcending manner; fabliau declares the certainty that they will always behave like animals. The one portrays men as superhuman, the other portrays them as subhuman. Neither is 'true' or realistic, though we might say that our understanding of what *is* true gains depth from having different slanting lights thrown upon reality, so that beneficial shock, enrichment, invigoration are given to our perception of the world. Romance and fabliau complement one another, and Chaucer encourages us to look at them thus by setting the *Knight's Tale* and the *Miller's Tale* side by side. Each type of story makes a selection of human experience in accord with its own narrative conventions or rules. Out of the interlocking of these and other different types of story, in the general medieval hierarchy of genres, or in the *Canterbury Tales* as a whole, grows the social relevance of literary forms, the fabliau amongst them.

The narrative structure of Chaucer's four fabliaux has already been briefly described. Before I go on to deal in detail with the manner in which he works variations on this structure in individual tales, it may be worth pausing to refine the model a little. The basic ingredients are three, a husband, a wife, and an intruder, though the functions of the last two may be duplicated in more complex plots. The intruder is always a man: it is possible to imagine a modern fabliau in which it was a woman, but not a medieval one. The husband belongs to the petit-bourgeoisie, or, if that term means nothing in the Middle Ages, to the world of successful tradesmen; the *Merchant's Tale* is, as often, exceptional, in that the husband is a 'knyght'. The wife is younger than her husband, or, if not younger, still with some unsatisfied sexual potential. This is briefly and devastatingly indicated, for instance, in an aside in the *Reeve's Tale*, when John leaps on the good wife: 'So myrie a fit ne hadde she nat ful yoore' (4230). The wife of the fabliaux is not, it must be stressed, promiscuous, and there is no suggestion that the affair in which she is engaged is a matter of regular occupation. This is not because Chaucer is mealy-mouthed where Boccaccio is (quite often) frank, but because he can thereby increase the amount and quality of the intrigue. The 'intruder' is usually younger than the husband, or at least, as in the *Shipman's Tale*, explicitly more sexually active. More importantly, he belongs to a different class, being usually a student or other kind of cleric or religious, and therefore more clever, flexible, and mobile than those with whom he is temporarily (as lodger or guest) accommodated. He is a member of a classless intellectual elite who, in being shown as a predator upon the conventional marital and materialistic values of the bourgeois, can be brought into an implicit alliance with the aristocracy. The *Merchant's Tale* is once more the exception, and there is no doubt that the nastiness of the tale is much increased by the fact that the intruder is a squire of January's own household, and furthermore one who plays a subordinate part in the intrigue to the wife.

It is not difficult to speak of Chaucer's fabliaux in this way, with the plot-elements and characters abstracted as functions, and it is not a distortion of the nature of the fabliaux to draw attention to the narrative rules upon which they operate. But the success of Chaucer's poetry is in the manner in which he works variations on these set patterns, defies expectation, tests the tolerance of the form and the habitual perceptions of the reader, and creates four poems which are as enjoyable for the ways in which each is unique as for the ways in which they fit a pattern.

The *Miller's Tale* is Chaucer's greatest achievement in the genre, and in many ways the most perfectly accomplished of all the *Canterbury Tales*. It seems to overflow with high spirits, and to convey, despite the nasty and painful events it describes, a sort of genial gusto. It is full of music and amorous serenading, whether Nicholas practising on his 'gay sautrie' (3213) and singing *Angelus ad Virginem* (thinking, perhaps, of himself as the angel Gabriel and Alison as the prospective 'virgin') or Absolon setting about his midnight 'gyternynge' (3363) at the famous 'shot-wyndowe'. The allusions to music often have a strong sexual suggestion, as when Nicholas turns his attention to his instrument after his exciting interview with Alison:

> Whan Nicholas had doon thus everideel
> And thakked hire aboute the lendes weel,
> He kiste hire sweete and taketh his sawtrie,
> And pleyeth faste, and maketh melodie.   (3303–6)

The most notable of these allusions, and the one that seems to capture the spirit of the tale, is the brief description of the love-making of Nicholas and Alison after they have tiptoed down from their tubs into the vacant marital bed: 'Ther was the revel and the melodye' (3652). The little touch of lyricism here is not dissipated by the further musical allusion that follows, when we are told that they went on enjoying themselves 'Til that the belle of laudes gan to rynge, / And freres in the chauncel gonne synge' (3655–6). A contrast between the two kinds of 'music' is implied, but with no more than genial perfunctoriness. The notion that some critics have that the religious reference acts as a reminder of Nicholas and Alison's wickedness is heavy-handed in the extreme. Nicholas and Alison have their 'bisynesse', and the friars have theirs: there is no competition. References to the church and the religious life of the community are frequent in the tale, but essentially as part of the unnoticed furniture of everyday urban life and part of the tale's incomparable substantiality. That Alison should go, after being well 'thakked aboute the lendes' by Nicholas, to the parish church, 'Cristes owene werkes for to wirche' (3308), is charmingly inapposite, but to call it 'ironical' would be to load the tale with a moral freight it has no purpose to bear.

The quality of lyricism in the tale is further enhanced by its exuberant travesty of courtly language and behaviour. It is a very 'literary' fabliau. The elaborate description of Alison, for instance, comes at just the point where the heroine would be described in a romance, and it is a beautifully observed parody of the conventional top-to-toe inventory. In itself, too, it is a subtle mixture of the vulgar and the artfully seductive: bedizened in black and white silk, in the latest out-of-date provincial fashion, and with a brooch planted in her cleavage 'As brood as is the boos of a bokeler' (3266), she is yet as lithe as a weasel, 'wynsynge' like a young colt, and her breath smells, unforgettably, one would think, of apples 'leyd in hey or heeth' (3262). To try to 'contain' such a picture within a moral or satirical frame of reference would be to deny the irresistible impression of animal vitality, indeed of innocence. So too when she acts out her little scene with Nicholas: he is the impassioned lover, ready to 'spille' if his desires are not satisfied (3278), and she is the coy mistress, threatening to cry out (but not too loud) if he does not remove his hand from her 'queynte'. She does not thoroughly understand why she should be, even temporarily, under this nice restraint (any more than a colt 'in the trave': 3282), but she obliges with a decent if brief show of reluctance.

Absolon, of course, is a more obvious satirical target, and his efforts to play the courtly lover are genuinely ludicrous. He has had some success with the flighty local barmaids, but he is a deal too circumspect for your true courtly lover, who would not expect to have to take a nap in order to prepare for his night's doings (3685) nor to chew 'greyn and lycorys' (3690) to make his breath sweet. When he arrives at the 'shot-wyndowe' to devastate Alison with his guitar, he gets everything wrong: the echoes of the Song of Songs (3698–707) are in a good courtly tradition, but not the emphasis on his 'sweating' for love nor on his desire for her as that of the 'lamb after the tete'. He also calls her, twice, his 'lemman', which is a coarse form of address, and hilariously inappropriate to his pretensions as a lover.[4]

In addition to the lyricism and gaiety that these allusions give to the tale, there is also an unexpected generosity, as well as a great fertility of comic invention, in Chaucer's portrayal of his characters. John the carpenter is the most notable example: set up at the start as that traditionally licensed victim of satire, the old man who marries a young wife, he is portrayed as richly complacent and gullible. The congratulations he offers himself on his simple honest Christian faith, and the way it has helped him avoid getting into the state Nicholas is in, are unforgettable:

> 'I thoghte ay wel how that it sholde be!
> Men sholde nat knowe of Goddes pryvetee.
> Ye, blessed be alwey a lewed man
> That noght but oonly his bileve kan!' (3453–6)

His readiness to accept Nicholas's fantastic story of the coming flood shows another kind of simple faith, and perhaps no great reluctance to be cast in the role of a second Noah. Yet his concern for Nicholas, who has been missing all weekend, is quite good-natured and unselfish, and his first reaction to the news of the flood is to think of his wife: "'Allas, my wyf! / And shal she drenche? Allas, myn Alisoun!'" (3522–3). There is enough here to give us a twinge of sympathy, but no more. Chaucer's control of our emotional responses of engagement and sympathy, responses such as are totally alien in the tradition of fabliau, is consummate. He allows us the delightful apprehension of a momentary intrusion of feeling, and then resumes his splendid fooling.

The high spirits of the tale are of course best exemplified in Nicholas, who has all the attributes of 'our hero', the master of plotting and connoisseur of intrigue. Notice what lengths he goes to in order to secure Alison's company on *Monday* night when the carpenter has been away in Oseney all the previous weekend. To have sneaked into bed with Alison then would have been, one feels, no challenge. When he is describing the escape from the flood, one senses that he has almost got carried away in the delighted contemplation of his own imaginative creation:

> 'Thanne shaltou swymme as myrie, I undertake,
> As dooth the white doke after hire drake.
> Thanne wol I clepe, "How, Alison! How, John!
> Be myrie, for the flood wol passe anon."
> And thou wolt seyn, "Hayl, maister Nicholay!
> Good morwe, I se thee wel, for it is day."' (3575–80)

Nicholas's wit and vitality carry all before them, but his downfall comes when he tries to repeat the trick Alison played on Absolon: this is a lapse from the high standard of cunning and inventiveness we expect of him, and he is duly punished. Absolon deserves his moment of triumph. Alison, by contrast, escapes scot-free, and quite properly so, according to the laws of the comic fabliau, not because she has done nothing wrong but because she has done nothing that betrays her nature. Throughout she behaves like the healthy animal she is, quick, alert, high-spirited, where Absolon has fantasies of the various animals he might be – a lamb seeking its mother's teat, or a cat playing with Alison-mouse (3347). The ending of the tale, with its catalogue of punishments (3850–3), has the air of justice meted out, but it is not a moral justice.

Fertility and richness of invention characterize the tale, but also a high degree of technical accomplishment. The dropping of hints is unobtrusively neat: the mention of Nicholas's skill in astrology and his ability to predict 'droghte or elles shoures' (3196) and of Absolon's unfortunate squeamish-ness of farting (3338) are delightful anticipations of significances still to be fulfilled. Absolon's certainty that the itching of his mouth is a sign of kissing 'at the leeste wey' (3680) is one of many prophetic puns that detonate by delayed action. The careful specification of the height above street-level of the 'shot-wyndowe' – 'Unto his brest it raughte, it was so lowe' (3696) – is of course vital to the ensuing action. Most cunningly devised is the long dor-mancy of the flood-plot, and the reader's sudden realization that Nicholas's cry for water will reactivate it. This is a sublime moment of almost pure aesthetic pleasure. Add to this what Muscatine has called the 'overpowering substantiality' of the tale,[5] and one sees the loving care Chaucer has lavished upon it. The density of detail, the sense of town life extending into deep perspective behind the foreground action, is extraordinary.[6] It is present in the architecture of John's house, down to the gable that looks out upon the garden, over the stable (3572); in the ramblingly uninformative account of John's whereabouts given by the anonymous 'cloisterer' (3661); in the noc-turnal activities of Gerveys the blacksmith (3761), who had to work at night, of course, because the things he was mending were needed by day; and per-haps above all in the series of references to the mystery plays. The bustle and business of the street-plays comes vividly alive in the allusions to the Miller himself speaking 'in Pilates voys' (3124) and to Absolon playing Herod 'upon a scaffold hye' (3384) – perhaps in a slightly 'camp', effeminate way? And Chaucer hints mischievously at the effect mystery plays might have on the average citizen in describing John's spectacular ignorance of the whole point of the Noah story.

The *Reeve's Tale* has much of this same substantiality, in its account of the Cambridge college background, the activity of flour-milling, the weary chase through the fens after the runaway horse, and above all in the evocation of the darkened bedroom of the night's encounters. It is remarkable, though, how a tale so similar in structure and technique can create such a totally different impression. Gusto and geniality give way to a spirit of meanness

and vindictiveness; the only music to be heard is the cacophony of the family
snoring (4165) and the only 'courtly' allusions are in the contemptuous reference to the miller's wife's absurd pretensions to be a lady (3942–3). Both
the *Miller's Tale* and the *Reeve's Tale* make a stronger impact individually
because of the effect of contrast, a measure of Chaucer's skill in juxtaposition
in his mature work on the *Canterbury Tales*.

The tale seems to be concentrated on its destructive purpose, and everything serves the Reeve's revenge upon the Miller. Where the *Miller's Tale*
began with a seductive description of Alison, the Reeve begins by presenting
the miller of his tale as a target to be attacked and destroyed. His violence,
his thievery, and his pride in his lineage are singled out for attention, and
then systematically rebuked and punished in the most painful and humiliating way. He himself is beaten up not only by the students but by his own
wife, his ill-gotten flour is restored to the students by his own daughter,
and that daughter herself, of whom he had such hopes, is now thoroughly
shop-soiled:

> 'Who dorste be so boold to disparage
> My doghter, that is come of swich lynage?'   (4271–2)

Even his hospitality in allowing the students to lodge with him is given no
chance to register sympathetically because of his sneering remarks about the
students' book-learning (4122–6). His wife is portrayed with open contempt,
and there is no hint of affection in the picture of his daughter and her coarsely
nubile charms:

> This wenche thikke and wel ygrowen was,
> With kamus nose and eyen greye as glas,
> With buttokes brode and brestes rounde and hye.
> But right fair was hire heer; I wol nat lye.   (3973–6)

The students themselves have nothing of Nicholas about them and are not
attractive in their own right. They are oafish fellows, and Chaucer takes some
care to present them as northerners and to have them speak in a passable
imitation of fourteenth-century northern dialect: that the miller can be shown
to be outwitted and put down by such bumpkins makes him even more to
be derided.

A particular edge is given to the tale's nastiness by the manner in which
sexual activity is portrayed. Chaucer has removed from the original story,
as told in a French fabliau,[7] the element of sexual attraction that first draws
the one student to the daughter and then the other to the wife. Aleyn and
John act simply out of revenge and because the family snoring is keeping
them awake. There are no musical allusions or lyrical overtones: they jump

on the women like animals: 'He priketh harde and depe as he were mad' (4231) and the fact that the women find they like it impugns only the miller's pride and virility. The little parody of the *aube*-scene (the lovers must part because of the approach of day) has Aleyn taking his leave of the daughter, Malyne, more because he is exhausted, it appears, than anything:

> Aleyn wax wery in the dawenynge,
> For he had swonken al the longe nyght.   (4234–5)

His vows of undying fidelity are perfunctorily echoed by Malyne, who has the grace 'almoost' to weep (4248), but who is chiefly concerned to hand over her father's hard-won cake of flour.

Systematically, it appears, those touches of lyricism and generosity that graced the *Miller's Tale* have been stripped away, and the fabliau used as a machine for the Reeve's vindictive purposes. Something of the tale's special tone might be related to the character of the Reeve, who seems bent on revenge even before he has heard the supposed attack on himself (also a carpenter) in the *Miller's Tale*. He is the kind of man who makes a profession of taking offence, and who makes a slimy pretence of self-righteousness to cover his envious and suspicious nature. His own prologue is a remarkably disgusting piece of self-ingratiating self-abasement. In pressing the narrator upon our attention in this way, Chaucer is bound to make us conscious of him, at least at one level, as we read his tale: certainly the sense of vindictive purpose is strong, and there are pointed allusions to the quasi-legal sanctions that justify getting one's own back (4181, 4321). But it would be wrong to make this 'the meaning' of the tale: the rumpus in the bedroom at the end is in the best manner of high-spirited fabliau, and the most we might say is that Chaucer has given our laughter an edge of uneasiness by having us share it with the Reeve. From a larger point of view, one might see the *Reeve's Tale* as the inseparable companion of the *Miller's Tale*. They are the Jekyll and Hyde of fabliau; the one necessarily belongs to and comments upon the other.

The *Shipman's Tale* has no dramatic context in the pilgrimage, and its brevity has often encouraged people to think of it as 'basic' fabliau. It is in fact a subtle and highly contrived variation on the form which has its own individual character. At first, by comparison with the Miller's and Reeve's tales, it seem easiest to characterize by negatives. It has no violence and no very explicit depictions of sexual activity, no courtly allusions, no lyrical fantasies, and no one seems very much upset by what happens. The narrator seems quite happy with the world he inhabits, and there is very little satirical comment, except such as is implicit in reporting such a world without comment.

It is in terms of such blandness that the tale is most acutely characterized. Throughout no one speaks openly or directly or honestly to anyone else, whether in rage, scorn or desire. Everyone is politely diplomatic, careful not to offend and not to reveal any real purpose or feeling. The scene between the wife and the monk in the garden is a beautifully decorous comedy of manners, with each delicate advance towards mutual understanding carefully planned and signalled. The monk's playful insinuation of her husband's inadequacy in bed (at which he has the grace himself to blush) encourages the wife to speak of her other dissatisfactions; they exchange vows of secrecy; the monk discovers that he has always been waiting for this moment of intimacy; the wife's need of money seals the bond. It is a market-driven seduction scene, and in some strange way the exchange of money seems to legitimize rather than corrupt the encounter. Nothing of this comes out in the open, of course. The wife sees what she does as a perfectly reasonable business transaction, and the monk, though there may be an element of calculation in his carefully regulated tipping of the members of the merchant's household (46), and certainly an accomplished skill in his technique of asking for a loan (269–80), is not portrayed as a scrounger or a predator.

The merchant, however, is the most unexpected beneficiary of the general complacency. He too is treated soberly, even generously. His avarice is not stressed, except by his wife, and he has a careful tedious explanation to his wife of why he has to spend so much time on his accounts:

> 'Wyf,' quod this man, 'litel kanstow devyne
> The curious bisynesse that we have' . . .   (224–5)

He speaks as if this is not the first time he has had to do this kind of explaining. The same quality of carefully fostered good nature comes over in his response to the monk's request for a loan. It is a generous response, of course, and the hundred francs are immediately promised. The promise, however, is followed by the careful qualification:

> 'But o thyng is, ye knowe it wel ynogh
> Of chapmen, that hir moneie is hir plogh.'   (287–8)

He wants to remind the monk that ready money is not easily come by in the finance business, that it is not a little thing for him to do, that it *is* a loan, at the same time that he wants to appear generous. One recognizes the desire to be thought well of, or to think well of oneself, and it comes out again in the merchant's later rebuke to his wife for not having told him of the return of the loan. He is annoyed because he feels he might have been thought by the monk to have arranged to meet him in Paris in order to ask for his money back. We are specifically told that this was not his intention (338), and the merchant cannot bear the thought of a generous intention wasted.

The wife has her own problem when she hears of what the monk has in fact done – that is, borrow the money from her husband to give to her (in exchange for a night in bed with her) so that she can pay her debts. She now owes the money to her husband too. But sex comes to the rescue again, and she pays her husband in the same coin as she paid the monk. So the hundred francs has gone the rounds, and so has the wife, and no one seems much the worse for the experience. In fact, there is hardly a ripple on the surface of surburban life. There is a good deal of insight in this tale into the power of money, into the nature of sex as a commodity, and into the subterfuges of self-deception. The tale is coldly exhilarating in its total disregard of familiar moral decencies.

The *Merchant's Tale* is quite different, and certainly Chaucer's most ambitious exercise in the fabliau form, so ambitious in fact that it threatens to explode the form into something like a modern 'black comedy'. It is a more powerful poem than the *Miller's Tale*, and expands on the technique of that tale with extensive lyrical interpolations (the marriage ceremony, 1709–41; January's love song, 2138–48), rhetorical digressions (e.g. 1783–94, 2057–68), a long mock-encomium on marriage at the beginning, and a mythological episode of Pluto and Proserpina at the end. There are, as in the *Miller's Tale*, many subtle verbal anticipations and echoings: January's comparison of his sexuality to the evergreen laurel (1466) is echoed in the laurel in the garden where he is cuckolded (2037); the wax to which he compares the pliability of the desired wife (1430) is echoed in the wax that the wife uses to make a copy of the key to the garden (2117). The fabliau nucleus is still there, in the episode of the pear-tree, but is almost an afterthought to a rich and strange performance.

One was aware of a sneering malevolence in the *Reeve's Tale*. Here that tone is continuous and raised to a high pitch of stridency. The opening account of January's desire to get married drips with contempt for such old fools, and the mock-encomium of marriage is openly sarcastic at times rather than mockingly ironical. The description of the marriage ceremony is cynically reductive: the priest comes forth,

> And seyde his orisons, as is usage,
> And croucheth hem, and bad God sholde hem blesse,
> And made al siker ynogh with hoolynesse.   (1706–8)

Not merely this travesty of marriage, but marriage as such, seems to be sneered at, and the same Thersitean voice is heard in the comments on January's energetic imitation of the Song of Songs: 'Swiche olde lewed wordes used he' (2149). The voice throughout is that of the clerical misogynist, and is expressive of that cynicism about sexuality generally which is the legacy of religious celibacy. It is the rhetoric of a disordered and mutilated conscious-ness, and Chaucer gives to it an extraordinary Swiftian power.

January himself is something more than the traditional *senex amans*. To the disgust traditionally associated with that figure Chaucer adds a lurid physical reality:

> And Januarie hath faste in armes take
> His fresshe May, his paradys, his make.
> He lulleth hire; he kisseth hire ful ofte;
> With thikke brustles of his berd unsofte,
> Lyk to the skyn of houndfyssh, sharp as brere –
> For he was shave al newe in his manere –
> He rubbeth hire aboute hir tendre face.   (1821–7)

The images of sexual possession as eating (1419), the fantasies of prolonged rape (1757–61), the haste, the barrelfuls of aphrodisiacs (1807), give a partly comic effect, but always with an undertone of disgust and repulsion. It is as if someone were telling a dirty story and insisting on going into detail, materializing every innuendo. The effect is shocking and disorientating, for there seems no centre of consciousness that we can draw to except the one that is disgusted and fascinated by sexuality. What is more, January is granted a kind of deformed moral consciousness, so that he is constantly preoccupied with whether what he is doing is right or lawful. Hence his long debates with his advisers, and with himself, and his pathetically confident explanation to May that what he is about to do to her, previously wrong, is now, by virtue of 'trewe wedlok', right: 'For we han leve to pleye us by the lawe' (1841). There is no need to be reminded how alien to fabliau is the stimulus to feeling and moral reflection, however perverted, that we are given in the *Merchant's Tale*.

A further strange twist to the tale is given by the portrayal of May and Damian. They would conventionally in a fabliau have the advantage and merit of youth, and some quality of gaiety and vigour would hang about their liaison. But they lack even January's vitality. God knows, says the narrator, what May thought of January's wedding-night performance, suggesting, in his prurient way, the unspeakable horrors of maidenly innocence violated – but then he tells us, with equally characteristic bluntness: 'She preyseth nat his pleyyng worth a bene' (1854). The coldness of the appraisal is as shocking as any of January's excesses, and the narrator's subsequent sneering remarks about her 'pitee' (1986, 1995), his gratuitous bit of information about the fate of Damian's love-letter (1954), suggest not a healthy animal vitality but a perverted cold sexuality. Damian is no more than a poodle to this lady dog-trainer and it is indeed to a fawning dog that he is compared when he returns to court and smothers January with his obsequious attentions (2014). January's own overheated sexual fantasies come to seem almost natural by comparison. His blindness, too, creates a grudging sympathy in us, and in him a kind of insight, as when he speaks to May of his 'unlikly elde' (2180) and his awareness of how he may appear to her. The corrupted understanding seems more and more to be that of the narrator.

The ending restores the lighter and more spirited mood of fabliau, and May's trick is a good one. If the ending suggests that January will do well to cherish the illusion she has put him under, and that happiness is truly the perpetual possession of being well deceived, then that is no more than we expect of fabliau. The sense of trespass, however, in the tale as a whole, remains. Chaucer, in suggesting to us all sorts of themes of moral and emotional significance, has violated all the expectations of the genre without creating any alternative order for the understanding of the tale. There is a character called Justinus, whose name suggests that he should represent some point of vantage in the story, some resting-place for the reader's bewildered moral consciousness; but he turns out to be wise only in the cynicism of embittered experience. There is no escape from the horror of sexuality. The attribution of the tale to the Merchant solves no problems, since there is no way in which the tale can be 'contained' within what we can legitimately assume about his character. The most we can say about the prologue, and its account of the plight of the unhappily married Merchant, is that it may be part of some process of revision in which this disturbing tale was accommodated to a more conventional complaint against marriage.

The Friar's and Summoner's tales lack something of the immediacy of appeal of the fabliaux, since they deal with specialized kinds of medieval corrupt practice, and not with sex and marriage, but they are both masterpieces of satirical anecdote. Though not strictly speaking fabliaux, they operate according to the same basic comic rules, namely, that the criterion by which human beings are judged successful is the extent to which they find means fully to satisfy their appetites and manipulate the world, by their smartness, to their will. What Chaucer has done is to absorb satire of the professional activities of summoners and friars into the dramatic comedy of the exchange of abuse between the Friar and Summoner. Moral outrage at what they describe each other as doing is a proper preliminary response, but it is swallowed up in laughter, since what the narrators try to do is to prove not that their victims are knaves but that they are fools. They know perfectly well that to demonstrate their opponent's success in villainy will cause no wound, since there is nothing to be ashamed of in following one's rapacious nature. To demolish one's victim effectively, he must be shown to be stupid, and both the Friar and the Summoner do this in the same way, by portraying their victims as pathetically gullible. Both the summoner of the *Friar's Tale* and the friar of the *Summoner's Tale* misunderstand things that would be obvious to the meanest intelligence, mistake the surface for reality, the letter for the spirit, and end up destroying themselves through their own stupidity.

The *Friar's Tale* is quite brief. It begins with the expected attack on the fictional summoner, but soon the story takes over, and we gradually forget the pilgrim-Friar and pilgrim-Summoner, engrossed as we are in the summoner's meeting with the mysterious yeoman. The revelation of his identity is gradual, with all sorts of hints and ironies to follow up; the summoner's embarrassment about his own profession, meanwhile, makes him more pathetically contemptible than being accused of robbing a hundred widows:

> He dorste nat, for verray filthe and shame
> Seye that he was a somonour, for the name. (1393–4)

The hilarity of the tale begins when the devil-yeoman reveals his identity. We naturally expect that the summoner will show some sign of apprehension, or at least some sign that he realizes something significant is happening. But no: he seems impenetrable to all understanding, and preoccupied with the devil's skill in shape-changing. He behaves like a con-man who has met a fellow trickster, and is so persistent in his trivial enquiries that the devil begins to show a certain exasperation, as if irritated that he has been sent on a special mission to capture a soul of such banality. Through all the subsequent incidents of the carter who curses his horse and does not mean what he says and the old widow who curses the summoner and does, the summoner remains impervious to any perception but of the grossly literal. Twice invited to think again or to repent (1522, 1629), he seems not even to understand what he stands to lose. The joke against the summoner is not that he is snatched off to hell but that he will not even realize where he is when he gets there.

The Summoner's response is violent, and his immediate riposte, concerning the dwelling-place of friars in the nether regions, is appropriately anal. This anality is wittily prolonged into the tale, with puns on 'ferthyng' (1967), 'fundement' (2103), and 'ars-metrike' (2222), and of course the denouement is a great fart. All this may seem very suitable to a man whose diet was all 'garleek, oynons, and eek lekes'(I, 634). However, the story he tells is not vile and reeking of the sewer, but cool, witty, and precisely judged. The portrait of the friar at his characteristic activities of hypocritical wheedling, and 'glosynge' ('Glosynge is a glorious thyng, certeyn': 1793) takes up the great bulk of the tale, and it is done with superb skill and panache. One notices the accustomed smoothness with which he shoos the cat off the most comfortable seat and takes its place (1775), the amorous suggestiveness of his address to Thomas's wife and the little variation he introduces into the fraternal kiss ('and chirketh as a sparwe / With his lyppes': 1804–5), the air of ascetic self-denial and true Franciscan charity ('But that I nolde no beest for me were deed': 1842) with which he orders his gourmet dinner. There is even something quite engaging about his quickness of wit in getting out of difficult situations. Suddenly realizing that the household of which he is such a close friend has suffered a bereavement of which he should have apprised himself, he lays on immediately an imaginary funeral service in which he galvanizes the whole brotherhood into activity,

> 'With many a teere trillying on my cheke,
> Withouten noyse or claterynge of belles'.   (1864–5)

The last detail is a shrewd bit of quick thinking: the bells, if they had sounded, would have been heard. So too when Thomas complains that all his gifts to the different friars have done him no good:

> The frere answerde, 'O Thomas, dostow so?
> What nedeth yow diverse freres seche?
> What nedeth hym that hath a parfit leche
> To sechen othere leches in the toun?
> Youre inconstance is youre confusioun . . .
> A, yif that covent half a quarter otes!
> A, yif that covent foure and twenty grotes!
> A, yif that frere a peny, and lat hym go!
> Nay, nay, Thomas, it may no thyng be so!
> What is a ferthyng worth parted in twelve?'   (1954–8, 1963–7)

He is a true ancestor of Falstaff, and we are obliged to pay laughing respect, in the very teeth of morality, to such vitality.

Towards the end of the tale, however, the friar seems to 'go into automatic'. His sermon on Ire is queasily irrelevant, and his demands on Thomas become more peremptory and blatant. He falls over-eagerly for Thomas's trick, and then, ridiculously, seems more put out by the absurdly impossible problem in 'ars-metrike' he has been set than by the grossness of his humiliation. All our memory of the quarrel between the Friar and the Summoner, all possibility of morally based satire on the friar, seem swallowed up in the conclusion of the story, in the posing of the puzzle of the divided fart and its fantastically imaginative solution. Humour gets the better of satire, and Chaucer, as often, seems to prefer complicity with the world of his creatures to moral criticism.[8]

NOTES

1. The essays of Henri Bergson ('Laughter') and George Meredith ('An Essay in Comedy') are conveniently available in *Comedy*, ed. Wylie Sypher (New York, 1956).
2. Mikhail Bakhtin, *Rabelais and His World*, trans. Helene Iswolsky (Cambridge, Mass., 1965). For skilful use of Bakhtin in relation to the *Miller's Tale*, see Alfred David, *The Strumpet Muse: Art and Morals in Chaucer's Poetry* (Bloomington, Ind./London, 1976), pp. 94, 104–5. See also, more recently, John Ganim, *Chaucerian Theatricality* (Princeton, N.J., 1991).
3. The traditional view is that of Joseph Bédier (*Les Fabliaux*, 1893) and is opposed by Per Nykrog, *Les Fabliaux: étude d'histoire littéraire et de stylistique médiévale* (Copenhagen, 1957). For a convenient summary of opinions, see D. S. Brewer, 'The Fabliaux' in *Companion to Chaucer Studies*, ed. Beryl Rowland (Toronto/ New York/London, 1968), pp. 247–67. There are important qualifications to Nykrog's view, suggestive of a looser and more heterogeneous audience for fabliau, in Charles Muscatine, 'The Social Background of the Old French Fabliaux', *Genre*, 9 (1976), 1–19.
4. See E. Talbot Donaldson, 'Idiom of Popular Poetry in the Miller's Tale' in *English Institute Essays 1950*, ed. A. S. Downer (New York, 1951), pp. 116–40; repr. in the author's *Speaking of Chaucer* (London, 1970), pp. 13–29.
5. Charles Muscatine, *Chaucer and the French Tradition: A Study in Style and Meaning* (Berkeley/Los Angeles, Calif./London, 1957), p. 226.
6. J. A. W. Bennett, *Chaucer at Oxford and at Cambridge* (Oxford, 1974), provides ample historical documentation to confirm this critical impression of the *Miller's Tale* and the *Reeve's Tale*.
7. For analogues to Chaucer's fabliaux, see Larry D. Benson and Theodore M. Andersson, *The Literary Contexts of Chaucer's Fabliaux: Texts and Translations* (Indianapolis, Ind./New York, 1971).
8. Since this essay was first published, most writing on the comic tales has been from the point of view not of genre, form, and style, but of the politics of class and gender. An example of the first is the discussion of the *Miller's Tale* as an expression of peasant class consciousness in Lee Patterson, *Chaucer and the Subject of History* (Madison, Wisc., 1991), pp. 244–79; of the second, the account of the same tale in Elaine Tuttle Hansen, *Chaucer and the Fictions of Gender* (Berkeley/Los Angeles, Calif./London, 1992), pp. 223–36, where the argument is that the imprisonment of female sexuality within a bitterly hostile antifeminism is no laughing matter. There is a collection of essays, old and new, of a more traditional kind, in *Chaucer's Humor: Critical Essays*, ed. Jean E. Jost (New York/London, 1994).

11

ROBERT WORTH FRANK, JR

The *Canterbury Tales* III: pathos

The narratives we may call 'tales of pathos' – the tales of the Man of Law, Second Nun, Clerk, Physician, Prioress, and Monk – make greater demands on a modern reader's historical sense and imaginative sympathies than probably any other grouping in the *Canterbury Tales*. An understanding reading can be rewarding, however, in several ways. They introduce us to modes of thinking and feeling central to fourteenth-century experience, illuminating aspects of Chaucer's world he otherwise left unexplored. They also testify to his passionate interest in the many forms of story flooding the late medieval world. Not of least importance, several of his greatest achievements are found here.

'Tales of pathos', however, are not a genre. No two narratives are the same: they include a saint's life, a miracle of the Virgin, a series of *de casibus* stories, a religious romance, an expanded exemplum, and a folktale. These tales vary, too, in the degree of pathos aimed for and achieved. The *Second Nun's Tale* and the *Monk's Tale* – with one striking exception – are only marginally pathetic, whereas the *Clerk's Tale*, the *Prioress's Tale*, the *Physician's Tale*, and the *Man of Law's Tale* are intensely so. Nevertheless, they may be properly considered together. They share a narrative mode and a method of treatment, they possess several features in common, and they make essentially the same demand on a modern reader, and are best understood and appreciated by reference to certain characteristics of fourteenth-century experience and mentality.

Unlike so many of Chaucer's narratives, they are in no way comic. Chaucerian irony is also absent. There is little or no complexity. Characters are generally one- or two-dimensional, motivated by a single virtue: constancy, patience, simple piety. The treatment of scene tends to be abstract. The action is played on a bare stage, so to speak. The narratives concentrate on crucial incident, moments of extreme threat, pain, distress, anguish. Or, if there is a happy ending, tearful bliss.

Chaucer's principal artistic concern (with the *Monk's Tale*, again, possibly an exception) is to produce a strong emotional effect. The situations – death of a child, separation of loved ones, being set adrift at sea, martyrdom – in themselves arouse feeling. Special attention is given to the emotional reaction of the central character, and, often, of witnesses and of the narrator as well. Additional devices to heighten feeling and involvement may be used: apostrophes, *exclamatio*, allusions charged with religious significance and emotional associations. Such non-narrative, rhetorical passages often alternate with dramatic scenes. The aim is to involve the audience and persuade them to an empathetic posture.

This, of course, is the essential nature of the pathetic. It is a mode of artistic representation that seeks to evoke pity and compassion in the beholder and to elicit tears of sympathy. Pathos, however, is out of fashion today. Except, perhaps, for the literature of brutality and violence, and for pornography, our age resents having its feelings worked upon, particularly its sense of pity. Appeals for food for starving children and funds for victims of disaster may make some use of pathos, but art may not. Receptivity to pathos is very much a matter of the taste of an age. Nineteenth-century British readers, Leigh Hunt, Wordsworth, Matthew Arnold, among others, responded with special enthusiasm to the tales considered here.

We will accept the tragic in art, but not the pathetic. The distinction between the two is helpful for a sharper understanding of this mode. The difference lies primarily in the nature of the central characters and of their relation to the action. In pathos, they must be victims, that is, they must be passive, not active agents who struggle in some fashion, however futile, against opposing forces and even contribute to their own destruction, as in tragedy. In pathos the central character is a suffering figure, and this suffering arouses our sympathy. If the suffering is totally undeserved, even stronger feeling is evoked, and so innocence is a characteristic of the pathetic victim. So also is weakness, an inability to struggle. The powerlessness of the victim is yet more dramatic if the hostile force acting on him or her is by contrast strong, brutal, evil, and immune to the claims of weakness and innocence.

Pathos, we have said, is dependent on the taste of the times, and Chaucer's age was unusually receptive to it, especially though not exclusively in the area of religion. In fourteenth- and fifteenth-century literature and art, religious pathos was powerful and pervasive. Three of our tales are religious in genre and subject, and there are references to 'icons' of religious pathos in two others. The account of Ugolino in the *Monk's Tale* is without overt religious allusion, but its language and imagery are rich in religious and biblical resonances.[1]

This deep vein of religious pathos has several sources. In a variety of ways religion in this period fed and aroused strong feelings of pity, joy, terror, hope. The Church did not depend on the teaching of formal doctrine alone. It also reached layfolk by appeals to feeling. The horrors of hell were graphically drawn in sermons and confessional manuals, in illuminations in Books of Hours, and in paintings on interior church walls. Sermons, lyrics, the mystery cycles, and art vividly recreated the sufferings of Christ and the anguish of the Virgin in the several stages of the Passion, the tender joy of the Nativity, the fearful flight into Egypt.

Behind much of this lay a phenomenon known as the humanization of Christ, well established by Chaucer's time. The human nature of Christ had become as significant for worshippers as the divine. Representations of the Crucifixion in the ninth and tenth centuries show a remote, austere God commanding awe and reverence. The thirteenth and fourteenth centuries present a suffering, dying man petitioning the beholder's compassion and tears, as do the swooning Virgin and the weeping Magdalene. Pictorial representations of this suffering, mortal God, loved and mourned by a mother and dear companions, call for a human, empathetic response. Lyrics report the Passion in lurid detail or express the sorrow of one meditating on the scene: in some, Christ speaks directly from the cross to the reader, bidding him see how He suffers. Many portray Mary's grief, often uttered directly by her.

A powerful agent in this humanization of Christ was the religious form called the meditation. Originally a monastic exercise, it was later adopted by lay persons. The meditant concentrated his or her thoughts on scenes or subjects that would bring home forcefully the crises of the human condition: death, the pains of hell, the bliss of heaven, one's sinfulness, God's goodness, the urgency of repentance. Scenes from the life of Christ, and of the Virgin, proved especially effective. Written meditations served as guides. One of the most popular was a thirteenth-century work, the *Meditations on the Life of Christ*. Anonymous through most of its history, or ascribed mistakenly to St Bonaventura, it is generally accepted today as the work of an Italian Franciscan, John of Caulibus, a native of San Gimignano. We know of over two hundred manuscripts of the work, and there are many translations of the Latin into the vernacular, including Middle English.[2]

Two facts about the *Meditations* are relevant here. First, it added freely to the Gospel accounts of Christ's life, drawing on apocryphal writings, the *Golden Legend*, and the author's fertile imagination. A complete 'domestic' history was created, in which the bond between the Virgin and Christ was stressed insistently. We learn how the infant cried in pain at the circumcision, and how Mary wept to hear him cry. We are told that during the years in Egypt the Virgin sewed and spun to earn money, and the five-year-old child

Jesus went about in search of work for his mother. The Gospels' silence on the years between Christ's twelfth and thirtieth years is filled by an account of his life with his family, sometimes helping his foster-father Joseph, sometimes assisting his mother by setting the table, making the beds, and doing other household chores. A Christ is created with whom the humblest can identify.

Secondly, the reader of the *Meditations* (and of other meditations) is constantly urged to participate in the action and to respond empathetically to the scene presented. The language is now vivid and detailed, now charged and emotive, and from time to time the reader is told to step into the scene. At the Nativity, the meditant is urged to 'kiss the feet of the child Jesus lying in the manger, and ask our Lady to hand him to you and even allow you to hold him. Take him and hold him fast in your arms; gaze at his face, kiss him with loving reverence and delight confidently in him' (p. 28). After visiting the Holy Family in Egypt, 'ask permission to leave; and after kneeling to receive a blessing first from the child Jesus, with compassionate tears bid them farewell. They were like exiles banished without just cause from their native land' (p. 48). On the road to Gethsemane, the meditant is urged to 'focus' his attention on Jesus 'closely as he makes his way, bent beneath the cross and gasping for breath. As much as you can, suffer with him, as he is placed in the midst of so much agony and renewed ridicule' (p. 250).

The influence of the *Meditations* was enormous. So also was the cult of the Virgin. She won adoring partisans as the most merciful resource in the pantheon. She became the mother not just of God but of all mankind. She could be turned to in desperation as one willing to intercede for a poor sinner when all else had failed. Her humility and her obedience made her a model for all; her compassion also invited imitation. As a human mother she shared the basic experience of womankind; as a mother who had witnessed her son's death at the hands of remorseless men she knew the bitterest agony of a parent. In her miracles she is seen to be especially alert to the tragedies of commonplace domestic life. She became an icon of pathos and a model of compassion.

The spirit of Franciscan piety also infuses this vein of late medieval spirituality. St Francis's devotion to the wounds and suffering of Christ and to the Virgin, his tears at the thought of their pain, his encompassing humanity and compassion, embracing the humblest and most despised – indeed, his love and tears for all created things, whether a leper, a cricket, or a stone – make him the patron saint of pathos. In reading these narratives, one should not forget his influence in these centuries. He might well have been Chaucer's ideal audience.

Finally, what can we deduce concerning Chaucer's own religious attitude? His primary image as a comic artist and an ironist may be difficult to reconcile with his role as an artist of the pathetic. (Charles Dickens, however, is not too remote a parallel.) But there is no reason to doubt that he shared the religious faith of his time. Such evidence as we have suggests that he was directly, devoutly religious, with a special love for the Virgin Mary. The faith and the fondness are demonstrated by his translation, probably early in his career, from the French, of 'An ABC to the Virgin'. The 'Retraction' attached to the conclusion of the *Canterbury Tales*, near the end of his life, is an explicit statement of faith and repentance. His fondness for the Virgin seems confirmed when the Prioress praises her reverently in her *Prologue* and then recounts one of her miracles. His translation of the life of St Cecilia, which eventually became the *Second Nun's Tale*, with its fervent, carefully fashioned invocation to the Virgin, suggests no wavering in his middle years. Let us turn to it first.

We know from the Prologue to the *Legend of Good Women* (F 426) that the translation of St Cecilia's life preceded the Canterbury project by several years. We should see it, therefore, as an act of personal devotion. Saints' lives were a popular form all through the medieval period, and the numerous translations into Old English and Middle English served an increasingly literate lay public for whom Latin was a closed book. In the second half of the thirteenth century Jacobus de Voragine had made an encyclopedic collection of saints' lives, the *Golden Legend* (*Legenda Aurea*) organized around the church calendar. This in some form was Chaucer's source for roughly the first two-thirds of his narrative, after which he switched to another version of the legend, the *Passio S. Caeciliae*.

Whatever his personal reasons, it was a good choice as a narrative. It is unified in theme: from beginning to end, St Cecilia is devoted to the work of conversion. It is climactic in its action, moving from the personal scene of her wedding night, when her vow of chastity leads to her husband's acceptance of her faith, through an ever widening circle of conversions and accompanying martyrdoms, to the dramatic confrontation with the Roman prefect Almachius and St Cecilia's martyrdom by fire and sword (beheading).

We know that Chaucer used basically 'two different Latin abridgements' of the legend of St Cecilia. The first half (lines 85–348) used the popular *Legenda Aurea* of the Dominican friar Jacobus de Voragine. The source for the second half (lines 349–558), only recently identified, was 'a liturgical version, ordinarily copied and circulated specifically for use in the liturgy at Matins on St Cecilia's feast day'; its author is unknown.[3] Chaucer's beautiful translation is a remarkable example of the translator's art, faithful to its original but with no evidence of strain or awkwardness. The language moves with the naturalness and ease of an original creation. This is especially evident in the handling of the verse form, the rhyme-royal stanza of his middle period (seven decasyllabic lines rhyming ababbcc). It is the stanza of the *Parliament of Fowls* and *Troilus and Criseyde*. He used it also for three other narratives in the present grouping, the tales of the Man of Law, Prioress, and Clerk. These are also translations essentially, though treated more freely. Whatever other reason Chaucer may have had for employing the stanza, it served him well as a translator.

Though St Cecilia's story ends in martyrdom, it qualifies only marginally as a tale of pathos. True, she is innocent, and she is helpless against Roman power and is, finally, a victim. Nevertheless, she is too strong a figure to evoke our pity in any insistent fashion. Valerian's affection for his brother is touching, as are Tiburce's simple, direct acceptance of his new faith and St Cecilia's chaste kiss of welcome on his breast. These human moments soften the tone. People weep at dramatic scenes. But St Cecilia's vigorous, contemptuous challenging of the Roman Almachius has a touch of the heroic. (Some readers think it unduly arrogant, but this is the standard posture of martyrs before their pagan accusers.) Her heroic stance continues through her martyrdom to the end. There may be some pathos in her isolation, but it is not stressed. The challenge to the reader of this tale is to search out and respond to the spirit of reverence which pervades the narrative and its language.

Like all saints' lives, its message is the special grace of God revealed in the saint's power of conversion, unshakeable faith, and the willing, even joyful, acceptance of the torments of martyrdom in witness of that faith's truth and power. The narrative pits simple faith against literal-mindedness and disbelief, and demonstrates the penetrating power of faith's vision as against the blindness of false or inadequate belief. This is done first engagingly, and in a low key, through St Cecilia's husband, Valerian, and his brother, Tiburce, and then, more dramatically, through the menacing, frustrated Roman prefect, Almachius. The simplicity of Valerian and Tiburce, both before and after conversion, is charming. They penetrate the illusion of the literal and see truth. Almachius never does. His power against St Cecilia can be exercised only with divine permission. She triumphs over him in her life and in her death.

Lucifer, Adam, Samson, Hercules, Nebuchadnezzar, Belshazzar, Zenobia; the 'Modern Instances': Pedro of Spain, Peter of Cyprus, Bernabò, Ugolino; Nero, Holofernes, Antiochus, Alexander, Caesar, Croesus.

The seventeen brief narratives that constitute the *Monk's Tale* are *de casibus* tragedies, telling of 'falls' (*casus*) from greatness. Boccaccio had compiled a great number of such narratives in his *De Casibus Virorum Illustrium*

(1363). Chaucer borrowed some of his information for the *Monk's Tale* from this work, and it may have inspired his much less extensive collection. Or perhaps it was the *Roman de la Rose* of the preceding century, which also had a brief *de casibus* passage. In the next generation after Chaucer, John Lydgate produced the lengthy *Fall of Princes*, working from a French translation of Boccaccio's work. The form continued to be popular into the sixteenth century, where the collection known as *A Mirror for Magistrates* went through many editions.

Chaucer collected his material from a variety of sources – the Bible, Boethius, Dante, the *Roman de la Rose*, as well as Boccaccio. For three of the four 'modern instances' he probably drew on the knowledge of contemporaries. It was a diligent and responsible selection, not a casual gathering. The individual narratives are, for the most part, interesting as stories. (They are best read one at a time, not all in one sitting.) Their greater appeal was as history in a popular, accessible form at a time when books were hard to come by. And they are presented here as history (VII, 1973–4), to which the *de casibus* genre gave a pattern.

More important, it presented history in the form most acceptable, as a moral guide. History's chief value was exemplary, to give men and women examples from the past by which they might be warned and advised. The moral taught is to beware of Fortune. The narratives tell of persons who stood in 'heigh degree' but fell from their position of power, wealth, or fame and lost all, including, finally, their lives. They are often responsible for their own destruction by their folly or their pride, but the active agent in their fall is Fortune.

Fortune and her wheel, on which kings and heroes rose and fell, were a medieval cliché, but a powerful image nonetheless. Life was terrifyingly uncertain in the fourteenth century. More to the point, Fortune had support in philosophy and had a role in the divine plan, spelled out for all to see in Boethius's *Consolation of Philosophy*. This was one of the most influential books of the Middle Ages and one Chaucer had translated and knew well; its importance to *Troilus* and the *Knight's Tale* has already been discussed in this volume by Jill Mann. Boethius defined the nature and role of Fortune. Ever changeable, Fortune rules over the mutable, impermanent, secondary 'goods' of this world, such as fame, riches, and power, as opposed to the immutable, eternal, primary good, the love and pursuit of goodness itself. No man can be secure until he has, in fact, been forsaken by Fortune (II pr. 1). But who can avoid giving some hostages to Fortune?

The leading figure in these narratives is neither helpless nor innocent and so hardly qualifies as an ideal subject for pathos. It is possible, however, that the 'fall' in itself produced a more emotional reaction then than it does today. In a culture so hierarchical, the spectacle of loss of power or fame or riches may have been radically threatening and distressing. Some of the illustrations in a manuscript of the French translation of Boccaccio's *De Casibus* verge on the pathetic and the sentimental. The Monk begins by saying, 'I wol biwaille . . .'. And the Knight stops the Monk, not because the stories are dull – Chaucer did not work in order to bore his audience – but because he found their 'hevynesse', that is, their sadness, disturbing. (The interruption is an ingenious way to bring a collection of brief stories to a dramatic conclusion.) The stories may then have been received with some intensity of feeling, even a sense of pathos.

This possibility is reinforced by the inclusion, without apology, of one of the most pathetic tales Chaucer ever told. He took it from a scene in the ninth circle of Dante's *Inferno* and, dropping the gruesome context, heightened the inherent pathos. It tells of the imprisonment and death by starvation of Count Ugolino of Pisa and his three children, the oldest only five. The youngest (aged three) voices his hunger (the last speech in Dante), cries from day to day, and dies. Seeing their father gnaw at his arms in his grief, the other two children misunderstand it as hunger and offer him their flesh. Chaucer, correctly, makes this the last speech we hear: 'And after that, withinne a day or two, / They leyde hem in his lappe adoun and deyde' (2453–4). Though the father's grief is not ignored, the focus is on the innocent children: 'Allas, Fortune, it was greet crueltee / Swiche briddes for to putte in swich a cage!' (2413–14). It is a beautifully carved cameo of the pathetic art. All the elements are there in perfect balance: extremity of situation, helplessness, innocence, powerful familial and emotional ties, sensitive language, and restraint.

The narrative assigned to the Man of Law had a long and complex history but came to Chaucer from a source close at hand, the Anglo-Norman *Chronicle* of Nicholas Trivet (*c.*1335). There are many versions in many languages. It recounts the adventures of a beautiful woman falsely accused, who in consequence suffers many trials but is ultimately exonerated and restored to happiness. Chaucer's fellow poet, John Gower, also using Trivet, told the story in his *Confessio Amantis* (II, 587–1598). In the next generation, Thomas Hoccleve told a variant version. *Emaré* and *Le Bone Florence of Rome* are two Middle English romances using the theme. The story obviously had strong contemporary appeal.

Trivet, including it in his *Chronicle*, presented it as an incident in the history of early England. The story is a romance; Trivet gave it a strong hagiographical colouring, making it a kind of secular saint's life. Chaucer disengaged the story from its chronicle setting but preserved and even intensified the religious elements.

The story is set in a distant time, before Christianity had come to England; and in exotic places – early Rome, pagan Syria, pagan Northumbria. The heroine, Custance, an emperor's daughter, is twice set adrift alone in the open sea. There are treacherous plots, providential rescues, separations of child from parent (Custance from her father), husband from wife and child (King Alla from Custance and his infant son), and tearful reunions.

The extraordinary adventures and reunions of romance do not require divine intervention, but they can be easily accommodated to it. The same situations can be found in a number of saints' lives, some of which have been labelled 'hagiographical romances'. The legend of St Eustace, for example, recounts the separation, first of wife from her husband and two sons, then of the sons from their father and from each other, with all parties finally united by a series of coincidences. There are dramatic adventures and rescues. In the life of Mary Magdalene, a king is forced to abandon his wife (believed dead) and newborn child on an alien shore; returning two years later, he finds both alive. The saints' lives merely emphasize the hand of God in these wondrous experiences. The marvellous becomes the miraculous.

The extreme situations of romance lead naturally to moments of pathos, heightened by the religious elements. There was also a scattered rhetoric of pathos, which Chaucer drew on, especially in this narrative.[4] To give added dignity and import to his heroine's misadventures, he supplies allusions to classical figures and events (190–203, 288–94, 400–3). The astounding survivals are placed in a dignifying pattern of divine protection by allusions to similar miraculous events in sacred history and hagiography (470–504, 639, 932–45). Rhetorical apostrophes further heighten emotional tension (at least fifteen: for example, 267–71, 295–315, 358–64, 631–7).

All these devices focus ultimately on Custance and her trials. She is a classically pathetic heroine, beautiful, saintly, innocent, helpless, victimized. Epithets applied to her – fair, innocent, humble, meek, wretched, weak, woeful (see 316, 682, 719, 918, 932, 978) – constantly remind us of her virtues and her pathetic circumstances. Chaucer gives her four dramatic scenes: her departure from Rome for Syria, her being set adrift there, the accusation of murder, and being set adrift again. Of these, the first and fourth are most fully developed. The first, building on a single sentence in Trivet, is elaborately worked up, especially by the use of rhetorical devices. It is a nicely calculated addition. It establishes her at once as a pathetic figure, giving her an emotional aura which never fades. The last, her departure from Northumbria, is her climactic scene. The method here is primarily dramatic. The compassion of the Virgin at the Crucifixion is invoked to equate, obliquely, with Custance's overwhelming fear for the safety of her infant son. There are pathetic tableaux: Custance lulling the weeping child and spreading her headscarf over its little eyes ('little' is a key adjective in Chaucer's vocabulary of pathos); her final walk across the sand quieting her child; her last words – 'Farewel, housbonde routhelees!' – not a speech of defiance but a final cry of pain that crystallizes the pathos of her plight. The scene is mounted with consummate skill, arousing and condensing feelings of pity and pain. The spectators' tears confirm the pathetic moment and they are also, in fact, a kind of stage direction to the reader.

The image of Custance that emerges is powerfully evocative, and its greatest power is inherent in the essence of her situation which Chaucer has perceived. His imagination was seized by the fact of her *aloneness*. In each scene we see how alone, how isolated, she is. The rhetoric and epithets merely reinforce a moving truth. 'Allas! Custance, thou hast no champioun' (631) the narrator is made to exclaim when she is falsely accused of murder, and Chaucer goes on to write one of his starkest, most moving passages:

> Have ye nat seyn somtyme a pale face,
> Among a prees, of hym that hath be lad
> Toward his deeth, wher as hym gat no grace,
> And swich a colour in his face hath had
> Men myghte knowe his face that was bistad
> Amonges alle the faces in that route?
> So stant Custance, and looketh hire aboute.   (645–51)

Even after her return to Rome she lives unknown to her parents for twelve years until King Alla's coming releases her from her spiritual isolation.

Custance embodies Chaucer's perception of the isolation of women in his day – or of upper-class women, at least – and his sense of its poignancy. Saying farewell to her parents as she departs for her marriage of conversion as well as convenience, she exclaims, 'Wommen are born to thraldom and penance, / And to been under mannes governance' (286–7). Used as counters in the games of power politics and economic manoeuvre, separated, possibly forever, from friends and family to marry, often, men they had never seen in countries totally alien, queens, duchesses, and ladies, whom the narrator appeals to for understanding of Custance's isolation, very probably would have understood all too well. And Chaucer here, and in the *Clerk's Tale*, seems to have understood too. It may even explain the rather awkward stanza about Custance's wedding night. The imaginative embodiment of isolation in the character of Custance is the narrative's real achievement.

Chaucer used a different technique of rhetorical elaboration to give weight to the *Physician's Tale*, an incident from Livy's *History of Rome*. He probably first found it in the *Roman de la Rose*, where it is used as an exemplum.

He attempts to turn it into a self-sufficient narrative; knowing it comes from Livy, he tells it as a true story (155–7). But in Livy, the father's desperate action, killing his daughter to save her from a tyrant's lust, dramatized the desperation of a political situation. As a purely human drama, however, it raises questions at a human level: Is the father's action justified? Is it responsible or merely cruel? The setting in pagan Rome rules out any appeal to Christian doctrine.

In consequence, the issue becomes abstract: the responsibilities of parental power and governance in relation to the priceless quality of youthful beauty and goodness, innocence and chastity. A long introductory passage poses the issue, using the rhetorical *descriptio* of so much courtly poetry, with its twofold division: here the *effictio*, describing the young daughter Virginia's beauty, though laudatory, is abstract (rose and white complexion, golden tresses); the *notatio* or moral description is more elaborate, endowing Virginia with manifold virtues: chastity, humility, abstinence, temperance, patience, eloquence, modesty, industry. Just as her name cannot help but suggest the Virgin, so also her virtues (and her beauty) are those invariably ascribed to Mary, making Virginia infinitely precious.

A long *digressio* establishes the theme of parental responsibility by addressing governesses and parents. It urges the latter not to slacken in teaching virtue, warning them that the worst treason is the betrayal of innocence. Setting a bad example or being negligent in chastising them may cause their children's destruction.

The narrative proper then begins and proceeds briskly. Chaucer summarizes the enthralment of the governor Apius by Virginia's beauty and his plot to possess her by the trumped-up charge that she is a stolen slave. Two 'courtroom' scenes follow. In one, Apius, sitting in his consistory, pronounces his false judgement (his 'sentence': 177, 190). In the other, Virginius, sitting in his 'halle' (207), pronounces *his* 'sentence' (224). The parallel scenes contrast false, corrupt judgement with responsible though unbearably painful true judgement.

This scene is the moment of pathos: parent and child, an impending cruel separation, expressions of strong feeling (218, 221, 223, 231, 235–6), Virginius's face pale as ashes, his aching heart (209, 211), Virginia's tears and swoons, and her final, touching plea to her father that 'with his swerd he wolde smyte softe' (252). There are no bystanders to heighten feeling. Father and daughter are alone. There is one biblical reference, to the parallel dilemma of Jephthah and his daughter. The Abraham–Isaac story would probably also have come to his audience's mind.

Chaucer's purpose seems to have been to tell a striking story in the pathetic mode. The long introduction is unwieldy, however, and the reader totally unsympathetic to pathos will find little to please. But Boccaccio told the same story in *De Claris Mulieribus* and Gower in the *Confessio Amantis* (VII, 5131–306). The very extremism that troubles a modern reader was no doubt part of its appeal and provides a further insight into the taste of the age.

The Prioress tells a miracle of the Virgin, a popular devotional form that often revealed a striking predilection for the weak and innocent and for the virtue of simplicity. In one miracle Mary saves from dismissal a priest who knows only one mass. In another, a simple-minded girl who can recite only *Ave Maria gratia plena Dominus tecum* receives a sign of special grace. The Virgin also protects those who show her special devotion: sinful monks, for instance, who forget their vows of chastity but not her worship. Her miracles also frequently deal with pathetic situations: a young wife, pregnant, who kills herself in a fit of mistaken jealousy, is revived; a mother's only son who dies is restored to life.

The miracle Chaucer selects combines the simplicity so greatly revered with the devotion to the Virgin so amply rewarded. The simplicity and devotion are demonstrated by a seven-year-old boy, who kneels before every statue of the Virgin he passes and recites the *Ave Maria*. They are revealed further in his determination to learn the *Alma redemptoris*, though he does not know what the Latin words mean. It is enough for him that it is an anthem in praise of the Virgin, and he sings it every day going to and from school through the Asian ghetto.

The simplicity and innocence, and the helplessness, are those of childhood, a fact we are never allowed to forget. The words 'litel', 'smal', 'yong', 'child', 'children', 'boy', 'innocent' are used again and again. (Perhaps here is the voice of the Prioress.) They solicit the reader's tender sympathy for the child and his devotion, horror, and pity at his manner of death.

Pathos is likewise elicited for the mother, a widow, alone and poor, in her anxious night of waiting and her journeys through the streets, as, half out of her mind, she searches for her child. It is a mirror-image of the Virgin's tearful search for the twelve-year-old Jesus when separated from him at the Temple. The many references to Mary as mother suggest an equation of the widow's suffering and the Virgin's compassion at the Crucifixion.

Feeling is further enhanced by the ruthless power and evil of the child's destroyers. The murder scene is swiftly rendered, the ruthlessness embodied in the rapid succession of verbs: 'hente', 'heeld', 'kitte', 'caste' (570–1). The repellent anti-Semitism is offensive to us, and some critics see it as a bitter comment on the Prioress. But it is an unhappy fact that anti-Semitism was endemic in the late Middle Ages. And the Virgin was the arch-enemy of heretics, and of Jews. They are targets in a number of her miracles, which often ended with massacres or enforced conversions. It is more reasonable to conclude, however reluctantly, that Chaucer did not see beyond the prejudice of his age and took the story simply because it served his purpose.

That purpose was to demonstrate the Virgin's power and her surpassing tenderness and mercy. The narrative does that, and so does the language. Constant references celebrate her name, her blessedness above all other mortals, her mercy (510, 532, 538, 543, 550, 556, 618–19, 654, 656, 664, 678, 690). And so does the pathos. For the tender feelings generated are transferred to the Virgin herself. Tears of sorrow and joy are a fitting and welcome tribute. In fourteenth- and fifteenth-century art she often floats in an aura of tenderness and tears. She does so here.

The Clerk tells an immensely popular narrative, originally a folktale. Boccaccio introduced it to the literary world as the last story in his *Decameron* (1353). Petrarch recast it into Latin (1373–4), and in the next twenty years there appeared another Italian version, two French translations, one of which was given even wider circulation by its inclusion in a Parisian merchant's book of guidance for his young wife (*Le Ménagier de Paris*, c.1393), and a French dramatization (1395). Chaucer used Petrarch's Latin and one of the translations. Clearly a nerve was touched by this story of a peasant's daughter who promised complete obedience to the marquis who married her and kept that vow without a murmur though he tested her obedience inhumanly.

Its appeal six hundred years ago can best be understood, first, by reference to the high value that religious teaching placed on humility, obedience, and patience, the virtues Griselda displays so abundantly. Pride is, of course, the deadliest of the seven deadly sins, and the remedy against pride is humility (see the Parson, x, 388, 476). The archetypal examples of humility, and its attendant virtue, obedience, were Christ and the Virgin. Christ is 'the Master of humility'. God's descending into human form and Christ's submitting to the indignities and torments of the Passion were the ultimate acts of patience and obedience. The Virgin was cited even more insistently as a practitioner of these virtues. In her years at the Temple, one of her seven requests was for 'humility, patience, benignity, and meekness'. Her humility, said one commentator, was the celestial ladder by which God descended to earth. Her obedience and humility at the Annunciation are a constant theme.

The Parisian merchant who copied the story for his wife did so in recommending wifely obedience, though he hastened to add he would never make such extreme demands on her. Griselda's story takes place, of course, within the context of a marriage, and in one sense it is about marriage. This fact alone makes her conduct unbearable to a modern reader. But the tale is neither foremost nor finally a demonstration lecture for husbands and wives. Its larger import, deriving from Petrarch's version, is the major reason it gripped so many. Her story dramatized for them the teaching that God tests his people. The tragedies of life are evidence enough for that. And it dramatized the humility required of the truly devout before God and the absolute obedience demanded in the face of that testing, a humility and obedience that frail mortality found difficult and, often, impossible. This is one source of the tale's poignancy. The racking demands on Griselda are extreme reflections of less drastic though surely painful testings of the faithful and devout. Her triumph chides them and reminds them how far short they have fallen.

Chaucer heightens this religious dimension. He adds the allusion to Job (932–8). More subtle are the touches by which he casts over the figure of Griselda the shadow of the Virgin. Her absolute humility is Mary's virtue. Her beauty and her early maturity (211–12, 218–20) are also reminiscent of Mary. Treatments of the Virgin stressed her beauty, and her maturity and wisdom even as a young girl in the Temple. Like the Virgin, Griselda is poor and never idle; the detail of her spinning while watching the sheep (223–4) is a pointed reference. There is an oblique allusion to the Nativity (206–7); the marquis's announcement that he wishes to take her as his wife on condition she obey him absolutely and her unquestioning acceptance arouses echoes of the Annunciation (see especially 292–4). To make this connection may seem blasphemous, but it is not. The scene is different in all but one or two details, and the echo is of the faintest, but the echo is there.

The association of Griselda with the Virgin draws to her much of the tender feeling surrounding Mary. It also makes more acceptable Griselda's patience and suffering by invoking the experience of that other rare mortal. The pathos depends on our believing in Griselda's agony. Her language and reactions with Walter conceal and deny any pain – they do so outrageously when he demands she give up her second child (617–72). But this is the obedience God demands. We penetrate to her real feelings in various ways: her farewell to her daughter (547–72) and to her son (679–83), her gentle admonitions to Walter when she leaves his house (813–89) and when she meets his new bride (1032–43).

Griselda's self-contained dignity is what finally exalts her. She is another of Chaucer's isolated women, isolated by her poverty, her low birth, her vows of obedience to her husband, her separations, her firmness, her suffering. She moves alone, in marriage, in childbirth, in bereavement, a powerful image of the isolation of the human soul. The narrative's method is accumulated pathos. She never weeps, nor are we urged to weep, until the climax. Then there is a storm of feeling, expressed most tellingly in the iron grasp on her two children, when Griselda at last is not alone with her love and her pain. And then she recovers her dignity, rising, abashed at her trance. And for the first time we have a sense of Walter and Griselda together (1113).

For some, Walter is an even greater problem than Griselda. Today we would call him obsessed. The narrator protests at his cruelty (460–2, 621–3), and this, together with Chaucer's humanization of the tale, his greater 'realism', it is claimed, make Walter's monstrous actions and Griselda's improbable obedience all the more implausible. But her alliance with the image of the Virgin roots her conduct in a laudable mode of action, and the realism makes her suffering a human suffering that we can respond to. As for Walter, critics forget that life at times can be monstrous.

We must remember, finally, that obedience was demanded not only by religion but by many social relationships in the fourteenth and fifteenth centuries: wife to husband, fief to feudal lord, subject to superior. Humility and subservience on one side, arrogance and outrageous demand on the other were often the order of the day in a society so hierarchical. The strain on psyche and ego may be imagined. And these were the centuries in which that hierarchy was beginning to show signs of stress and change. In religion many hungered after a more personal relationship with divinity. The increased circulation of money, the growth of trade, a slightly accelerated social mobility must have called into question in many instances the absolute rigidity of former relations of inferiority. This may be the real nerve the story touched. Though the narrative holds up absolute obedience as the ideal, it also acknowledges the terrible demands that can be made in its name and their irrationality, and above all it gives imaginative and sympathetic recognition to the price of obedience, the suffering it can entail. Griselda captures the imagination not only for her 'patience', her obedience. She does so even more because of her great pain. We can identify with that. Chaucer's restraint and his sensitivity make it possible. Griselda is his greatest triumph in the pathetic mode.

In *The Anatomy of Criticism* Northrop Frye places pathos in the category of the low mimetic, of domestic tragedy. Most of us will live our lives in the low mimetic mode. We shall not dwell or end in epic or heroic tragedy. Pathos, then, is rooted in a level of experience common to most humankind. Behind the melodramatic and extreme situations which it employs and which we hope we shall never know are experiences that are commonplace and familiar: the loss of a parent, the death of a child, a separation of husband and wife. The emotions dramatized in pathos are emotions we shall know:

terror, grief, overwhelming joy. We shall probably never know the agony of the loss of a kingdom, but we shall all know, at some time, the grief caused by the loss of someone we love.

Pathos may seem alien because it works with extremes. It willingly tramples over probability if need be to portray these extremes – of goodness, of evil, of suffering, of faith, of innocence. From this pushing to extremes arises its abstract character. Qualifications and complexities do not interest it. Pure innocence, pure evil, pure goodness, are what it wants, and it cuts away everything extraneous to get them. It needs them in order to get the strong emotional effect it aims for. This employment of extremes and this pursuit of emotional impact are precisely what the modern reader objects to as forced and dishonest. But the truth is that at moments of strong feeling we do simplify and exaggerate. When we weep for a dead friend we forget all faults and he or she becomes for the moment pure generosity, or pure goodness. When we explode with anger the object of our wrath becomes villainy personified. Pathos is more honest about, and less afraid of, raw feeling than is irony.

The simplicities of the tales of pathos are what is most difficult for a modern reader to accept. Yet simplicity is their essence, and they demand a corresponding simplicity in the reader if they are to receive a proper response – T. S. Eliot's 'condition of complete simplicity / Costing not less than everything'. The tears that flow in such abundance in these narratives and the tears so ardently sought from the reader are valued as cleansing, redeeming, and above all revelatory. The mask dissolves and the shared humanity and weakness are declared. When the hero weeps, he becomes one with the least of his followers.

And if the art of the pathetic is not the highest art, it is not necessarily a cheap or easy art. True, the effect of pathos may be achieved easily, or cheaply. But what a particular culture will accept as legitimate devices for achieving pathos – what it is truly strongly moved by – must be allowed the artist as legitimate resources. And there can be a skilful and an honest art of the pathetic, where situation, language, and mode of treatment justify the emotional effect sought for. That skilful and honest art may be found in Chaucer's tales of pathos.

NOTES

1. See Jill Mann, 'Parents and Children in the "Canterbury Tales"' in *Literature in Fourteenth-Century England*, eds. Piero Boitani and Anna Torti (Tübingen/Cambridge, 1983), pp. 165–83.
2. See 'The Author' (pp. xiv–xxiv) and 'The Manuscripts' (pp. xxiv–xxv) in the English translation of John of Caulibus, *Meditations on the Life of Christ*, trans.

and eds. Francis X. Taney, Sister Anne Miller, OSF, and C. Mary Stallings-Taney (Asheville, N.C., 2001), referred to hereafter as *Meditations*. One set of illustrations from an Italian manuscript is included in the older translation, *Meditations on the Life of Christ: An Illustrated Manuscript of the Fourteenth Century*, trans. Isa Ragusa, eds. Isa Ragusa and Rosalie E. Green (Princeton, N.J., 1961). The Latin text can be found in *Meditaciones Vite Christi*, ed. Mary Stallings-Taney, *Corpus Christianorum Continuatio Medievalis* 153 (Turnhout, 1997).

3. Sherry L. Reames, 'The Second Nun's Prologue and Tale' in *Sources and Analogues of the Canterbury Tales*, vol. 1, eds. Robert M. Correale and Mary Hamel (Cambridge, 2002), pp. 491–528. The quotations are on p. 494. See also Sherry L. Reames, 'A Recent Discovery Concerning the Sources of Chaucer's "Second Nun's Tale"', *Modern Philology*, 87 (1989–90), 337–61.

4. Thomas H. Bestul, 'The *Man of Law's Tale* and the Rhetorical Foundations of Chaucerian Pathos', *Chaucer Review*, 9 (1974–5), 216–26.

I2

A. C. SPEARING

The *Canterbury Tales* IV: exemplum and fable

In medieval culture an accepted hierarchy of discourses set moral teaching above narrative yet established strong expectations that the two would be connected. Stories were necessary to illustrate general truths and make them memorable, while, in an age suspicious of the dangers of fiction, the claim to teach was necessary as justification for story-telling. The two most obvious forms the link could take are named in this essay's title. The exemplum has been defined as 'a short narrative used to illustrate or confirm a general statement'.[1] Exempla or 'ensamples' usually purport to be stories that are or could be true and thus to offer evidence in support of doctrine, while 'A fable (*fabula*) is something which neither happened nor could happen'.[2] Fables – invented fictions or pagan myths – were often seen as allegories, requiring interpretation to uncover a truth hidden beneath the surface. Boccaccio defines 'fabula' as 'a form of discourse, which, under guise of invention, illustrates or proves an idea; and, as its superficial aspect is removed, the meaning of the author is clear'.[3] From early times, classical mythology had been so interpreted: Jupiter was taken to represent some aspect of the Christian God, or, as Boccaccio, following earlier commentators, explains, Mercury's visit to rebuke Aeneas means that Aeneas was roused by 'remorse, or the reproof of some outspoken friend'.[4] A common type of invented fiction is the beast-fable: stories of the cock and fox or the lion and mice, manifestly untrue but devised to teach truths amusingly, especially to schoolboys beginning Latin: 'to delight and also to recall irrational human nature to its true self by a comparison with brute beasts'.[5] By a translation back into human terms of behaviour attributed to animals, beast-fables could illustrate prudential morality: 'beware of flattery' or 'never trust a woman' – for medieval schoolboys learned antifeminism with their Latin. Chaucer shows little interest in hidden meanings or allegorical interpretation. He is a literalist, and for him the beast-fable tends to become a fictional exemplum, while classical myths are 'fables' in the sense of being the mistaken truths of 'olde tyme . . . / While men loved the lawe of kinde' (*Book of the Duchess*, 52–6).

For Chaucer 'fable' usually means simply fiction, as opposed to 'historial thyng' (*Physician's Tale*, 155–6) or 'storyal soth' (*Legend of Good Women*, 702).

The idea that doctrines can best be taught by stories has a long history in Christian thought. St Gregory wrote that 'there are many who are drawn to love of the Heavenly Kingdom more by exempla than through direct preaching',[6] and exempla became increasingly common in sermons. Chaucer's Pardoner grasps Gregory's point and evidently owes to it much of his success as a preacher: first he shows his listeners his forged credentials, next his spurious relics, and

> Thanne telle I hem ensamples many oon
> Of olde stories longe tyme agoon.
> For lewed peple loven tales olde;
> Swiche thynges kan they wel reporte and holde.   (VI, 435–8)

Chaucer or his characters repeatedly follow the same practice in the *Canterbury Tales*, whether or not for homiletic purposes. 'Ensamples many oon' can also provide the basis for complete literary works. Robert Mannyng's *Handlyng Synne* is a penitential handbook in which schemes such as the commandments and sins are expounded through exemplary narratives, all allegedly true. Gower's *Confessio Amantis* uses the penitential framework, adapted to the 'religion of love', for a collection of stories exemplifying sins against Cupid. And Chaucer himself made exemplification the basis for two story-collections: the *Legend of Good Women*, where, despite his claim that elsewhere he wrote of unfaithful women only to discourage infidelity 'By swich ensample' (Prologue F 474) – just the counter-exemplary function that medieval commentators saw in Ovid's *Heroides* – Cupid imposes on him the penance of collecting stories of faithful women; and the *Monk's Tale*, a collection of 'ensamples trewe and olde' (VII, 1998) relentlessly demonstrating Fortune's unreliability.

Similarly, Chaucer frequently exploits the idea that stories can be justified if they exemplify doctrines. Several of the least edifying *Canterbury Tales* end by claiming to have demonstrated some instructive truth. The *Reeve's Tale* allegedly endorses the proverbs that 'Hym thar nat wene wel that yvele dooth' and 'A gylour shal hymself bigyled be' (I, 4320–1); the *Merchant's Tale* purports to show that 'He that mysconceyveth, he mysdemeth' (IV, 2410); and from the *Canon's Yeoman's Tale* we are to learn that God's enemies never prosper (VIII, 1476–9). It does not take such questionable cases, though, to suggest that the link between story and doctrine is likely to be tense. Sufficient ingenuity in the teller can make any story illustrate some doctrine or other; yet stories retain an energy of their own that resists subordination to doctrinal purposes. The very details that make a narrative vivid and memorable may well diverge from the doctrine supposedly served and lead us to question it. Conversely, while the teller's ingenuity in adapting his story to an exemplary purpose may help to make it stick in our minds, the more conspicuous that ingenuity the more we may resist it.

Modern readers are apt to be biased against the very possibility of exemplary narrative by scepticism about the validity of general truths. Traditional societies live on proverbs, pithy generalizations that transmit the structure of their culture, and cannot therefore be repeated too often. In our culture, the concept of general truth last flourished in the Augustan age, and it is over two centuries since Blake angrily opposed that concept with his assertion that 'to Generalize is to be an Idiot. To Particularize is the Alone Distinction of Merit'.[7] Even though much literary interpretation still, and perhaps inevitably, involves the processing of narrative particulars into general truths, modern readers are likely to doubt whether stories can effectively teach doctrines. (We need to remember, too, that the 'slow-motion attention'[8] devoted to medieval texts by modern critics may unearth discrepancies unnoticeable to medieval readers or listeners.) We should not assume that Chaucer shared our scepticism about exemplification. Nevertheless, his clearest instances of exemplum or fable do seem to involve tensions in the relationships between stories and doctrinal truths. Whatever his conscious intentions, the four tales considered here (those of the Friar, the Pardoner, the Nun's Priest, and the Manciple) can be read as demonstrations of ways in which stories do something other than convey the meanings to which they are explicitly yoked. I examine the four in the accepted manuscript order simply to avoid imposing on them a sequence of my own. What emerges may be a growing scepticism on Chaucer's part about the link his age expected between narrative and moral wisdom; but the *Canterbury Tales* is too rich and various a collection to serve as an exemplum or fable illustrating the 'truths' of more recent thought about literature.

The *Friar's Tale*, often described as a fabliau, is best considered as an exemplum. Its story, of a grasping ecclesiastical official who enters into partnership with a devil in human disguise and is eventually carried off to hell as his prey, was used as an exemplum by medieval preachers. The closest analogue, in a Latin sermon by a Durham monk, describes it as a merry tale which nevertheless teaches the avoidance of certain vices;[9] and there as in Chaucer the victim's anonymity enhances the exemplary effect. The *Friar's Tale* lacks the boisterous sexual and excretory humour of fabliaux, relying instead on ironic wit and quiet inevitability. The devil in it distinguishes between 'sleyghte' and 'violence' as methods of earning his keep (III, 1431), and the whole tale is one of 'sleyghte': the victim's eagerness to rush towards damnation makes 'violence' unnecessary.

The tale's moral is explicit: we should pray for help in resisting diabolic temptation, for

> 'The leoun sit in his awayt alway
> To sle the innocent, if that he may.'   (1657–8)

This compressed version of Psalm 10.8–9 – 'He sitteth in ambush . . . in private places, that he may kill the innocent./ . . . he lieth in wait in secret like a lion in his den' – serves adequately as a general moral, but difficulty arises if we attempt to relate it closely to the story, for the summoner who is the devil's victim is plainly *not* innocent. Chaucer presents the tale as motivated by the Friar's contempt for the pilgrim-Summoner; accordingly the summoner in the tale is unquestionably guilty, and his guilt matches the medieval reputation of the archidiaconal court he serves. A study of the records of such courts notes their 'singleminded concentration on profit from sexual offences'.[10] The archdeacon tried people for moral and other ecclesiastical infractions, 'But certes, lecchours dide he grettest wo' (1310). For those convicted, corporal punishment was normal – 'They sholde syngen if that they were hent' (1311) – but might be avoided by paying a fine. The summoner's task was to find sinners and bring them to court or collect the fines; the one in the tale surreptitiously keeps half for himself. He is, in the tale's coolly insulting words, 'A theef, and eek a somnour, and a baude' (1354) – a bawd in procuring immorality in order to uncover it. No 'innocent', then; and to ambush him the devil need only be a patient lion. Medieval devils are generally boisterous figures, given to oaths and fireworks, but this one is not 'the devel blak and rough of hewe' (1622) imagined by the widow, but a smart yeoman, wearing huntsman's green, with only the black fringes on his hat to hint at his true nature. He answers the summoner's questions 'in softe speche' (1412) and even prefaces the announcement of his damnation with a soothing 'be nat wrooth' (1634). Yet 'the devel Sathanas' (1526) and 'The peynes of thilke cursed hous of helle' (1652) are only just offstage, and the story gains piquancy from our awareness of the horrors concealed by its restrained and elegant surface.

It is that surface, polished with irony, that makes it such an effective exemplum. Irony depends on differing levels of understanding, and in the *Friar's Tale* there are several. Unusually, Chaucer does not take us into his confidence, and at first we know no more than the summoner that the yeoman he meets is a devil. There are the black fringes, to be sure, huntsman's garb suits a devil, and they meet 'under a forest syde' (1380), a liminal area where supernatural encounters can be expected – in the immediately preceding *Wife of Bath's Tale* (990) that was where fairies appeared. But at first we are simply amused at the summoner's calling himself a bailiff because his true occupation is so shameful. Even when his fellow bailiff explains that he lives 'fer in the north contree' (1413), Lucifer's dwelling according to Isaiah 14.13, and that he expects to see the summoner there eventually, the penny may not drop, until he announces, smiling slightly, 'I am a feend; my dwellyng is in helle' (1448). The parallels the summoner has delightedly noted between his way of life and his new companion's now take on extra force, and we see how appropriate it is that a devil should inspire him to such ready disclosure of his lack of conscience and desire to be shriven.

A gap in understanding remains. The summoner preys ruthlessly on others, and has been described in images that link him with predatory animals – hawks, hunting-dogs, shrikes. The devil too is a huntsman, and one who readily admits it: 'ryde wolde I now', he says, 'Unto the worldes ende for a preye' (1454–5), and to the summoner's question whether devils have fixed shapes he answers that they assume such appearances 'As moost able is oure preyes for to take' (1472). The summoner cannot emulate such shape-shifting, yet it never strikes him that the prey his new companion now seeks could be himself. He curiously questions him – why do devils work so hard? do they create new bodies for their human appearances? – and even when warned that

> Thou shalt herafterward, my brother deere,
> Come there thee nedeth nat of me to leere,   (1515–16)

he still sticks to his agreement to share takings. Next, when they encounter a carter whose cart is temporarily stuck and who is consigning 'hors and cart and hey' (1547) to the devil, but doing so 'in easy, unthinking forgetfulness of eternity',[11] the summoner foolishly urges the devil to take them. Last, as culmination of his stupid complacency, he proposes to show the devil how to extract twelve pence from the old widow. 'Taak heer ensample of me' (1580), he patronizingly urges, not grasping that *he* is to be the subject of an exemplum constructed (under divine providence) by the devil. And when she consigns him most sincerely to the Devil unless he repents, and he answers with equal sincerity that he never will, the devil takes him, and there is still no sign that he grasps what has happened.

The devil has explained that 'somtyme we been Goddes instrumentz' (1483), and the tale seems shaped by providence to bring the summoner his just reward. The neatness of the plot suggests this; so does the way in which he unconsciously conspires in the irony against himself by making remarks with double meanings. The devil assures him that

> 'I wole holde compaignye with thee
> Til it be so that thou forsake me.'
> 'Nay,' quod this somonour, 'that shal nat bityde!'   (1521–3)

And when, trying to persuade the widow to part with her shilling, the summoner remarks, 'My maister hath the profit and nat I' (1601), he is thinking of the archdeacon, while really his master is already the 'hard . . . and daungerous' lord of hell (1427). Finally, he rashly vows, 'the foule feend me fecche / If I th'excuse . . .!' (1610–11).

The emotional coolness and formal elegance of the *Friar's Tale* are matched by a more marked intellectual content than its sermon analogues possess. The summoner's curiosity about hell receives learned answers, distinguishing the purposes the devils serve, their degrees of power over human bodies and souls, and the means by which they adopt human forms. Such learning is vain because unnecessary, for the devil warns,

> . . . thou shalt, by thyn owene experience,
> Konne in a chayer rede of this sentence
> Bet than Virgile, while he was on lyve,
> Or Dant also.   (1517–20)

But the warning is itself learned, with its reference to a professorial chair and to pagan and Christian authorities on hell. The tale focusses on 'entente', a concept crucial to penitential theology. Friars specialized in hearing confessions, and the *General Prologue* stresses the Friar's claim to possess 'power of confessioun' (I, 218) greater than a parish priest. This theme is reflected in the tale. The source of sin is not deed but 'entente'; that is what any confessor must scrutinize to assess the penance necessary before absolution can be granted. The tale has many casual references to 'entente' in the general sense of 'purpose', but it eventually isolates the word's penitential sense. The devil, more scrupulous than the summoner, declines to accept what the carter offers because 'It is nat his entente, trust me weel' (1556); and when the cart is freed and the carter blesses his horses instead, the devil explains that 'The carl spak oo thing, but he thoghte another' (1568). For intention to be complete, thought must correspond to words; this fundamental principle of the trade of both is understood only by the devil. The widow, infuriated by the summoner's claim to her new pan 'For dette which thou owest me of old' (1615), consigns him and the pan to the Devil; the devil, kneeling, asks her, 'Is this youre wyl in ernest that ye seye?' (1627); she confirms that it is, the summoner confirms that it is not his 'entente' (1630) to repent, and, all necessary conditions being satisfied, the devil carries off the widow's donations.

We are left to imagine what the pan's use will be in hell – perhaps to boil the summoner.

Q.E.D. seems the appropriate conclusion to this neat demonstration of sin and punishment, but the tale has another layer which complicates its exemplary function. The Friar's antagonism towards the pilgrim-Summoner has been manifest since they threatened tales against each other's professions in the *Wife of Bath's Prologue*. What provokes him is not, as satirists and preachers like to claim, 'The strong Antipathy of Good to Bad' (for both are equally guilty of perverting the Church's penitential apparatus), but rather the contempt of a smooth-talking extortioner for a bullying one. The Summoner threatens that his tale will grieve the Friar's heart; the Friar promises that his will arouse laughter. The *Friar's Tale*, like most of the *Canterbury Tales*, cannot helpfully be regarded as an expression of its teller's individual character, but a *professional* animus runs through it. 'We' friars, the Friar proudly claims, are exempt from summoners' jurisdiction, and the Summoner angrily responds that prostitutes too are 'out of oure cure' (1333). The tale reveals a professional *parti pris* in the studied insolence with which the fictional summoner is treated, disclosing his insatiable greed but also emphasizing his stupidity in failing, right to the last, to grasp his role as chosen victim. But gradually something more disturbing emerges: this contempt for the summoner shades into admiration for the devil who so coolly tricks him. As readers, enjoying the restraint of the devil's language, his weary tolerance of fatuous questions, his easy theological learning, we are liable to find ourselves identifying with his intelligence against the summoner's stupidity, and thus ambushed by the murderous lion. Re-entering his tale at the end, the Friar impudently begs us to pray that summoners repent before the devil seizes them. We laugh in his company, perhaps not noticing how he exemplifies the truth of the pilgrim-Summoner's later accusation: small marvel that he knows so much about hell, for 'Freres and feendes been but lyte asonder' (1674).

In one way the *Pardoner's Tale* is a simpler case than the Friar's. A pardoner was licensed by the Church to transmit absolution to sinners whose willingness to make financial contributions confirmed their penitence. This system, in theory a means by which sinners could gain access to the Church's 'treasury of grace', was in practice open to gross corruption, and Chaucer's Pardoner is among the most disreputable pilgrims. He preaches to incite desire for his wares; asked to tell a tale, but urged by the respectable pilgrims to make it 'som moral thyng' (VI, 325), he pauses to drink, and then offers them a sample of his preaching. His prologue describes his preaching technique, and his tale is a specimen sermon, or rather an exemplum that has subsumed the sermon. The general truth this 'moral tale' (460) illustrates is defined in the text on which he preaches: *Radix malorum est cupiditas* (the desire for money is the root of all evils) (1 Timothy 6.10). His purpose in preaching is to gain money, yet, just as the 'lewed peple' are taken in by the rags and bones he calls relics, so they are moved by his exemplum against *cupiditas*, and with good reason.

The tale is a perfect instance of exemplary narrative. Its characters are anonymous and its landscape symbolic.[12] Three revellers, learning that a companion has been slain by 'a privee theef men clepeth Deeth' (675), set off drunkenly to find and kill Death, are directed down a 'croked wey' (761) by an old man whom they meet 'Right as they wolde han troden over a stile' (712), find a heap of coins under a tree, and end by killing each other to possess them. As in the *Friar's Tale*, the story is shaped with extreme neatness. The revellers do 'find death' under the tree, and the self-destruction of sinners seems to disclose the working of divine providence to punish *cupiditas*. Like the Friar's summoner, they are blind to the ironies they enact: one exclaims that if he could possess all the treasure himself,

> Ther is no man that lyveth under the trone
> Of God that sholde lyve so murye as I!   (842–3)

without recognizing that he is even then before God's judgement-seat. It is 'the feend, oure enemy' (844) who suggests that he should poison his fellows; but, except that the tavern where it begins is 'that develes temple' (470), that is the tale's only mention of the Devil. Diabolic intervention is unnecessary when men are so set on damning themselves. Their story is driven by a feverish energy quite different from the restraint of the *Friar's Tale*. Their life is crammed with 'riot, hasard, stywes, and tavernes' (465); learning of their companion's fate, they leap up 'al dronken in this rage' (705) to seek Death; they run to the tree the old man points out; one agrees to 'renne to the town' (796) to fetch refreshments, and, having purchased 'strong and violent' poison (867), he runs again to borrow bottles for it; the others 'ryve hym thurgh the sydes tweye' (828) and then drink the poison. Only in recounting the triple death is the tale restrained (and then only to break out in violent exclamations against the sin that caused it); otherwise its narrative style enacts a life restlessly driven by appetite.

Yet the tale's imaginative power exceeds its exemplary function. The old man is uncanny in a way rarely found in a poet more given to complexity than to mystery. Asked why he lives so long, he answers that it is because no one will exchange youth for his age, and goes on to describe in chilling and suggestive detail the misery of a life spent searching for death:

> . . . on the ground, which is my moodres gate,
> I knokke with my staf, bothe erly and late,
> And seye, 'Leeve mooder, leet me in!'   (729–31)

The old man, 'al forwrapped save [his] face' (718), is like a swaddled baby trying to re-enter the womb. There are hints about him of the Wandering Jew, of the Pauline 'old man', of Death himself; but the impossibility of assigning him to any pre-existing category leaves us baffled and disturbed as by a dream rather than instructed as by an exemplum.

Again, though the tale claims to illustrate the specific danger of *cupiditas*, it does not separate this sin from others, but mingles sins together, evoking the metamorphic energy of a sinfulness that eludes categorization. The Pardoner's homiletic 'interlude' passes through drunkenness, lechery, gluttony, gambling, blasphemy – intricately interconnected sins of the tavern. Blasphemy receives special emphasis, especially in the form of swearing by the parts of Christ's body. Of the three revellers we are quickly informed that

> Oure blissed Lordes body they totere –
> Hem thoughte that Jewes rente hym noght ynough,   (474–5)

and the tale echoes with such oaths:

> 'By Goddes precious herte,' and 'By his nayles,'
> And 'By the blood of Crist that is in Hayles,
> Sevene is my chaunce, and thyn is cynk and treye!'
> 'By Goddes armes, if thou falsly pleye,
> This daggere shal thurghout thyn herte go!'   (651–5)

The idea that oaths repeat the mutilation of Christ's body makes them blasphemous indeed, but at the price of a literalistic materialism comparable to the imagining of Death as a person. The tale discloses a world dominated by such materialism: like a Bosch painting, it is full of dismembered bodily parts possessing a hideous life of their own. In the prologue the Pardoner's neck, hands, and tongue seem to operate autonomously as he preaches, and the tale gives independent life to belly, throat, mouth, gullet, tongue, nose, face, 'flessh, and blood, and skyn' (732), bones, sides, neck, and finally 'fundement' and 'coillons' (950–2). The Pardoner's false relics are similarly mutilated parts of pigs and sheep, but even if genuine they would still be bits of bodies. The Pardoner's world is not only one of carnal and carnivorous materialism, where marrow is knocked out of bones to 'go thurgh the golet softe and swoote' (543); it is one where the Church itself presents holiness in the form of bodily fragments.

The *Pardoner's Tale* is about blasphemy; it also enacts blasphemy. The revellers' aim that 'Deeth shal be deed' (710) is an attempt to usurp Christ's role, as prefigured in Hosea 13.14: 'O death, I will be thy death.' The three form an unholy Trinity, and when 'the worste of hem' (776) embarks on his plan to kill the youngest he sends him to fetch 'breed and wyn' (797), the eucharistic elements that become Christ's body and blood. When two murder the third, they 'ryve hym thurgh the sydes tweye' (828), as Christ's body was riven on the cross and as oaths tear it once more. A current blasphemy saw the Crucifixion as a conspiracy by two members of the Trinity against the third;[13] the *Pardoner's Tale* acts out this blasphemy, followed by a sacramental meal that kills its participants.

All this enriches without contradicting the tale's exemplary function: it remains a vision of the power and self-destructiveness of sin that is surely effective in arousing fear and repentance. But the exemplary narrative is framed by a narratorial purpose that complicates matters. Preaching against *cupiditas*, the Pardoner says, 'I preche of no thyng but for coveityse' (424), and his prologue is a detailed exposition of his motives and methods. It derives from a non-realistic literary convention of confession, to which Chaucer adds both theological and psychological dimensions. He is characterized in the *General Prologue* and his own prologue as shamelessly flaunting his abnormal appearance and dubious gender. Much recent criticism has been preoccupied with his possible homosexuality, often in ways that throw little light on his tale,[14] though emphasis on the Pardoner's 'queerness' in the larger sense of 'unfittingness, disjunctiveness . . . uncategorizability'[15] may help us to respond to its uncanny quality. His power derives from a persistent self-exposure, but exposure of a self that always eludes definition: calculated histrionicism cannot be distinguished from psychopathological compulsion.

The Pardoner's account of his pulpit techniques may be amusing, but his callousness about the spiritual consequences is horrifying: what does he care if his listeners' souls 'goon a-blakeberyed' (406) when they die? What is most frightening, though, is that his techniques work. The demonstration-sermon becomes a real sermon: we cannot remain comfortably separated from the 'lewed' audience; we too are gripped by the exemplum of the three revellers, and when the Pardoner concludes we are all too ready to be deceived by his promise not to deceive us, a promise in which truth itself is 'queered':

> And lo, sires, thus I preche.
> And Jhesu Crist, that is oure soules leche,
> So graunte yow his pardoun to receyve,
> For that is best; I wol yow nat deceyve.　　　　(915–18)

His whole way of life is a blasphemy, of which his tale is but a further display; but suppose it leads us not a-blackberrying but to Christ's pardon? Suppose the damned preacher can really bring us to salvation? The Pardoner is not a priest, but the question raised is analogous to that in contemporary controversies as to whether a priest lacking grace could truly grant absolution or perform the eucharistic miracle. In terms of the exemplum, the doubt produces a fundamental disturbance in the relation between narrative and moral teaching. Perhaps the power of narrative is merely aesthetic, and poetry is reduced to those culinary effects the Pardoner contemptuously attributes to his use of Latin,

> To saffron with my predicacioun,
> And for to stire hem to devocioun. (345–6)

The separation of fiction from moral purpose leaves even exemplary narrative exposed as mere lies – an insight that will be taken up by the Parson as the tales close.

The *Pardoner's Tale* itself, however, ends with a characteristically Chaucerian swerve away from the darkness it has opened up. The Pardoner overreaches by inviting the Host to be the first to kiss his relics. Harry angrily rejects them for the fakes they are –

> Thou woldest make me kisse thyn olde breech,
> And swere it were a relyk of a seint,
> Though it were with thy fundement depeint! (948–50)

– yet in doing so he comes dangerously near to calling in question the pilgrimage's goal, for St Thomas's breeches were among the relics at Canterbury.[16] As often in this tale, we seem on the verge of a Protestant conclusion; but instead the Host turns on the Pardoner, with his dubious sexuality, and proposes that his testicles should be severed and enshrined as a relic 'in an hogges toord' (955). This last and most violent image of dismemberment goes too far for the Knight, who insists that they should make peace. 'Anon they kiste, and ryden forth hir weye' (968) – leaving behind a fearsome apprehension.

The *Nun's Priest's Tale*, Chaucer's only beast-fable, tells how the cock Chauntecleer is frightened by a nightmare in which he is seized by a dog-like yellowish-red beast with black-tipped ears and tail. His wife Pertelote argues that dreams have merely physiological causes; thus he has no reason to fear, and should simply take 'digestyves / Of wormes' and 'laxatyves' (VII, 2961–2). But Chauntecleer has learned from his extensive reading that dreams are prophetic, and he devotes 176 lines to 'ensamples olde' (3106) demonstrating this. His first two exempla are of considerable length and have many properties of the exemplary tales we have discussed: unnamed characters, authenticating detail, skilful development towards a climax that seems predetermined and perhaps divinely ordained. The first is especially absorbing, 'close . . . to the excellences of the Pardoner's exemplum',[17] a horror story in miniature of a pilgrim to whom his separately lodged travelling companion appeared thrice in dreams, the first time to prophesy that he would be murdered and the last, 'With a ful pitous face, pale of hewe' (3023), to say that the prophecy was fulfilled and his body was in a dung-cart. So it proved to be. This perfect exemplum is also perfect proof of the tense relationship between narrative and doctrine. Chauntecleer himself, moved by his own story, declares what it teaches: 'Mordre wol out; that se we day by day' (3052). We may well agree, for the more completely the story engages us, the more likely we are to forget its intended moral – not 'Murder will out' but, as Chauntecleer then hastily recalls, 'Heere may men seen that dremes been to drede' (3063). This pattern of forgetfulness is repeated by Chauntecleer in respect of his whole collection of exempla. Its 'conclusioun' for him is that 'I shal han of this avisioun / Adversitee' (3151–3), so we might expect it to leave him depressed and wary. In fact he is so pleased with himself for having defeated his wife by his masculine display of learning that he is greatly cheered, and, having patronizingly disposed of her with a mistranslated Latin quotation, he summons his obedient hens, copulates 'twenty tyme' (3177) with Pertelote, and struts about, not deigning 'to sette his foot to grounde' (3181), a marvellous parody of male complacency. For Chauntecleer, then, a collection of exempla has led to a conclusion quite contrary to his original purpose in telling them.

Exempla collections, as we have seen, can form complete works, and the tale preceding the Nun's Priest's is such a collection. The Monk proposes to recount a series of 'tragedies'. They tell of falls from high estate to misery, and he repeatedly urges us to 'Be war by thise ensamples trewe and olde' (1998) of Fortune's unreliability. Whatever Chaucer's intentions when he began this collection, its effect as it grows becomes one of both monotony and incoherence. The exempla all illustrate the same truth, yet the exemplary purpose blunts the point of each individual story, failing even to distinguish between deserved and undeserved falls. We are relieved when, after the seventeenth tragedy, the Knight interrupts, saying that such stories are depressing (and boring, adds the Host), and the Nun's Priest is named as the next teller. The Monk's final exemplum is that of Croesus, also one of Chauntecleer's list of exempla, so we may assume that the interruption and the juxtaposition of the two tales are not random.

The *Nun's Priest's Tale* is designed as a parody of exemplary tragedy. The tragedy of Croesus tells how he had a dream which was correctly interpreted by a female as foretelling his death; in the tale of Chauntecleer, the hero has a dream which is misinterpreted by a female as foreboding no harm. In the latter tale, the tragic outcome, having been extensively lamented in advance, is then narrowly averted, but the moral remains the same:

> Lo, how Fortune turneth sodeynly
> The hope and pryde eek of hir enemy! (3403-4)

The Monk's exempla are 'trewe and olde'; the story of Chauntecleer is only as true as that of Lancelot, 'That wommen holde in ful greet reverence' (3213). A tragedy comparable to the destructions of Troy, Carthage, and Rome, and, in a witty parody of Geoffrey of Vinsauf's rhetorical textbook, to the death of Richard Lionheart, but which has a cock as its hero and then does not occur after all, is hardly to be taken at face value. The full apparatus of rhetorical high style is applied to Chauntecleer's story. It is related to history, scientific learning, elevated theological debate, and the language in which this is done is genuinely impressive; yet a powerful contextual irony operates through reminders that 'My tale is of a cok' (3252) and of other animals, whose similarity to human beings may indeed, by reminding us of the absurdity of our claim to be taken seriously, 'recall irrational human nature to its true self'.

'Taketh the moralite', the Nun's Priest finally urges those who think his tale 'a folye, / As of a fox, or of a cok and hen' (3438-40) – which is just what he has been at pains to insist it is. Some have seen the closing injunction as implying hidden allegorical significance. The cock, it has been suggested, is the priest, the widow who owns him the Church, and the fox is the Devil. (Perhaps indeed its black tips may remind us of the black fringes in the *Friar's Tale*.) Or perhaps the fox is a heretic or a friar rather than the Devil – perhaps all three. Or the tale may be an allegory of the Fall, with the cock as an Adam misled by his wife, but this time avoiding expulsion from the garden at the last moment. Many such suggestions have been made, but their multiplicity and contradictoriness tell against them, and there is no obvious evidence that Chaucer intended any of them.[18] We are left to be amused by the occasional hints of hidden meaning and their utter incongruity with a farmyard world in which the only morality is instinctive and prudential – eating, copulating, avoiding death.

The story in the form Chaucer tells it was probably known to him as a sermon exemplum.[19] An appropriate tale for a priest, it does not lack non-allegorical moral applications. There is that concerning Fortune quoted above. There are conflicting generalizations about dreams: Pertelote's 'Ne do no fors of dremes' (2941) and Chauntecleer's 'no man sholde been to recchelees / Of dremes' (3107-8). There is a cluster of antifeminist morals: *Mulier est hominis confusio* (woman is man's ruin), which Chauntecleer mistranslates as 'Womman is mannes joye and al his blis' (3164-6), and the

Nun's Priest's generalization that 'Wommennes conseils been ful ofte colde' (3256), which he then hastily blames on Chauntecleer. There is advice about flatterers, addressed specifically to 'ye lordes' (3330) and then stated more generally at the conclusion. There is a further pair of divergent morals drawn by the protagonist and antagonist: Chauntecleer's

> For he that wynketh, whan he sholde see,
> Al wilfully, God lat hym nevere thee!

and then the fox's

> God yeve hym meschaunce,
> That is so undiscreet of governaunce
> That jangleth whan he sholde holde his pees.　　　　(3431–5)

The Nun's Priest advises, 'Taketh the fruyt, and lat the chaf be stille' (3443), but his tale offers such a selection of fruits that we are at a loss to know which to select as '*the* moralite'. The beast-fable has become a mock-exemplum as much as a mock-tragedy, mocking that determination to find meaning in stories that seems to be a permanent part of human culture.

Though the shortest completed *Canterbury Tale*, the *Manciple's Tale* is one of the most baffling, and though it seems the clearest instance of an exemplum, with a sixty-four-line moral, beginning 'Lordynges, by this ensample I yow preye, / Beth war . . .' (IX, 309–10), its exemplary function is strangely distorted. A sense of cross-purpose begins with its prologue. The Host jeers that the Cook has fallen drunkenly asleep and says his penance must be to tell a tale, but the Manciple intervenes with an offer to take his place, followed by a violently sarcastic verbal assault. The Host, however, warns him that if he tells a tale against the Cook, the latter may later take revenge by revealing the Manciple's dubious accounting practices. The Manciple instantly claims that he was only joking, degrades the Cook by offering him yet more drink, and proceeds with a tale of a quite different kind. Chaucer has appeared to be preparing for another pair of tales motivated by professional antagonism, but the Manciple prefers discretion to valour. The power of drink, often associated with conviviality and uninhibited self-expression, is now debasing and leads to silence, and Harry's comment –

> O Bacus, yblessed be thy name,
> That so kanst turnen ernest into game!
> Worshipe and thank be to thy deitee!　　　　(99–101)

– can only be read as savagely ironic on Chaucer's part.

Like Bacchus in the prologue, the Phoebus Apollo who is the tale's 'hero' is no real deity, and classical fable becomes little different from exemplary narrative. Living on earth as a 'lusty bachiler' (107), he had a white crow that could speak and sing beautifully, and a wife whom he guarded jealously but who deceived him with a worthless lover. The crow witnessed this and told Apollo; he angrily slew his wife with his bow, but then in remorse broke his bow and musical instruments, and punished the crow by turning it black and depriving it of speech and song. The moral, learned, the Manciple says, from his mother, is 'Kepe wel thy tonge and thenk upon the crowe' (362).

This simple story, ultimately derived from Ovid, is amplified in a way apparently designed to enrich its moral force but actually serving to confuse interpretation. Apollo is praised for his singing, playing, archery, 'his manhede and his governaunce' (158), but his role is utterly undignified, as a jealous husband who is cuckolded and then foolishly punishes the truth-teller. Denouncing the crow, he apostrophizes his dead wife:

> O deere wyf! O gemme of lustiheed!
> That were to me so sad and eek so trewe,
> Now listow deed, with face pale of hewe,
> Ful giltelees . . .   (274–7)

Yet the wife's guilt is a narrative datum, of which the crow had offered 'sadde tokenes' (258). The operatic pathos of Apollo's speech works only if we forget that his view of his wife is self-deceptive fantasy. Where then should our sympathy lie? With the wife, as victim of jealousy? Far from it: the tale is rancid with antifeminism. The impossibility of governing natural impulses is demonstrated by the insertion of three exempla into the exemplum: a caged bird always tries to escape, however luxuriously kept; a cat will reject dainty food, 'Swich appetit hath he to ete a mous' (180); a she-wolf on heat will accept any mate, even the 'leest of reputacioun' (185). The Manciple adds,

> Alle thise ensamples speke I by thise men
> That been untrewe, and nothyng by wommen,   (187–8)

but this is another expedient withdrawal. Why otherwise should the last 'ensample' concern a *she*-wolf, and why should the wife's lover then be paralleled with the she-wolf's mate as 'of litel reputacioun' (199)? Yet the nameless rival, mentioned only with contempt, can clearly expect no more approval than the wife; thus the crow remains as the sole possible recipient of our sympathy. He at least, evidently an exception to the generalization about caged birds, does his duty to his master and suffers for it, but his way of revealing the truth is ludicrously tactless: 'This crowe sang "Cokkow!

Cokkow! Cokkow!"' (243). Even he seems infected by the malice of the prologue, and it is hardly surprising that Apollo denounces his 'tonge of scorpioun' (271), that he is consigned to the Devil (307), and that the moral concerns guarding one's tongue.

A story may perhaps be an effective exemplum although its characters are all foolish or contemptible, but even the moral of the *Manciple's Tale* is self-cancelling. A sixty-four-line speech in favour of silence is absurd, and still more so, in this antifeminist context, when its garrulity is attributed to a woman. The mother monotonously repeats 'My sone'; she finds innumerable long-winded ways of saying, 'Don't talk'; and this praise of silence, like its source in the Epistle of St James,[20] leaves the impression of a gigantic tongue babbling uncontrollably.

To determine Chaucer's purpose in the *Manciple's Tale* is difficult, especially in the absence of contextual guidance such as that provided for the *Nun's Priest's Tale* by the *Monk's Tale* and its interruption. Various speeches pull in opposing directions; the tale seems to offer not a stable, even if inverted, hierarchy of story and meaning, but a cluster of divergent discourses in unstable equilibrium. Something similar might be said of the *Canterbury Tales* as a whole, but there the overall effect is of plenitude – 'God's plenty', in Dryden's famous phrase – while in the *Manciple's Tale* it is of exhaustion, sour verbalism from which the only exit is silence. The end of the collection is near, and those critics may be right who see self-reference in this penultimate tale. Like the Manciple, though on a higher social level, Chaucer held positions in which success must have depended on guarding his tongue, and the Manciple, whose words express not truth but self-interest, may be an unflattering self-portrait. Apollo is the god of poetic inspiration: shot down in mid-flight by the Franklin's interruption of the *Squire's Tale* (v, 673ff), he is now an earthly, demythologized figure, who ends by destroying his divine attributes. Apollo's crow, able to 'countrefete the speche of every man / . . . whan he sholde telle a tale' (134–5), sounds like the poet of the *Canterbury Tales*, while as the voyeur who tells of an illicit love-affair, he recalls Chaucer's situation in *Troilus and Criseyde*.[21] Self-reference is suggested, too, by the long discourse on language inserted after Apollo's cuckolder has been described as the wife's 'lemman' (205). Apologizing for such 'knavyssh speche' (205), this first quotes a proverb employed in the *General Prologue* in defence of artistic freedom – 'The word moot nede accorde with the dede' (208, cf. I, 742) – then argues (with a characteristic antifeminist switch) that, though an unfaithful wife of noble rank is conventionally called her lover's 'lady' and one of low rank 'his wenche or his lemman' (220), the services they perform are identical. The effect of the speech is now to devalue artistic freedom, by reducing stylistic variety to social prejudice and the matter of courtly poetry to mere coarseness. If this is all the poet can say, silence may be the best outcome; yet even the argument for silence is cancelled by uncontrollable garrulity. What follows is the *Parson's Prologue*, in which the Parson, about to tell the final tale, denounces 'fables and swich wrecchednesse' (X, 34), offers instead 'Moralitee and vertuous mateere' (38), and proceeds to tell, in prose, the only tale with no narrative element. The attempt, embodied in exemplum and fable, to make narrative serve general truth is finally abandoned; and it is tempting to see the self-destructive cynicism of the *Manciple's Tale* as a springboard designed to project the collection towards the Parson's austerity and its own end.[22]

NOTES

1. J. A. Mosher, *The Exemplum in the Early Religious and Didactic Literature of England* (New York, 1911), p. 1. A more recent though less lucid definition is that of Larry Scanlon, *Narrative, Authority, and Power: The Medieval Exemplum and the Chaucerian Tradition* (Cambridge, 1994), p. 34: 'a narrative enactment of cultural authority'.

2. Conrad of Hirsau, *Dialogue on the Authors* in *Medieval Literary Theory and Criticism c.1100–c.1375: The Commentary Tradition*, eds. A. J. Minnis and A. B. Scott (Oxford, 1988), p. 44.

3. *The Genealogy of the Gentile Gods* in *Medieval Literary Theory and Criticism*, p. 423.

4. *The Genealogy of the Gentile Gods*, p. 436.

5. Conrad of Hirsau, *Dialogue on the Authors*, p. 48.

6. *Dialogues* 1, Prol. 9, cited by Charles Runacres, 'Art and Ethics in the *Exempla* of *Confessio Amantis*' in *Gower's Confessio Amantis: Responses and Reassessments*, ed. A. J. Minnis (Cambridge, 1983), p. 107, n. 2.

7. *Marginalia to Reynolds's Discourses*, from *Poetry and Prose of William Blake*, ed. Geoffrey Keynes (London, 1939), p. 777, also cited by Runacres, 'Art and Ethics', p. 112. For fuller discussion of exemplification and the reaction against it, see J. A. Burrow, *Ricardian Poetry* (London, 1971), pp. 82–92, and *Medieval Writers and Their Work* (Oxford, 1982), pp. 107–18.

8. Peter W. Travis, 'Reading Chaucer *Ab Ovo*: Mock-*Exemplum* in the *Nun's Priest's Tale*' in *The Performance of Middle English Culture: Essays on Chaucer and the Drama in Honor of Martin Stevens*, eds. James J. Paxson *et al.* (Cambridge, 1998), pp. 161–81, at p. 170.

9. G. R. Owst, *Literature and Pulpit in Medieval England* (Cambridge, 1933), pp. 162–3.

10. Thomas Hahn and Richard W. Kaeuper, 'Text and Context: Chaucer's *Friar's Tale*', *Studies in the Age of Chaucer*, 5 (1983), 67–101, at p. 74.

11. V. A. Kolve, '"Man in the Middle": Art and Religion in Chaucer's *Friar's Tale*', *Studies in the Age of Chaucer*, 12 (1990), 5–46, at p. 15.

12. On the latter see Bruce A. Johnson, 'The Moral Landscape of the Pardoner's Tale' in *Subjects on the World's Stage: Essays on British Literature of the Middle*

Ages and the Renaissance, eds. David G. Allen and Robert A. White (Newark, Del., 1995), pp. 54–61.

13. *Piers Plowman: The B Version*, eds. George Kane and E. Talbot Donaldson (London, 1975), X. 52–4.

14. An exception is Steven F. Kruger, 'Claiming the Pardoner: Toward a Gay Reading of Chaucer's *Pardoner's Tale*', *Exemplaria*, 6 (1994), 115–39, who notes that, with one exception, this is 'the only one of the *Canterbury Tales* that focuses solely on male characters' and that the deadly struggle among the three revellers is described as 'a violent parody of [homo]sexual intercourse' (pp. 130–1).

15. Carolyn Dinshaw, *Getting Medieval: Sexualities and Communities, Pre- and Postmodern* (Durham, N.C., 1999), p. 158.

16. Daniel Knapp, 'The Relyk of a Seint: A Gloss on Chaucer's Pilgrimage', *ELH*, 39 (1972), 1–26. For a quite different explanation of the reference to breeches, see Richard Firth Green, 'The Pardoner's Pants (and Why They Matter)', *Studies in the Age of Chaucer*, 15 (1993), 131–45.

17. Derek Pearsall, ed., *The Nun's Priest's Tale* (Norman, Okla., 1984), p. 10.

18. Unconscious meanings remain an intriguing possibility: see, e.g., R. James Goldstein, 'Chaucer, Freud, and the Political Economy of Wit: Tendentious Jokes in the *Nun's Priest's Tale*' in *Chaucer's Humor: Critical Essays*, ed. Jean Jost (New York, 1994), pp. 145–62.

19. A. Paul Shallers, 'The *Nun's Priest's Tale*: An Ironic Exemplum', *ELH*, 42 (1975), 319–37.

20. Sheila Delany, 'Doer of the Word: The Epistle of St. James as a Source for Chaucer's *Manciple's Tale*', *Chaucer Review*, 17 (1983–4), 250–4.

21. A. C. Spearing, *The Medieval Poet as Voyeur: Looking and Listening in Medieval Love-Narratives* (Cambridge, 1993), ch. 6.

22. Studies by which I have been influenced in writing this essay but which are not mentioned in the preceding notes include the following:

Piero Boitani, '"My Tale is of a Cock" or, The Problems of Literal Interpretation' in *Literature and Religion in the Later Middle Ages*, eds. Richard G. Newhauser and John A. Alford (Binghamton, 1995), pp. 25–42.

Carolyn Dinshaw, *Chaucer's Sexual Poetics* (Madison, Wis., 1989), ch. 6.

Peter Dronke, *Fabula* (Leiden, 1974).

Alan J. Fletcher, 'The Preaching of the Pardoner', *Studies in the Age of Chaucer*, 11 (1989), 15–35.

H. Marshall Leicester, *The Disenchanted Self: Representing the Subject in the Canterbury Tales* (Berkeley, 1990), chs. 1, 6.

R. T. Lenaghan, 'The Irony of the *Friar's Tale*', *Chaucer Review*, 7 (1972–3), 282–94.

Monica E. McAlpine, 'The Pardoner's Homosexuality and How it Matters', *PMLA*, 95 (1980), 8–22.

Jill Mann, 'The *Speculum Stultorum* and the *Nun's Priest's Tale*', *Chaucer Review*, 9 (1974–5), 262–82.

Stephen Manning, 'The Nun's Priest's Morality and the Medieval Attitude toward Fables', *Journal of English and Germanic Philology*, 59 (1960), 403–16.

Anne Middleton, 'The *Physician's Tale* and Love's Martyrs: "Ensamples mo then Ten" as a Method in the *Canterbury Tales*', *Chaucer Review*, 8 (1973–4), 9–32.

Alastair Minnis, 'Chaucer's Pardoner and the "Office of Preacher"' in *Intellectuals and Writers in Fourteenth-Century Europe*, eds. Piero Boitani and Anna Torti (Cambridge, 1986), pp. 88–119.

Lee Patterson, *Chaucer and the Subject of History* (Madison, Wis., 1991), ch. 8.

Lee Patterson, 'Chaucer's Pardoner on the Couch: Psyche and Clio in Medieval Literary Studies', *Speculum*, 76 (2001), 638–80.

Derek Pearsall, 'Chaucer's Pardoner: The Death of a Salesman', *Chaucer Review*, 17 (1982–3), 358–65.

Malcolm Pittock, 'Chaucer's Pardoner and the Quest for Death', *Essays in Criticism*, 24 (1974), 107–23.

V. J. Scattergood, 'The Manciple's Manner of Speaking', *Essays in Criticism*, 24 (1974), 124–46.

J.-Th. Welter, *L'Exemplum dans la littérature religieuse et didactique du moyen âge* (Paris, 1927).

13

BARRY WINDEATT

Literary structures in Chaucer

'Th'ende is every tales strengthe . . .' as Pandarus tells Criseyde, and the *Canterbury Tales* as a whole and in many of its parts – as well as some of Chaucer's other works – suggest both the significance and also the challenge and strain that Chaucer found in inventing an appropriate close to the structures that he had created in his poems.[1] This essay outlines Chaucer's characteristic uses of such literary structures, and the particular place of an ending as the 'strengthe' in the distinctive forms of artistic wholeness that Chaucer's poetic structures represent. It is not only in Chaucer's many poems that are not brought to a close – the *House of Fame*, the *Anelida*, the *Legend of Good Women*, the *Cook's Tale*, the *Squire's Tale* – but also in those works where Chaucer does provide a conclusion, such as the ending of the *Troilus*[2] or the ending of the whole *Canterbury Tales* with the *Parson's Tale*, that the poet's sense of the ending as a difficult and special part of the 'strengthe' of a literary structure is felt.[3]

While *Troilus and Criseyde* is Chaucer's greatest single completed work and his most fully achieved and accomplished literary structure, the nature and extent of completedness in the *Canterbury Tales* is uncertain, and poses special problems in analysis. It is a work which is completed in different ways at different levels. The individual tales are highly finished within themselves, but the interlinking structure that frames them – of which enough has been written to establish the course of the whole – still bears signs of work in progress. Chaucer's last literary will and testament in the *Retractions*[4] at the end of the *Canterbury Tales* does, however, suggest that at some point, perhaps perforce, the poet saw himself as having finished with the tales, presumably much in the state reflected in the Ellesmere manuscript, where the structure and order of the series of 'Fragments' which form the *Canterbury Tales* most probably represent the state of composition that Chaucer had reached and then rounded off.[5]

But if, by comparison with the more characteristically 'Gothic' structures of many of his other works, the *Troilus* is Chaucer's most symmetrically constructed poem, reflecting in its five-book symmetry the lessons of classical models,[6] the range of Chaucer's literary structures only confirms the underlying patterns in his structural techniques. In most of his poems, as in the *Troilus*, Chaucer builds the old story into a new structure marked by his distinctive disposition of prologues, interpolated passages, and framing structures, which contain the narrative within a commentary that has transformed meaning by the time the poem reaches its resolution in the structure Chaucer has devised ('That thow be understonde, God I biseche!' *Troilus* v, 1798).

To begin with beginnings is to notice Chaucer's recurrent introduction of prologues into the structures of his poems, and also of various kinds of prefatory section more broadly defined. In this, it has been suggested, Chaucer is working within the structural principles of much Gothic art, with its disposition towards effects achieved by juxtaposition, and such comparisons with the procedures of medieval artists and builders seem true to the daring and subtlety of Chaucer's own approach to structure.[7] The construction of the dream poems strikes the modern reader as Chaucer's most 'Gothic' structural technique, where phases and episodes of the dreamer's observing experience are juxtaposed with others in the manner of the 'panels', 'masses', and 'blocks' juxtaposed in the plastic arts. In poems of this sort, as in pictures, to juxtapose materials is to suggest some thematic relation, and it is precisely in this creation of a new structure, by conjoining and co-ordinating elements drawn from a range of his reading, that Chaucer's dream poems are original.[8] The dream poems make distinctive use of a prefatory or prologue phase, which establishes a theme against which subsequent reading experience in the poem is registered and played off. The dreamer's bedtime reading in the *Book of the Duchess* of the story of how a loving wife, Alcyone, comes to acknowledge the death at sea of her husband Ceyx, forms a poignant prologue and mirroring precedent for the dreamer's subsequent conversation in his dream with the Man in Black, who is grieving for a dead wife. In the *Parliament of Fowls* the dreamer's initial reading of the *Dream of Scipio* forms a comparably appropriate prologue to the thematic structure of the poem, just as in the *House of Fame* the poet's vision in dream in Book I of a kind of mural of the Dido legend establishes awareness of problems of literary truth-telling as an important thematic first movement to the poem, which is drawn upon during the rest of the poem's structure.[9]

Indeed, when we are talking of the poet of the *General Prologue*, it is scarcely necessary to stress how much literary potential Chaucer clearly saw in the play between some decisively established body of initial information and the work that follows. The whole conception of the *Canterbury Tales* as a collection of stories within the framework of the tale-telling on the pilgrimage to Canterbury is the most ambitious instance of Chaucer's inclination throughout his artistic career to reinterpret received materials by setting them within 'frames' of various forms, 'frames' which through Chaucer's structural devising enable the received story to be read within a context constructed to extend and give superadded meaning to the borrowed story-shape.[10] As the Fragments of the *Canterbury Tales* now stand, it is only the Physician's and Shipman's tales at the openings of Fragments VI and VII which baldly open without an introduction of some kind, and the interplay between such prologues and what follows will often suggest ironic discontinuities which are one of Chaucer's characteristic ways of exploiting his prologues and prefaces.

Apart from Chaucer's distinctive use of prologues in the framework to the *Tales*, he also develops comparable structural techniques within the construction of some of the tales themselves, as with the tales of the Physician, Merchant, and Pardoner. Part of the creative process in structuring such tales involves Chaucer's conjoining of his narration of some pre-existing story with an ample and thematically important first phase or preface, so that the received story can be reinterpreted within a new context. In the *Physician's Tale* the story – of how the Roman father kills his beloved young daughter rather than allow her to be dishonoured by a corrupt judge – is provided in Chaucer's new structural disposition with an opening discourse on the balance between nature and nurture and on the upbringing of children (9–104). In a short tale this preface takes up some first third of the whole structure and, by thus establishing a context, gives more substance to what is only a brief brutal incident in Livy and a passing exemplum in the *Roman de la Rose*. Whatever ironic incongruities may be seen between this 'education prologue', the character of the Physician, and the logic of the borrowed story, such added possibility for layers of meaning has been created by Chaucer's interpolation of this prefatory phase before the narrative itself. Similarly in the *Canon's Yeoman's Tale*, the lengthy first 'Part' is a hectic account of the processes of alchemy, followed in the second 'Part' by the narrative of the tale itself, which stands in pointed juxtaposition with this technical first 'movement' of the Yeoman's utterance as a whole.

Even more striking as a comparable structural disposition is the way Chaucer develops the opening phase of the *Merchant's Tale*. Before the narrative begins to fulfil its fabliau pattern, Chaucer has introduced the lengthy prefatory discourse of well over a hundred lines ('To take a wyf it is a glorious thyng . . .': 1268ff), enumerating the joys and by implication the sorrows of marriage. This substantial 'panel' of generalization is interpolated between January's initial inclination to marry, in the first lines of the tale, and the teller's eventual pursuit of the narrative line suspended during this theoretical quasi-preface ('For which this Januarie, of whom I tolde . . .': 1393). Indeed, the prejudiced debate on matrimony which January now conducts (1399ff) – which opens up a range of reference and comparison unlikely to slip from the reader's awareness during the rest of the tale – also fits with a wider pattern in Chaucer's structural techniques, which involves the early introduction of some substantial passage to give a new context to the unfolding of the ensuing story-shape. In the *Nun's Priest's Tale*, Chaucer's version of the fable of the cock and fox, the cockerel's prescient dream of his fate prompts a discourse and dispute on the truth of dreams which is almost a third of the length of the whole tale, so that the narrative of the tricking of the cock does not get under way until sometime past the mid-point of the tale (3187ff). This virtuoso 'preface' of prejudiced argument and anecdotage so establishes the question of predestination that the unfolding story-pattern of the familiar fable cannot but be seen in relation to what has gone before, just as in the *Summoner's Tale* – by the interpolation of the friar's preaching against anger into the spare narrative of fabliau – a distinctive 'block' of discourse is held in ironic juxtaposition with the narrative inside the newly constructed whole and so extends the meaning of the fabliau.

It is through his use of the structural possibilities of prologue and frame for a borrowed story-line that Chaucer achieves such decisive effects in the *Pardoner's Tale*. The very old tale of the fools who set off to seek and kill Death is provided with two consecutive 'prefaces': not only the Pardoner's confession of his preaching practices in his prologue, but then the full and exclamatory exposition of the relevant sins, on which the Pardoner embarks between briefly introducing the characters of his tale and then returning to them, hundreds of lines later, to set the narrative going (483–660). The juxtaposition between this prefatory phase and the ensuing story has a dreadful aptness, and lends a moral momentum to the exemplary tale which the Pardoner knows how to bring to a rhetorical climax (895–903), although the framing structure of the tale then leads through a series of different experiences of ending, frames within frames, boxes within boxes: the first, accomplished ending with the Pardoner's 'sample' exemplum; the second, jagged ending with his attempt to transfer the closing effects of the exemplum to the pilgrims, and the angry débâcle with the Host; the third and imposed ending in reconciliation and continuity, at once sublime and ludicrous ('Anon they kiste, and ryden forth hir weye'). It is through the structure of such a frame that Chaucer releases the fullest force in the traditional tale which serves as his 'source'.

When Chaucer's structural technique in using his sources and analogues is examined, it becomes clear that there is no paradox in the fact that he invents so few stories yet is so inventive a story-teller. Chaucer's inventiveness will often consist in an 'art of context', of creating a structure which enables an interaction between materials which he has had the perceptiveness to bring together. In this sense his most innovative wielding of structure lies in his technique of 'contextualizing' received materials.

While it is evidently a simplification of the creative process, it is perhaps helpful to think of the story-shape, the narrative pattern of his 'original', as an outline structure held within Chaucer's imagination as he invents his own version through such techniques as constructing a frame, emphasizing or suppressing certain parts, interpolating substantial passages both narrative and non-narrative, within the overall shape of the original or traditional story. While Chaucer also creates his own interpretation of received matter through closer stylistic effects, some of his most characteristic reinterpretation of sources is achieved through structural techniques, as in such diverse tales as the Man of Law's and the Manciple's. In the *Man of Law's Tale* Chaucer is at work interpolating added passages into the received story-line in a way that punctuates but respects the structure of the original narrative. In the *Manciple's Tale* the teller's interpolations into the original story-line are so lengthy and substantial that it is the 'framework' of intervention into the narrative which now provides the main continuity and holds the story-shape within its structure.

As Chaucer in the *Man of Law's Tale* composes into his own stanzas from the uninterrupted prose of his source in Trivet's Anglo-Norman chronicle, he also punctuates thematically by inserting a succession of interpolations at key points, such as the exclamations on the lessons of the stars (197–203, 295–315), on Satan (358–71), on God's miraculous powers to preserve His servants (470–504), on Custance's predicaments (645–58), on drunkenness (771–7), on lechery (925–31). Through such formal non-narrative interpolations, and the elaborate added prayers (449ff, 841ff), the tale of Custance is taken over substantially unchanged – and even highlighted – as a story-shape, but restructured from within by an added pattern of commentary.

If the *Man of Law's Tale* story is interpolated by commentary, in the *Manciple's Tale* commentary is interpolated by the received story from *Metamorphoses*. First, the narrative scene is set: that Phoebus has a caged crow and that he jealously loves his wife, hoping to keep her faithful. But now intervenes a lengthy discourse on the impossibility of thwarting natural instincts (160–95). The narrative resumes long enough to relate that the wife indeed had a lover, but before anything can happen another passage of commentary discusses the appropriate use of words for things, including lovers (207–34). Eventually the narrative is resumed and the crow punished for its pains by the ungrateful god. The last third of the tale's whole structure is now occupied by the Manciple's prudent moralization of his fable

(309–62), a passage which expresses the cautiousness and limitedness of his character.

As a narrative of metamorphosis set within a framework of moralization the *Manciple's Tale* ends, at the level of both story and interpretation, with a resolution that puts it at one extreme of the wide range of relatively open and closed forms of ending in Chaucer's works. The genres where narrative arrives at perhaps the most resolved conclusions are fabliau and hagiography, while some of Chaucer's other poems are variously open-ended, both by design as in the *Book of the Duchess*[11] and the *Parliament of Fowls*,[12] and by default, as in the poems which Chaucer left uncompleted.

In some of these unfinished works the natural point of ending seems so close to the point at which Chaucer's writing breaks off that the absence of that ending is all the more intriguing. The *Legend of Good Women* is evidently incomplete as a series, but the last legend of *Hypermnestra* breaks off unfinished even though the source material has been used up in what exists and the narrative seems effectively at an end. Perhaps that was the problem: the source in *Heroides*, couched as a letter from the heroine, by definition could not narrate the writer's own end, and that Chaucer evidently stalled at the task of providing an appropriate conclusion suggests his sense of the need and the difficulty of an ending. More famously unfinished and difficult, the *House of Fame* breaks off just as it teasingly anticipates the arrival of some authoritative figure who may have resolved the impasse the poem has reached, and the anticipation of a conclusion beyond the confines of the existing poem resembles the ending of the *Parliament of Fowls*, whether or not the lack of a formal close reflects Chaucer's difficulty in providing a resolution of the issues raised in the *House of Fame*.

Whether the much more fragmentary state of *Anelida and Arcite* or the *Squire's Tale* reflects Chaucer's unwillingness or inability to complete them, they also resemble each other precisely in an open-ended structural pattern by starting with the promise of action but moving into the essential immobility of a set-piece 'complaint', itself a closing device in some of Chaucer's short poems (like the *Complaint of Mars*), where a brief narrative prefaces and provides the context for an elaborate concluding 'complaint', in a transition in pace and focus which achieves a closural effect.[13]

If these fragmentary structures of poetic openings suggest difficulties in closing poems that Chaucer turned away from, in few narrative poems could closure be more fittingly and climactically achieved than in such fabliaux as the Miller's, Reeve's, or Shipman's tales, where a vigorous plot of 'tricks' is worked through to its resolution.[14] With Nicholas's cry of 'Water!' (I, 3815) or the *double entendre* of 'taille' (VII, 416), the plot 'clicks' satisfyingly shut and completes the reader's expectations of the tale, just as the *Friar's Tale* comparably 'turns' upon the fulfilment of the literally meant force of an oath, which is prepared for and anticipated in the earlier agreement between summoner and devil. With such tales the falling out of sheer plot bulks larger in the reader's pleasure than in most other types of story in the *Canterbury Tales*, and the closure of the *Summoner's Tale* shows both Chaucer's relish for fabliau and the special role he accords the ending of a story as the solving of a problem, the answering of a question. Through the incongruously elaborate and pseudo-scientifically precise arrangements for dividing the donation of the fart, the tale finds its resolution in an image in the mind's eye of the cartwheel, here focussed and defined with the dignity of an invention, almost a piece of machinery, the mechanism of a 'process', which resolves the problem set in the tale and brings it to an achieved close beyond which the fabliau could not be continued. Such use of the image left in the mind's eye by the pear tree at the ending of the *Merchant's Tale* comparably brings that tale to a close upon a 'memorial' image of the action[15] to which the dispute between Pluto and Proserpina affords a framing reinforcement of meaning. Indeed, the closing of the *Franklin's Tale* as it paces itself towards its final *demaunde* 'Which was the mooste fre . . .?' suggests that endings are sometimes to be savoured in the posed deliberateness of their patterns, not rushed or pre-empted until their shape is complete: 'Herkneth the tale er ye upon hire crie . . . / And whan that ye han herd the tale, demeth' (v, 1496–8).

Working on looser plots, some of Chaucer's other tales – like the lives of the saintlike – rest more on patterns of enduring than intervening in events. But the differences in Chaucer's art of closure between the *Prioress's Tale* and the *Second Nun's Tale* on the one hand, and the *Man of Law's Tale* and the *Clerk's Tale* on the other, underline the important role of the ending in resolving such tales. As the central figures of the Prioress's and Nun's tales are candidates for sainthood, both story-patterns complete themselves with a sense of triumphant deliberateness: the miraculous discovery of the body of the little 'clergeon' and its ceremonious enshrinement bring the tale to a conclusion in ritual confirmation of the new saint, while in the Nun's tale, as in many saints' legends, the violent scene of Cecilia's martyrdom – with its iconography of the three wounds – concludes the tale with a powerful image. By comparison, in the *Man of Law's Tale*, the story of the saintly wife Custance with its patterns of endurance and survival generates no such climactic concluding action but has a succession of 'discoveries' and endings – reunion of husband and wife, reunion of daughter and father, death of husband and return to father, death of father, death of heroine – as the tale quietly follows the cycles of human life to exhaustion. A comparable pattern in Griselda's endurance in the *Clerk's Tale*, because of Chaucer's alteration of the internal balance of the tale, demands a more complex form of closure, drawing on the structural techniques of some of his most distinctive conclusions through handling of juxtaposition and framing devices.

Although it follows the structural pattern of Petrarch's version of the Griselda story, the *Clerk's Tale* encourages an emotional involvement with the characters which is in uneasy tension with the structure of the original tale. There is no moment of actual martyrdom for Griselda to end the tale with a climax, but at the denouement in her rediscovery of her children – once the testing embodied in the story-shape is past – Chaucer works up to a climax of pathos in the mother's repeated swoons. The narrative climax brims with a fullness of released emotion, but the poem of the *Clerk's Tale* is larger and longer than the old story of Griselda it contains,[16] and before the poem's structure releases us we must first step successively through several frames, turning to look back at the story itself now framed within frames. First, the narrative is framed by sinking back into an exemplary past: Griseldas are no longer made; anyway, it would be intolerable if women were to follow her example literally. But the marvellously spirited 'Envoy', which then rounds off the tale by instead urging women to terrorize their husbands, seems by its very excess to allow space retrospectively to the value of Griselda's provoking example. In their structural juxtaposition, the striking transition from framed story into an adjuring envoy allows an exhilarating effect of release, as is also experienced through the device of the final envoy in some of Chaucer's short poems like the poised *Envoy to Bukton*, with its ironic closing advice on freedom: 'The Wyf of Bathe I pray yow that ye rede . . .'

If the framed structure to the tale of Griselda subverts the Wife of Bath's view that 'it is an impossible / That any clerk wol speke good of wyves' (III, 688–9), the idiosyncratic structure of her own romance tale reflects both the Wife's inclination to clerkly talk and the different role of some of Chaucer's endings as the attempted resolution of a problem – particularly in such romances as the tales of the Wife, Franklin, and Knight. The climax to the structure of the Wife's version of her traditional tale is less the knight's discovery of the answer to the question about what women most desire (for this occurs around the middle of the tale), but rather his acceptance of his wife's arguments. To correct the knight's objection to his wife's low birth and old age Chaucer here introduces for the lady the lengthy 'pillow-lecture' (roughly a quarter of the whole tale's volume). The presence of this long lecture within the tale's structure rests more on thematic than psychological aptness. Size is emphasis. Proportion effects reinterpretation. By including this moral speech within the traditional story-shape of the romance, Chaucer attempts to lift the original fairy-tale resolution of the story through a magical transformation on to a new level of reward, from which the Wife, however, briskly moves to her pragmatic final prayer ('and Jhesu Crist us sende / Housbondes meeke, yonge, and fressh abedde': 1258–9).

Variations – however ironic or perfunctory – on the deeply traditional medieval device of ending with a prayer conclude many of the *Canterbury Tales*,[17] for the very act of ending prompts a prayerful sense of all ending, just as an ending usually promises a conclusion, which completes and fulfils the meaning of the preceding structure. Chaucer's bold structural techniques within his poems set up a momentum which the ingenuity of his framing structures can catch and bring to memorable conclusion. Yet to find a way of resolving the questions prompted by his restructuring of a received story is demanding in proportion to the ambiguities created through Chaucer's reconstruction of a poem.[18]

At the close of the *Knight's Tale*, Chaucer's problem in concluding reflects the implications of the structural pattern he has crystallized out from a less pointedly structured source.[19] Chaucer releases the force he sees in the *Teseida* by replacing the essentially external structural features of Boccaccio's poem with structural patterns that expose much more intensely the conflicting feelings and interests intrinsic to the story's shape. The trappings of *Teseida* are relinquished, and whole books and episodes disappear, while the patterns of pairing, division, and juxtaposition in the lives of the characters swim up much more sharply into focus. The proportional relation between the parts that he keeps expresses Chaucer's thematically important structural decisions: the third quarter of his poem actually involves the construction of magnificent buildings which project the conflict within the story in the solidity of symbolic architectural structures. Yet such attempted imposition of order and structure only emphasizes the arbitrary injustice of Arcite's end, and the difficulty for Chaucer's Theseus to make some concluding sense of the ending. To that difficulty Chaucer rises by interpolating Theseus's oration, another large set-piece 'block' within one of Chaucer's structures. But by using the flight of Arcite's soul to the eighth sphere at the end of *Troilus* instead, Chaucer has removed one kind of certainty and knowledge about the afterlife, while adding for Theseus an attempt within the limits of human knowledge and experience to make sense of Arcite's death. Within a much less reassuring structure, formal assurance is to be attempted, and the juxtaposition of Theseus's rhetoric of resignation with the symbolic structure of the preceding tale brings an uneasy close to the opening tale of the pilgrimage of the *Canterbury Tales* – that collection of poems evidently planned to be one poem as well, in a structure which shows Chaucer building with the structural techniques that distinguish all his poems, while moving towards a unity at once ambitious yet casual, finished yet fragmentary.

That the *Canterbury Tales* as it stands is a work frozen at a certain stage of the composition of its whole structure is suggested by the survival of some evidently authentic inconsistencies which presumably any final authorial revision would have resolved. The largest inconsistency in structure involves the tale-telling agreement itself, whereby each pilgrim is to tell two tales on the way to Canterbury and two on the way back to London (I, 791–5). But when Harry Bailly invites the Parson to tell his tale and close the collection 'as we were entrying at a thropes ende' and presumably drawing towards Canterbury, the Host declares, 'For every man, save thou, hath toold his tale' (X, 25). As the *Tales* stand, most pilgrims have in fact told just one tale, although some have not yet told any, and it is hard to imagine how the Knight, or indeed many of the pilgrims, could follow the effect of their first tale.[20] Two incompatible structures for the story-telling are thus apparently accepted at either end of the work, just as in the *Manciple's Prologue* the Host speaks as if in ignorance of the *Cook's Tale*, for which a slot has clearly been created much earlier in the whole structure.

Signs of an unrevised but authentic text similarly emerge from matchings of tale to teller so hasty that even the gender or profession of the teller has not been brought into line with the tale. The *Shipman's Tale* – probably originally to be told by the Wife of Bath – has been shifted to its new teller without revision of the internal signs of a female teller (VII, 11–19). The Second Nun in her prologue refers to herself as an 'unworthy sone of Eve' (VIII, 62), presumably because Chaucer did not look through line by line to remove inconsistencies in a work possibly written before the *Tales* and reused here. Such oversights suggest a busy artist, concerned at some stage in shifting and linking blocks of familiar material, and preoccupied then with larger rather than smaller connections and effects, which may also explain the survival within the *Merchant's Tale* of signs that it was originally intended for a religious teller (1251, 1322).[21]

It was perhaps such a shifting about of existing tales within the structure of the whole that has left the Man of Law in his Introduction announcing his intention to tell a tale in prose, but then telling the tale of Custance in stanzaic verse. This interesting prologue, in which the Man of Law makes disparaging remarks about Chaucer's abilities as a poet, apparently reflects several authentic layers of authorial intention, and was possibly once intended to introduce the opening tale of the whole pilgrimage, for the elaborate passage of time-telling by the Host (II, 1–14) is matched in the *Tales* only by the comparably elaborate passage when the Host calls on the Parson to tell the last tale (x, 2–11). Chaucer perhaps once thought of these two time-tellings standing symmetrically at either end of the tale-telling, for the Man of Law's discussion in his prologue of the proper subjects for literature, and his enumeration of Chaucer's other works, focus on matters very fitting for the outset of the *Tales*. His own tale in prose which once was to follow and perhaps open the whole *Canterbury Tales* was very possibly the prose *Melibee* – which the poet himself now tells – or even Chaucer's lost translation of *De Contemptu Mundi* mentioned in the Prologue to the *Legend of Good Women* (G 414), so that the *Man of Law's Prologue* apparently reflects a mixture surviving there together of several layers or strata of the poet's intentions for the structure of the *Tales*.

It is striking that such apparent survivals of Chaucer's uncancelled draftings occur not within the tales but in the link passages, the prologues, epilogues, and endlinks, where the disposition of the Host – which itself contributes powerfully to the structure of how the *Tales* connect together – evidently prompts Chaucer to write and rewrite. The first ending of the *Clerk's Tale* – Harry Bailly's response (1212a–g) – is later replaced by the Clerk's envoy. The prologue to the *Monk's Tale* and the epilogue to the *Nun's Priest's Tale* reveal how a framing idea which strikes Chaucer in one place is shifted to another context with more potential: the Host's innuendo about the teller as himself a 'trede-foul' in the sketchy yet authentic epilogue to the Priest's tale of the cock (VII, 3451) achieves its full realization as the Host's teasing in the *Monk's Prologue* (1945), but the unacceptably repetitious overlap between the two contexts is unlikely to have survived a final revision of the structure of the *Canterbury Tales*.

It is another of Chaucer's drafted link-passages built around the Host's responses – the epilogue to the *Man of Law's Tale* – which has stimulated much debate about what structures and order of tales Chaucer envisaged. After the *Man of Law's Tale*, when the Host calls on the Parson to tell a tale and is rebuked for his swearing, another pilgrim interrupts to insist on telling a livelier tale. Some manuscripts attribute this interjection to the Summoner or the Squire, but it is unlikely that Chaucer would ever have intended so to introduce their existing tales here. One otherwise undistinguished manuscript, however, attributes this intervention to the Shipman (whose tale, after all, was probably the Wife's first tale), and upon this slender evidence it has been conjectured that the whole Fragment VII, which is opened by the *Shipman's Tale*, should be shifted forward to follow the *Man of Law's Tale* and precede the Wife's present tale, although this particular sequence is found in no extant manuscript.[22]

The appeal of such conjectural emendation lies not simply in finding a coherent role for the evidently authentic epilogue to the *Man of Law's Tale* (which now stands like a staircase without a house), but in structuring the sequence of tales so that the sporadic allusions to geographical place in the links occur in their proper geographical sequence. The Summoner's threat to tell 'tales two or thre / Of freres er I come to Sidyngborne' (III, 846–7) could then follow instead of preceding the Host's comment in the *Monk's Prologue*: 'Loo, Rouchestre stant heer faste by!' (VII, 1926). To shift Fragment VII forward would thus remove an apparent confusion over geographical sequence – for of course Rochester comes before Sittingbourne on the road to Canterbury – although this is to interpret the Summoner's blustering words very literally to mean that Sittingbourne is actually the next place on the itinerary.

Chaucer's references to time and place as structuring features of the *Canterbury Tales* are in fact so imprecise as to suggest he lacked time or interest to work through the links plotting a careful structure of chronological and geographical references, foregrounding the *Tales* as an actual pilgrimage on a particular route. Indeed, in the *Man of Law's Prologue* the Host notices that it is 18 April, yet many tales later in the *Parson's Prologue* the date is indicated to be 17 April,[23] although this is only in keeping with the vagueness of allusions to time and place throughout. Chaucer gives little sense of the days of the journey, none of places visited or lodged in. The beginning at the Tabard is realized, but on a pilgrimage to Canterbury the pilgrims' arrival at the shrine is never enacted or described.

Taking the 'meta-tale' of Canterbury – which aims to enable all the tales to be read both in themselves and as one work – as the tale of a pilgrimage during which a collection of stories are related by the pilgrims, modern conceptions of the structure of the whole *Tales* have stressed both dramatic and symbolic unity: the dramatic continuum of the frame of links, and the spiritual unity provided by the purpose and associations of pilgrimage. Whether or not the forgetfulness of spiritual pilgrimage and absorption in story-telling between the beginning and end of the whole structure of the *Tales* reflects on the pilgrims' need for true pilgrimage, these dramatic and spiritual structures operate differently in different parts of the *Canterbury Tales*. The electricity released by Chaucer's conception of a socially very mixed group of tellers involved in a competitive story-telling has often been favourably compared with the socially homogeneous party who tell tales as a pastime in the more two-dimensional frame of Boccaccio's *Decameron*. But the dramatic continuum that Chaucer constructs is of a sharply focussed kind, spotlighting two- or three-way exchanges between the pilgrims.

In the inter-tale continuity passages of the *Canterbury Tales* it is indeed interruption which forms one of the most dramatic devices of structuring: plans and patterns are recurrently not allowed to pursue their course to a conclusion. Most pointedly, the poet-figure himself is brusquely interrupted in relating his *Thopas* and forbidden to continue it. The Host's intention that the Monk should follow the Knight is overborne by the drunken Miller (I, 3118ff). The Pardoner interrupts the *Wife of Bath's Prologue* (III, 163ff), and at its conclusion the Friar and Summoner have an altercation (829ff), not long after which the Summoner breaks into the *Friar's Tale* (1332ff). The *Monk's Tale* is cut short by the Knight (VII, 2767ff), and the whole sudden arrival and tale-telling of the Canon's Yeoman is an interruption into the pilgrimage. Whether the response to the *Squire's Tale* which Chaucer has written for the Franklin (V, 673ff) was positively intended to act as an interruption of the *Squire's Tale* – which stands in the manuscripts unfinished and perhaps unfinishable – is an instance of the ambiguity of interpreting an unfinished unity like the *Canterbury Tales*, in which dramatic unity often lies in such juxtaposition of tales, in interruption and the denial of an ending.

Juxtaposed pairings, into which tales are structured by the responses of their tellers or the Host, form one of the most recurrent patterns in the structure of the *Canterbury Tales*. The Miller's and Reeve's tales, and the Friar's and Summoner's, are locked together by the antagonism of their tellers, the determination of the second teller to 'quit' or pay back the first for his tale. In the prologues to the Cook's and Manciple's tales there are hints that such clashes of tales might have been developed between the Cook and Host, and the Cook and Manciple, because of professional rivalries. The *Clerk's Tale* may be seen as a response to the Wife's comments about clerks, while the *Merchant's Tale* follows on as a response to the Clerk's preceding tale. It is Harry Bailly's responses which link the Physician's and Pardoner's tales, and the tales within Fragment VII. Indeed, it is striking how – as the Fragments of the *Canterbury Tales* stand – Chaucer seems to have been working out towards the continuity of the *Tales* as a whole from local unities first established in sequences of pairs. Four (or five) fragments out of the existing nine (or ten) work on this principle; (IV) Clerk–Merchant; (V) Squire–Franklin; (VI) Physician–Pardoner; (VIII) Second Nun–Canon's Yeoman; (IX and X) Manciple–Parson. This apparent pattern of the poet-at-work, preserved in the structure of the completed links, suggests how for Chaucer the essential continuum of the *Canterbury Tales* arises out of the potential for dialogue and pairing between tellers and tales, unities which may be dramatic or thematic, pairings of juxtaposed tales which complement and comment on each other and, cumulatively, on those which have already been told by previous tellers.

These structural patterns in Chaucer's exploiting of the devices of inter-ruption and of pairing can be seen in the placing of the *Melibee* as the poet-figure's second attempt at a tale after the interruption of his *Thopas*. If the structure of the whole *Canterbury Tales* as it stands represents a cross-section of a particular stage of the poet at work, then the altered role of the *Melibee* offers a clue to Chaucer's shifting conception of the unity of the *Tales*. The use of dramatic interruption can allow within the wholeness of the *Tales* some instances (like the *Monk's Tale*) of forms and attitudes which anticipate no necessary end and might continue interminably. The poet's *Thopas*, although comparably directionless and irreversibly cut short, does already anticipate a progressively diminishing structural pattern.[24] It would have dwindled away to nothing, if it had not been interrupted and paired with the *Melibee*, a structure of an altogether different completedness and resolution. In the *Melibee* an opening allegorical narrative, in which enemies break into Melibeus's house and wound his daughter, provides the impetus for the rest of the tale's structure as a book of moral counsel, through his wife Prudence's eventually successful persuading of Melibeus to overcome with forgiveness his impulse for revenge, and to seek reconciliation.[25] If this noble and beautifully written work, with its lesson of patient and loving forbearance, did indeed once initiate the *Canterbury Tales*, it would have contributed to a distinctly different thematic structure for the whole poem. That it should now be positioned very much in the midst of the sequence of tales, and voiced by the poet as his second-choice attempt, points to the strik-ingly open form of structure which Chaucer was working on for the tales. The humiliating interruption of the poet-figure's own bad poem, and the difficulty even for a strong character like the Host in keeping the company in order, only emphasize how local and relative seems all authority within the framework of the *Tales*. In the Knight's and Parson's tales Chaucer has clearly demarcated in particular ways an opening to the tale-telling and a close to the pilgrimage,[26] but between these two points there is more sense of the local unities of juxtaposition and pairing in the 'quitting' of tales than in a structure 'progressive' in time, place, or moral 'development' among the pilgrim-tellers. In this sense, the framework of the *Tales* aims at a structure 'realistic' in reflecting the unpredictable, accidental, disconnected qualities of life, although patterns of theme both within and across the existing Frag-ments point to an underlying structure of reiterated concerns and approaches (like those brought together in the *Melibee*) that counterpoints the continu-ity of clash and quarrel but does not surface into a linear progress of formal debate and resolution.[27]

Yet in having the Host invite the Parson at the end of the tale-telling to 'knytte up wel a greet mateere', and in making the Parson respond by declining to tell a tale as such at all but instead providing a treatise on penance, Chaucer closes the structure of the whole *Canterbury Tales* with the resolution of faith.[28] In the context of contemporary penitential manuals of its type, the *Parson's Tale* shows a careful and serious structure of its own, reflecting Chaucer's thoughtful co-ordination of a number of sources into an analysis of sinfulness and the potential for emendation, which in medieval terms offers a very full understanding of human experience.[29] Indeed, the universal relevance of its application has inevitably prompted attempts to interpret the role of the *Parson's Tale* in the structure of the *Canterbury Tales* as one that unifies backwards from a finally achieved vantage-point of spiritual values, by offering retrospective commentary and judgement upon the relevant instances of sin in the preceding tales and their tellers.[30] But the scope of the *Parson's Tale* makes an overlap with aspects of the tales inevitable rather than specific, while the *Parson's Prologue* with its renunciation of the fiction of 'fables' suggests a decisive turning-point of transition and transcendence from the preceding continuum of the tale-telling, a change of plane borne out in the changed demands on the reader in the instructional mode of this 'tale' which is no tale. This instructive strategy of the tale in promoting a penitent sense of purpose itself anticipates a spiritual movement which is the true fulfilment of the idea of pilgrimage in the whole structure of the *Canterbury Tales* (as the Parson undertakes: 'To shewe yow the wey, in this viage, / Of thilke parfit glorious pilgrymage / That highte Jerusalem celestial': 49–51).[31] The outward and literal end of that particular fictional pilgrimage to Canterbury is never completed, but to end in a penitential manual offers to each reader the opening of a true inward pilgrimage beyond the experience of this book of tales. In this spiritual authority as teaching the *Parson's Tale* draws together the closural and judgemental associations of its context and its content, leaving irreversibly behind as evening falls the idiosyncrasies and divisions of temporal experience in the *Tales*, and through the very orderliness and comprehensiveness of its analytical mode projecting those timeless and unchanging verities which should be the goal of all.

For Chaucer – to whom the artistic problems of concluding seem to have been a symptom of the significance he created in his fictional structures – the placing of the *Parson's Tale* at the conclusion of the *Canterbury Tales* must be an ending to all endings, an absolute ending, for it ends with the absolute, with that truth which is our ultimate end. As Chaucer had read, and himself translated into English, in Boethius's *Consolation of Philosophy*: 'of things that han ende may ben maked comparysoun, but of thynges that ben withouten ende to thynges that han ende may be makid no comparysoun . . .' (*Boece* II, pr. 7, 106–9).

NOTES

1. Cf. Elizabeth Salter, *Fourteenth-Century English Poetry: Contexts and Readings* (Oxford, 1983), p. 116: '[Chaucer's] endings and reconciliations are often made in a spirit of stoicism or weariness, with rarely the sense that they are the ineluctable consequence of what has gone before, and often coming with surprising suddenness'. See also Barbara Herrnstein Smith, *Poetic Closure* (Chicago, 1968) and E. R. Curtius, *European Literature and the Latin Middle Ages*, trans. W. R. Trask (London, 1953), pp. 89–91 ('Topics of the Conclusion').

2. On the traditional context of the ending of the *Troilus*, cf. John M. Steadman, *Disembodied Laughter: Troilus and the Apotheosis Tradition* (Berkeley, Calif., 1972), and J. S. P. Tatlock, 'The Epilog of Chaucer's *Troilus*', *Modern Philology*, 18 (1921), 625–59. For critical discussion, see Barry Windeatt, *The Oxford Guides to Chaucer: 'Troilus and Criseyde'* (Oxford, 1992), pp. 298–313 ('Ending(s)').

3. Piero Boitani, *Chaucer and the Imaginary World of Fame* (Cambridge, 1984), p. 208, notes that the *Parliament of Fowls*, *Troilus*, the *Legend*, and the *Canterbury Tales* 'have disturbing, unsatisfactory, ambiguous, problematic, incomplete conclusions. This is perhaps the reason why twentieth-century readers – used as they are to "open" forms of art – feel that his failures are, beginning with this infinite *House of Fame*, his most exciting successes'.

4. For the background, see Olive Sayce, 'Chaucer's "Retractions": The Conclusion of the *Canterbury Tales* and Its Place in Literary Tradition', *Medium Aevum*, 40 (1971), 230–48; Douglas Wurtele, 'The Penitence of Geoffrey Chaucer', *Viator*, 11 (1980), 335–59; and Míceál F. Vaughan, 'Creating Comfortable Boundaries: Scribes, Editors, and the Invention of the *Parson's Tale*' in *Rewriting Chaucer: Culture, Authority, and the Idea of the Authentic Text, 1400–1602*, eds. Thomas A. Prendergast and Barbara Kline (Columbus, Ohio, 1999), pp. 45–90.

5. The Ellesmere manuscript's order of tales is:

I (A) General Prologue, Knight, Miller, Reeve, Cook
II (B1) Man of Law
III (D) Wife, Friar, Summoner
IV (E) Clerk, Merchant
V (F) Squire, Franklin
VI (C) Physician, Pardoner
VII (B2) Shipman, Prioress, Thopas, Melibee, Monk, Nun's Priest
VIII (G) Second Nun, Canon's Yeoman
IX (H) Manciple
X (I) Parson.

Cf. Larry D. Benson, 'The Order of the *Canterbury Tales*', *Studies in the Age of Chaucer*, 3 (1981), 77–120; E. T. Donaldson, 'The Ordering of the *Canterbury Tales*' in *Medieval Literature and Folklore Studies: Essays in Honor of Francis Lee Utley*, eds. Jerome Mandel and Bruce A. Rosenberg (New Brunswick, N.J., 1970), pp. 193–204; Helen Cooper, *The Structure of the Canterbury Tales* (London, 1983), ch. 2 ('The Ordering of the *Canterbury Tales*'); Derek Pearsall, *The Canterbury Tales* (London, 1985), ch. 1.

The authority of the tale order has been part of a broader debate about the relative merits of two early manuscripts: the Ellesmere (now Huntington Library,

California, MS EL 26 C9) and the Hengwrt (now National Library of Wales, Aberystwyth, MS Peniarth 392D). See *The Ellesmere Chaucer: Essays in Interpretation*, eds. M. Stevens and D. Woodward (San Marino, Calif., 1995), especially Helen Cooper, 'The Order of the Tales', pp. 245–61. On the Hengwrt manuscript, see *The Canterbury Tales: A Facsimile and Transcription of the Hengwrt Manuscript*, ed. Paul G. Ruggiers (Norman, Okla., 1979), and *The Canterbury Tales by Geoffrey Chaucer Edited from the Hengwrt Manuscript*, ed. N. F. Blake (London, 1980).

6. See Windeatt, *Oxford Guide*, pp. 180–211 ('Structure'). The page-format of my edition, *Geoffrey Chaucer: 'Troilus and Criseyde': A New Edition of 'The Book of Troilus'* (London, 1984), is designed to illustrate Chaucer at work on structuring the *Troilus* as he composes from his source, Boccaccio's *Filostrato*.

7. See R. M. Jordan, *Chaucer and the Shape of Creation: The Aesthetic Possibilities of Inorganic Structure* (Cambridge, Mass., 1967). For a more general study, William W. Rydyng, *Structure in Medieval Narrative* (The Hague, 1971).

8. Cf. Robert O. Payne, *The Key of Remembrance* (New Haven, Conn., 1963), ch. 4, 'The First Structural Stereotype', p. 145: 'The great originality of these [dream] poems is in their attempt to exploit the possibilities of *dispositio* – overall structural arrangement – in ways more complex and meaningful than anything the [rhetorical] manuals suggest in their perfunctory treatments of it.' See also *Chaucer's Dream Poetry: Sources and Analogues*, ed. and trans. B. A. Windeatt (Cambridge, 1982), pp. ix–xvii.

9. Cf. Sheila Delany, *Chaucer's House of Fame: The Poetics of Skeptical Fideism* (Chicago, 1972), p. 49: 'Explicit content, then, may be less central to meaning than method or structure, and that structure may be grasped at various points in the work.' See also J. M. Davidoff, *Beginning Well: Framing Fictions in Late Middle English Poetry* (London, 1988).

10. See Helen Cooper, 'The Frame' in *Sources and Analogues of The Canterbury Tales*, vol. 1, eds. Robert M. Correale and Mary Hamel (Woodbridge, 2002), pp. 1–22.

11. George Henderson, *Gothic* (Harmondsworth, 1968), p. 115: 'A Gothic building cannot simply stop, it has to fade away. Hence the familiar flurry of curves and spikes, by which the physical presence is gradually withdrawn and the dense material mass is dissolved into the empty air'; quoted in discussion of the *Book of the Duchess* in A. C. Spearing's *Medieval Dream-Poetry* (Cambridge, 1976), p. 53.

12. Cf. *The Parlement of Foulys*, ed. D. S. Brewer (London, 1960), p. 25: 'Nothing has been resolved – ordinary logic is defeated or unimportant – but we are aware of a completed structure, of opposites balanced if not entirely reconciled.'

13. Cf. W. A. Davenport, *Chaucer: Complaint and Narrative* (Cambridge, 1988).

14. See Derek Brewer, 'Structures and Character-Types of Chaucer's Popular Comic Tales' in his *Chaucer: The Poet as Storyteller* (London, 1984), pp. 80–9.

15. Cf. V. A. Kolve, *Chaucer and the Imagery of Narrative: The First Five Canterbury Tales* (London, 1984), especially ch. 2 ('Chaucerian Aesthetic: The Image in the Poem').

16. Cf. Derek Brewer, *Chaucer: The Poet as Storyteller*, ch. 4 ('Towards a Chaucerian Poetic') and ch. 6 ('The Nun's Priest's Tale as Story and Poem').

17. On prayers as endings, see Matthew of Vendôme, *Ars Versificatoria* in *Les Arts poétiques du XIIe et du XIIIe siècle*, ed. E. Faral (Paris, 1924), p. 192.

18. Cf. P. M. Kean, *Chaucer and the Making of English Poetry*, 2 vols. (London, 1972), vol. 2, ch. 2 ('The *Canterbury Tales*: The Problem of Narrative Structure'): 'It seems likely that [Chaucer] would have understood . . . a type of structure in a long narrative work which depended on the development of ideas and of themes, rather than on the devising of a plot with appropriate characters. If so, this would have reinforced any feeling that narrative structure was dependent on a more total and intimate organization of the material than could be achieved by a construction which was based on the story line alone' (p. 71).

19. Cf. Elizabeth Salter, *Chaucer: The Knight's Tale and the Clerk's Tale* (London, 1962), pp. 35–6, and *The Knight's Tale*, ed. A. C. Spearing (Cambridge, 1966), pp. 75–8.

20. For an argument that Chaucer did not abandon the two-way journey scheme, see Charles A. Owen, *Pilgrimage and Storytelling in the Canterbury Tales* (Norman, Okla., 1977), and *The Manuscripts of the Canterbury Tales* (Cambridge, 1991). Cf. also *The Canterbury Tales: Fifteenth-Century Continuations and Additions*, ed. John M. Bowers (Kalamazoo, Mich., 1992).

21. Cf. Jordan, *Chaucer and the Shape of Creation*, p. 117: 'Such imperfections of adjustment . . . reveal the essential character of Chaucer's art. It is an art of superimpositions, adjustments, accommodations.'

22. This is the 'Bradshaw Shift', suggested by the reading 'Shipman' in Bodleian MS Arch. Selden. B. 14.

23. Cf. Sigmund Eisner, 'Chaucer's Use of Nicholas of Lynn's Calendar', *Essays and Studies*, 29 (1976), 1–22.

24. Cf. J. A. Burrow, 'An Agony in Three Fits' in his *Essays on Medieval Literature* (Oxford, 1984): 'The poem seems to narrow away, section by section, towards nothingness' (p. 65).

25. See Dolores Palomo, 'What Chaucer Really Did to *Le Livre de Melibee*', *Philological Quarterly*, 53 (1974), 304–20; Lee Patterson, '"What Man Artow?": Authorial Self-Definition in *The Tale of Sir Thopas* and *The Tale of Melibee*', *Studies in the Age of Chaucer*, 11 (1989), 117–76; Carolyn C. Colette, 'Heeding the Counsel of Prudence: A Context for the *Melibee*', *Chaucer Review*, 29 (1995), 416–33.

26. Cf. Paul G. Ruggiers, *The Art of the Canterbury Tales* (Madison, Wisc., 1965), pp. 42–50 ('The Range of the Middle'), and also his 'The Form of the *Canterbury Tales: Respice Fines*', *College English*, 17 (1955–6), 439–44.

27. Cf. Cooper, *Structure of the Canterbury Tales*, ch. 5 ('Links within the Fragments'). Cf. also Donald R. Howard, *The Idea of the Canterbury Tales* (Berkeley/Los Angeles, Calif., 1976) ch. IV ('Memory and Form') and ch. V ('The Tales: A Theory of Their Structure'); Judson Boyce Allen and Theresa Anne Moritz, *A Distinction of Stories: The Medieval Unity of Chaucer's Fair Chain of Narratives for Canterbury* (Columbus, Ohio, 1981); Rosemarie P. McGerr, *Chaucer's Open Books: Resistance to Closure in Medieval Literature* (Gainesville, Fla., 1998); and Thomas J. Reed, Jr, *Middle English Debate Poetry and the Aesthetics of Irresolution* (Columbus, Mo., 1990).

28. Cf. Traugott Lawler, *The One and the Many in the Canterbury Tales* (Hamden, Conn., 1980), ch. 5 ('Closure') and ch. 7 ('Closure II: The Parson's Tale and

Chaucer's Retraction'). See also *Closure in the Canterbury Tales: The Role of the Parson's Tale*, eds. L. T. Holley and D. Raybin (Kalamazoo, Mich., 2000).

29. Cf. *Summa Virtutum de Remediis Anime*, ed. and trans. Siegfried Wenzel (Athens, Ga., 1984), and Siegfried Wenzel, 'The Source of Chaucer's Seven Deadly Sins', *Traditio*, 30 (1974), 351–78. See also Lee W. Patterson, 'The "Parson's Tale" and the Quitting of the "Canterbury Tales"', *Traditio*, 34 (1978), 331–80, for a valuable discussion. In his 'Notes on the *Parson's Tale*', *Chaucer Review*, 16 (1981–2), 237–56, Siegfried Wenzel comments: 'In writing [the *Parson's Tale*] Chaucer translated substantial sections from the identified sources. But it is equally accurate to point out that in doing so he not only worked selectively, but also made changes and additions which reveal intelligence, purposiveness, and a fairly exact familiarity with the pastoral-theological thought and language of his time.' Cf. also Richard Newhauser, 'The Parson's Tale' in *Sources and Analogues*, eds. Correale and Hamel, pp. 529–613.

30. Professor Patterson ('The Quitting of the "Canterbury Tales"', pp. 357–70) lists some thirty-five passages in the *Parson's Tale* which echo passages in the preceding tales. Ten such echoes are of conventional phrases and ideas: *ParsT* 1068, *MerchT* 1315, *ShipT* 9; *ParsT* 940, *WBProl* 129–30, *MerchT* 2048; *ParsT* 957, *KnT* 1323; *ParsT* 472, *KnT* 1255–6, *PardProl* 294–6; *ParsT* 473, *ClT* 995–1001; *ParsT* 389, *MerchT* 1640–1; *ParsT* 857–8, *RvProl* 3879–81, *WBProl* 291; *ParsT* 630, *WBProl* 244; *ParsT* 603, *PardProl* 350–1; *ParsT* 368, *Mel* 1079. A further twenty-one passages show the *Parson's Tale* overlapping with some of the preceding tales in drawing on the same traditional homiletic materials: (1) *ParsT* 93, *PhysT* 286; (2) *ParsT* 155–7, *WBProl* 784–5; (3) *ParsT* 407, *GP* 377, 449–52; (4) *ParsT* 484, *PhysT* 114–16; (5) *ParsT* 564, *SumT* 2009; (6) *ParsT* 589, 592, *PardT* 633–7; (7) *ParsT* 591, *PardT* 472–5; (8) *ParsT* 593, *PardT* 648–50; (9) *ParsT* 617, *SumT* 2075; (10) *ParsT* 631–4, *WBProl* 278–80, *Mel* 1086; (11) *ParsT* 710, 714, *SNProl* 1–3; (12) *ParsT* 721, *PhysT* 101–2; (13) *ParsT* 793, *PardT* 591–4; (14) *ParsT* 819, *PardT* 504; (15) *ParsT* 819–20, *PardT* 529–33; (16) *ParsT* 822, *PardT* 558–9; (17) *ParsT* 836, *PardT* 481–4, *PhysT* 59, *WBProl* 464; (18) *ParsT* 859, *MerchT* 1839–40; (19) *ParsT* 884, *MerchT* 1438–40; (20) *ParsT* 929, *MerchT* 1384; (21) *ParsT* 100, *Mel* 1054. The four remaining echoes are rather more substantial: *ParsT* 464, 154, 73, *WBT* 1158; *ParsT* 600, *PardT* 631–2; *ParsT* 1008, *SumT* 2098; *ParsT* 938–9, *MerchT* 1441–51.

31. Cf. Ralph Baldwin, *The Unity of the Canterbury Tales*, Anglistica, 5 (Copenhagen, 1955); Thomas H. Bestul, 'Chaucer's Parson's Tale and the Late Medieval Tradition of Religious Meditation', *Speculum*, 64 (1989), 600–19; and Dee Dyas, *Pilgrimage in Medieval English Literature, 700–1500* (Woodbridge, 2002).

14

CHRISTOPHER CANNON

Chaucer's style

Any description of Chaucer's style is complicated by the two distinct and conflicting meanings the term 'style' now has. The first of these is a product of Romanticism and can be described as the belief that word forms and grammars are aspects of human character. Where 'the attunement of the soul' is thought to 'exer[t] a particular influence upon the language', as Wilhelm von Humboldt (1767–1835) believed, languages will seem to differ from one another in the very same ways, and in the very forms, as people differ.[1] When developed as a method of literary analysis, as it was by philologists such as Leo Spitzer (1887–1960), this view can also discover the 'soul of the artist' in the smallest linguistic detail (the habitual use of a conjunction, for example).[2] Although we do not understand ourselves to be thinking along these lines now, we still employ this theory every time we say that a line of poetry, or a particular turn of phrase, is 'Chaucerian'. For the subtle but sure consequence of assuming that language and 'the artist' are equivalent is the belief that a writer's work is as cohesive as personhood (its parts are so integral that they form an indivisible whole) and just as distinctive (entirely unlike the work of any other person). In the case of Chaucer, such 'style' is the 'peculiar complexity' which sets his writing apart as if it were itself an individual. It is 'the meanings and values that make him Chaucer'.[3]

But Chaucer would not himself have recognized 'style' in this sense, and, although he used the word, it was with a meaning derived from classical and medieval treatises on rhetoric. We retain this meaning in modern English translations of such treatises where we use it to translate the Latin *elocutio*, defined in the *Ad Herennium* (86–82 BC) as 'the adaptation of suitable words and sentences to the matter devised'. This 'style' is a measurement of the degree to which a given language is 'ornate' (*ornata*) or – as ornament is conventionally specified in rhetoric – the quantity and kind of those tropes and figures (metaphor, metonymy, hyperbole, synecdoche, etc.) which it contains. A natural byproduct of such an understanding of language is a hardening or stratification of such measurements, with the result that this sense of 'style' also tends to carry with it the belief that language comes in 'levels' or 'types' (*genera*).[4] Classical rhetoric specified three such types, the 'high' (*gravis*), consisting of words which are 'impressive' in an 'ornate arrangement', the 'middle' (*mediocris*), consisting of words which are 'lower' but not yet 'colloquial', and the 'low' (*adtenuatus*), consisting of words which match the 'most current idiom of standard speech'.[5] It is this hierarchy that Chaucer evokes when he uses the word 'stile', since he always pairs it with 'heigh' in some way (IV, 18, 41, 1148; V, 106). He also embraces the concept of *elocutio* responsible for such gradations – the belief that language must (and can) be suited to the material it conveys – when he says that 'the wordes moote be cosyn to the dede' (I, 742; see also IX, 208 and *Boece* III pr. 12).

Overlaying these difficulties of terminology is a much larger confusion about the significance of Chaucer's style in history, for it is often said that Chaucer invented the habits of his language more or less out of whole cloth – that he was, as Dryden (1631–1700) put it, the 'Father of English Poetry' because he 'first adorn'd our Native Tongue'.[6] The view is intractable if only because it is so old: a version of it appeared in the years just after Chaucer died, and even Chaucer can be seen to nudge his immediate audience toward this notion when he frequently mocks and dismisses the very English literature to which he owed his most significant debts. The analysis of style on which such a presumption is based has often been casual, and almost always self-proving: in the fifteenth century the standard method was for poets who imitated Chaucer to say that he had begun everything of importance; subsequently, we have had both a canon of literature and literary histories which demonstrate Chaucer's originality by excluding most of what preceded him. Scholarship on Middle English in the last fifty years has gradually turned up precedents for most of what is consequential in Chaucer's linguistic and poetic practice, but it has been very difficult to amalgamate these particular discoveries into a general understanding because the term 'style' is at once essential to and ill-suited to the task. Where a category is, in a sense, internal to itself, where a term may refer to either the whole of a writer's work *or* to the various types of language which comprise that work, it is difficult to make clear that Chaucer's whole style is *only* distinct from the whole styles of other writers in the articulation and deployment of its parts – in the styles it assembles from precedent. This is, nevertheless, the view I shall advance in the rest of this essay, focussing primarily – and at some length – on the debt Chaucer's techniques owe to earlier writing, before turning in conclusion to an account of how these techniques were reassembled into a form at once characteristic and unique. This emphasis is necessary to set a very muddled record straight, but it is in no way meant to denigrate Chaucer's capacities as a writer. The particularly 'Chaucerian' is rich and remarkable precisely because it draws so fully on the great variety of past achievement. It can be studied, not only for that richness, but as a window onto the larger literary world which Chaucer himself so valued that he absorbed it more comprehensively than any other Middle English writer.

The undistinguished style

Because poets and literary historians have been so eager to say just how new Chaucer's language was, it has almost never seemed worth saying that it had to be quite *usual* if Chaucer was ever to be understood. This means that for every extraordinary image or expression in the poems ('Nas never pyk walwed in galauntyne / As I in love am walwed and ywounde': *To Rosamounde* 17–18), for every memorably compressed simple sentiment ('pitee renneth soone in gentil herte': I, 1761),[7] Chaucer had to produce hundreds of workmanlike lines and phrases which conveyed simple meanings in a straightforward way. Of course standard forms can themselves become distinctive when they appear often enough. Chaucer uses the verb 'bifallen' with a temporal marker so frequently for example (see I, 19; III, 1713; VI, 52; VII, 2423), that a line such as 'But so bifel, this marchant on a day' in the *Shipman's Tale* (VII, 53) will seem like a linguistic signature to anyone familiar with Chaucer's writing. A quick glance at the relevant entries in the *MED* shows however that such a use of the verb is not unusual in the languages of the romances written in the generation before Chaucer, and that the particular temporal marker Chaucer has chosen is itself a kind of formula: 'Bifel so þat . . .' can be found in a similar context in *Richard Coeur de Lyon* (c.1300) and 'on a day' in *Sir Orfeo* (c.1330).[8] Chaucer's language was, on the whole, the language of these romances, and that language was, more generally, the language of London. Chaucer has also seemed foundational, then, because this London dialect eventually became Standard English: any difference between Chaucer's English and writers of only a few generations earlier has seemed like progress toward this particular form of modernity, and it has also been easy to see the language of those contemporary Middle English writers who did not share Chaucer's dialect (such as the *Gawain*-poet and William Langland) as either backward or eccentric.

It is true that, in Chaucer's hands, the most basic materials yield extraordinary variety, but it is almost always by acts of discovery rather than acts of invention, by exploring the uses inherent in a form rather than by making something completely new. There is no space here to prove this claim fully because it is most abundantly true at the level of particular words and phrases, but a single example can serve to illustrate the enormous possibility for development that Chaucer can discover in grammatical givens.[9] The raw material in this case is a set of similar but alternative forms, which Middle English employed in a number of categories. These include past participles with or without the prefix 'y-' (*slayn* or *yslayn*), the infinitive with or without 'to' or 'for to' as a marker (*ben* or *to ben*, or *for to ben*), double versus single negation (*ne* + verb + *no* + complement or verb + *no* + complement), *gan* + infinitive as a periphrasis for the preterite (*gan synge* or *sang*), and any word with an etymological or inflectional final *-e* which could be pronounced or left silent (so '*name*' pronounced as either two syllables or one).[10] Such basic (and therefore pervasive) forms, which differed by a syllable or two but still meant the same thing, gave Chaucer enormous flexibility in the creation of metrical patterns, and it was his careful deployment of these alternatives which allowed him to stabilize the relatively rough metre of the romances. A poem such as *Guy of Warwick* (c.1300) used these forms (for example, *ygon* in the quotation below) but its lines tend to imply, more often than they actually achieve, a norm of eight-syllable lines with four stresses:

> Wel glad and blithe than ben he,
> and al that weren in that cité.
> To her innes thai ben ygon,
> Wel glad ben hii everichon.[11]

By contrast, Chaucer ensured that the pattern of his own lines ran smooth by choosing the appropriate form (here, *gan . . . shoute* instead of *shouted*, *for to lawghe* instead of *laughen* or *to laughen*), and by exploiting the possibility of pronouncing an *-e* in one word ('*game*') while it was left silent in another ('*fonde*'):

> And that wente al the world aboute,
> That every wight *gan* on hem *shoute*
> And *for to lawghe as they were wod*,
> Such game fonde they in her hod.   (*House of Fame*, 1807–10)

Chaucer's octosyllabics are not themselves wholly 'regular', since there are exceptional lines in his poems as well as variations repeated often enough to form their own standard, but the careful deployment of this variety of forms also assures that Chaucer's verse rhythms are much *more* regular than those of any of his predecessors.

In addition to the outlines of a metrical pattern, it was also the English romances such as *Guy of Warwick*, *Sir Orfeo*, and *Richard Coeur de Lion* which provided Chaucer with a whole set of key terms ('hende', 'lemman', 'druerie') as well as a corresponding fund of stock phrases ('bright in bour') for describing the kinds of courtly persons and situations he initially wrote about. Because these romances were the longest poems written in English up to this point, their writers had also acquired the habit of finding rhymes by means of relatively meaningless phrases at line's end, and Chaucer inherited both a tolerance for such fillers and some of their conventional vocabulary ('so as I gesse', 'as I trowe', 'for the nones').[12] It is a measure of the extent of this debt that the first lines of the *Book of the Duchess* translate the first lines of *Le Paradys d'Amour* by Froissart (1338–1410) but achieve their rhymes entirely by means of such phrases:[13]

Je sui de moi en grant merveille	I have gret wonder, *be this lyght,*
Comment je vifs quant tant je veille	How that I lyve, for *day ne nyght*
Et on ne point en veillant	I may nat slepe *wel nygh noght;*
Trouver de moi plus traveillant . . .	I have so many an ydel thoght . . .
(1–4)	(1–4)

Chaucer even relied on this method when he moved away from romance subjects, as in the *House of Fame*, where a filler is used to flesh out an otherwise exact translation of the first lines of the *Aeneid*:

> 'I wol now synge, *yif I kan,*
> The armes and also the man . . .'   (143–4)

It is more likely that Chaucer writes 'yif I kan' here in order to have a rhyme for 'man', than that he wishes to suggest that Virgil might not be up to the challenge of this story. But such a superimposition of the casual and the serious is a characteristic that Chaucer also absorbs from the romances, where the roughness of metre, the homogeneity of diction, and the preponderance of filler can often seem similarly inappropriate to the weighty subjects treated. This debt is also easy to miss because Chaucer sometimes uses the diction of the romances to convey the awkward idealism of the foolish (Absolon in the *Miller's Tale*, for example),[14] and he mocked the whole of the genre in the *Tale of Sir Thopas*, but, as I shall show in more detail below, it is precisely the relaxed assumption of such casual speech which is generally characteristic of Chaucer's verse.

What is usually given much more emphasis than such English precedent, however, is the influence of writing from the Continent. Although this too is a debt to the past, it has been customary to see it as a form of rarity (of a scope or of a type 'new' to English) and so almost every account of Chaucer's English produces a sentence like this:

> The great work of his life was the development of an English poetic tradition; this involved transference into English of the French tradition fed and supplemented by the greater literatures in Latin and Italian.[15]

The extent and inventiveness of this 'transference' has sometimes been demonstrated by counting the number of borrowings from French and Latin recorded in Chaucer's English for the first time (there are 1,102 such words out of Chaucer's total vocabulary of 9,117 words), or by enumerating the wide variety of French, Italian, and Latin sources that Chaucer relied upon. The facts in such illustrations are not wrong, but those facts can also be used to prove exactly the opposite point if it is noted that the *technique* of such borrowing, if not Chaucer's specific importations, was itself the founding practice of the prior English tradition. The borrowing of Continental words had actually reached its peak in the generation *before* Chaucer wrote, and such lexical exchange was extensive within the earlier Middle English romances because these texts were for the most part translations of some French source. It is true that Chaucer borrowed certain aspects of his versification from French for the first time (he took rime royal from the *ballades* of Machaut (d. 1377)), but it is also earlier English writing that would have inspired this adaptation, since the very octosyllabics which Chaucer found in English were, in origin, a French form too – borrowed by Middle English romances, from their sources, in earlier generations. It is not always necessary to cross the Channel to find a model for the forms Chaucer used either. Although it has been claimed, for example, that 'several of Machaut's individual complaints are among the few significant predecessors of Chaucer's decasyllabic couplets',[16] the only inspiration Chaucer would have needed for the extension of the octosyllabic to ten syllables was the long line of earlier alliterative verse. Such verse had already absorbed the courtly language of romance and had begun to rhyme, and the lines of a lyric such as 'Annot and John' (*c*.1325) are already approximating the necessary shape:

> Ichot a burde in a bour ase beryl so bryht,
> ase saphyr in seluer semly on syht . . .[17]

Writers of the fifteenth century thought that Chaucer's primary innovation lay in his use of rhetoric, that he was, as Lydgate (d. 1449) put it, the 'firste' to bring 'Retoryke' to a 'Rude speche'.[18] This debt is also sizeable and important, but, since rhetoric is, at root, a set of normative principles (teaching how a writer's style or *elocutio* can be adjusted to its subject), its general tendency is to make writing *less* original. When we discover in Chaucer an unusual abundance of those tropes and figures which popular treatises such as Geoffrey of Vinsauf's *Poetria Nova* (*c*.1210) catalogued and recommended, we are also measuring the extent to which he conformed to a set of fixed patterns and recommended shapes. However striking the first lines of the *Parliament of Fowls* may seem, then, they are, from this perspective, an expansion of a very old subject (the Latin proverb *ars longa, vita brevis*) by means of *contentio* (the comparison of antithetical positions), *expolitio* (dwelling on the same subject by means of variation), and *similitudo* (finding similarities in the dissimilar):[19]

> The lyf so short, the craft so long to lerne,
> Th'asay so hard, so sharp the conquerynge,
> The dredful joye alwey that slit so yerne:
> Al this mene I by Love . . .   (1–4)

It is precisely because Chaucer's style could be said to be less original on these grounds that some literary critics have held that his poetry is only most effective and original where it avoids rhetoric. Chaucer invites this estimation in a variety of ways and most memorably when he mentions Geoffrey of Vinsauf in the *Nun's Priest's Tale* (VII, 3347) only to introduce a parody of rhetorical invention in which the most complex figures and tropes are wheeled out to elaborate the lives of chickens. But it is an important, if paradoxical, consequence of the concern with ornament in rhetoric that it actually *de*values language: rhetoric recommends figures and tropes because it believes that poetry 'is a process of manipulating language so that the wisdom evolved in the past will become available, applicable, and operative in the present', and it is therefore in the story which is revived, and not in its verbal decoration, that value must lie.[20] It is this form of conservatism which Chaucer sets out at some length in the Prologue to the *Legend of Good Women*:

> Than mote we to bokes that we fynde,
> Thurgh whiche that olde thinges ben in mynde,
> And to the doctrine of these olde wyse,
> Yeve credence, in every skylful wise,
> That tellen of these olde appreved stories . . .   (F 17–21)

The early dream visions may be said to take this view as their theme when they begin with the search for the old story which will form the basis for what follows. Such a principle is also basic to Chaucer's practice on all those occasions when he departs from one old story, not for free invention, but to retell yet another: thus, the first *canticus Troili* (I, 400–20) departs from Boccaccio only to translate a sonnet by Petrarch, and the second *canticus Troili* (III, 1744–71) turns away again only to adapt the eighth metre from Book II of Boethius's *Consolation of Philosophy*. To be so in thrall to the past and so chary of the new is of course to believe that the backward glance is itself creative, that a retrospection rapt enough will release new meanings in what is the most old.[21] But, because the earlier English romances were themselves translations or adaptations of 'olde appreved' stories, they were therefore rhetorical in just this fundamental sense, and Chaucer is even following long-standing English precedent in embracing this principle of re-creation.

Chaucer did not take only whole narratives from the traditions he relied upon, however: the most important aspect of his inherited technique are the 'two basic conventional styles' he took wholesale from the 'French tradition', two prepackaged adjustments of 'word' to 'deed'.[22] Because they map onto the levels of style recommended by the rhetorics, it is partly the case that the elements of these styles are no more than a mediated version of the techniques which Chaucer could have learned from someone like Geoffrey of Vinsauf. The portrait of 'Blanche' in the *Book of the Duchess*, for example (817–1040), could be described as an extended *effictio* ('to depict or represent corporeal appearance') since it portrays her body from top to toe ('every heer on hir hed' (855) to 'al hir lymmes' (959)), with interleaved remarks on her manners ('And which a goodly, softe speche / Had that swete' (919–20)), and probity ('She used gladly to do wel' (1013)).[23] But Chaucer lifts this figure, its material, as well as the general setting in which these elements are deployed in his own poem, from Machaut's *Jugement dou Roy de Behaigne*.[24] Chaucer's debt in this case is therefore to the *whole* of a style, an adjustment of technique to subject which Muscatine called 'courtly' because it involved a set of interdependent habits for portraying the lives of aristocratic persons, usually in an 'exotic setting' where 'undramatic discourse and semiotic gesture' were 'designed to evoke invisible worlds'.[25] Chaucer was not unusual in such borrowing, for the courtly style was also foundational for Middle English romance. There is, for example, a useful parallel between Chaucer's and Machaut's shared *effictio* and the description of 'Dame Herodis' in *Sir Orfeo* where an anatomy of a 'body', face (or 'rode'), 'fingers', and 'lovesum eygen two' are carefully shaped to evoke the exotic and invisible world of the afterlife (which 'Herodis' has just witnessed).[26] It is also fair to say, however, that, even if the possibility of borrowing such stylistic units was prepared by an English tradition, such borrowings were more visible in Chaucer's case because he relied on their rich combination of elements more extensively.[27]

These elements are also clearer to see in his verse because they are so frequently thrown into relief by a second set of carefully adjusted elements and techniques. Muscatine called this style 'realistic' or 'naturalistic' because it gives 'the impression of dealing with life directly, with something of life's natural shape and vitality'.[28] But the key word here is 'impression', since it is crucial to Muscatine's definitions that such a style is not presenting reality itself, but, rather, a set of conventions which create such an illusion or effect. This is the style of the French fabliau, but Chaucer discovered it where it sits right alongside the courtly style in poems such as the *Romance of the Rose*. It is there that the 'dreamland' setting is so often interrupted by 'a colorful piece of everyday domestic life', as here, when 'Shame' is awakened from her sleep:[29]

'Por quoi dormez vos a cest hore,'	'Why slepist thou, whanne thou
Fet Honte, 'par mal auanture?	shulde wake?'
Fox est qui en vos s'aseüre	Quod Shame; 'thou doist us vylanye!
De garder rose ne boton	Who tristith thee, he doth folye,
. . .	To kepe roses or botouns . . .'
'En tel heure vos chouchiez?	. . .
Leuez vos sus, e si bochiez	Art thou now late? Ris up in hy,
Touz les pertuis de cele haie,	And stop sone and delyverly
E ne portez nului menaie.'	All the gappis of the haye.
(3678–81, 3691–4)	Do no favour, I thee praye.'
	(4008–11, 4021–4)

It is not just the domesticity in a case such as this but the *obtrusion* of such different circumstances and diction in a courtly context that is the technique Chaucer absorbs, and this is why he first employs such naturalism in the most courtly of his poems. After the pastiche from Froissart which begins *The Book of the Duchess*, on the way to that extended *effictio* inspired by Machaut, there is, for example, Chaucer's own spirited description of an awakening:

> This messager com fleynge faste
> And cried, 'O, how! Awake anoon!'
> Hit was for noght; there herde hym non.
> 'Awake!' quod he, 'whoo ys lyth there?'
> And blew his horn ryght in here eere,
> And cried 'Awaketh!' wonder hyë.
> This god of slep with hys oon yë
> Cast up, and axed, 'Who clepeth ther?'   (178–85)

Comedy is generated here by the allegorical perversity of waking 'Sleep', but it is also a function of the conversational repetition and the directness of action (a horn blown 'ryght' in an ear) which are the procedures of realism here. There were also precedents for the use of this style in courtly contexts in the Middle English romances. When Floris is told that Blancheflour is dead (wrongly, as it happens) in *Floris and Blancheflour*, informality obtrudes in his conversation with the queen:

> 'Thou gabbest me,' he saide tho;
> 'Thy gabbing doth me muche wo!
> Tell me where my leman be!'

> All weeping saide thenne she,
> 'Sir,' she saide, 'deede.' 'Deed!' saide he.
> 'Sir,' she saide, 'for sothe, ye.'
> 'Allas, when died that swete wight?'
> 'Sir, withinne this fourtenight
> The erth was laide hur abo[ve]
> And deed she was for thy love.'[30]

The realism is sporadic in this case, since some of these exclamations are proper *apostrophe* of the most elevated kind, and such rapid intercutting of dialogue was itself a feature of the courtly style. But the simplicity and bluntness of some words here ('gabbest', 'gabbing') is enough to indicate that strong emotion has stripped away some proprieties, and Floris's reaction (accusing the queen of joking when she tells him his lover is dead) is painful precisely because it is so raw. The general lack of polish in the whole of such Middle English romances can be attributed to such diffusion of elements of the natural style into courtly circumstances, and it is the awkwardness of such a mixture, which is (like octosyllabic in these romances) yet another native inheritance, that Chaucer stabilized by his care.

As will be seen below, the deployment of the distinction between these two types of style was more important to Chaucer than 'courtliness' and 'naturalism' *per se*, but no inheritance was more important in the making of Chaucer's style than the *possibility* of such a distinction. It is therefore the very extent of this influence which can actually cause us to miss the variety of levels at which this technique operates. We may notice that the *Canterbury Tales* is built round the juxtaposition of various forms of court-liness or naturalism (the *Knight's Tale* as against the *Miller's Tale*, say), but we may miss the fact that these styles are also juxtaposed within such tales as well. The most homely image may erupt even in the most elaborate de-scription of the 'hertes' of lovers in the *Knight's Tale* ('Now up, now doun, as boket in a welle': 1533). And, although the Reeve thinks the Miller's language is so coarse that he describes it as 'cherles termes' (I, 3917), the courtly style obtrudes everywhere into the naturalism of the *Miller's Tale*. While the description of Alisoun is in significant part naturalistic since it asso-ciates Alisoun with the most common living things (weasels, kids and calves, colts, a pear tree), and the most ordinary activities (skipping and 'making game'), it is also 'courtly' as it too takes the shape of an *effictio*, moving from Alisoun's head ('ful smale ypulled were hire browes two': 3245) down the whole of her body ('Long as a mast, and upright as a bolt': 3264). Although we might be so conditioned by what the Wife of Bath tells us about herself to expect the oaths, curses, or colloquial turns of phrase which mark her language ('Abyde!' quod she, 'my tale is nat bigonne': 169), the idealization of Criseyde in *Troilus* may cause us to overlook the coarser aspects of her conversation:

> 'I! God forbede!' quod she. 'Be ye mad?
> Is that a widewes lif, so God yow save?
> By God, ye maken me ryght soore adrad!
> Ye ben so wylde, it semeth as ye rave.'   (II, 113–16)

Chaucer's most important debt to the past was the way he enchained these two modes as a constant set of alternatives and contrasts, a style that was not simply mixed but which was wholly defined by the activity of *mixing*.

The distinctive style of types

What Chaucer learned most consequentially from the past forms he studied so carefully was, then, the way that *division* itself might have an expressive function which exceeded that of either of the parts divided. Because Chaucer's debt to the 'courtly' and 'naturalistic' styles was therefore more to the line between them than to any of their constituent elements, the elements of his own styles were hardly limited to the techniques of the French tradition, and it is common to signal this difference by returning to rhetorical classifications and describing Chaucer's two styles as 'high' and 'low'. These terms helpfully broaden the relevant categories but they also bring with them the impression that they are distinguished not only in kind, but in quality – that the 'high' is somehow *better* than the 'low' in Chaucer, as it often was in rhetoric. Chaucer helps in this confusion too since he presented the 'heigh style' as something difficult to achieve (as, for example, when the Squire is too modest to attempt 'so heigh a style': V, 106) or difficult to understand (as when the Host forbids a 'heigh style' to the Clerk because he doesn't feel the general run of pilgrims are up to it: IV, 15–20). The problem intensifies when this terminological misunderstanding combines, by means of a rather vicious structural pun, with a similar distinction between 'innovation' and 'tradition'. In scholarship of the past, in fact, it has been a deceptively short step from understanding that Chaucer had two styles to the view that his more elevated style was 'new' and his lower style was 'old', that he 'adorned the Native Tongue' by grafting a language of sophistication and ornament onto the stalk (or stump) of a native language of natural colloquial simplicity. This mistake is both widespread and long-standing because it is fuelled by all the enthusiasms of the old foundationalist myth, and it is, of course, also based upon an accurate and crucial sensitivity to the divisions which are so important to Chaucer's style. It has been very damaging, however, insofar as it has so misaligned Chaucer's debt to past practice that it has often been impossible to discern those ways in which he actually was original.

Where that originality lies is not in fact in any aspect of these types of style, but in the clarity of their *articulation* and the particularities of their *combination*: Chaucer makes the whole of his style a complex intermixture of the 'high' and the 'low', not only by moving between the various elements of these styles in sequence, but by layering their elements so as to create a simultaneity which is finally basic to his every use of language and his broadest themes. The first sentences of the *General Prologue* to the *Canterbury Tales* offer a good point at which to isolate the most important elements of this general practice. The famous first sentence is 'high' in its style, rhetorically complex (it could be described as an *expolitio* on the theme of the fecundity of nature in springtime), syntactically varied as well as extended (it postpones its main clause until line twelve, and adds supplementary clauses for a further six lines), with a vocabulary that is both heavily polysyllabic and recherché, consisting of words that Chaucer did not use very often ('licour', 'veyne', 'holt', 'heeth', 'strondes', 'halwes') or that he uses here in unusual ways ('tendre', 'vertu', 'engendered'):

> Whan that Aprill with his shoures soote
> The droghte of March hath perced to the roote,
> And bathed every veyne in swich licour
> Of which vertu engendred is the flour;
> Whan Zephirus eek with his sweete breeth
> Inspired hath in every holt and heeth
> The tendre croppes, and the yonge sonne
> Hath in the Ram his half cours yronne,
> And smale foweles maken melodye,
> That slepen al the nyght with open ye
> (So priketh hem nature in hir corages),
> Thanne longen folk to goon on pilgrimages,
> And palmeres for to seken straunge strondes,
> To ferne halwes, kowthe in sondry londes;
> And specially from every shires ende
> Of Engelond to Caunterbury they wende,
> The hooly blisful martir for to seke,
> That hem hath holpen whan that they were seeke.   (1–18)

The second sentence of the *General Prologue* is, on the other hand, shorter, syntactically straightforward, more homely and local in its detail, and lexically constrained (for it is, at least initially, heavily monosyllabic):

> Bifil that in that seson on a day,
> In Southwerk at the Tabard as I lay
> Redy to wenden on my pilgrymage
> To Caunterbury with ful devout corage,
> At nyght was come into that hostelrye
> Wel nyne and twenty in a compaignye
> Of sondry folk, by aventure yfalle
> In felaweshipe, and pilgrimes were they alle,
> That toward Caunterbury wolden ryde.   (19–27)

But, as generally with Chaucer's styles, the most crucial aspect of the difference between these sentences is the carefully erected boundary – the distinction – *between* them. This line does not wholly coincide with sentence division: complex vocabulary has died out and monosyllables have fully encroached by the last line of the first sentence, and its syntax grows simpler after line twelve. However, at the beginning of the second sentence Chaucer also sets down a clear marker for change by using those two standard phrases mentioned above ('bifel that' and 'on a day'), thereby offering a linguistic figure for the shift from the unusual to the familiar, and the change in focus of this sentence, as well as its immediate concretion of description, are themselves abrupt enough to create a new stylistic area. As I have already suggested, moreover, it is in the nature of Chaucer's stylistic distinctions that the principal elements of one style actually *can* be found in the other. The second sentence may begin with monosyllables but it has its share of polysyllables and it even repeats the polysyllabic rhyme 'corage/pilgrimage'; its syntax, although less complicated than that of much of the first sentence, grows increasingly complex (we do not find out what actually 'befell' on this day until the fifth and sixth lines of the sentence). Conversely, although the second sentence seems to proceed with the narrative simplicity of the older romances, it is in fact the abstraction of the first sentence which is more conventional, since a description was a standard procedure for scene-setting in the old romances. A surprisingly similar passage can be found in *Kyng Alisaunder* (c.1300):

> Averylle is mery and langeth the daye:
> Leuedyes dauncen and thai playe.
> Swaynes justeth, knightes tournay,
> Syngeth the nigttyngale, gradeth the jay.[31]

Such mixing is a form of richness rather than of blurring precisely because boundaries are articulated carefully enough to bring out the different tendencies of each style. Here, as elsewhere, moreover, Chaucer is less interested in particular stylistic attributes than in the *idea* of some distinction itself; rather than create strictly segregated linguistic kinds he tries to press difference from similarity, to construct the *sense* of a 'high' style in the first sentence and the *sense* of a 'low' style in the second as much by means of the contrasts they offer to each other as by an inherent set of linguistic properties. It is this extraordinary capacity to generate dynamism in language by the nature of its arrangement rather than by its constituents which is Chaucer's unique linguistic signature.

In fact this capacity for finding movement in stasis, or distinctions in the same, was so basic to Chaucer's language that we may suspect it of being a fundamental habit of his mind – the way he said things because it was the way he thought of them – and it is certainly fair to say that this double structure was as much a signature of his meanings as it was of his sentences. One way to move toward some understanding of the wider role such a structure played is to examine what Chaucer might have meant by the interesting word he took from Boccaccio to describe a particularly rich example of its use. The root of 'ambages' is the Latin *ambages*, which means 'winding or circuitous paths', but it is also related to Latin *ambiguitas*, which the *Ad Herennium* and Geoffrey of Vinsauf use to describe a word which 'belies its appearance' (*haec vox transvertit visum*).[32] The word occurs only once in Chaucer (in the stanza in *Troilus* where it also occurs in the *Filostrato*) and it is given to Diomede who uses it to describe Calkas to Criseyde:

'And but if Calkas lede us with ambages –
That is to seyn, with double wordes slye,
Swiche as men clepen a word with two visages –
Ye shal wel knowen that I naught ne lie . . .'   (v, 897–900)

Ambiguitas in rhetoric is a fault, and Chaucer certainly denigrates it here, but, as we have seen, it is itself a characteristic 'ambage' of Chaucerian self-presentation to name a productive source by means of contempt. And, as defined here, the 'ambage' or 'double word' once again makes a distinction (here between seeming truth and actual falsehood) by means of layering, where the resulting richness is also seen to take residence in a single instance of language (here the word 'with two visages'). This would be no more than to describe the structure of any lie were it not the case that the meaning Chaucer is pointing to extends far beyond Diomede's overt statement: not only do we have one man telling us that another may speak falsehoods, but we have a 'slye' character trying to persuade Criseyde of this as he 'woos' her, thereby also suggesting that *he* may be lying.[33] This marking of the boundary between two meanings again serves to proffer the idea of a distinction, thereby creating even further distinctions beyond these circumstances:

it serves to suggest, for example, that Troilus's earlier persuasiveness might have been a kind of 'slyness', and that Criseyde's 'betrayal', since the 'giving of her herte' to Diomede is only a repetition of her earlier commitment to Troilus, might also be described as 'love'. In these larger forms this structure has been described as a double point of view or 'double vision' which results from the assembling of 'incongruous and inharmonious parts into an insep-arable whole which is infinitely greater than its parts', and in this form it is understood, not as a phenomenon of words or sentences only, but also of character, situation, and narrative shape.[34] Another term which bridges this large distance is *ironia*, and it is in terms of 'irony' that critics of Chaucer have most commonly connected the smaller linguistic examples I have given to the larger thematic effects of this technique, sometimes speaking of 'struc-tural irony' when talking about poetic wholes.[35] Such irony can involve, for example, the celebration and critique of courtly idealism by means of a naturalism itself prized for its practicality but deplored for its futilities in *Troilus*. It can be activated around a single line such as 'pitee renneth soone in gentil herte' so that its use to praise Theseus in the *Knight's Tale* (1761) can be inverted in the *Merchant's Tale* as a sarcastic description of the heartless May (1986) – where that inversion itself undermines its own foundations (as we might come to realize, pity did not run *so* soon in Theseus). Taken in these broad terms such examples could be multiplied endlessly – but that is of course the point. Chaucer's *whole* style is characterized by the discovery, in language – by means of language – of the two in the one.

There is some danger in proposing irony as the key to Chaucer's style, since there has been such cavalier application of this term and a consequent haziness about its meaning ever since George Kittredge used it so freely in *Chaucer and His Poetry* (1915). As Derek Pearsall has rightly said, the poten-tial for irony to license absolutely any meaning is pernicious: 'if everything is ironical, nothing is interesting' since 'the very complexity that was sought through variation in point of view becomes imperiled'.[36] And yet, just like the confusion about the origins of Chaucer's two styles, the danger exists be-cause the structure is both omnipresent and foundational – to get it wrong in this particular way is at least to get something important right. For this same reason the specific richness of much that Chaucer wrote will remain unde-tected if 'double words' are never sought. Chaucer comes closest to telling us this on those occasions throughout his writing where he contrasts 'earnest' with 'game',[37] or when he organizes the whole tale-telling competition of the *Canterbury Tales* around the contrast between 'sentence' and 'solaas' (I, 798). His point in each of these cases must be that such oppositions contain one another, that it is worth making such distinctions because there is earnest in game and pleasure to be had in the serious – and vice versa in each case. The still larger claim embedded in the variety and extent of such doubleness must therefore be that the 'ambage', or the irony, is the ideal form not only of language but of the very meanings language conveys: it is, for Chaucer, the shape truth has, whatever truth may be discovered to be.

NOTES

1. Wilhelm von Humboldt, *Linguistic Variability and Intellectual Development*, trans. George C. Buck and Frithjof A. Raven (Coral Gables, Fla., 1971), p. 16.
2. Leo Spitzer, 'Linguistics and Literary History' in *Linguistics and Literary History: Essays in Stylistics* (Princeton, 1967), pp. 1–29, at pp. 18–19.
3. Charles Muscatine, *Chaucer and the French Tradition* (Berkeley, Calif., 1957), p. 8.
4. *Ad Herennium*, ed. and trans. Harry Caplan (Cambridge, Mass., 1981), I.ii.3 and IV.xiii.
5. *Ad Herennium*, IV.viii.
6. Caroline F. E. Spurgeon, *Five Hundred Years of Chaucer Criticism and Allusion, 1357–1900*, vol. I (Cambridge, 1925), pp. 276 and 284.
7. Chaucer was very fond of this line and also used it in the *Legend of Good Women* (F Prologue 105), the *Merchant's Tale* (1986) and the *Squire's Tale* (479).
8. See *MED*, s.vv. 'bifallen' v. 2b and 'dai' n., 12c (j).
9. On the grammar of Chaucer's language see Norman Davis, 'Chaucer and Fourteenth-Century English' in *Writers and Their Background: Geoffrey Chaucer*, ed. Derek Brewer (London, 1974), pp. 58–84, and David Burnley, *The Language of Chaucer* (London, 1989), esp. pp. 10–99.
10. For these examples see Davis, 'Chaucer and Fourteenth-Century English', pp. 67–8 (on the past participle), 68–9 (on final -*e*), and Burnley, *The Language of Chaucer*, pp. 28–30 (on the infinitive), 53–4 (on the *gan*-periphrasis), 61–4 (on negation).
11. *The Romance of Guy of Warwick*, 3 vols., ed. Julius Zupitza, EETS os 42 (1883), 49 (1887), and 59 (1891), lines 2259–62. I have normalized the spelling and typography of this edition for the sake of clarity.
12. Larry D. Benson, 'The Beginnings of Chaucer's English Style' in *Contradictions: From Beowulf to Chaucer*, eds. Theodore M. Andersson and Stephen A. Barney (Aldershot, 1995), pp. 243–65, esp. pp. 248–56.
13. I draw this example (which is extended and more fully discussed there) from D. S. Brewer, 'The Relationship of Chaucer to the English and European Traditions' in *Chaucer and Chaucerians*, ed. D. S. Brewer (London, 1966), pp. 1–38, at pp. 2–6.
14. E. T. Donaldson, 'The Idiom of Popular Poetry in the *Miller's Tale*' in *Speaking of Chaucer* (London, 1970), pp. 13–29.
15. James I. Wimsatt, 'Chaucer and French Poetry' in *Writers and Their Background*, ed. Brewer, pp. 109–36, at p. 111.
16. Wimsatt, 'Chaucer and French Poetry', p. 125.
17. For this poem see *The Harley Lyrics: The Middle English Lyrics of MS. Harley 2253*, ed. G. L. Brook, 4th edn (Manchester, 1968), pp. 31–2.

18. *Chaucer: The Critical Heritage*, ed. Derek S. Brewer, 2 vols. (London, 1978), vol. 1, p. 46.
19. For these figures see Geoffrey of Vinsauf, *Poetria Nova*, trans. Margaret F. Nims (Toronto, 1967), p. 61.
20. Robert O. Payne, *The Key of Remembrance: A Study of Chaucer's Poetics* (New Haven, Conn., 1963), p. 89.
21. On translation as a species of rhetorical invention in Chaucer, see Rita Copeland, *Rhetoric, Hermeneutics and Translation in the Middle Ages: Academic Traditions and Vernacular Texts* (Cambridge, 1991), esp. pp. 186–202.
22. Muscatine, *Chaucer and the French Tradition*, p. 4.
23. Geoffrey of Vinsauf, *Poetria Nova*, trans. Nims, p. 62 (line 1261). For an example of this technique see pp. 36–7 (lines 562–99).
24. For the passage in the *Jugement* see *Chaucer's Dream Poetry: Sources and Analogues*, ed. and trans. B. A. Windeatt (Woodbridge, Suffolk, 1982), pp. 7–9.
25. Muscatine, *Chaucer and the French Tradition*, pp. 17–18 and 40.
26. *Sir Orfeo* in *Middle English Verse Romances*, ed. Donald B. Sands (Exeter, 1986), pp. 185–200 (lines 81–92).
27. The emphasis here and throughout this essay may seem to scant Chaucer's discovery of an 'Italian tradition', but the English precedent with which I am concerned must be oriented to French literature because this is the only Continental form Chaucer's predecessors looked to. It is not easy to distinguish 'Italian' from 'French' influences in this context, moreover, because Dante and Boccaccio were themselves so deeply influenced by the very French writing I am referring to. On the 'common French ancestry' of both Chaucer and Boccaccio see David Wallace, *Chaucer and the Early Writings of Boccaccio* (Woodbridge, 1985), and, on the pervasiveness of 'French patterns of thinking . . . in European culture' more generally, see Ardis Butterfield's essay in this volume ('Chaucer's French Inheritance', esp. pp. 26–8).
28. Muscatine, *Chaucer and the French Tradition*, p. 59.
29. The example is derived from Muscatine, *Chaucer and the French Tradition*, pp. 45–6. The Middle English translation given here is one that has sometimes been attributed to Chaucer (as 'Fragment B') but now thought not to be his work. I quote the French from *The Romaunt of the Rose and Le Roman de la Rose: A Parallel-Text Edition*, ed. Ronald Sutherland (Oxford, 1967).
30. *Floris and Blancheflur*, lines 235–44, in *Middle English Verse Romances*, ed. Donald B. Sands (Exeter, 1986), pp. 279–305.
31. *Kyng Alisaunder*, ed. G. V. Smithers, 2 vols., EETS os 227 (1952) and 237 (1957), lines 139–42. I have also normalized the spelling of this passage for the sake of clarity.
32. See *Ad Herennium*, IV.53.75ff and Geoffrey of Vinsauf, *Poetria Nova*, lines 1545–8.
33. On this passage see B. A. Windeatt, *Oxford Guides to Chaucer: Troilus and Criseyde* (Oxford, 1992), p. 325.
34. E. T. Donaldson, 'Chaucer the Pilgrim' in *Speaking of Chaucer*, pp. 1–12, at pp. 11–12.
35. On *ironia* in the rhetorical tradition see Cicero, *De Oratore*, 2 vols., eds. and trans. E. W. Sutton and H. Rackham (London, 1942; repr. 1967), II.67, §§ 269–71

and Quintilian, *Institutio Oratoria*, 4 vols., ed and trans. H. E. Butler (London, 1920–2), VIII.6, line 54 (in vol. 3). On 'structural irony' in *Troilus*, see, for example, Muscatine, *Chaucer and the French Tradition*, p. 132.

36. Derek Pearsall, *The Canterbury Tales* (London, 1985), p. 63.

37. See *House of Fame* 822; *Troilus and Criseyde* III, 254; and IV, 1465; *Legend of Good Women* 2703; *Canterbury Tales* I, 3186; IV, 609, 733, 1594; IX, 100.

15

JAMES SIMPSON

Chaucer's presence and absence, 1400–1550

Chaucer and Malory are the only Middle English writers whose literary afterlife has been pretty well continuous from the fifteenth to the twenty-first centuries. Study of Chaucer in particular reveals the pressures and contours of Middle English studies with especial clarity. Many recent studies have focussed on aspects of Chaucer's reception, especially in the fifteenth and sixteenth centuries,[1] and the present chapter is devoted to that same period. It will in part confirm the conclusions of previous work, in part challenge them. In particular, I challenge the notion that Chaucer's fifteenth-century followers were inertly unresponsive to the possibilities opened up by Chaucer's *œuvre*. Indeed, it is precisely the need to isolate Chaucer's genius that produces a dismissive account of Chaucer's fifteenth-century followers; that need began in earnest in the sixteenth century.

A complete conspectus of the way in which Chaucer's works were revised and remade would need to cover the following areas: the changing nature of the texts in which his works were presented; the way in which he was cited in broadly 'literary' texts; the way in which his name was deployed in political and religious controversy.[2] I give examples of each of these areas, but a complete conspectus would occupy a large book. Instead, I propose an argument designed to account for the structure of Chaucer's reception between 1400 and 1550 (the date of the third edition of William Thynne's *Workes of Geffray Chaucer*).

Chaucer died in 1400. Biological death is, however, only part of the story, and in this section I outline the two decisive models by which Chaucer's death was received across the fifteenth and sixteenth centuries. Everyone was persuaded, needless to say, that Chaucer was dead, but by one model he lives on as a guiding personal presence, whereas by the other he is definitively absent, available only through archaeological remains in need of reconstruction. These two models exist side by side only in the last decades of the fifteenth, and the first decades of the sixteenth centuries, which were precisely the decades in which the 'presence' model gave way to the archaeological model. I therefore begin with an example of each model drawn from these critical years.

The presence model is visible in the *Comfort of Lovers*, written by Stephen Hawes (d. 1511) very soon, apparently, after the accession of Henry VIII in 1509 (it was published in 1510). Composed by a narrator dependent on yet thoroughly estranged from court, it opens with complaint about an unspecified grief, before the narrator sleeps and dreams of a lady to whom he dare not reveal the name of his lover. The poem fairly brims with the expression of intense threat and insecurity: the narrator seems to have acted as a spy, and yet now to be implicated in the treachery of those for whose surveillance he was responsible. Looking into the mirror of his future he sees that 'preuy malyce his messengers had sent / With subtyll engynes to lye in wayte' (404–5). Hawes was a groom of the King's Privy Chamber from 1503; the last payment in which he is listed as a poet is dated 1506. *The Comfort of Lovers* must refer to Hawes's circumstances as a court poet to Henry VII, and, presumably, to his loss of position even before the accession of the new king in 1509.

Whatever the precise biographical content of this poem, Hawes's representation of history in these paranoid conditions of threat and loss is revealing. In particular, he imagines time and tradition in strangely distorted ways, pointing wholly to Hawes himself. He is at once massively dependent on yet spectacularly opportunistic with literary traditions. In his Prologue he declares his homage to the triumvirate of Gower, Chaucer, and Lydgate, by way of generating his own humble enterprise:

> First noble Gower moralytees dyde endyte,
> And after hym Cauncers [*sic*] grete bokes delectable
> Lyke a good phylosophre meruaylously dyde wryte;
> After them Lydgate the monke commendable
> Made many wonderfull bokes moche profytable.
> But syth they are deed and theyr bodyes layde in chest
> I pray to god to gyue theyr soules good rest.[3]

The last two lines here would suggest that this is a triumvirate of definitively dead poets, leaving Hawes bereft in much the same way he is socially bereft in court. Once in the tower where he meets his fate, however, he makes a remarkable claim about the ongoing *presence* of these three poets. Under threat, he is comforted, he says, by 'bokes made in antyquyte':

> By Gower and Chauncers poetes rethorycall
> And Lydgate eke by good auctoryte
> Makynge mencyon of the felicyte
> Of my lady and me.   (283–6)

Literary tradition exists to legitimate Hawes; in important ways it is *about* Hawes. Connections between past and future hang dangerously by a thread in this poem, and Hawes reacts to this fragility with an understandable but extreme account of poetic lineage. The very logic of paranoia is to intuit connections of exceptional tenuousness precisely because the lonely figure cannot perceive connections of a more substantial kind. Hawes represents himself as simultaneously on the extreme margin and at the epicentre of great affairs. He is clearly not waving but drowning, invoking literary tradition as an act of personal desperation. Gower, Chaucer, and Lydgate may be dead, but they continue to be a personal resource for the suffering poet, since they prophesied the alleviation of his suffering. They exist, that is, not so much as a body of texts whose existence will fortify a poet drawing on a particular tradition, but as a body of people who express a personal solidarity that, by virtue of their texts, survives them. However tenuous, then, Hawes's reception of earlier poets, including Chaucer, is clearly personal. Chaucer exists as a presence on whom Hawes can continue, just, to draw.

Contrast that posture with the kind of thing we find in Caxton's prologue to his 1484 reprinting of the *Canterbury Tales*, where Chaucer is definitively absent. Caxton praises Chaucer as 'that noble and grete philosopher . . . the which for his ornate writyng in our tongue may wel have the name of a laureate poete'. He then recounts the editorial history of his first edition of the *Tales*, which he had printed six years earlier, on the basis of what he now realizes was a defective copy. A 'gentleman', Caxton (d. 1492) tells us, complained to him about this first edition, since the gentleman's father had a copy 'that was very trewe and accordyng unto hys owen first book by hym [Chaucer] made'. Caxton responds that he had printed the first edition in good faith, according to a copy then in his possession, 'and by me was nothyng added ne mynusshyd [diminished]'. Once the gentleman's old manuscript has been delivered, he recognizes that the first edition was seriously defective, 'in settyng in somme thynges that he [Chaucer] never sayd ne made and levyng out many thynges that he made whyche ben requysite to be sette in it'.[4]

For Caxton, Chaucer is dead and gone. Only textual remains survive, which must be subject to collation, the aim of which is to reproduce the same text that Chaucer wrote, no more nor less. Certain obvious differences from the model exemplified by Hawes present themselves: Caxton reproduces the text of Chaucer, not Chaucer's presence, and he aims to reproduce the exact text that Chaucer wrote, excising accretions and repairing deletions. In short, Caxton acts as philological editor, not as compiler-poet.

Chaucer's death is clearly the premise of this enterprise, but that merely begs the question of how that death is represented. This enterprise needs its poets definitively dead, in order to create its own object of enquiry. Caxton's project, that is, may be described as 'philological', in however nascent a form of that practice. Caxton points the way to all the skills of the textual editor (e.g. codicology, history of the language, and textual criticism). The transmitter of the dead poet is no longer someone who feels in personal contact with him, but rather an expert who rescues and reconstructs the past 'as it was' from the predations of time. For that recovery even to begin demands that the poet is *not* a readily available and personal presence.

In the same way that Italian 'humanist' scholars were beginning to recover the texts of Classical antiquity from what they projected as the ravages of time, so too does Caxton recover Chaucer from the fifteenth century. In its inchoate way, his project squares with that of philological humanism and its insistence on the 'historical solitude' of the present, cut off from the living presence of past masters. Such consonance with humanist practice is suggested by Caxton's earlier citation of the Italian humanist Steven Surigonus's effusive Latin epitaph for Chaucer. In the epilogue to his edition of Chaucer's *Boece* (1478), Caxton cites the epitaph, which begins by bewailing buried Chaucer's death over his tomb:

> Pyerides muse si possunt numina fletus
> Fundere diuinas atque rigare genas
> Galfridi vatis chaucer crudelia fata
> Plangite sit lacrimis abstinuisse nephas
> Vos coluit viuens at vos celebrate sepultum.[5]

[Pierian Muses, if heavenly powers can weep and dampen divine cheeks, bewail the cruel fate of the bard Geoffrey Chaucer. Let it be shameful to abstain from weeping: he cultivated you when he was alive; celebrate him now that he is buried.]

The posture of frankly pathological melancholy ('sit lacrimis abstinuisse nephas') underwrites the philological reconstruction: the fact of death creates the philologist's object, by giving him a lost object to reconstitute; the intensity of the grief produces the moral passion of his enterprise. Weeping at the funeral monument underwrites reconstruction of the fragmented textual monument.

As Seth Lerer has so aptly said, in the last decades of the fifteenth century 'Chaucer's authority shifts between a remembered presence and a buried absence'.[6] Both are accounts of Chaucer's death, but each gives rise to a very distinct treatment of Chaucer's texts. The 'remembered presence' is a figure without precise delineation: his texts are available as materials for new poetry, which builds on accretively, in almost conversational manner, to Chaucer's poetry; Chaucer's name need not be cited when borrowing.

The master of this model is the reader, who uses the author's words at will. The product of this model is a new literary work. The 'buried absence', or philological model, by contrast, delineates a textual corpus in very precise ways, excising accretion, and reconstituting exactly what the poet said. The master is, ostensibly, the poet himself, in the delineation of whose sovereign intentions the technically proficient editor works. Its product is a new text of Chaucer, a textual monument available for the construction of a national literary tradition. Biography, too, is the product of that textual monumentalization: the textual project's correlative is the reconstitution of the exceptional authorial life.

These two models of textual reception are, of course, embedded in Chaucer's own *œuvre*, though with a massive weighting towards the 're-membered presence' model. This applies not only to Chaucer's reception of his own sources, but also to the ways in which Chaucer offers his text, in Dante's words, to his own future readers, to 'questi che chiameranno questo tempo antico' [those who will call this time antique] (*Paradiso* XVII, 20). Certainly Chaucer exhibits a concern for the accurate transmission of his *ipsissima verba*: he only half-jokingly curses Adam his scribe should Adam fail to 'wryte more trewe' when he comes to reproducing 'Boece or Troylus'.[7] And in *Troilus and Criseyde* itself, Chaucer likewise prays for accurate scribes immediately after he lays claim, for the first time in English poetic history, to have written a work whose status will bear comparison with the works of Classical antiquity. Immediately after, that is, he commands his 'litel bok' to 'kis the steppes' where Virgil, Ovid, Homer, Lucan, and Statius tread, so too does he pray that 'non myswrite the, / Ne the mysmetre for defaute of tonge' (V, 1795–6).

These correlative indications of a care for textual stability and a sense of joining a definable, monumental literary tradition with its attendant fame are, however, rare in Chaucer's *œuvre* as a whole. No sooner does Chaucer broach the question of poetic fame in his relatively early *House of Fame* (?late 1370s) than he loses interest in it. Rejecting the arbitrary operations of poetic and historical fame in Fame's palace, 'Geffrey' declares his indifference to fame. 'Sufficeth me, as I were ded, / That no wight have my name in honde' (1876–7), he says, by way of gaining admittance to the poetic locus that really interests him, the improvised, unstable *bricolage* of the House of Rumour. This locus destabilizes all secular sources of authority, Chaucer's own no less than all others. Chaucer's *House of Fame* is a fame poem in reverse, a manifesto for the modes of poetic production and reception of the *Canterbury Tales*, modes that privilege an audience's power to appropriate and accretively build on to prior poems. Caxton may have wished to produce an edition of the *Canterbury Tales* in which there was 'nothyng added ne mynusshyd', but the *Canterbury Tales* itself was constructed precisely on the basis of poetic competition and conversation that permitted free addition and diminution of the received work.[8]

The status of courtly-bureaucratic vernacular poetry, and the system by which it was produced, changed in the early fifteenth century. Above all, the relation of vernacular poets and politically powerful patrons became much closer and more explicit. None of Chaucer's poetry has explicit patronal reference except his first and possibly last datable works, the *Book of the Duchess* (c.1368) and 'The Complaint of Chaucer to His Purse' (1399–1400). Both were written to Lancastrian patrons, and both, especially the last, point the way to the pattern of Lancastrian patronage. Early fifteenth-century court poets often imagined, and in many cases no doubt enjoyed, the patronage of powerful (often royal) figures, who were clearly interested in the promotion of a vernacular tradition, in ways that Richard II seems not to have been. A nameable patron produces a named, payable poet, who is, accordingly, obliged to write within the limits of such patronage. On the face of it, this situation might produce a more sober, politically sensitive poetry, and a more sober reception of Chaucer's works. Certainly the Chaucerian works most frequently copied independently in the fifteenth century were the *Clerk's Tale* (6 copies), the *Prioress's Tale* (5), and *Melibee* (5). It seems also to have been the case that the readership of Chaucer's works changed from the highly literate, quite small bureaucratic circle within which his works may first have circulated. The class of owners of Chaucer's full works in the fifteenth century 'seems to have been primarily a secular mercantile or gentry one'.[9]

The tally of such copying is, however, quite low in any case, and we should not forget that the very 'Chaucer' so excerpted is himself a product of the fifteenth century: all the fifty-six complete texts of the *Canterbury Tales*, for example, were copied in the fifteenth century, for the most part in the years 1425–75.[10] We only know that some fifteenth-century readers excerpted from the fact that other fifteenth-century copyists did not. Many scribes copied and readers presumably read their texts whole, and, if the evidence of the scribes is anything to go by, they responded vigorously to those texts.

Earlier fifteenth-century readers may have read some of their texts whole, some in excerpts, but they did not read their author whole. The technological and economic conditions of sharply defined authorial corpora simply did not exist in this period. The closer relation of poet and patron produced, as one might expect, some sharpened sense of a definable corpus. It is surely significant that the fullest fifteenth-century list of Chaucer's works was produced by Lydgate in the *Fall of Princes* (1431–9) by way of reminding Lydgate's own patron, Duke Humphrey of Gloucester, of the value of patronage (I, Prologue, 274–399). One manuscript (Cambridge, University Library Gg.4.27, *c.*1420) clearly also aims for some notion of a collected Chaucer, including as it does both *Troilus* and the *Canterbury Tales*, but not much is, as far as one can see, made of Chaucer's name, and non-Chaucerian works are also included in the collection. More typical, according to A. S. G. Edwards, was an anthologizing tendency 'to mingle his [i.e. Chaucer's] own works with those of the emergent Chaucerian tradition, linking him with Hoccleve, Clanvowe, Roos and particularly Lydgate'.[11]

Anthologizing involves the creation of new compilations, with a much lower level of respect for authorial integrity than is characteristic of the 'philological absence' model. The 'remembered presence' model is dominant in the fifteenth-century literary response to Chaucer, as some characteristic examples will show. Each expresses a love for Chaucer, although none is overwhelmed by him. Precisely by virtue of building onto his achievement, without underrating or monumentalizing it, these responses reveal a confident readiness to enter into often competitive and productive conversation with Chaucer, freely adding to his works. As one considers these responses, it should also be borne in mind that they represent only one section of fifteenth-century writing. A great deal of literary writing in this century remained almost entirely untouched by Chaucer's work. This is clearly true of a range of areas that Chaucer himself held at arm's length: popular romance; Arthurian writing; alliterative poetry, including texts of the '*Piers Plowman*' tradition; and dramatic writing, in both the professional and amateur traditions.

Hoccleve's *Regement of Princes* was produced in 1412, in close proximity to the time and place in which one of the most beautiful manuscripts of the *Canterbury Tales*, the so-called Ellesmere manuscript, was produced. Both present beautiful, sober, apparently verisimilar illuminations of Chaucer, the Ellesmere manuscript placing its image beside the sober *Melibee* (not *Thopas*). Images often serve to recall the dead; the function of the portrait in the Hoccleve manuscript is indeed, on the face of it, to bring Chaucer back to a life of sorts:

> Although his lyf be qweynt, the resemblance
> Of him hath in me so fressh lyflynesse
> That to putte othir men in remembrance
> Of his persone, I have heere his liknesse
> Do make, to this ende, in sothfastnesse,
> That they that han of him lest thoght and mynde
> By this peynture may ageyn him fynde.[12]

Scholars have placed different, though to my mind not mutually exclusive, valuations on this striking investment in the recovery of Chaucer: he is

deployed as a prompt for patronage; as a representative of religious ortho-
doxy; as a model for poetic counsel.[13] In the context of the present essay, the
significance of the stanza and the image is the attempt to overcome death,
but the death to be postponed is less Chaucer's than Hoccleve's. In both
the *Regement* and in his later *Complaint* (1420), Hoccleve complains of being forgotten, unpaid, and heading for death. It is surely significant that it
should be Hoccleve, the poet most articulate about the evanescence of ex-
ploited writers, who should bring the dead poet so forcefully to life. Earlier in
the poem Chaucer had served the same function, bringing Hoccleve's name
to life. The old man whom Hoccleve meets in the Prologue finally persuades
him that he write something for the Prince, bringing to public notice the
private complaints of poverty and exploitation that are draining Hoccleve
of life. The promise of a renewed vigour is followed by this exchange:

> 'What shal I calle thee, what is thy name?'
> 'Hoccleve, fadir myn, men clepen me.'
> 'Hoccleve, sone?' 'Ywis, fadir, that same.'
> 'Sone, I have herd or this men speke of thee;
> Thow were aqweyntid with Chaucer, pardee –
> God have his soule, best of any wight!' (1863–8)

This heavily underlined signature marks the point, then, at which Hoccleve
recovers himself. And as soon as Hoccleve and the Prince are put into
the same frame, Chaucer's name also appears, reinvigorating Hoccleve's
previously drained presence in the imagined presence of the Prince. Being
'aqweynted' with a living Chaucer temporarily disposes of the threat of being
'qweynt' by death. Hoccleve might lament Chaucer's death, but Chaucer's
'hy vertu astertith [escapes]', and 'ay us lyfly hertith / With bookes of his
ornat endytyng' (1961–74).

Hoccleve, then, is clearly using Chaucer as a name with which to conjure.
This is all the more interesting given the *lack* of Chaucerian borrowing in
the *Regement*. Hoccleve is much more indebted to the regiminal poetics and
material of Gower, whom he also calls 'my maister' (1975).

Lydgate provides a much more significant, concerted, and intelligent engagement with Chaucer's *œuvre*. Derek Pearsall has rightly characterized
this engagement as competitive: he suggests that 'Lydgate's career, poem by
poem, is a determined effort to emulate and surpass Chaucer in each of
the major poetic genres that Chaucer had attempted'.[14] Lydgate's *romans
antiques*, his *Troy Book* (1412–20) and *Destruction of Thebes* (1422–3),
exemplify this most clearly: Chaucer might write *Troilus and Criseyde*, but
Lydgate gives the whole Trojan narrative, prequel and sequel to Chaucer's

story; so, too, the *Destruction of Thebes* gives the whole Theban narrative right up to the point at which the *Knight's Tale* begins.

This enlargement of the historical frame of the Trojan and Theban narratives is not merely a matter of overwhelming one's competitor by superior weight of line numbers. More interestingly, Lydgate's enlargement of the historical frame is also a way of revealing the micro-pattern of Chaucer's more personal narratives within the ongoing, entropic histories of Troy and Thebes. The *Destruction of Thebes* reveals that the personal rivalries of the *Knight's Tale* are but part of a much wider, fratricidal historical pattern embedded in the vortex of Theban history. The *Troy Book* reveals that Troilus's disaster is of a piece with the much larger, intensely destructive patterns of military and sexual rivalry between Greeks and Trojans.

Are these destructive patterns of historical rivalry also pertinent to the relation between Chaucer and Lydgate? It has been suggested that Lydgate's narrative of Oedipus figures his own relationship with father Chaucer. Certainly the Prologue to the *Destruction of Thebes* marks Chaucer's presence and absence in heightened, revealingly conflicted ways. On the one hand Chaucer must be there, since Lydgate happens to join the pilgrims in Canterbury, when it is agreed that he will tell the first tale on the return journey to London. Before this meeting, however, Lydgate has opened the poem with resounding praise of the dead Chaucer, whose poetry 'never shal appallen in my mynde / But alwey fressh ben in my memoyré' (44–5).[15] Chaucer is there but not there, vibrantly remembered by Lydgate who seems conveniently to have forgotten that Chaucer was among the pilgrims.

This spectacular lack of fit within the authenticating fiction of the poem might suggest unresolvable Oedipal rivalry, by which fathers are at once honoured and eliminated. If one were, however, to use familial models within *The Destruction of Thebes* as figures for Lydgate's relation with Chaucer, then fraternal rather than Oedipal rivalry is much more central to the narrative. And fraternal rivalry seems much more accurately descriptive of the relation between Lydgate's and Chaucer's poems. Chaucer is *not* eliminated at the end of *The Destruction of Thebes*. On the contrary, Lydgate's narrative returns to and recognizes Chaucer's text at its end. Certainly there has been some 'quiting': whereas Chaucer's Knight had halted the Monk's tragedies, monk Lydgate appears to produce a tragedy that can stand comparison with the *Knight's Tale*. And whereas the *Knight's Tale* avoids the direct representation of history and war, Lydgate's poem ships the full, ghastly freight of Theban history. The effect of this enlargement of perspective in both length and breadth is not, however, to minimize let alone eliminate the *Knight's Tale*. Lydgate instead provides the first reading of that poem. It is a deeply pessimistic reading that harnesses Chaucer's energies to address the dangers of civil war in England as the Canterbury pilgrims head back towards London. It is no less a penetrating critical and creative response to the *Canterbury Tales* than the other example of a post-Chaucerian poet imagining a continued *Canterbury Tales*, the *Tale of Beryn* (*c.*1420). In its thoroughly divided affiliations to both romance and to fabliau, *Beryn* is an exceptionally shrewd response to the *Canterbury Tales*.[16]

The same kind of argument could be mounted for the relation of Lydgate's *Troy Book* and *Troilus and Criseyde*, with especial focus on the former's astonishing and deeply shocking description of Criseyde as a Greek in Book II. Lydgate makes an elaborately deferential bow to Chaucer, saying that Chaucer's poetry is like the royal ruby set within the copper ring 'among oure bokis of Englishe' (II, 4710); he cannot add anything to Chaucer's description of Criseyde's beauty, he says, before citing in very precise detail Chaucer's description at *Troilus and Criseyde* v, 806–26. Lydgate *is* 'adding', however, since, without comment, he places Criseyde among the Greeks, radically abbreviating a long, sympathetic narrative of departure in Chaucer's poem, and so offering a powerful critique of that sympathy (*Troy Book* II, 4677–762). Lydgate draws attention to the 'copper' of his own poem, questioning the value of, but not removing, the Chaucerian 'ruby'. The shock of *Troilus and Criseyde* continued to reverberate throughout the fifteenth century, provoking accretive responses, the greatest of which is unquestionably Henryson's *Testament of Cresseid* (*c.*1475). All of these responses, Lydgate's included, seek not to eliminate father Chaucer; neither do they seek to isolate the stable, true, Chaucerian text. On the contrary, as examples of the 'remembered presence' model, they build accretively and conversationally onto Chaucer's profoundly open-ended text.

There are many examples of this accretive, confidently competitive response to Chaucer in Lydgate's poetry and in the fifteenth century more generally. One final example must suffice. Lydgate produces a moving threnody for Chaucer in his *Life of Our Lady* (*c.*1420), in which the dead Chaucer's ongoing presence is registered in complex and productive ways. As he approaches the Incarnation, Lydgate falters as he recognizes that no help will be forthcoming from 'my maister Chaucer', who is now 'ygrave' (II, 1628). It was Chaucer who 'made firste, to distille and rayne / The golde dewe dropes of speche and eloquence / Into our tonge' (II, 1632–4). Chaucer is as the sun in whose presence no star may appear. Given all this, it is no wonder that

> . . . my hert pleyne
> Vpon his dethe, and for sorowe blede
> For want of him, nowe in my grete nede

> That shulde, alas, conveye and direct
> And with his supporte amende and corecte
>
> The wronge traces of my rude penne
> There as I erre.   (II, 1644–50)[17]

Even as Lydgate grieves for Chaucer as an absent near-presence, as someone who should be there to 'conveye and direct' Lydgate's own work, he distances himself from Chaucer. He does so not only by insisting that Chaucer 'lieth nowe in his cheste' (II, 1654), but more subtly by counterpointing the terms of praise used for Chaucer with those used for his chosen source of inspiration here, the Virgin Mary. Chaucer might be the unique 'sun' who 'enlumined' English rhetoric, beside whom no star may appear, but Lydgate's real inspiration here is the Virgin Mary, that 'sterre that bare the bright sonne' (I, 43). All the language used of Chaucer, that is, picks up, and is put delicately into question by, the alternative, living source of inspiration, to whom Lydgate prays that her 'dewe', or 'licour' of grace fall to Lydgate's pen, 'tenlumyne this dyte / Thorough thy supporte that I may procede' (I, 58–9). This is not the language of stumbling deference; it marks, instead, the ongoing presence of Chaucer's rhetorical ambition even as Chaucer is set at a distance.

From the 'remembered presence' model, let us now turn to the philological, 'absence' model. Set the two models into any historical scene, and we might expect the reputation of *all* writers who become canonical to undergo a move from the 'presence' to the 'absence' model. After all, the 'presence' model depends on acquaintance, either real or at least plausibly imagined. After a dead writer recedes from the interpretative community's living memory, we might expect the technical ministrations of philology to come into play. And before a writer is treated as canonical, he or she is treated with less philological respect; the work is part of the ongoing conversation of the relevant interpretative community. It is surely significant that Chaucer's own fullest account of his works is in his *Retractions*, evidently written in the knowledge of his approaching death: as Chaucer knows he is about to die, that is, he provides the bibliography, first tool of the philologist.

This passage from one model to the other may thus be inevitable in the move to canonicity. I suggest, nevertheless, that this predictable historical passage was subject to exceptional pressures in Chaucer's case across the years 1470–1550. During these years what may be called the literary system itself changed. The system, that is, whereby authors are connected to their texts by their publics underwent a series of interdependent and powerful changes. Authors became more professional by being more economically dependent on their literary work; this required a stable and identifiable corpus of work attachable to a payable name. In addition, the introduction of printing in the 1470s allowed for the possibility of a much more stable form of textual reproduction which was, at the same time, much more economically fruitful. The influence of Continental philology encouraged writers to seek, while living, the laureate fame (and its attendant patronage) awarded by philologists to the dead poets of antiquity.[18] So it is not merely that Chaucer's texts moved into the purview of philology; more to the point, they did so precisely as philology began to define itself as a practice in these years.

All these changes reconfigured the way in which Chaucer was received. Occasionally he was censured for not having conformed to the new philological model. Thus in his *Eneados* (1513) Gavin Douglas attacks Chaucer for his sympathetic presentation of Dido (in the *Legend of Good Women*), in flagrant divergence from the one authoritative presentation, Virgil's *Aeneid*.[19] Despite his reverence for Chaucer, Douglas effectively lays charges against him for having 'gretly the prynce of poetis grevit' in the Ovidian account of Dido in the *Legend*. For, he says, in that work Chaucer at the same time claims to follow Virgil, and yet calls Aeneas a traitor. Douglas stands incredulous at the charge of treachery against Aeneas, since 'Virgill dyd diligens / But [without] spot of cryme, reproch or ony offens / Eneas for to loif [praise] and magnify' (I, Prologue, 419–21). He goes on to excuse Aeneas before excusing Chaucer's own weakness, 'For he was evir, God wait [knows], all womanis frend' (I, Prologue, 449). In this Douglas shows himself the philological author for whom the text is what an author wrote, rather than what a reader makes of it. This contrasts starkly with the narratorial reader of the *Aeneid* in Chaucer's *House of Fame*, who reads the narrative of Dido with such intense sympathy as entirely to rewrite it, without citation of any previous author: 'Non other auctour alegge I' (314).

Criticism of Chaucer is, however, extremely rare. Much more common is the representation of Chaucer as the proto-model of the kind of writer who emerged in the last decades of the fifteenth century. He is, as the first biography of Chaucer has it, a humanist, university-educated scholar who resided in France for a time, gaining glory for himself through literary performance, in intimate contact with kings and all the nobility of England; his principal object was rhetorical refinement of the language in order to bring England into fit comparison with her main competitors for cultural prestige, Italy and France.[20] Written by the antiquarian John Leland (?1503–52), this biography is revealingly much closer to Leland's own than it is to Chaucer's.

Changes in the literary system that produced Leland's invented biography were themselves powerful and enduring. Chaucer's reputation was subject, however, not only to changes in the literary system. The broader historical situation provoked by the Act of Supremacy in 1534 also placed stringent pressures on what was now required of him. Chaucer, that is, became the key literary counter in the radical reshaping of the English past necessitated by the English Reformation. In short, Chaucer became a Protestant and a champion of English insularity. This Protestant and proto-nationalist cultivation of Chaucer also necessitated, however, an assiduous separation of Chaucer from all his coevals and pre-Reformation followers. The medieval past could not be rejected *en bloc*, but if Chaucer was to be rescued from obscurity, his case had to prove the rule by exception. In the decades 1530–50, then, Chaucer was increasingly represented as unique and inimitable by 'followers' doomed only to attempt imitation.

William Thynne's edition of Chaucer was produced just on the verge of the break with Rome, in 1532; it exemplifies all the pressures, both literary and historical, that Chaucer's reputation had subsumed from the 1470s. Above all, this is the first edition of Chaucer's collected works, unlike the printed editions of single works, or at most the *Canterbury Tales*, produced by Caxton, de Worde, and Pynson.[21] Chaucer's career now becomes visible as a whole for the first time, in either manuscript or print. Very much an example, in terms of his claims at any rate, of the 'philological absence' model, Thynne articulates his editorial practice as one of sifting through textual remains and expelling false textual accretions. At first he only had prints, wherein he 'deprehended . . . many errours, falsyties and deprauacions, which euidently appered by the contrarietees and alterations found by collacion of the one with the other'. This, he says, provoked him to search out any 'true' copies of Chaucer's works, both printed and manuscript, 'remaynyng almost vnknowen and in oblyuion'.[22]

Thynne presents the grieving posture of the textual editor, accentuating the level of loss in order, perhaps, more powerfully to authorize his own act of arduous reconstruction: he laments the 'neglygence of the peple that haue ben in this realme who doutlesse were very remysse' (1, p. 89).

He also presents his work as an act of nationalist pride, describing the project of restoring Chaucer's works as part of a larger antiquarian recollection of English accomplishment in sciences, 'of whiche . . . it hath plesed god as highly to nobilytate this yle as any other regyon of christendome' (1, p. 89). He dedicates the book to Henry VIII as its ideal recipient, Henry and Chaucer being a patron/poet couple made for each other and only each other. There has, says Thynne, been no other person 'syns or in the tyme of Chaucer [who] was or is suffycient but only your maieste royall, whiche by discrecyon and iugement as moost absolute in wysedome . . . could . . . adde or gyue any authorite hervnto' (1, p. 89).

Finally, Thynne goes to extreme lengths to isolate Chaucer as the only pre-'modern' poet worthy of notice. Given, he says, that Chaucer lived in a time when 'all good letters were layde a slepe throughout the world', it is nothing short of a miracle that 'suche an excellent poete in our tonge shulde as it were (nature repugnynge) spryng and aryse' (1, p. 88). Chaucer is a poet decidedly *not* part of a tradition by this account; he is, instead, 'in the tyme of the author in comparison as a pure and fyne tried precious or policyed iewell [that emerged] out of a rude or indigest masse or mater' (1, p. 89). For Hawes the great sustaining poets were Gower, Chaucer, and Lydgate, while in Thynne's account all but crystalline Chaucer have receded into shapeless 'masse'.

If Thynne's edition was receptive to the new philology, it was also sensitive to the broader historical situation of England in the early 1530s. Published in 1532, before the ecclesiastical position of England had become clear, Thynne had to be circumspect about religious controversy in his dedication to the king. Writing in 1599, Thynne's son Francis reported that his father had originally printed a certain *Pilgrim's Tale* in the first edition. This text (not in fact by Chaucer and evidently written post-1536), had, by the younger Thynne's account, to be excised because, although Thynne senior had the king's support, he was under threat from Cardinal Wolsey, who, along with the bishops, 'heaved at' Thynne and forced him to retract. Even Parliament, Thynne younger relates, was about to ban Chaucer's works.[23]

Francis Thynne's story is confused in various ways, but it points to a truth. William Thynne certainly did wish to remake Chaucer into an unambiguously evangelical writer. Once England's position had become clear, the anti-papal, Lollard *Ploughman's Tale* was included in the 1542 reprint of the 1532 edition, though remaining outside the *Tales*. By the time of the (?)1550 reprint, the *Ploughman's Tale* had been incorporated *within* the *Tales*, just before the *Parson's Tale*. Thynne was clearly not the only one to promote Chaucer's evangelical credentials. *The Ploughman's Tale* had been published under Chaucer's name in 1535 and 1548.[24] The Lollard *Jack Upland* (written between ?1389 and 1396), was also attributed to Chaucer in its 1536 printing.[25]

The historical influence of Thynne's edition is hard to overestimate. It formed the basis of the Chaucerian canon for all editions of Chaucer's works up to but not including that of Skeat (1897).[26] Its continuing influence may still be visible in the decision of the *Riverside Chaucer* to place the *Canterbury Tales* first, out of chronological order. Its influence is most powerfully visible, however, in the ways in which it spectacularly infringes its own philological aims of, in Caxton's words, not 'settyng in somme thynges that he [Chaucer] never sayd'. This applies not only to Thynne's inclusion of much extra matter by Gower, Usk, Hoccleve, Lydgate, and Henryson that survived in later pre-Skeat editions, but, more influentially I think, the inclusion of the evidently spurious evangelical text.

The inclusion of this matter points to an almost inevitable and potentially disabling paradox embedded in the philological model. Insofar as the philological model creates a textual monument, that is, it offers up that clearly defined monument for national consumption. And as it offers up a poetic *œuvre* for national use, it commits the nation to invest heavily in it, thereby provoking accretions. The philological model ends up provoking, that is, precisely what it had set out to eliminate. The accretions now are, however, of a different kind: they are ideologically saturated with national needs.

That Chaucer had become a vital national resource after Thynne's edition is visible in his appearance as poet in, for the first time, semi- and fully official documents. A straw in the wind is Richard Morison's *Remedy for Sedition* (1536),[27] written as Henrician apologetics for the brutal repression of the northern-centred Pilgrimage of Grace of 1536, the most concerted rebellion against Henry's religious reforms. The text is a rather simple call to obedience to the king's laws. The most striking exhibition of humanist learning in the name of popular repression comes in the citation and deformation of Chaucer's *Clerk's Tale* (995–1001). While the Clerk expresses these sentiments in support of Griselda oppressed by the tyrannical Walter, Morison's use and alteration of Chaucer would put him on the side of Walter. The text he cites rewrites all Chaucer's lexis that had become difficult by the sixteenth century, each change emphasizing criticism of the insurgents. He addresses them thus:

> O sterne people uniuste and untrewe
> Ay undiscrete, and chaungynge as a fane
> Delytynge ever in rumours that be newe:
> For lyke the mone ever waxe ye and wane
> Your reason halteth, your iugement is lame
> Youre doom is false, youre constance evyll preveth
> A full great foole is he that on yow leveth.   (B.i^r)

Of course Chaucer continued to be used in unofficial environments.[28] Morison's striking deployment of Chaucer as spokesman for (an unstable) official policy briefly precedes, however, a much more draconian and entirely official deployment of Chaucer as nearly the sole survivor of the discursive uprooting necessitated by the break with Rome. Thus in 1542 an act was passed to purge the kingdom of false doctrine. It banned Tyndale's Bible, along with 'all other bookes and wrytinges in the English tongue, teaching or comprysing any matiers of Cristen religion, articles of the faithe or holy scripture . . . contrarye to that doctrine [established] sithens the yere of our Lorde 1540'. All these banned books 'shalbe . . . clerlie and utterlie abolished, extinguished and forbidden to be kepte or used'.[29] This might sound like a matter of religious books alone, but as the act proceeds, its extraordinary scope emerges, designed as it was to restructure nothing less than the entire geography of English discursive history. The only survivors of this textual purge are as follows: Bibles in English not translated by Tyndale, and all of the King's 'proclamations, injunctions, translations of the Pater Noster, Ave Maria, and Crede, psalters, primers, prayers, statutes and lawes of the Realme, Cronicles, Canterburye tales, Chaucers bokes, Gowers bokes and stories of mennes lieves'. These shall remain licit reading matter, unless, the act continues, the King should change his mind.[30] These exceptions made the import of the act only more draconian, since they excluded, by implication, any other English literature printed before 1540 apart from the King's official publications, histories, and the works of Chaucer and Gower. By 1542, then (the year in which Thynne's second edition appeared), Gower and Chaucer have become very nearly the only the acceptable pre-1534 voices for a highly labile official policy.

The 'philological absence' model, then, insists on Chaucer's death. In its theory, at any rate, Chaucer's absence is the cue for a good deal of elimination. False readings and spurious works are to go, even if, as we have seen, this model introduces its own accretions of a more highly charged kind. Philological practice, as distinct from its theory, added works to the Chaucer corpus for various reasons: it added comparable works by near-contemporary poets, and, for different reasons, it added highly polemical, evangelical works to bolster positions of national importance.

The 'absence' model not only provoked elimination of corrupt readings and spurious works; it also tended to eliminate Chaucer's competitors. 'Syncrisis', or the literary-critical practice of setting two poets contemporary with each other into competition, is an ancient feature of literary culture. In the first half of the sixteenth century, however, the pressure to select the one great poet was magnified, as the ground around Chaucer had to be cleared, eliminating his 'barbarous' followers. Both evangelical and humanist perspectives provoked writers, for distinct but equally powerful reasons, to create and thereafter dismiss a corrupting 'middle age' that stands in the way of pure, originary sources of enlightenment. Faced with the necessity of resuscitating Chaucer as the one great figure of the later 'Middle Ages' in England, sixteenth-century critics tended to institute the fifteenth century as a mini-Middle Age, obscuring access to the pure Chaucerian source. Some other pre-Act of Supremacy writers were sporadically selected as prophets of the brilliant present, including, briefly, Langland and some Lollard texts, but

Chaucer received by far the most consistent praise as the pre-Reformation champion of the Reformation.

If Chaucer's *House of Fame* is a fame poem in reverse, Skelton's *Garland of Laurel* is a fame poem in fast forward.[31] Written at different times between 1495 and 1523 when it was printed, Skelton arranges the scene for his own laureation. In it, for the last time in English poetic history, Chaucer is invoked as a presence. In an ecstasy, Skelton beholds the splendidly dressed Gower, Chaucer, and Lydgate, who themselves 'wantid [lacked] nothynge but the laurell' (397); they approach Skelton and confirm that he is worthy to become a 'star' 'in our collage [college] above the sterry sky', for having 'brutid Britons of Brutus Albion' (403–5). Each poet addresses Skelton. Chaucer gives the details of court protocol: the three poets will 'brynge you personally present' before Fame, 'in whose court poynted is your place' (418–20). Chaucer, then, is certainly present here, but the very terms of his location have rendered the 'remembered presence' model untenable. In the context of laureation, in Fame's palace, for having created a national poetic monument, Skelton creates the terms of a philological reception. Only three years after the publication of Skelton's poem, Richard Pynson introduced his edition of the *Canterbury Tales* (1526) by describing it as a book 'diligently and trewly corrected by a copy of Willyam Caxton's impryntyng according to the true making of the said Geffray Chaucer'.[32] By the 1520s Chaucer has, then, definitively gone, leaving only textual remains.

NOTES

1. A. C. Spearing, *Medieval to Renaissance in English Poetry* (Cambridge, 1985); John M. Bowers, 'The *Tale of Beryn* and the *Siege of Thebes*: Alternative Ideas of the *Canterbury Tales*', *Studies in the Age of Chaucer*, 7 (1985), 23–50; *Chaucer Traditions: Studies in Honour of Derek Brewer*, eds. Ruth Morse and Barry Windeatt (Cambridge, 1990); Seth Lerer, *Chaucer and His Readers: Imagining the Author in Late-Medieval England* (New Haven, Conn., 1993); Nicholas Watson, 'On Outdoing Chaucer: Lydgate's *Troy Book* and Henryson's *Testament of Cresseid* as Competitive Imitations of *Troilus and Criseyde*' in *Shifts and Transpositions in Medieval Narrative: A Festschrift for Dr Elspeth Kennedy*, ed. Karen Pratt (Cambridge, 1994), pp. 89–108; Kevin Pask, *The Emergence of the English Author: Scripting the Life of the Poet in Early Modern England* (Cambridge, 1996); Seth Lerer, *Courtly Letters in the Age of Henry VIII* (Cambridge, 1997); *Refiguring Chaucer in the Renaissance*, ed. Theresa M. Krier (Gainesville, Fla., 1998); *Writing after Chaucer: Essential Readings in Chaucer and the Fifteenth Century*, ed. Daniel J. Pinti (New York, 1998); Scott-Morgan Straker, 'Deference and Difference: Chaucer, Lydgate, and the *Siege of Thebes*', *Review of English Studies*, 52 (2001), 1–21.

2. For compendia of allusion and criticism, see both *Five Hundred Years of Chaucer Criticism and Allusion (1357–1900)*, ed. Caroline F. E. Spurgeon, 3 vols. (London, 1908–10) and *Chaucer: The Critical Heritage*, ed. Derek Brewer, 2 vols. (London, 1978).

3. Stephen Hawes, *Comfort of Lovers*, in *Stephen Hawes, The Minor Poems*, eds. Florence W. Gluck and Alice B. Morgan, EETS os 217 (London, 1974), lines 22–8. I have lightly punctuated the text. All further line references are cited in the body of the text.

4. Cited from *Caxton's Own Prose*, ed. Norman Blake (London, 1973), pp. 61–3, at p. 62.

5. Cited from *Chaucer: The Critical Heritage*, ed. Brewer, 1, p. 78. I have slightly altered the translation.

6. Lerer, *Chaucer and His Readers*, p. 151. I am deeply indebted to this excellent chapter.

7. 'Chaucer's Words Unto Adam, His Own Scribe'.

8. See Jill Mann, 'The Authority of the Audience in Chaucer' in *Poetics: Theory and Practice in Medieval English Literature*, eds. Piero Boitani and Anna Torti (Cambridge, 1991), pp. 1–12.

9. A. S. G. Edwards, 'The Early Reception of Chaucer and Langland', *Florilegium*, 15 (1998), 1–22, at p. 9.

10. See M. C. Seymour, *A Catalogue of Chaucer Manuscripts*, 2 vols. (Aldershot, 1995, 1997), vol. 2.

11. A. S. G. Edwards, 'Fifteenth-Century Middle English Verse Author Collections' in *The English Medieval Book*, eds. A. S. G. Edwards, Vincent Gillespie, and Ralph Hanna (London, 2000), pp. 101–12, at p. 103.

12. Thomas Hoccleve, *The Regement of Princes*, ed. Charles R. Blyth (Kalamazoo, Mich., 1999), lines 4992–8. I have preserved the reading 'lest' at line 4997.

13. See Nicholas Perkins, *Hoccleve's 'Regiment of Princes': Counsel and Constraint* (Cambridge, 2001), pp. 117–21 for a survey of views and his own contribution.

14. Derek Pearsall, 'Chaucer and Lydgate' in *Chaucer Traditions*, eds. Morse and Windeatt, pp. 39–53, at p. 47.

15. John Lydgate, *The Siege of Thebes*, ed. Robert R. Edwards (Kalamazoo, Mich., 2001). I argue that the title is more properly *The Destruction of Thebes* in James Simpson, '"Dysemol daies and Fatal houres": Lydgate's *Destruction of Thebes* and Chaucer's *Knight's Tale*' in *The Long Fifteenth Century: Essays in Honour of Douglas Gray*, eds. Helen Cooper and Sally Mapstone (Oxford, 1997), pp. 15–33.

16. See *The Canterbury Tales: Fifteenth-Century Continuations and Editions*, ed. John M. Bowers (Kalamazoo, Mich., 1992).

17. John Lydgate, *A Critical Edition of John Lydgate's 'Life of Our Lady'*, eds. Joseph A. Lauritis, Ralph A. Klinefelter, and Vernon F. Gallagher (Pittsburgh, Ill., 1961). I have repunctuated the edited text. Reference to further citations is made in the body of the text.

18. For these developments, see especially David R. Carlson, *English Humanist Books: Writers and Patrons, Manuscripts and Print, 1475–1525* (Toronto, 1993).

19. Gavin Douglas, *Virgil's 'Aeneid', Translated into Scottish Verse*, ed. David F. C. Coldwell, 4 vols., Scottish Text Society, 3rd series, 25, 27, 28, 30 (Edinburgh, 1957–64). Reference to further citations is made in the body of the text.

20. *Chaucer, The Critical Heritage*, ed. Brewer, I, pp. 91–6.
21. These editions of the *Canterbury Tales* are as follows: *Canterbury tales* (William Caxton, 1483), listed in *A Short-Title Catalogue of Books Printed in England, Scotland and Ireland and of English Books Printed Abroad 1475–1640*, eds. A. W. Pollard and G. R. Redgrave, 2nd edn rev. W. A. Jackson *et al.*, 3 vols (London, 1976–91) (hereafter *RSTC*), 5083; *Canterbury tales* (Richard Pynson, 1492), *RSTC*, 5084; *The boke of Chaucer named Caunterbury tales* (Wynkyn de Worde, 1498), *RSTC*, 5085; *Canterbury tales* (Richard Pynson, 1526), *RSTC*, 5086.
22. Thynne's preface is available in *Chaucer: The Critical Heritage*, ed. Brewer, I, pp. 87–90. I have punctuated the text. The text is ostensibly written by Sir Brian Tuke, but the voice of the actual text shifts between that of Tuke and that of Thynne. I attribute the whole text to Thynne as a matter of convenience. Reference to further citations is made in the body of the text. See J. E. Blodgett, 'William Thynne (d. 1546)' in *Editing Chaucer: The Great Tradition*, ed. Paul Ruggiers (Norman, Okla., 1984), pp. 35–52.
23. Francis Thynne, *Animadversions*, ed. G. H. Kingsley, EETS os 9 (London, 1865), p. 7.
24. *The Ploughman's Tale* (T. Godfray, 1535), *RSTC*, 5099.5; and *The Plouumans tale compylled by syr G. Chaucher [sic] knyght* (W. Hyll, 1548), *RSTC*, 5100.
25. *Jack uplande compyled by the famous G. Chaucer* (J. Nicholson, 1536), *RSTC*, 5098.
26. For all these editions, see the articles in *Editing Chaucer*, ed. Ruggiers.
27. *RSTC*, 18113.5.
28. For the 'official' versus the 'unofficial' versions of Chaucer in Henrician England, see especially John Watkins, '"Wrastling for this World": Wyatt and the Tudor Canonization of Chaucer' in *Refiguring Chaucer*, ed. Krier, pp. 22–39, and Lerer, *Courtly Letters*, especially ch. 5.
29. *Statutes of the Realm*, ed. T. E. Tolmins *et al.*, 11 vols. (London, 1810–28; repr. 1963) (hereafter *SR*), 34 Henry 8, Chapter 1.1, III, p. 895. I have punctuated the text.
30. *SR*, 34 Henry 8, Chapter 1.1, III, p. 895.
31. In *John Skelton, The Complete English Poems*, ed. John Scattergood (Harmondsworth, 1983).
32. Cited in *Five Hundred Years of Chaucer Criticism*, ed. Spurgeon, I, p. 76.

16

CAROLYN DINSHAW

New approaches to Chaucer

Chaucer at Ground Zero

This essay was begun on the day that the last load of debris was removed from the site of the World Trade Center disaster of September 11, 2001. My desk at New York University is about a mile from Ground Zero, as the site became known. I easily could have attended the ceremony that day marking the end of recovery and clean-up, but I did not go to that vast literal and metaphorical pit. In fact I *would* not revisit it, lest I never return from all that loss. Instead, I wrote about the Middle Ages.

If I attempted – however unintentionally – to regain via the medieval a measure of wholeness, safety, and grounding lost in the trauma of September 11, it certainly wasn't the first time the past era has been invoked to perform such a recovery. Indeed, it has been recently argued that British historians in the 1950s undertook 'an obsessive search for the archival identity of Robin Hood' upon 'the loss of the raj'.[1] Not long after that postcolonial grieving, a leading American Chaucerian hoped that 'the recognition of valid realities established by earlier generations' might provide protection against another gaping hole, what he called 'that rancid solipsistic pit' of modernity.[2] In these scholarly instances the medieval, and particularly Chaucer, was used in a process of mourning, or rather, if we accept Freud's distinctions, in a melancholic refusal of loss, the putative modern-day loss of good love, revealed truth, and fullness of being.[3]

No scholar nowadays would explicitly create a fantasy Middle Ages to supply what is perceived as missing in the present day (though in retrospect it seems always possible to uncover implicit melancholy). The role of the medieval in popular discourse around September 11 was much more complex as well: President Bush called the war on terrorism a 'crusade', invoking an ominously continuous history of colonialism and bloodshed from the European Middle Ages to the American twenty-first century; if the White House subsequently backed away from that rhetoric, the mainstream media referred to Osama bin Laden as 'primitive' and the Taliban as 'medieval', imposing a Western chronology on the enemies that had wreaked such havoc on our modernity, and in this way trying propagandistically to control them. September 11 in the most extreme way made many Americans (if not Westerners in general) question the importance of what they were spending their time on, and that questioning often involved turning to the past for answers.

For those of us who teach Chaucer – and those of us who learn about him in the classroom – this questioning was an exaggerated version of the query we often confront in one guise or another: How does Chaucer matter now? How does reading Chaucer's texts relate to the world in which we live? Such questions can lead to the contemplation of new approaches to Chaucer insofar as new approaches specifically highlight and problematize the relationship of past texts and the present day. In this essay I shall first discuss possible models of relating the past and the present, and then shall go on to discuss new critical approaches to one Chaucerian text, the *Man of Law's Tale*. My point about these approaches – I have highlighted feminist, queer, and postcolonial analyses in my admittedly partial selection here – is that they presume a certain openness of the text: the significance of texts changes in time, with changing contexts. I have chosen the *Man of Law's Tale* because it is the Chaucerian work that deals most thoroughly with Christian–Islamic relations, a core concern motivating the events of September 11. It is not only a text that offered clear opportunities in the late twentieth century for critical re-evaluation, but also, I shall finally suggest, a text whose significance post-September 11 became deadly.

One further acknowledgement before we begin: the meaning of September 11 is certainly not unitary, and neither is it agreed upon even among Americans, let alone the rest of the world. Indeed, the meaning of 'the present day' or 'now' varies with one's location in time and space. But the issues raised by September 11 – and at least some general issues of 'the present day' for likely readers of this essay – can be delineated: including East–West and Islamic–Christian relations and the roles of religion, of violence, and of women, these issues provide a framework for re-evaluation of Western cultural monuments such as Chaucer. Such re-evaluation is made possible, as we shall see, by the complex nature of the literary text and in fact of time itself.

Past and present

How does Chaucer matter now? A panicked or simply impatient judgement holds that in fact Chaucer doesn't matter any more, that his texts are too historically distant to be relevant in these times. For the modernist whose historical sense is punctuated by breaks and ruptures, the medieval period is drastically separated from subsequent eras by changes wrought by humanism and the Enlightenment. Foucault, whose *History of Sexuality*, volume 1, charts discursive shifts beginning in the seventeenth century, sees the Middle Ages in several different ways, but one major thread is that it is a time very different from our own modernity. In an interview discussing his developing work on the next volumes of the *History of Sexuality*, Foucault was asked if he were looking in the past for an alternative to the modern day: 'No!' he replied. '[Y]ou can't find the solution of a problem in the solution of another problem raised at another moment by other people.'[4] The complexity of Foucault's projects (which are not histories of solutions but genealogies of problems, as he put it) is beyond the explanatory scope of this essay, but there is obvious truth to his statement: of course we cannot map, say, what we might view as Chaucer's benevolent view of social diversity in the *General Prologue* onto our own policies of tolerance in the American melting-pot. 'The past is seldom usefully examined by assuming that its specific questions or their settings are the same as those of the present,' writes historian Caroline Bynum.[5]

If differences in historical contexts frustrate a desire to find a relationship between the present day and Chaucer – a desire not limited to the post-Vietnam War era but evinced even in the tougher critical climate of the Cold War era in the USA as well – we could choose to ignore context altogether and regard Chaucer's texts as a kind of sacred scripture, a repository of universal truths and examples for all time.[6] This approach would treat literature as a phenomenon that draws on archetypes, mythic cycles, or some other source of transhistorical meaning. If we choose to turn to Chaucer as an antidote for our current toxins, we would have our historically contingent reasons for doing so (September 11, in this case) but we would be drawing on the text as a non-contingent truth for all times.

Alternatively, we may be suggesting in this gesture that there are specific similarities between the conditions of the late fourteenth and those of the late twentieth/early twenty-first centuries, and thus that Chaucer's texts are particularly historically suited to our troubled times. In this case, we would choose to explore similarities between, say, the world-views produced by accelerated change and the technology-driven militarism of the late fourteenth century, with its longbow battles and ugly, compromised crusades, on the one hand, and by the precision missile warfare and CIA-trained Taliban of the late twentieth and early twenty-first centuries, on the other. What Chaucer said about his times could be specifically meaningful, therefore, to ours: Theseus's speech at the end of the *Knight's Tale*, for example, would have special applicability to the horrors of war in our era.

A subtler historicism would not insist on contextual *similarity* as a basis for relevance. It would delineate the context in which Chaucer was writing, finding the terms in which he expressed concepts of violence, say, and would delineate our contexts and concepts as well; it would then chart the differences and similarities, finding analogies between approaches to violence in Chaucer's time and our own. A 'large and developing issue' with which both medieval and modern are preoccupied – in this case, violence – would then emerge into view. Caroline Bynum writes, 'It is not only possible, it is imperative to use modern concerns when we confront the past. So long as we reason by analogy rather than merely rewriting or rejecting, the present will help us see past complexity and the past will help us to understand ourselves.'[7] In this view, though continuities emerge, the historian's interest is in diversity – diversity of conceptualizations *within* each period, in fact, as well as *between* medieval and present day.

Bolder assertions, typically by literary scholars, emphasize more direct and continuous histories of our modern preoccupations. Thus we could argue that the Wife of Bath's discussion of gender relations in her *Prologue* and *Tale*, for example, provides a prehistory of the celebration of masculine heroism on September 11. In this case, feminist theory – positing structures of gender – would allow us to see not only *analogies* between the way the Wife of Bath approaches gender and the way journalists do but *continuities* in gender approaches between then and now: while we would acknowledge the differences between conditions and expectations for women in Chaucer's day and in our own, we would trace a continuity of gender structures, in this instance misogyny. Such theory does not necessarily float transcendentally above historical contingency; in fact, the medieval text can correct theory. Shifting examples from feminist to postcolonial theory: Chaucer's *Man of Law's Tale*, informed by his knowledge of vigorous commercial and cultural interactions between East and West, crucially corrects Said's *Orientalism* with its notion of the 'purely antiempirical' medieval construction of Islam.[8]

Hypotheses of historical continuity have been important for literary scholars answering the question, 'Why read Chaucer now?' Chaucer's elegiac works (such as the *Book of the Duchess*) have been found to participate in a long tradition – including psychoanalysis – of psychic coercion, forbidding grief, defending against loss, and insisting on transcendence.[9] Reading his work now could help us understand the politics of grief management around September 11. Reading the *Pardoner's Prologue* and *Tale* as imaginative renderings of an outcast allows us to speculate on the historical roots of othering in a present-day American culture that is increasingly closed in on itself.

Yet analogy and continuity are only two forms of relationship between past phenomena and present-day ones, only two answers to the question about the relationship between Chaucer's texts and the present day. As in other fields of literary criticism, an intense interrogation of the 'we' in phrases like 'we readers of Chaucer' has widened the scope of Chaucerian analyses; the process of reading historical texts has increasingly come to be understood not as a universal exercise but as a situated, contingent one, to some degree inevitably subjective. Some approaches to Chaucer have indeed developed the subjective element, the more particular, individual, and intimate: thus affective relations between literary character and reader, for example, have been explored – between, say, the Pardoner and me as two queers (and Foucault makes three) linked only by our shared condition of being left out of our respective cultures.[10] An empathic relation to texts of the past has also been experienced: medieval texts, it has been suggested, teach a mode of 'feeling thinking' that helps us understand not only the texts but also our desire for them, our desire for the past.[11] Recognizing the insight of psychoanalysis that the past is in us, others have seen the importance of repetition in our relations with the past, hauntings making the past present.[12] A radically discontinuous history is postulated, famously, by Walter Benjamin: history is not constituted by sequences of events like 'beads of a rosary', he asserts, but by 'constellation[s]' of present eras and specific past ones.[13]

Basic assumptions underlie these latter approaches: time is not fixed, and texts are not, either. Linear time is only one way of reckoning chronology, after all; Aron Gurevich discusses different and sometimes contradictory kinds of time perception operating all at once in the Middle Ages: agrarian, genealogical, cyclical, biblical, historical.[14] And such heterogeneity of time perception obtains for the modern world as well, as the earlier example of the mainstream media's calling the Taliban 'medieval' suggests. Further, as Hans-Georg Gadamer writes, 'The experience of history, which we ourselves have, is . . . covered only to a small degree by that which we would name *historical consciousness*.'[15] There is no clear cut-off between then and now in a world in which the past is *in* you, psychoanalytically or hermeneutically speaking.

Texts, meanwhile, 'are always getting ready to fly apart in time', as Paul Strohm writes, 'to decompose into their own heterogeneous materials'. A text can be made up of materials whose role in literary history has yet to be played out, like Petrarch's 'Renaissance' sonnet embedded squarely in Chaucer's 'medieval' *Troilus and Criseyde*; the Chaucerian text forms 'an unstable amalgam of unexhausted past and unaccomplished future'.[16] The open-ended nature of the linguistic sign contributes to the conceptualization of textual meaning as somewhat unfixed or shifting in time: 'meaning is context-bound', as Jonathan Culler put it in an influential deconstructive formulation, 'but context is boundless'.[17] As Strohm puts it, 'texts are valued not only for what they were but also for what they have become'; they await 'retrospective illumination' in new contexts.[18] The medieval text viewed in this way can hardly serve as a safe haven or grounding for traumatized postmodernists.

The judgement of anachronism in an interpretation of Chaucer's texts is therefore neither entirely easy nor automatically damning. A safely conservative approach to Chaucer holds that discourses 'specifically contemporary to Chaucer' are the proper ones in which interpretively to set his works.[19] But there is no pure moment of contemporaneity within which to situate Chaucer's texts. One may well maintain that everything in Chaucer's texts must be understood somehow to 'pertain to, or be realized within', the moment of their composition. Yet a narrow concept of contemporaneity, or of the way a text exists in time, should not inhibit us from seeking in Chaucer's texts a 'usable past'.[20]

Granted, some worries about anachronism, or more precisely here, 'presentism', have merit, as Caroline Bynum and William Jordan, among others, have persuasively demonstrated.[21] It doesn't get us very far in comprehension of the fourteenth century or the twenty-first to ask what Chaucer thought of 'race', to take another example relevant to September 11, if we use that term to mean a post-Enlightenment conception of biological and geopolitical difference. But we can analyse the concepts that are meant by terms he did know or use (*gens*, 'peple', etc.), terms with dense histories and philosophies of their own. We can analyse the clusters of attributes associated with descriptors of skin colour, with geographical diversity, and with religious difference, *inter alia*, in Chaucer's world. We can track the relationships of difference and similarity between Chaucer's approach to these concepts and our own approaches in the USA; we can thus see how a large field of interest in something we call race has been developing over time. We can isolate analogies between approaches then and approaches now, or we can seek more direct connections between developing concepts of race. We can as well focus on the conceptual diversity we find in both periods to decompose a supposedly universal (but really only modern and Western) concept of 'race'. Or we can explore how modern racial categories are indeed haunted by the medieval.

Should we use the modern term 'race' in referring to the concerns in Chaucer's texts? If we do, we risk the imposition of modernity on the medieval; we risk obliterating the Chaucerian with our own concerns. But the modern and the medieval are not absolutely separable, as we have seen, and there are great potential gains that offset these risks: if we understand the term as historically contingent and broad enough to use in historical enquiry, and if we are mindful not to allow its modern meanings to narrow or distort our investigations – admittedly so difficult that some scholars think this is not possible – we will be able to take the term away from racists who aver that it is a universal concept with a fixed meaning for all time.[22] The same methodological discussion of risks and benefits holds true for 'gender' and 'sexuality', two more terms that bring up concerns about presentism – not to mention 'queer': 'gender', unlike 'race', was used in the Middle Ages (see the *Middle English Dictionary* 'gendre [n.]'), but its range of medieval meanings and connotations must be investigated. 'Sexuality' and 'queer' are not Middle English terms, and are likewise risky – but potentially beneficial – for historically sensitive discussion.

Misogynist Constance, feminist Constance

The significance of a Chaucerian text can be illuminated by succeeding events. Well before September 11, preoccupations of the later twentieth century had already made scholars enquire anew of Chaucer's works: September 11 changed the contexts of enquiry again and thus shed new light on the old texts, but twentieth-century traditions of feminism, gay liberation, and post-colonial activism had already reframed them. The *Man of Law's Tale* is a signal text for this kind of re-evaluation, with its narrative of a pale, saintly woman cast about on rough seas from Rome to Syria to England and back again to Rome, victim of murderous plots and – at least in the analogues – unnatural desire.

Constance, the long-suffering heroine of the *Man of Law's Tale*, was ripe for feminist reconsideration. A long critical tradition read her as a saintly figure, or, more specifically, as 'a typical heroine of hagiographical romance', combining a virtuous demeanour with far-flung adventures.[23] The journeys to faraway lands, smitten husband-to-be of high estate, murderous mothers-in-law, counterfeit letters, air of the supernatural, surprise encounters, and tearful reconciliations – all these motifs had been identified as typical of the romance genre, as had the dilatory, episodic nature of the narrative and its doublings of character and scene. The historical model for Constance, Constantia, daughter of Byzantine emperor Tiberius Constantinus, was not in fact a saint, but her exemplary deportment in Chaucer's source was saint-*like*, putting her in the company of figures such as Saint Mary Magdalene whose lives had been recounted in romance-like works.

A romance heroine is subject to the whims of Fortune. A hagiographical romance heroine puts her trust, rather, in the Providential disposition of the cosmos, having learned the lesson Boethius taught in his *Consolation of Philosophy*.[24] In this critical tradition, the tale is interpreted as showing 'the absolute power of God and his love for those who serve him'.[25] Thus the image of Constance on the sea in a rudderless boat conveys the sense of her inner stability in settings of extreme contingency and lack of control. It has also been argued that her narrative, with its temporal setting in the sixth century and its geographical range, represents not only a philosophical or spiritual principle but also the historical spread of the Christian Church; Constance in her boat images the steady ship of the Church, disseminating the truth.[26]

But just as scholars tuned into the pain voiced by Boethius in his dialogue with Lady Philosophy,[27] scholars tuned into Constance's pathetic and unheeded lament to her parents when she must leave home for a foreign land to marry a man she has never met:

> Allas, unto the Barbre nacioun
> I moste anoon, syn that it is youre wille;
> But Crist, that starf for our redempcioun
> So yeve me grace his heestes to fulfille!
> I, wrecche womman, no fors though I spille!
> Wommen are born to thraldom and penance,
> And to been under mannes governance. (281–7)

Influenced by the atmosphere of women's liberation – the first significant politically driven article analysing Constance's femininity as an emblem of social relations was published in 1974–5 – scholars began to read Constance's representation as powerless female subjected to masculine control in terms of sexual politics.[28] The *Tale*'s narrative conventions, which had been so neatly explained by generic categorization as romance, were interrogated for gender values and ideologies. Thus the dilatory nature and doublings of romance narrative, for example, have been characterized as a particularly feminine disruption of narrative linearity, teleology, and closure identified with the masculine.[29]

Based on anthropologist Gayle Rubin's influential analysis – also published in 1975 – of the role of women in anthropological theories of culture, my reading in *Chaucer's Sexual Poetics* of the *Man of Law's Tale* (which I adduce here as an example of a standard feminist reading) found the representation of Constance to be continuous with treatments of women built into twentieth-century theories of the structure of patriarchal culture; that is, it found the *Man of Law's Tale* to participate in a long tradition of patriarchal texts.[30] Rubin took up Marcel Mauss's theory of gift exchange, particularly as it was followed and extended by Claude Lévi-Strauss. Mauss hypothesized that the exchange of gifts constitutes society, indeed liberates culture itself; Lévi-Strauss built on this, suggesting that women are the most precious gifts, and that marriage should be seen as 'the archetype of exchange'. The regulation of this particular exchange of women in marriage is the very basis of social organization, finds Lévi-Strauss; thus the universal prohibition of incest. The power asymmetry bewailed by Constance is intrinsic to a society based on the exchange of women. As Rubin observes, 'if it is women who are being transacted, then it is the men who give and take them who are linked, the woman being a conduit of a relationship rather than a partner to it'.[31] And if the incest taboo is found to be universal, so is the power asymmetry between giver and gift, man and woman.

Trade and exchange, particularly the 'traffic in women', describe the dynamics of the *Man of Law's Tale*. Constance, traded in marriage by her father, the Roman Emperor, to the Sultan of Syria, is like the 'chaffare' traded by merchants who have travelled to Rome from Syria and back again with their goods and tales. Moreover, just as this tale itself has been told to the Man of Law by a merchant, Constance is the story told to the Sultan by merchants; it is by hearing about her that the Sultan purposes to marry her. She is a conduit in a relationship – the proposed linking of West and East – rather than participant in it; consequently, any agency she has is downplayed in the narrative. Even the conversion of the Northumbrian pagans effected through her influence occurs without her direct intervention – in a startling contrast to, say, the vociferous, even sardonic Cecilia in the *Second Nun's Tale*.

The murderous mothers-in-law, those women in the tale who exhibit agency, who have active and independent desires, are characterized as completely evil. The Sultan's mother refuses to convert to Christianity, and King Alla's mother rejects his wife as foreign, 'strange' (700). Both mothers-in-law must be killed off – and indeed are revealed, rhetorically at least, to be not women at all: 'O feyned womman,' cries the Man of Law in castigating the Sultaness; 'fy!' he exclaims at Donegild's 'mannysh' spirit (362, 782). Proper women in this world must conform their desires to the desires of others; for the smooth operation of the system, woman will desire the man to whom another man has traded her. Women of independent wills threaten this system.[32] Female passivity is structurally required in patriarchal society, according to this reading focussing on Constance's blankness.

Patriarchal power in this view is a historically continuous structure, however locally specified, of male domination. In my analysis a feminist theory of the exchange of women shows continuities in gender politics in all kinds of discourses (anthropological, literary) past and present. In this focus on continuity there is of course the danger, discussed earlier, of eliding crucial differences in discursive contexts that have had an impact on the historical and social particulars of the construction of gender and patriarchy; a similar danger has been pointed out in critiques of Rubin's article itself, which boldly asserts 'examples of trafficking in women' throughout history and across cultures.[33] While there may always be tension between historical and social particulars, on the one hand, and larger theoretical claims on the other, as my discussion above implies, in the context of feminist criticism of the *Man of Law's Tale* advances have been made in at least making the theoretical model of patriarchal power more complex: patriarchal power operates not only by means of gender politics – establishing and controlling women's difference from men – but also by creating and controlling other kinds of differences as well (religious and territorial, to name two of importance in this tale) against which it can consolidate itself. So argues Susan Schibanoff, in an important analysis of the *Man of Law's Tale*.[34]

A crucial advance in feminist literary criticism, starting in the early 1980s, has been to relate gender to other forms of social organization, understanding that gender is always constituted in relation to other social categories.[35] Thus Schibanoff construes Constance's passivity in terms of a co-ordinated Western patriarchal system of othering women, Muslims, the East, and heretics: women are seen to be threatening not because they are so different from men but because they are so similar, built, after all, out of Adam's side; Islam is seen by some as a Christian heresy, 'an internal perversion of the putatively true faith', and thus a threat; the East is 'insidious'; and *all* these dangers must be 'resituate[d]' as identifiable and distanced Others so as to be controlled, curtailed, or destroyed.[36] The Man of Law's narrative strategies perform such a resituation, and in so doing, the tale fosters among its audience on the road to Canterbury 'the sense of a common vested interest among English men who . . . imagine themselves crowded on several fronts by the proximate Other – the woman, the heretic, the Oriental'.[37] Schibanoff is developing an argument about Chaucer's society here, but she could as well be writing of the threatened white male of the late twentieth century: the structures of psychic threat are analogous, if not continuous.

Constance's agency – or lack thereof – has been an issue of considerable feminist debate. Readings against this patriarchally dominated grain will find evidence of agency for the heroine. At the crux of arguments about Constance's power is a quandary for Western feminists, debated energetically in the 1980s: Is the position of the Other necessarily, entirely, always disempowering? Can marginalization result somehow in empowerment? Quoting Hélène Cixous, to wit, that marginality can be 'a position of maximum maneuverability . . . a border in which outmoded male logic ceases to speak', Elizabeth Robertson finds Constance's power in her 'strangeness', her ambiguity, her obscurity, her unknowability.[38] Her Otherness renders her superior, not subordinate, and it emanates not only from her gender but also from a spirituality that is non-violent and non-hieratic, an extra-institutional apostolic Christianity that in fact implicitly criticizes the masculine violence and the institutional Christianity in the tale.

There is no imminent resolution of this critical debate about Constance's power or weakness – or the gender politics of Chaucer in this tale. Much depends on the larger framework of each reading in the *Canterbury Tales* or Chaucer's *œuvre*, and has some relation, as I have been suggesting, to the moment in which the critic is writing. As feminist analyses have developed, they have become more inclusive, bringing more and more into the orbit of gender's workings. And one vital correction of general feminist literary practice on which medievalists can insist is attention to the pressure that religion or spirituality (so often ignored in the secular US academy) applies to that critical triumvirate of gender, race, and class.

Queerness taints the *Man of Law's Tale*

The shift from feminist to queer analysis of medieval texts is not necessarily a huge one, insofar as gender and sex are interlinked (proper gender behaviour specifies the kind of person with whom you may licitly have sexual relations, for example), and insofar as queer analysis seeks disruptions of binary logics (natural/unnatural; reproductive/non-reproductive; licit/illicit), just as feminist analysis does, as I have intimated above (beginning/end, margin/centre, same/other). A queer analysis should draw other social categories into sex's orbit, just as feminist analysis should do for gender. But the analytical foregrounding of sex and its whole range of associations (sex acts, desire, the erotic, the amatory) over gender will distinguish the two approaches. Though analyses of sex sometimes had their roots in gender analyses, the distinction between sex and gender was influentially formulated and pursued in the 1980s, as feminisms diversified and took different directions. In this section I shall take the analysis of incest in the *Man of Law's Tale* as an example: in my earlier feminist analysis, incest is seen as a manifestation of gender dynamics, and the significance of the sexual act in the narrative is absorbed into its gender significance. In my more recent queer reading, illicit sex, including incest, is found to be stereotypically associated with Islam, but the sexual is not entirely absorbed by another particular significance, be it religious (or racial) or gendered.[39]

To use the term 'queer', of course, raises the issues of presentism I discussed earlier. 'Queer' is not a Middle English word, and it emerged into widespread use in specific Anglo-American contexts in the late 1980s. Moreover, its use in reference to the present day is somewhat inconsistent: sometimes it denotes gays and lesbians, sometimes all sexual outlaws. But in either case, we must not assume that what we typically mean now by 'gay', 'lesbian', or 'sexual outlaw' can be mapped onto, say, London in the late fourteenth century. Gay history, as practised by its foremost early scholar, John Boswell, was marred by its implicit assumption that relationships between men of similar ages constituted gayness – much as we assume today of gay relationships – thus leaving aside the complicated but widespread social phenomenon of pederasty.[40] And if we mean by 'queer' sexual outlaws, that is, those people or behaviours falling outside sexual norms – see the recent book *The Trouble with Normal* – we must consider that the concept of a 'norm' is itself a nineteenth-century invention, born of the field of statistics and linked with eugenics.[41] I use the term in the latter way, but rather than think in terms of sexual norms and their violation, then, I try to discern the terms and categories associated with the sexual, erotic, and amatory, both valued and denigrated, in the text; in this way I attempt to overcome a distortion of the past text by imposition of present-day sexual norms or categories. That which in the realm of the sexual cannot be categorized, the residue, the leftover, is queer.

In the *Man of Law's Tale*, incest is just that kind of residue. Unnatural sexuality has been a flashpoint of criticism on the tale for almost a century, since it was found that in a large number of its folktale sources and analogues the narrative of Constance's adventures is motivated by incest. Though in Chaucer's direct sources, Nicholas Trivet's Anglo-Norman *Chronicle* and Gower's *Confessio Amantis*, the incest has been removed, Chaucer must have known versions of the Constance legend that begin with the exile of the heroine by a father who makes sexual demands. Oddly enough, the Man of Law specifically states in the Introduction to his tale (when asked by the Host to tell a tale, and responding that Chaucer has told all the good ones) that Chaucer does not tell tales of incest. If we recall Lévi-Strauss's theory, the incest *prohibition* is universal – but that does not mean that incest doesn't happen. It is clearly no violation of masculine prerogative if a father makes advances on his daughter, but it does violate the cultural rule of the necessary exchange of women. Father–daughter incest, that is, violates patriarchy's own rules, and thus *stories* of such incest will not be told.

By drawing attention to what has been suppressed, the Introduction suggests in fact that incest may still haunt the narrative. And even as traces of father–daughter incest linger in the 'till-death-do-them-part' reunion of Emperor and Constance at the end of the tale, so does a much more disruptive incestuous possibility arise: the desire of the mothers for their sons, the Sultaness for the Sultan and Donegild for Alla. Such desire (the motive, I suggested, for the mothers' violence against Constance) interrupts the smooth cultural operation of the exchange of women. Independent, disruptive feminine desire is not tenable in the patriarchal arrangements of the narrative; therefore, the mothers-in-law are forcibly eliminated.

Sex, in this view, is made significant within the gender dynamics of the tale. But if we want to understand this sexual act more fully (rather than take it solely as meaning gender), we will want to investigate other factors: how does religious difference, for example, affect the representation of incest here? Steven Kruger has suggested that 'efforts at keeping religious communities segregated', efforts that flourished in, for example, the decrees of the Fourth Lateran Council in 1215, were based on some conviction that Jewish and Saracen bodies were different from Christian bodies. Some difference that was unincorporable into the community of Christians remained even in the bodies of converts: Kruger writes of 'Christian anxieties about Jewish and Muslim bodies and . . . uncertainty about whether religious conversion truly transformed those bodies, cleansing them of their impurities, repairing their imperfections, and removing the tinges of animality that clung to them in Christian fantasies'.[42]

The threat of Jews in the *Man of Law's Tale* is dispelled by their safe assimilation into Christian scriptural history. The Man of Law's rhetorical outbursts include 'the Judaic past within the Christian present', as John Fyler remarks: Jonah, Susannah, David, Judith, and the 'peple Ebrayk' all figure as examples of God's power adduced by the Man of Law.[43] And any potential threat posed by the pagans in Northumberland, where Constance lands after her expulsion from Syria, is diffused by their representation as precursors of Christianity: it is taken as a matter of course, for example, that the court of King Alla, so virtuous is he, should have and revere a book of the Christian gospels, 'a Britoun book, written with Evaungiles' (666). It is only a matter of time before the virtuous pagan converts to Christianity, and converts without a residue of paganness; in the view of the narrative he has been a Christian in some sense all along.[44]

But the Saracens, in all their corporeal difference, hold out the threat in the tale. Converts are slaughtered mercilessly at the Sultan's wedding banquet, and Constance is pictured (in the Sultaness's evil imaginings) stained by their lost blood: 'For thogh his wyf be cristned never so white, / She shal have nede to wasshe awey the rede, / Thogh she a font-ful water with hire lede' (355–7). That blood is the remainder, unconverted and materially resistant, of the converted Saracens, something where the imprint of Christianity didn't take. According to medieval Christian writers, Saracen blood circulates incestuously: incest was one of the stereotypical, illicit pleasures of the Saracens. And it was a pleasure thought (by anxious Christians, at least) to extend Saracen blood lines, to control and extend alien religious strength: as

Petrus Alphonsi put it in his twelfth-century *Dialogue*, 'they are permitted to have wives from their own kin, so that the offspring of their blood may increase, and the bond of friendship among them be vigorous'.[45] Incest is a manifestation of gender relations, certainly, but also of anxieties about religion, and they are played out in a sexual medium that has, moreover, its own unassimilable, uncontrollable, desirous aspects. As the Saracen blood stains the Christian Constance, incest taints Christians and proto-Christians alike in the tale.

This analysis sees that religious difference is rendered in bodily terms. Religion factors into something we might call *racial*, insofar as race encompasses (as Thomas Hahn puts it) 'conscious and conventionalized distinctions based on appearance, territorial and geopolitical diversity, and power relations'.[46] And further, religion cannot be detached from gender or sex in this tale; they are in fact its media. Indeed, we might see the whole incest formation here as a queerness, understanding queerness not as narrowly sexual but as a phenomenon that shakes up, confuses, exceeds, or otherwise renders irrelevant operant categories of sex – categories that are gendered and racial/religious as well. My analysis here has suggested that queerness circulates in the *Man of Law's Tale* as the sexual residue of racial/religious difference. Queerness in the *Man of Law's Tale* is incest, that racial remainder of the unconverted that taints with illicit desire not just the evil Sultaness but even the staunchest Christian, the Roman Emperor. In the end, Constance returns to the arms of her father in the narrative's ultimately ironic effort to contain that taint.

The categorical excess that is queerness takes us back to other category collapses we have considered, including the discussion of time wherein we observed the past's inextricability from the present and the concomitant disruption of linear, serial chronology. It takes us back to the disruption of the masculine by the feminine posited by analyses of romance, returning us to basic assumptions (shared by new critical approaches to Chaucer) about texts and, finally, signs: that they are not fixed in hierarchies and binary oppositions. Rather, they circulate, contact, disrupt, or – as I shall finally suggest – create new possibilities.

The *Man of Law's Tale* and the deadliness of Western historical narratives

Themes of racial/religious difference were available to and productive for Chaucerians writing about the *Man of Law's Tale* well before September 11. But on that day a need for information became urgent; many Americans felt the need to understand Western traditions in relation to the East, and the stakes were much higher than they had been a day before. Islamic–Christian relations had suddenly become deadly again on a very large scale, and it was clear that interpreting the history of these relations could have fatal consequences. The main pillars of Western culture – in the literary tradition, Chaucer, Shakespeare – would be re-evaluated anew. What is Chaucer's role in the development of the discourse of East–West relations?

This question serves to reanimate a critical dispute over the meaning and value of Chaucer's representation of Islam in the *Man of Law's Tale*. A mid-twentieth-century critical tradition, expounding on Chaucer's modernity, observed that Chaucer's sense of history – following the Renaissance of the twelfth century – included 'a more accurate sense of chronology' and a greater 'sense of cultural diversity' than earlier classical and medieval temporal understandings.[47] Thus the whole tale is notable for its clearly marked placement in the historical past, as distinct from the present and the future, and the representation of the Sultaness is remarkable for its portrayal of her fierce devotion; the tale presents her religious conviction from the 'Saracen point of view' ('oure lawe sweete', one of the Sultan's privy council calls it: 223). While Muslims are sometimes valued only because of their potential for conversion,[48] the strength of the Sultaness, intransigent in her faith, marks Chaucer's interest in cultural difference. Moreover, the Sultaness does not rehearse the oaths typical of other representations of Saracens, nor does she stereotypically worship idols.

But we have already noted Schibanoff's less positive interpretation of the tale's representation of Islamic–Christian and East–West relations. Critics recently have considered hostile rather than sympathetic the Sultaness's characterization, focussing not on Chaucer's putative interest in cultural diversity but on his representation of her homicidal actions and the Man of Law's hyperbolically negative rhetoric (e.g., 'O Sowdanesse, roote of iniquitee! . . . this scorpioun, this wikked goost, / The Sowdanesse': 358, 404–5). And attention to the chronology of the tale has revealed not accuracy but a discrepancy that scholars have found to be meaningful distortion, a discrepancy proceeding not from respect for cultural diversity but from what one critic, following Said, calls 'orientalism' – 'a Western style for dominating, restructuring, and having authority over the Orient'.[49] The dates for the historical King Alla's reign are 560–88; Mohammed, invoked by the Sultaness as 'Goddes message Makomete' (333), lived from 570? to 632. Thus Islam had not achieved its status as 'lawe' by the time of Alla's reign. Instead, as Kathleen Davis has argued, in the tale Islam has been projected backwards. This is the Islam in the past that Chaucer's Western Christendom needs in the fourteenth-century present to write its own history of emergence and consolidation: 'late medieval European historiography . . . must remember Islam as murderous and so incapable of eradicating its error that contact with it spawns only violence and death, rather than the shared life of spiritual conversion or human progeny'.[50] Even before Chaucer's rendition, Trivet in his chronicle version had already manipulated chronology and fact, linking a romance fable to historical events – revisions motivated by the crusading fervour in early fourteenth-century England.[51] Chaucer at the end of the century chooses to cut Trivet's more ostensibly crusading rhetoric – he eliminates Trivet's contention that Constance's first marriage would recover access for Christians to the Holy Land – but a claim about the tale's ideological role in a developing Western world-view nonetheless emerges from Chaucer's subtler representations: associating Saracens with the corporeally different and perverse, as we have seen; back-dating Islam and quickly laying waste to the Syrians; absorbing paganism and gradually consolidating a Western Europe inclusive of England in the poem, Chaucer creates a story of the inevitable, necessary, and blessed historical triumph of Western Christendom.

Is this Chaucer's view? Or is this the Man of Law's, and not Chaucer's at all? Is it even possible, let alone desirable, to separate out the speaker's view from the author's?[52] The structure of the *Canterbury Tales* has always muddied the issue of authorial responsibility and intention. Indeed, Fyler suggests that Chaucer's project in the *Tales* is to explore the ethical potentials of impersonation: 'Chaucer reveals the ethical nature of his characters by their degree of magnanimity in the ways they people their tales.' The Man of Law may respond with 'xenophobic alarm at the world outside Christian Europe', but Chaucer stands outside – beyond, above – his limited, sometimes narrow-minded characters.[53]

The issue of Chaucer's intention here will never be clear, given the multivocalic nature of the *Tales*. But different assumptions about literature separate Fyler's formalist view from, say, Davis's: while the former assumes an author who is the ground of meaning of a text, the latter treats the text as it participates in discursive structures – like orientalism – that are larger than any individual author. And it is, finally, the discourse as the individual author deploys it (and is deployed by it) that is of interest in the latter approach. Here, with emphasis on analysis of colonization and its effects, the displacement of the dominance of Christianity, and the decentring of Europe, Davis's approach is inspired by postcolonial studies.[54] Further, as we see in Davis's work, postcolonial concerns intersect with feminist and queer concerns, as all these approaches seek to understand ways that subjugated peoples (women, 'perverts', the colonized) can have agency and subjectivity.

Postcolonial studies arose in response to twentieth-century decolonization. But its analytical reach is not limited to the twentieth century and after. Postcolonial studies problematize (among other things) time: when exactly does the *post*colonial start, if the colonial has never not been? Why should linear, Western Enlightenment expectations of pre and post, cause and effect structure the study?[55] The field thus has much to offer medievalists, who are also interested in understanding modes of temporality and non-dualist, non-essentialist philosophical modes not dictated by Western Enlightenment protocols. Indeed, melding the insights of medievalists and postcolonial theorists, we can try to understand how the cosmic armature of the *Man of Law's Tale* – non-rational, not bound by natural laws of cause and effect – might disrupt masculine imperialist rule.[56] The interests of medievalists importantly intersect with those of thinkers more immediately engaged in understanding September 11: medievalists can help imagine a future in the West that is less imperialist because less bound to a single chronology, a logic of causality, binary or dualist expectations – because medievalists understand a Western past in which these Enlightenment parameters did not obtain.

The narrative of the *Man of Law's Tale* entered a history of fatal discourses after September 11. I mean by this strong assertion that the significance of the tale's orientalist representations changed in the new context of extreme Islamicist violence carried out on Western soil: they became part of a long tradition of Western relations to the East that has proved deadly. But if a postcolonial reading leads us to a broad conclusion about the orientalist discourse of the *Man of Law's Tale* – or if a feminist reading leads us to an interpretation of its misogynist discourse, or a queer reading to straightening moves of the narrative – we need not let that be the end of our enjoyment of Chaucer's texts. It may be harder, in the atmosphere post-September 11, to enjoy what Derek Pearsall calls Chaucer's aestheticization of 'difficult social realities'.[57] More generally, it may be indeed impossible to use these Middle Ages as a retreat from the horrors of the present. But through efforts to understand our Western cultural history, of which Chaucer is a vivid part, we can be enabled to think differently – not nostalgically, but nonetheless pleasurably, insofar as there is pleasure in imagining the possibility of a new world.[58]

NOTES

1. Kathleen Biddick, *The Shock of Medievalism* (Durham, N.C., 1998), p. 59.
2. D. W. Robertson, Jr, 'Some Observations on Method in Literary Studies' in his *Essays in Medieval Culture* (Princeton, N.J., 1980), pp. 73–84, at p. 82.
3. Louise O. Fradenburg, discussing Chaucer and Chaucerians, has analysed the Freudian distinction in her essays '"Voice Memorial": Loss and Reparation in Chaucer's Poetry', *Exemplaria*, 2 (1990), 169–202, and 'Criticism, Anti-Semitism, and the *Prioress's Tale*', *Exemplaria*, 1 (1989), 69–115.

4. Michel Foucault, 'On the Genealogy of Ethics: An Overview of Work in Progress' in *The Foucault Reader*, ed. Paul Rabinow (New York, 1984), pp. 340–72, at p. 343.

5. Caroline Bynum, 'Why All the Fuss about the Body? A Medievalist's Perspective', *Critical Inquiry*, 22 (Autumn 1995), 1–33, at p. 29.

6. E. N. Johnson, addressing the Mediaeval Academy in the Cold War 1950s, issued a passionate call for medievalists to justify their interests with reference to contemporary issues, in 'American Mediaevalists and Today', *Speculum*, 28 (1953), 844–54.

7. Bynum, 'Why All the Fuss?', pp. 29, 31.

8. Kathleen Davis, 'Time behind the Veil: The Media, the Middle Ages, and Orientalism Now' in *The Postcolonial Middle Ages*, ed. J. J. Cohen (New York, 2000), pp. 105–22, at p. 113.

9. See Fradenburg, '"Voice Memorial"'.

10. See my *Getting Medieval: Sexualities and Communities, Pre- and Postmodern* (Durham, N.C., 1999), pp. 100–42.

11. Nicholas Watson, 'Desire for the Past', *Studies in the Age of Chaucer*, 21 (1999), 59–97.

12. See, for example, Biddick, *The Shock of Medievalism*.

13. Walter Benjamin, 'Theses on the Philosophy of History' in *Illuminations*, ed. Hannah Arendt, trans. Harry Zohn (New York, 1969), pp. 253–64, at p. 263.

14. A. J. Gurevich, 'What is Time?' in *Categories of Medieval Culture*, trans. G. L. Campbell (London, 1985), pp. 93–151.

15. Hans-Georg Gadamer, 'Kant and the Hermeneutical Turn' in his *Heidegger's Ways*, trans. J. W. Stanley (New York, 1994), p. 58, quoted by Dipesh Chakrabarty in his *Provincializing Europe: Postcolonial Thought and Historical Difference* (Princeton, N.J., 2000), p. 112.

16. Paul Strohm, *Theory and the Premodern Text* (Minneapolis, Minn., 2000), pp. 65, 80.

17. Jonathan Culler, *On Deconstruction: Theory and Criticism after Structuralism* (Ithaca, N.Y., 1982), p. 123.

18. Strohm, *Theory and the Premodern Text*, pp. 95, 81.

19. Lee Patterson, 'Chaucer's Pardoner on the Couch: Psyche and Clio in Medieval Literary Studies', *Speculum*, 76 (2001), 638–80, at p. 638.

20. Strohm, *Theory and the Premodern Text*, pp. 93, 77.

21. See Bynum, 'Why All the Fuss?' and William Jordan, 'Why "Race?"' in Thomas Hahn, ed., *Race and Ethnicity in the Middle Ages*, special issue of *The Journal of Medieval and Early Modern Studies*, 31 (2001), 165–73.

22. See Hahn, ed., *Race and Ethnicity in the Middle Ages*, particularly the essays by Hahn and Robert Bartlett as well as Jordan.

23. Patricia J. Eberle's notes in *The Riverside Chaucer*, gen. ed. Larry D. Benson (Boston, 1987), p. 858, citing Clogan.

24. See Eugene Clasby, 'Chaucer's Constance: Womanly Virtue and the Heroic Life', *Chaucer Review*, 13 (1978–9), 221–39.

25. V. A. Kolve, *Chaucer and the Imagery of Narrative: The First Five Canterbury Tales* (Stanford, Calif., 1984), p. 297.

26. Kolve, *Chaucer and the Imagery of Narrative*, pp. 297–358.

27. See, for example, Winthrop Wetherbee, *Platonism and Poetry in the Twelfth Century: The Literary Influence of the School of Chartres* (Princeton, N.J., 1972), pp. 74–82.

28. Sheila Delany, 'Womanliness in *The Man of Law's Tale*', *Chaucer Review*, 9 (1974–5), 63–72; repr. in *Writing Woman: Women Writers and Women in Literature, Medieval to Modern* (New York, 1983), in which she discusses the political contexts of her analysis.

29. For romance narrative as deferral, see Patricia Parker, *Inescapable Romance: Studies in the Poetics of a Mode* (Princeton, N.J., 1979); for the gendering of delay and dilation, see her *Literary Fat Ladies: Rhetoric, Gender, Property* (New York, 1987).

30. *Chaucer's Sexual Poetics* (Madison, Wisc., 1989), pp. 88–112. I have reused several sentences from that text in this essay. For lack of space here, I have not reproduced the bibliographic references; the reader is encouraged to consult the original.

31. *Chaucer's Sexual Poetics*, p. 97.

32. The exchange of women between men does not rule out female agency altogether; all sorts of mischief can happen outside the exchange, as long as patriarchal structure (with its clear lines of inheritance ensured by marriage and legitimate offspring) is maintained.

33. Rubin, 'The Traffic in Women: Notes on the "Political Economy" of Sex', *Toward an Anthropology of Women*, ed. R. R. Reiter (New York, 1975), p. 175. For critiques, see, for example, Marilyn Strathern, *The Gender of the Gift: Problems with Women and Problems with Society in Melanesia* (Berkeley, 1988); in a Chaucerian context, see Jill Mann, *Feminizing Chaucer*, new edn (Cambridge, 2002), pp. 153–4.

34. Susan Schibanoff, 'Worlds Apart: Orientalism, Antifeminism, and Heresy in the *Man of Law's Tale*', *Exemplaria*, 8 (1996), 59–96.

35. Delany in her 1983 *Writing Woman* makes clear that gender politics must be part of a comprehensive social analysis.

36. Schibanoff, 'Worlds Apart', pp. 72, 69.

37. Schibanoff, 'Worlds Apart', p. 94.

38. Elizabeth Robertson, 'The "Elvyssh" Power of Constance: Christian Feminism in Geoffrey Chaucer's *The Man of Law's Tale*', *Studies in the Age of Chaucer*, 23 (2001), 143–80, at pp. 166, 159–65.

39. 'Pale Faces: Race, Religion, and Affect in Chaucer's Texts and Their Readers', *Studies in the Age of Chaucer*, 23 (2001), 19–41. I have reused several sentences from that text here.

40. The term 'gay' thus seems to have imposed its modern-day values onto the medieval evidence. See John Boswell, *Christianity, Social Tolerance, and Homosexuality: Gay People in Western Europe from the Beginning of the Christian Era to the Fourteenth Century* (Chicago, 1980), and my discussion of Boswell's *œuvre* in *Getting Medieval*, pp. 22–34. Judith Bennett has recently tried to overcome this problem with respect to lesbian history: '"Lesbian-Like" and the Social History of Lesbianisms', *Journal of the History of Sexuality*, 9 (2000), 1–24.

41. Michael Warner, *The Trouble with Normal: Sex, Politics, and the Ethics of Queer Life* (New York, 1999). On norms, see Amy Hollywood, 'The Normal, the

Queer, and the Middle Ages', *Journal of the History of Sexuality*, 10 (2001), 173–9.

42. Steven F. Kruger, 'Conversion and Medieval Sexual, Religious, and Racial Categories' in *Constructing Medieval Sexuality*, eds. Karma Lochrie, Peggy McCracken, and James A. Schultz (Minneapolis, 1997), 158–79, at pp. 169, 167.

43. John M. Fyler, 'Chaucerian Romance and the World beyond Europe' in Donald Maddox and Sara Sturm-Maddox, eds., *Literary Aspects of Courtly Culture* (Cambridge, 1994), pp. 257–63, at p. 261.

44. Don-John Dugas, 'The Legitimization of Royal Power in Chaucer's *Man of Law's Tale*', *Modern Philology*, 95 (1997), 27–43, at pp. 31–2.

45. Petrus Alphonsi, *Dialogi*, PL 157: 598: 'Conceditur insuper eis de propria cognatione habere uxores ut sanguinis proles accrescat, et fortius inter eos amicitiae vinculum vigeat.' Quoted and translated in Kruger, 'Conversion', p. 174.

46. Hahn, 'The Difference the Middle Ages Makes: Color and Race before the Modern World', in *Race and Ethnicity*, p. 6.

47. Morton Bloomfield, 'Chaucer's Sense of History', *Journal of English and Germanic Philology*, 51 (1952), 301–13, at p. 304.

48. On the 'Saracen point of view', see Bloomfield, 'Chaucer's Sense', pp. 309–10. On the value of Muslims as potential converts, see Robertson, 'The "Elvyssh" Power of Constance', p. 153.

49. Davis, 'Time behind the Veil', following Edward W. Said, *Orientalism* (New York, 1979), p. 3.

50. Davis, 'Time behind the Veil', p. 116.

51. Lillian Herlands Hornstein, 'Trivet's Constance and the *King of Tars*', *Modern Language Notes*, 55 (1940), 354–7, at p. 356. See *The Riverside Chaucer*, p. 857, for Trivet's revisions.

52. On the problems of the dramatic interpretation of the *Tales*, see the essay by C. David Benson in this volume.

53. Fyler, 'Chaucerian Romance', pp. 258, 261. See also Glory Dharmaraj, 'Multicultural Subjectivity in Reading Chaucer's "Man of Law" [*sic*] Tale', *Medieval Feminist Newsletter*, 16 (Fall 1993), 4–8.

54. See Jeffrey Jerome Cohen, 'Introduction: Midcolonial' in *The Postcolonial Middle Ages*, ed. Cohen, pp. 1–17, esp. pp. 6–7.

55. Cohen, 'Introduction: Midcolonial', p. 3.

56. On premodern philosophical modes, see Bynum, 'Why All the Fuss?', p. 30. On the force of the cosmic hierarchy in this tale see Mann, *Feminizing Chaucer*, pp. 100–12.

57. Derek Pearsall, 'Chaucer's Englishness', *Proceedings of the British Academy*, 101 (1999), 77–99, at p. 85.

58. Thus Foucault's explorations in his *History of Sexuality*, vol. 2: 'The object was to learn to what extent the effort to think one's own history can free thought from what it silently thinks, and so enable it to think differently' (*The Use of Pleasure*, trans. Robert Hurley (1985; repr. New York, 1990), p. 9).

17

JOERG O. FICHTE

Further reading: a guide to Chaucer studies

1 *Bibliography*

The first six items in section 1.1, listed in chronological order, are comprehensive surveys of Chaucer criticism up to 1996; for works published after that date, the annual bibliographies published in the journals listed in section 1.2 should be consulted. *Studies in the Age of Chaucer* and the *Year's Work in English Studies* are particularly useful because the items listed are annotated.

Selected bibliographies follow in alphabetical order. The annotated Chaucer Bibliography by Leyerle and Quick contains about 1,200 items, and that by Allen and Fisher contains 924 items. The other volumes in this section belong to the Chaucer Bibliographies series; they will facilitate access to the prodigious amount of Chaucer criticism produced in this century.

A Chaucer MetaPage designed to provide access to Chaucer studies on the worldwide web can be reached at http://www.unc.edu/depts/chaucer/.

1.1 *Collections*

Hammond, E. P. *Chaucer: A Bibliographical Manual* (New York, 1908; repr. New York, 1933).

Griffith, D. D. *Bibliography of Chaucer, 1908–1953* (Seattle, 1955).

Crawford, W. R. *Bibliography of Chaucer, 1954–63* (Seattle, 1967).

Baird, L. Y. *A Bibliography of Chaucer, 1965–1973* (Boston, 1977).

Baird-Lange, L. Y. and H. Schnuttgen. *A Bibliography of Chaucer, 1974–1985* (Hamden, Conn., 1988).

Bowers, B. K. and M. Allen, eds. *Annotated Chaucer Bibliography, 1986–1996* (Notre Dame, Ind., 2002).

Allen, M. and J. H. Fisher. *The Essential Chaucer: An Annotated Bibliography of Major Modern Studies* (Boston, 1987).

Beidler, P. G. and E. M. Biebel, eds. *Chaucer's Wife of Bath's Prologue and Tale: An Annotated Bibliography* (Toronto/Buffalo, N.Y./London, 1998).

Burton, T. L. and R. Greentree. *Chaucer's Miller's, Reeve's, and Cook's Tales: An Annotated Bibliography 1900 to 1992* (Toronto/Buffalo, N.Y./London, 1997).

Eckhardt, C. D. *Chaucer's General Prologue to the Canterbury Tales: An Annotated Bibliography, 1900–1984* (Toronto/Buffalo, N.Y./London, 1990).

Leyerle, J. and A. Quick. *Chaucer: A Bibliographical Introduction* (Toronto/Buffalo, N.Y./London, 1986).

McAlpine, M. E. *Chaucer's Knight's Tale: An Annotated Bibliography, 1900–1985* (Toronto/Buffalo, N.Y./London, 1991).

Peck, R. A. *The Chaucer Bibliographies: Chaucer's Lyrics and Anelida and Arcite: An Annotated Bibliography 1900 to 1980* (Toronto/Buffalo, N.Y./London, 1983).

Peck, R. A. *Chaucer's Romaunt of the Rose and Boece, Treatise on the Astrolabe, Equatorie of the Planetis, Lost Works, and Chaucerian Apocrypha: An Annotated Bibliography, 1955–1985* (New York, 1987).

Sutton, M. *Chaucer's Pardoner's Prologue and Tale: An Annotated Bibliography 1900 to 1995* (Toronto/Buffalo, N.Y./London, 2000).

1.2 Annual bibliographies

Studies in the Age of Chaucer

The annual bibliographies published in the above journal are also available as the Chaucer Bibliography Online, a database maintained by Mark Allen at the University of Texas at San Antonio. Connection may be made at http://uchaucer.utsa.edu.

Year's Work in English Studies

2 Editions

The standard one-volume edition of Chaucer's works is *The Riverside Chaucer*, a collaborative effort produced under the general editorship of Larry D. Benson. This was based on the second edition of Chaucer's works by F. N. Robinson. Skeat's edition, though now outdated, was the first modern edition of Chaucer, and much later scholarship is based on its voluminous notes. Manly and Rickert's critical edition of the *Canterbury Tales*, published in 1940, was based on all surviving manuscripts. The *Variorum Edition* project, initiated under the general editorship of Paul G. Ruggiers, and now directed by Daniel J. Ransom, was planned as a series of volumes each of which would be devoted to a particular work of Chaucer, and would provide by way of commentary on the text very full syntheses of scholarship and criticism on the work in question. Of the eleven volumes that have appeared so far, eight are devoted to the *Canterbury Tales*; since the Hengwrt MS is used as a base text in these volumes, a facsimile of this manuscript, with accompanying transcription and details of variants in the Ellesmere MS, was published as volume 1 in the *Variorum* series.

John H. Fisher's edition is designed for classroom use; it uses one base MS for every text with emendations from collations of texts by earlier editors. Also designed for classroom use are the selective editions by Baugh and Donaldson, who print almost identical selections – that is, all of Chaucer's verse with the exception of the *Legend of Good Women*, *The Romaunt of the Rose*, *Anelida and Arcite*, and the prose writings. Donaldson's edition also features good discussions of the individual works.

The continuing popularity of the *Canterbury Tales* is attested to by the great number of modern editions. Blake is based on the Hengwrt MS; Pratt uses the text of the Robinson edition with occasional variants; and Cawley uses the Robinson edition without alterations. A separate edition of the *Canterbury Tales*, adapted from the *Riverside Chaucer* with the needs of students in mind, was produced by Larry Benson in 2000. Selected tales with good introductions and glossaries have been edited by Hussey, Spearing, and Winny (*General Prologue, Miller's Tale, Reeve's Tale, Cook's Tale, Wife of Bath's Tale, Nun's Priest's Tale*, and *Franklin's Tale*) and by Andrew and Cawley (*General Prologue, Miller's Tale, Reeve's Tale, Cook's Tale, Shipman's Tale*, and *Nun's Priest's Tale*).

The standard edition of the *Troilus* is that by Barry Windeatt, which superseded the edition by Robert K. Root. The edition by Helen Phillips and Nicholas Havely of Chaucer's *Dream Poetry* (*Book of the Duchess, House of Fame, Parliament of Fowls* and portions of the *Legend of Good Women*) contains a general introduction, glosses, commentary, and selected source material. Helen Phillips's edition of the *Book of the Duchess* is excellent, featuring a good introduction with bibliography, the text plus readings from different MSS, copious notes, a translation of the French sources and analogues, and a complete glossary. A new electronic edition of the *Book of the Duchess* that includes a reading text, a critical edition, facsimiles, and texts and translations of all major sources has been compiled by M. McGillivray. Derek Brewer's edition of *The Parliament of Fowls* contains an excellent introduction, bibliography, text, notes, and glossary. Nicholas Havely's edition of the *House of Fame* is a collation of all five witnesses together with an introduction and glosses. Cowen and Kane's completely fresh edition of the *Legend of Good Women* provides an introduction, variants, and textual commentary.

2.1 Complete editions

Benson, L. D. *et al.*, eds. *The Riverside Chaucer* (Boston, 1987).

Fisher, J. H., ed. *The Complete Poetry and Prose of Geoffrey Chaucer* (New York, 1977).

Robinson, F. N., ed. *The Works of Geoffrey Chaucer*, 2nd edn (Boston/London, 1957).

Ruggiers, P. G., ed. *A Variorum Edition of the Works of Geoffrey Chaucer* (Norman, Okla., 1979–) [*General Prologue*, ed. M. Andrew, 2 vols., 1993; *Miller's Tale*, ed. T. W. Ross, 1983; *Summoner's Tale*, ed. J. F. Plummer III, 1995; *Squire's Tale*, ed. D. C. Baker, 1990; *Physician's Tale*, ed. H. S. Corsa, 1987; *Prioress's Tale*, ed. B. Boyd, 1987; *Nun's Priest's Tale*, ed. D. Pearsall, 1984; *Manciple's Tale*, ed. D. C. Baker, 1984; *The Minor Poems, Part One*, eds. G. B. Pace and A. David, 1982; *The Romaunt of the Rose*, ed. C. Dahlberg, 1999; *A Treatise on the Astrolabe*, ed. S. Eisner, 2002]. The progress of this series can be followed in the Variorum web-site, http://www.ou.edu/variorum.

Skeat, W. W., ed. *The Complete Works of Geoffrey Chaucer*, 2nd edn, 7 vols. (Oxford, 1899).

2.2 Selected editions and individual works

Andrew, M. and A. C. Cawley, eds. *Geoffrey Chaucer: Comic and Bawdy Tales* (London, 1997).

Baugh, A. C., ed. *Chaucer's Major Poetry* (New York, 1963).

Benson, L. D., ed. *The Canterbury Tales Complete* (Boston/New York, 2000).

Blake, N. F., ed. *The Canterbury Tales by Geoffrey Chaucer* (London, 1980).

Brewer, D. S., ed. *The Parlement of Foulys*, 2nd edn (Manchester, 1972).

Cawley, A. C., ed. *The Canterbury Tales*, rev. edn (New York, 1975).

Cowen, J. and G. Kane, eds. *Geoffrey Chaucer: The Legend of Good Women* (East Lansing, Mich., 1995).

Donaldson, E. T., ed. *Chaucer's Poetry: An Anthology for the Modern Reader*, 2nd edn (New York, 1975).

Havely, N., ed. *Chaucer: The House of Fame* (Durham, N.C., 1994).

Hussey, M., A. C. Spearing, and J. Winny, eds. *Selected Tales from Chaucer* (Cambridge, 1965–).

McGillivray, M., ed. *Geoffrey Chaucer's Book of the Duchess: A Hypertext Edition* (Alberta, 1997).

Manly, J. M. and E. Rickert, eds. *The Text of the Canterbury Tales*, 8 vols. (Chicago/London, 1940).

Phillips, H., ed. *The Book of the Duchess*, 2nd rev. edn (Durham/St Andrews, 1993).

Phillips, H. and N. Havely, eds. *Chaucer's Dream Poetry* (London/ New York, 1997).

Pratt, R. A., ed. *The Tales of Canterbury* (Boston, 1966).

Root, R. K., ed. *The Book of Troilus and Criseyde* (Princeton, N.J., 1926).

Windeatt, B. A., ed. *Troilus and Criseyde: A New Edition of 'The Book of Troilus'* (London/New York, 1984).

3 Chaucer's life and world

Approximately five hundred documents referring to Chaucer, the man and civil servant, have been collected by Crow and Olson in the *Chaucer Life-Records*. Biographies drawing on these life records and the poet's works are the books by Chute, Brewer (*Chaucer*; *Chaucer and His World* – a book featuring many fine illustrations), Pearsall, and Stone. Brewer's third study, *Chaucer in His Time*, is an account of the political and social conditions of Chaucer's England, courtly life, domestic life, and religious life, as are the studies of Howard and Strohm, who position Chaucer within a specific social status group. D. W. Robertson complements this general outline by a specific study dealing with the economic, political, social, and intellectual conditions of Chaucer's London. Two richly illustrated pictorial companions to the *Canterbury Tales* in particular and to Chaucer's works in general are the books by Hussey and by Loomis. Rickert *et al.*'s volume, finally, presents a fine collection of contemporary documents illustrating such widely divergent areas as London life, training and education, commercial life, entertainment, travel, warfare, and religion.

Brewer, D. S. *Chaucer in His Time* (London, 1963; repr. Westport, Conn., 1977).
Brewer, D. S. *Chaucer*, 3rd edn (London, 1973).
Brewer, D. S. *Chaucer and His World* (London, 1978).
Chute, M. *Geoffrey Chaucer of England* (New York, 1946; repr. London, 1977).
Crow, M. M. and C. C. Olson, eds. *Chaucer Life-Records* (Austin, Tex., 1966).
Howard, D. R. *Chaucer: His Life, His Works, His World* (New York, 1987).
Hussey, M. *Chaucer's World: A Pictorial Companion* (Cambridge, 1967).
Loomis, R. S. *A Mirror of Chaucer's World* (Princeton, N.J., 1965).
Pearsall, D. *The Life of Geoffrey Chaucer: A Critical Biography* (Oxford, 1992).
Rickert, E., C. C. Olson, and M. M. Crow, eds. *Chaucer's World* (New York, 1948).
Robertson, D. W., Jr. *Chaucer's London* (New York, 1968).
Stone, B. *Chaucer* (Harmondsworth, 1989).
Strohm, P. *Social Chaucer* (Cambridge, 1989).

4 Language and style, dictionaries and glossaries, concordances

Section 4.1 contains a list of studies on the language, style, and vocabulary of Chaucer's poetry. Purely linguistic analyses – that is, studies of the phonology, morphology, and syntax of Chaucer's language – are offered by Kerkhoff, Kökeritz, Sandved, and Ten Brink. For the position of Chaucer's language in the wider context of Middle English the interested reader should consult the handbook by Mossé, and the study of syntax by Mustanoja in section 4.2. The studies by Eliason, Elliott, Masui, and Roscow investigate primarily stylistic features, while Burnley's excellent treatments combine both historical linguistics and stylistics. Cannon reassesses the traditional claims for Chaucer as a linguistic innovator; Part 2 of his study provides an index of Chaucer's vocabulary, with details of the linguistic derivation and first recorded use of each word and its first use in Chaucer's works.

Fundamental for the understanding of Chaucer's language is the *Middle English Dictionary*. A special glossary of the words appearing in Chaucer's works has been assembled by Davis *et al.*, while Ross has provided an index of (allegedly) lewd words and phrases. The older concordance by Tatlock and Kennedy is based on the text of the old Globe Chaucer but is still useful, since Benson's concordance to the *Riverside Chaucer* is not widely available. The computer-generated concordance of Oizumi (based on the *Riverside Chaucer*) treats each of Chaucer's works separately, and is not lemmatized (i.e., it does not distinguish between 'dere' = 'dear' and 'dere' = 'harm').

4.1 Language, style, and vocabulary (Chaucer)

Benson, L. D. *A Glossarial Concordance to the Riverside Chaucer* (New York, 1993).

Burnley, J. D. *Chaucer's Language and the Philosophers' Tradition* (Cambridge, 1979).

Burnley, J. D. *The Language of Chaucer* (London, 1989).

Cannon, Christopher. *The Making of Chaucer's English: A Study of Words* (Cambridge, 1998).

Davis, N., D. Gray, P. Ingham, and A. Wallace-Hadrill. *A Chaucer Glossary* (Oxford, 1979).

Eliason, N. E. *The Language of Chaucer's Poetry: An Appraisal of the Verse, Style and Structure* (Copenhagen, 1972).

Elliott, R. W. V. *Chaucer's English* (London, 1974).

Kerkhoff, J. *Studies in the Language of Geoffrey Chaucer* (Leiden, 1966).

Kökeritz, H. *A Guide to Chaucer's Pronunciation* (Stockholm/New Haven, Conn., 1954; repr. New York, 1962).

Masui, M. *The Structure of Chaucer's Rime Words: An Exploration into the Poetic Language of Chaucer* (Tokyo, 1974; repr. Folcroft, Pa., 1975).

Oizumi, A., ed. *A Complete Concordance to the Works of Geoffrey Chaucer*, 10 vols. (Hildesheim/Zurich/New York, 1991).

Oizumi, A. and H. Yonekura, eds. *A Rhyme Concordance to the Poetical Works of Geoffrey Chaucer, A Complete Concordance to the Works of Geoffrey Chaucer*, XI–XII, Supplement Series, I–II, 2 vols. (Hildesheim/Zurich/New York, 1994).

Roscow, G. H. *Syntax and Structure in Chaucer's Poetry* (Cambridge, 1981).

Ross, T. W. *Chaucer's Bawdy* (New York, 1972).

Sandved, A. O. *Introduction to Chaucerian English* (Cambridge, 1985).

Tatlock, J. S. P. and A. G. Kennedy, eds. *A Concordance to the Complete Works of Geoffrey Chaucer and to the Romaunt of the Rose* (Washington, D.C., 1927; repr. Gloucester, Mass., 1963).

Ten Brink, B. *The Language and Metre of Chaucer*, trans. M. Bentinck Smith (London, 1901; repr. New York, 1969).

4.2 *Language (Middle English)*

Middle English Dictionary, eds. H. Kurath, S. M. Kuhn *et al.* (Ann Arbor, Mich., 1954–).
Mossé, F. *A Handbook of Middle English*, trans. J. A. Walker (Baltimore/London, 1952).
Mustanoja, Tauno F. *A Middle English Syntax* (Helsinki, 1960).

5 Prosody

The study of Chaucer's prosody is hampered by certain conditions which make it difficult to provide definitive answers in this area of investigation. First, we do not know whether he meant his poetry to be read or recited, or precisely what alterations the scribes made when they copied Chaucer's poetry. Secondly, we do not know enough about the spoken language of Chaucer's time to make unassailable statements about his prosody. And thirdly, modern editors have provided us with texts which reflect their own principles of prosody rather than those that Chaucer may have subscribed to. For these reasons it is not surprising that a protracted debate has been carried on, a debate based on certain assumptions about the prosodic principle of Chaucer's poetry. There are two approaches: (1) the hypothesis of iambic decasyllabic verse as the basis of Chaucerian prosody and (2) word-stress and speech rhythms as determinants of the metre of Chaucer's verse. Closely connected with these two approaches are the question of how far Chaucer modelled his verse on contemporary Italian and French verse, and the controversy over the pronunciation of the final unaccented *-e*. Proponents of the decasyllabic iambic verse theory often subscribe to the influence of Italian and French verse on Chaucer's prosody, Romance poetry being fundamentally syllabic in character; while adherents to the speech-rhythm hypothesis would discount this influence, pointing to the accentual nature of English poetry. The same holds true for the pronunciation of the final unaccented *-e*, which some will pronounce for metrical reasons, while others will not, arguing the obsoleteness of this sound in the London standard of Chaucer's time and the dominance of natural speech rhythms.

There is also debate over the meaning of the punctuation in the MSS. Do the virgules (/), colons, and dots placed either above or on the line indicate caesuras or rising intonation? Are the lines divided into two half-lines or not? And is Chaucer thinking in terms of a single line-unit at all?

Finally, the question of how far Chaucer's prose is influenced by the Latin cursus – that is, the cadenced medieval prose characterizing the Latin writings of his time – is still unanswered.

Conflicting views on these and other matters will be found in the studies cited below analysing Chaucer's prosody. The essay by Gaylord is the best assessment of the strengths and weaknesses of the respective positions.

Baum, P. F. *Chaucer's Verse* (Durham/Cambridge, 1961).
Gaylord, A. T. 'Scanning the Prosodists: An Essay in Metacriticism', *Chaucer Review*, 11 (1976), 22–82.
Gaylord, A. T., ed. *Essays on the Art of Chaucer's Verse* (New York, 2001).
Glowka, A. W. *A Guide to Chaucer's Meter* (Lanham, Md., 1991).
Halle, M. and S. A. Keyser. 'Chaucer and the Study of Prosody', *College English*, 28 (1966), 187–219.
Mustanoja, T. F. 'Chaucer's Prosody' in *Companion to Chaucer Studies*, ed. B. Rowland, rev. edn (New York/Oxford, 1979), pp. 65–94.
Robinson, I. *Chaucer's Prosody: A Study of the Middle English Verse Tradition* (Cambridge, 1971).
Schlauch, M. 'Chaucer's Prose Rhythms', *PMLA*, 65 (1950), 568–89.
Schlauch, M. 'The Art of Chaucer's Prose' in *Chaucer and Chaucerians: Critical Studies in Middle English Literature*, ed. D. S. Brewer (London, 1966), pp. 140–63.
Southworth, J. G. *Verses of Cadence: An Introduction to the Prosody of Chaucer and His Followers* (Oxford, 1954).
Southworth, J. G. *The Prosody of Chaucer and His Followers: Supplementary Chapters to Verses of Cadence* (Oxford, 1962).
Youmans, G. 'Reconsidering Chaucer's Prosody' in *English Historical Metrics*, eds. C. B. McCully and J. J. Anderson (Cambridge/New York, 1996), pp. 185–209.

6 Sources and analogues

The standard work on sources and analogues for the *Canterbury Tales* was until very recently the collection by Bryan and Dempster. The first volume of a revised version, edited by Correale and Hamel, appeared in 2002; it contains facing-page translations of texts in languages other than English. A second volume will complete the work. Hanna and Lawler edit and translate the key texts of the clerical antifeminist tradition used in the *Wife of Bath's Tale*. This volume, like those edited by Eisner, Lewis, Mooney, and Wenzel, belongs to the series called the Chaucer Library, which aims to present the classical and medieval works that Chaucer knew as nearly as possible in the form that he knew them, with accompanying translations. For the fabliaux in the *Canterbury Tales* Benson and Andersson's collection of the French, German, Italian, and Latin analogues, accompanied by an English translation, is a valuable reference book. R. K. Gordon prints a translation of the Troilus section of the *Roman de Troie* and of the *Filostrato* together with the text of *Troilus* and Henryson's *Testament of Cresseid*. Havely provides a new translation of those sections from Boccaccio's works comprising the basis of the *Troilus*, the *Knight's Tale*, and the *Franklin's Tale*. Windeatt makes available in translation the French, Latin, and Italian texts that lie behind Chaucer's dream poems, for example passages from Froissart, Machaut, Deschamps, Cicero, and Boccaccio.

A source book of a different sort is that by Miller, which combines translations of passages from works Chaucer is known to have used with selections from the works of a large number of writers regarded by Chaucer and his contemporaries as authorities in matters ranging from reading to romantic love, chivalric ideals to antifeminism, and the estates of society to the Last Judgement.

Benson, L. D. and T. M. Andersson, eds. *The Literary Context of Chaucer's Fabliaux: Texts and Translations* (Indianapolis, Ind./New York, 1971).

Bryan, W. F. and G. Dempster, eds. *Sources and Analogues of Chaucer's Canterbury Tales* (Chicago, 1941; repr. New York, 1958).

Correale, R. M. and M. Hamel, eds. *Sources and Analogues of the Canterbury Tales*, vol. 1 (Cambridge, 2002) [contains the Frame, *Clerk's Tale*, *Cook's Tale*, *Franklin's Tale*, *Friar's Tale*, *Melibee*, *Monk's Tale*, *Nun's Priest's Tale*, *Pardoner's Prologue and Tale*, *Parson's Tale*, *Reeve's Tale*, *Second Nun's Prologue and Tale*, *Squire's Tale*].

Eisner, S., ed. *The Kalendarium of Nicholas of Lynn* (Athens, Ga./London, 1980).

Gordon, R. K., ed. *The Story of Troilus as Told by Benoît de Sainte-Maure, Giovanni Boccaccio, Geoffrey Chaucer, Robert Henryson* (New York, 1934; repr. Toronto, 1979).

Hanna, R., III, and T. Lawler, eds. *Jankyn's Book of Wikked Wyves*. Vol. 1: *The Primary Texts. Walter Map's "Dissuasio," Theophrastus' "De Nuptiis," Jerome's Adversus Jovinianum* (Athens, Ga./London, 1997).

Havely, N. R., ed. and trans. *Chaucer's Boccaccio: Sources of Troilus and the Knight's and Franklin's Tales* (Cambridge, 1980; repr. 1992).

Lewis, R. E., ed. *Lotario dei Segni (Pope Innocent III). De Miseria Condicionis Humane* (Athens, Ga., 1978; London, 1980).

Miller, R. P., ed. *Chaucer: Sources and Backgrounds* (New York, 1977).

Mooney, L. R., ed. and trans. *The Kalendarium of John Somer* (Athens, Ga./London, 1998).

Wenzel, S., ed. *Summa Virtutum de Remediis Anime* (Athens, Ga., 1984).

Windeatt, B. A. *Chaucer's Dream Poetry: Sources and Analogues* (Cambridge, 1982).

7 Introductions, handbooks, anthologies, and collections of essays in criticism

Within the past forty years a number of general introductions have been written to facilitate access to Chaucer's poetry. Most of the books in section 7.1 are designed to do just that – that is, to introduce students to the Chaucer canon. The volumes by Norton-Smith and Mehl, though likewise introductory in nature, are suitable for the more advanced student of Chaucer's poetry. Also within the same period a number of companions to Chaucer studies have been assembled to help both students and teachers familiarize themselves with major aspects of Chaucer studies. The five works listed here reflect different approaches as well as different levels, ranging from selective (Cawley) to all-inclusive (Rowland) and from introductory (Allen and Axiotis; Hussey, Spearing, and Winny) to advanced (Brewer).

Section 7.3 lists nine anthologies of Chaucer criticism. The older collections by Wagenknecht and by Schoeck and Taylor contain some important critical essays from the first half of the twentieth century. The anthologies by Andrew, Barney, and Benson reprint influential essays ranging from the beginning of the twentieth century up to the 1980s. The collection edited by Shoaf combines reprinted essays from the 1970s and 1980s with a large number of new contributions.

In section 7.4 a number of collections of original essays are listed ranging from specific topics like 'Chaucer and the Italian Trecento' to general discussions such as 'Chaucerian Problems and Perspectives'.

7.1 Introductions

Aers, D. *Chaucer* (Atlantic Highlands, N.J., 1986).
Brewer, D. *A New Introduction to Chaucer*, 2nd edn (London/New York, 1998).
Coghill, N. *The Poet Chaucer*, 2nd edn (London, 1968).
Dillon, J. *Geoffrey Chaucer* (Basingstoke/London/New York, 1993).
Howard, E. J. *Geoffrey Chaucer* (New York, 1964).
Hussey, S. S. *Chaucer: An Introduction* (London, 1971).
Knight, S. *Geoffrey Chaucer* (Oxford, 1986).
Lawlor, J. *Chaucer* (New York, 1968).
Mehl, D. *Geoffrey Chaucer: An Introduction to His Narrative Poetry* (Cambridge, 1986).
Norton-Smith, J. *Geoffrey Chaucer* (London, 1974).
Rudd, G. *The Complete Critical Guide to Geoffrey Chaucer* (London/New York, 2001).

7.2 Handbooks

Allen, V. and A. Axiotis, eds. *Chaucer* (New York, 1996).
Brewer, D. S., ed. *Writers and Their Background: Geoffrey Chaucer* (London, 1974).
Cawley, A. C., ed. *Chaucer's Mind and Art* (Edinburgh/London, 1969).
Hussey, M., A. C. Spearing, and J. Winny. *An Introduction to Chaucer* (Cambridge, 1965).
Rowland, B., ed. *Companion to Chaucer Studies*, 2nd edn (Toronto/New York/London, 1979).

7.3 *Anthologies of essays in Chaucer criticism*

Andrew, M., ed. *Critical Essays on Chaucer's Canterbury Tales* (Toronto, 1991).

Barney, S. A., ed. *Chaucer's Troilus: Essays in Criticism* (Hamden, Conn./London, 1980).

Benson, C. D., ed. *Critical Essays on Chaucer's Troilus and Criseyde and His Major Early Poems* (Toronto, 1991).

Ellis, S., ed. *Chaucer: The Canterbury Tales* (London/New York, 1998).

Jost, J. E., ed. *Chaucer's Humor: Critical Essays* (New York/London, 1994).

Schoeck, R. J. and J. Taylor, eds. *Chaucer Criticism*, 2 vols. (Notre Dame, Ind., 1960).

Shoaf, R. A., ed. *Chaucer's Troilus and Criseyde: "Subgit to alle Poesye": Essays in Criticism* (Binghamton, N.Y., 1992).

Stillinger, T. C., ed. *Critical Essays on Geoffrey Chaucer* (New York/London, 1987).

Wagenknecht, E. C., ed. *Chaucer: Modern Essays in Criticism* (New York, 1959).

7.4 *Collections of original essays in criticism*

Arrathoon, L. A., ed. *Chaucer and the Craft of Fiction* (Rochester, Mich., 1986).

Beidler, P. G., ed. *Masculinities in Chaucer: Approaches to Maleness in the Canterbury Tales and Troilus and Criseyde* (Cambridge/Rochester, N.Y., 1998).

Benson, C. D. and E. Robertson, eds. *Chaucer's Religious Tales* (Cambridge, 1990).

Boitani, P., ed. *Chaucer and the Italian Trecento* (Cambridge, 1983).

Brewer, D. S., ed. *Chaucer and Chaucerians: Critical Studies in Middle English Literature* (London, 1966).

Dean, J. M. and C. Zacher, eds. *The Idea of Medieval Literature: New Essays on Chaucer and Medieval Culture in Honor of Donald R. Howard* (Newark, N.J., 1992).

Economou, G. D., ed. *Geoffrey Chaucer: A Collection of Original Articles* (New York, 1975).

Fein, S., D. Raybin, and P. C. Braeger, eds. *Rebels and Rivals: The Contestive Spirit in the Canterbury Tales* (Kalamazoo, Mich., 1991).

Fichte, J. O., ed. *Chaucer's Frame Tales: The Physical and the Metaphysical* (Tübingen/Cambridge, 1987).

Hahn, T., ed. *Reconceiving Chaucer: Literary Theory and Historical Interpretation, Exemplaria*, 2 (1990), 1–353.

Hermann, J. P. and J. J. Burke, Jr, eds. *Signs and Symbols in Chaucer's Poetry* (University, Ala., 1981).

Koff, L. M. and B. D. Schildgen, eds. *The Decameron and the Canterbury Tales: New Essays on an Old Question* (Madison, Wisc./London, 2000).

Mitchell, J. and W. Provost, eds. *Chaucer the Love Poet* (Athens, Ga., 1973).

Morse, R. and B. Windeatt, eds. *Chaucer Traditions: Studies in Honour of Derek Brewer* (Cambridge, 1990).

Robbins, R. H., ed. *Chaucer at Albany* (New York, 1975).

Rose, D. M., ed. *New Perspectives in Chaucer Criticism* (Norman, Okla., 1981).

Salu, M., ed. *Essays on Troilus and Criseyde* (Cambridge, 1979).

Stevens, M. and D. Woodward, eds. *The Ellesmere Chaucer: Essays in Interpretation* (San Marino, Calif./Tokyo, 1995).

Vasta, E. and Z. P. Thundy, eds. *Chaucerian Problems and Perspectives: Essays Presented to Paul E. Beichner CSC* (Notre Dame, Ind./London, 1979).

Wasserman, J. N. and R. J. Blanch, eds. *Chaucer in the Eighties* (Syracuse, N.Y., 1986).

8 Criticism

Responses to Chaucer and his works from the medieval period to the twentieth century are comprehensively documented in the volumes by Spurgeon (up to 1900) and Brewer (up to 1933); Burrow's much smaller volume offers a useful selection of critical responses from medieval to modern times. Within the past fifteen years, as a glance at one of the annual bibliographies will quickly convince anyone, Chaucer criticism has become not only a veritable industry but also well-nigh unmanageable. To give it adequate treatment within the limited scope of this bibliography is impossible. Consequently, the interested reader is advised to consult the essays listed below (8.1), which will sketch the history of Chaucer criticism from the Middle Ages to the present when read in the following order: Brewer (2), Baugh and Purdy, Crawford, Ridley, Baird-Lange, and Leicester. Benson's, Rooney's, and Rudd's treatments are more general.

Although a survey of Chaucer criticism cannot be produced here, it is still possible to establish groupings to which the book-length studies cited below can be assigned. They can be allocated to the following three categories: 8.2 general criticism; 8.3 literary tradition; and 8.4 historical criticism. Under the heading of 'general criticism' are included studies on rhetoric, stylistics, genre theory, narratology, hermeneutics, and gender, or combinations thereof. In the category 'literary tradition' the works on Chaucer and his place in literary history are assembled, be they native English, French, Latin, or Italian. And the grouping 'historical criticism', finally, embraces those studies which focus primarily on the theological, philosophical, art-historical, historical, and socio-economic conditions and their supposed influence on Chaucer's poetry. Needless to say, the boundaries between these three divisions are not always clear-cut because studies on Chaucer tend to be multifaceted and occasionally multimethodological. In these cases assignment has been made according to what appears to be the dominant character trait. In general, studies from the post-war era have been included here, since the foundations of contemporary Chaucer criticism rarely go back further than that. Seminal books which appeared in this epoch of criticism are marked by an asterisk (*) – the choice made by the present author being, of course, a subjective one.

8.1 Surveys of Chaucer reception and criticism

Baird-Lange, L. Y. 'Chaucer Studies: Continuations, Developments, and Prognostications' in *A Bibliography of Chaucer, 1974–1985*, eds. L. Y. Baird-Lange and H. Schnuttgen (Hamden, Conn., 1988), pp. xi–liv.

Baugh, A. C. 'Fifty Years of Chaucer Scholarship', *Speculum*, 26 (1951), 659–72.

Benson, L. D. 'A Reader's Guide to Writings on Chaucer' in *Writers and Their Background*, ed. D. S. Brewer (Athens, Ga., 1975), pp. 321–72.

Brewer, D. S. 'The Criticism of Chaucer in the Twentieth Century' in *Chaucer's Mind and Art*, ed. A. C. Cawley (Edinburgh/London, 1969), pp. 3–28.

Brewer, D. S. *Chaucer: The Critical Heritage*, 2 vols. (London/ Henley/Boston, 1978) [discussion of the history of Chaucer criticism in vol. 1, pp. 1–29; vol. 2, pp. 1–23].

Burrow, J. A., ed. *Geoffrey Chaucer: A Critical Anthology* (Harmondsworth, 1969).

Crawford, W. R. *Bibliography of Chaucer 1954–63* (Seattle/London, 1967), pp. ix–xl.

Leicester, H. M., Jr. 'Chaucer Criticism in 1996: Report to the Plenary Session of the New Chaucer Society, July 29, 1996', *Envoi*, 6 (1997), 1–14.

Purdy, R. R. 'Chaucer Scholarship in England and America: A Review of Recent Trends', *Anglia*, 70 (1952), 345–81.

Ridley, F. H. 'The State of Chaucer Studies: A Brief Survey', *Studies in the Age of Chaucer*, 1 (1979), 3–16.

Rooney, A. *Geoffrey Chaucer: A Guide through the Critical Maze* (Bristol, 1989).

Rudd, G. *The Complete Critical Guide to Geoffrey Chaucer* (London/New York, 2001), pp. 153–82.

Spurgeon, C. F. E., ed. *Five Hundred Years of Chaucer Criticism and Allusion, 1357–1900*, 3 vols. (Cambridge, 1925; repr. New York, 1960).

8.2 General criticism

Burlin, R. B. *Chaucerian Fiction* (Princeton, N.J., 1977).

Corsa, H. S. *Chaucer: Poet of Mirth and Morality* (Notre Dame, Ind., 1964).

Cox, C. S. *Gender and Language in Chaucer* (Gainesville, Fla., 1997).

David, A. *The Strumpet Muse: Art and Morals in Chaucer's Poetry* (Bloomington, Ind./London, 1976).

*Dinshaw, C. *Chaucer's Sexual Poetics* (Madison, Wisc., 1989).

Donaldson, E. T. *Speaking of Chaucer* (London/New York, 1970).

Ferster, J. *Chaucer on Interpretation* (Cambridge, 1985).

Fichte, J. O. *Chaucer's 'Art Poetical': A Study in Chaucerian Poetics* (Tübingen, 1980).

Ganim, J. M. *Chaucerian Theatricality* (Princeton, 1990).

Grudin, M. P. *Chaucer and the Politics of Discourse* (Columbia, 1996).

Hansen, E. T. *Chaucer and the Fictions of Gender* (Berkeley/Los Angeles, Calif./London, 1992).

Jordan, R. M. *Chaucer and the Shape of Creation: The Aesthetic Possibilities of Inorganic Structure* (Cambridge, Mass./London, 1967).

Jordan, R. M. *Chaucer's Poetics and the Modern Reader* (Berkeley/Los Angeles, Calif./London, 1987).

Kelly, H. A. *Chaucer and the Cult of Saint Valentine* (Leiden, 1986).

Koff, L. M. *Chaucer and the Art of Storytelling* (Berkeley/Los Angeles, Calif./London, 1988).

Lawton, D. *Chaucer's Narrators* (London, 1986).

Mann, J. *Feminizing Chaucer* (Cambridge, 2002).

Martin, P. *Chaucer's Women: Nuns, Wives, and Amazons* (Iowa City, 1990).

Minnis, A. J. *Chaucer and Pagan Antiquity* (Cambridge, 1982).

*Payne, R. O. *The Key of Remembrance: A Study of Chaucer's Poetics* (New Haven, Conn./London, 1963).

Rigby, S. H. *Chaucer in Context: Society, Allegory, and Gender* (Manchester/New York, 1996).

Weisl, A. J. *Conquering the Reign of Femeny: Gender and Genre in Chaucer's Romances* (Cambridge, 1995).

8.2.1 General criticism: *Canterbury Tales*

Benson, C. D. *Chaucer's Drama of Style: Poetic Variety and Contrast in the Canterbury Tales* (Chapel Hill, N.C./London, 1986).

Bishop, I. *The Narrative Art of the Canterbury Tales: A Critical Study of the Major Poems* (London, 1987).

Blake, N. *The Textual Tradition of the Canterbury Tales* (London/Baltimore, 1985).

Brown, P. *Chaucer at Work: The Making of the Canterbury Tales* (London/ New York, 1994).

Condren, E. I. *Chaucer and the Energy of Creation: The Design and Organization of the Canterbury Tales* (Gainesville, Fla., 1999).

Cooper, H. *The Structure of the Canterbury Tales* (London, 1983).

Cooper, H. *Oxford Guides to Chaucer: The Canterbury Tales* (Oxford/New York, 1989).

Crane, S. *Gender and Romance in Chaucer's Canterbury Tales* (Princeton, N.J., 1994).

Ellis, R. *Patterns of Religious Narrative in the Canterbury Tales* (London, 1986).

Frese, D. W. *An Ars Legendi for Chaucer's Canterbury Tales* (Gainesville, Fla., 1991).

*Howard, D. R. *The Idea of the Canterbury Tales* (Berkeley/Los Angeles, Calif./ London, 1976).

Kendrick, L. *Chaucerian Play: Comedy and Control in the Canterbury Tales* (Berkeley/Los Angeles, Calif./London, 1988).

*Kolve, V. A. *Chaucer and the Imagery of Narrative: The First Five Canterbury Tales* (London, 1984).

Laskaya, A. *Chaucer's Approach to Gender in the Canterbury Tales* (Cambridge, 1995).

Leicester, H. M., Jr. *The Disenchanted Self: Representing the Subject in the Canterbury Tales* (Berkeley/Los Angeles, Calif./London, 1990).

Lumiansky, R. M. *Of Sondry Folk: The Dramatic Principle in the Canterbury Tales* (Austin, Tex., 1955).

Mandel, J. *Geoffrey Chaucer: Building the Fragments of the Canterbury Tales* (Rutherford, N.J., 1992).

Pearsall, D. *The Canterbury Tales* (London/Boston, Mass./Sydney, 1985).

Phillips, H. *An Introduction to the Canterbury Tales: Reading, Fiction, Context* (London, 2000).

Richardson, J. *'Blameth nat me': A Study of Imagery in Chaucer's Fabliaux* (Paris/The Hague, 1970).

Ruggiers, P. G. *The Art of the Canterbury Tales* (Madison, Wisc., 1968).

Wetherbee, W. *Geoffrey Chaucer: The Canterbury Tales* (Cambridge, 1989).

8.2.2 General criticism: dream visions

*Clemen, W. H. *Chaucer's Early Poetry*, trans. C. A. M. Sym (London, 1963).

Delany, S. *The Naked Text: Chaucer's Legend of Good Women* (Berkeley/Los Angeles, Calif./London, 1994).

Edwards, R. R. *The Dream of Chaucer: Representation and Reflection in the Early Narratives* (Durham, N.C., 1989).

Frank, R. W., Jr. *Chaucer and the Legend of Good Women* (Cambridge, Mass., 1972).

Minnis, A. J., V. J. Scattergood, and J. J. Smith, *Oxford Guides to Chaucer: The Shorter Poems* (Oxford, 1995).

Percival, F. *Chaucer's Legendary Good Women* (Cambridge, 1998).

Rowe, D. W. *Through Nature to Eternity: Chaucer's Legend of Good Women* (Lincoln, Nebr., 1988).

Traversi, D. *Chaucer. The Earlier Poetry: A Study in Poetic Development* (Newark, N.J., 1987).

Winny, J. *Chaucer's Dream-Poems* (New York, 1973).

8.2.3 General criticism: *Troilus and Criseyde*

Benson, C. D. *Chaucer's Troilus and Criseyde* (London/Boston, 1990).

Gordon, I. *The Double Sorrow of Troilus: A Study of Ambiguities in Troilus and Criseyde* (Oxford, 1970).

Kaminsky, A. R. *Chaucer's Troilus and Criseyde and the Critics* (Athens, Ga., 1980).

Meech, S. B. *Design in Chaucer's Troilus* (Syracuse, N.Y., 1959; repr. New York, 1969).

*Windeatt, B. *Oxford Guides to Chaucer: Troilus and Criseyde* (Oxford, 1992).

8.3 Literary tradition

Besserman, L. *Chaucer and the Bible: A Critical Review of Research, Indices, and Bibliography* (New York, 1988).

Calabrese, M. A. *Chaucer's Ovidian Arts of Love* (Gainesville, Fla., 1994).

Davenport, W. A. *Chaucer: Complaint and Narrative* (Cambridge, 1988).

Fyler, J. M. *Chaucer and Ovid* (New Haven, Conn./London, 1979).

Kean, P. M. *Chaucer and the Making of English Poetry*, 2 vols. (London, 1965).

Kelly, H. A. *Chaucerian Tragedy* (Cambridge, 1997).

Miskimin, A. S. *The Renaissance Chaucer* (New Haven, Conn., 1975).

*Muscatine, C. *Chaucer and the French Tradition* (Berkeley/Los Angeles, Calif., 1975).
Nolan, B. *Chaucer and the Tradition of the 'Roman Antique'* (Cambridge, 1992).
Schless, H. H. *Chaucer and Dante: A Reevaluation* (Norman, Okla., 1984).
Taylor, K. *Chaucer Reads the Divine Comedy* (Stanford, Calif., 1989).
Wallace, D. *Chaucer and the Early Writings of Boccaccio* (Woodbridge, 1985).

8.3.1 Literary tradition: *Canterbury Tales*

Boitani, P. *Chaucer and Boccaccio* (Oxford, 1977).
Cooke, T. D. *The Old French and Chaucerian Fabliaux. A Study of Their Comic Climax* (Columbia, S.C./London, 1978).
Hertog, E. *Chaucer's Fabliaux as Analogues* (Leuven, 1991).
Hines, J. *The Fabliau in English* (London/New York, 1993).
*Mann, J. *Chaucer and Medieval Estates Satire: The Literature of Social Classes and the General Prologue of the Canterbury Tales* (Cambridge, 1973).
Neuse, R. *Chaucer's Dante: Allegory and Epic Theater in the Canterbury Tales* (Berkeley/Los Angeles, Calif./London, 1991).
Thompson, N. S. *Chaucer, Boccaccio, and the Debate of Love: A Comparative Study of The Decameron and The Canterbury Tales* (Oxford, 1996).

8.3.2 Literary tradition: dream visions

Bennett, J. A. W. *The Parlement of Foules: An Interpretation* (Oxford, 1957).
Bennett, J. A. W. *Chaucer's Book of Fame* (Oxford, 1968).
*Boitani, P. *Chaucer and the Imaginary World of Fame* (Cambridge, 1984).
Delany, S. *Chaucer's House of Fame: The Poetics of Skeptical Fideism* (Chicago/London, 1972).
Koonce, B. G. *Chaucer and the Tradition of Fame* (Princeton, N.J., 1966).
Payne, R. L. *The Influence of Dante on Medieval Dream Visions* (New York, 1989).
Russell, J. S. *The English Dream Vision: Anatomy of a Form* (Columbus, Ohio, 1988).
Wimsatt, J. I. *Chaucer and the French Love Poets: The Literary Background of the Book of the Duchess* (Chapel Hill, N.C., 1968).

8.3.3 Literary tradition: *Troilus and Criseyde*

Fleming, J. V. *Classical Imitation and Interpretation in Chaucer's Troilus* (Lincoln, Nebr., 1990).
McAlpine, M. E. *The Genre of Troilus and Criseyde* (Ithaca, N.Y./London, 1978).
Steadman, J. M. *Disembodied Laughter: Troilus and the Apotheosis Tradition* (Berkeley/Los Angeles, Calif./London, 1972).
Stillinger, T. C. *The Song of Troilus: Lyric Authority in the Medieval Book* (Philadelphia, Penn., 1992).

8.4 *Historical criticism*

Chance, J. *The Mythographic Chaucer: The Fabulation of Sexual Politics* (Minneapolis/London, 1995).

Curry, W. C. *Chaucer and the Mediaeval Sciences*, 2nd edn (New York, 1960).

Fisher, J. H. *The Importance of Chaucer* (Carbondale, Ill., 1992).

Howes, L. L. *Chaucer's Gardens and the Language of Convention* (Gainesville, Fla., 1997).

Klassen, N. *Chaucer on Love, Knowledge and Sight* (Cambridge, 1995).

Knapp, P. *Chaucer and the Social Contest* (New York, 1990).

North, J. D. *Chaucer's Universe* (Oxford/New York, 1988).

*Patterson, L. *Chaucer and the Subject of History* (Madison, Wisc., 1991).

*Robertson, D. W., Jr. *A Preface to Chaucer: Studies in Medieval Perspectives* (Princeton, N.J., 1962).

*Wallace, D. *Chaucerian Polity: Absolutist Lineages and Associational Forms in England and Italy* (Stanford, Calif., 1997).

Wood, C. *Chaucer and the Country of the Stars: Poetic Uses of Astrological Imagery* (Princeton, N.J., 1970).

8.4.1 Historical criticism: *Canterbury Tales*

Astell, A. W. *Chaucer and the Universe of Learning* (Ithaca, N.Y./London, 1996).

Bowden, M. *A Commentary on the General Prologue to the Canterbury Tales*, 2nd edn (New York/London, 1967).

Brown, P. and A. Butcher. *The Age of Saturn: Literature and History in the Canterbury Tales* (Oxford, 1991).

Lawler, T. *The One and the Many in the Canterbury Tales* (Hamden, Conn., 1980).

Olson, P. *The Canterbury Tales and the Good Society* (Princeton, N.J., 1986).

INDEX

CAMBRIDGE COMPANIONS TO LITERATURE

CAMBRIDGE COMPANIONS TO CULTURE